THE SATOSHI ENIGMA

THE SATOSHI ENIGMA

THE SEARCH FOR BITCOIN'S CREATOR

STEPHEN LAURIE

Published by Hypostasis Ltd.
71-75 Shelton Street, Covent Garden
London WC2H 9JQ

www.hypostasis.co
Email: info@hypostasis.co

Writing as S.P. Laurie

THE THOMAS CODE:
Solving the Mystery of the Gospel of Thomas

THE GOSPEL OF DOMITILLA:
Did the Emperor's niece write Luke?

THE JUDAS WAR:
How an Ancient Betrayal Gave Rise to the Christ Myth

THE ROCK AND THE TOWER:
How Mary Created Christianity

ISBN Print 978-1-912029-96-9
ISBN eBook 978-1-912029-95-2

NOTE ON TEXT

The body text of this book is in British English, but I have kept the original language for posts and quotes. This approach matches Satoshi, who wrote in British English with a sprinkling of American spellings.

Regardless of language, the many quotes from internet forums and mailing lists are full of misspellings and idiosyncratic grammar. There is an attraction to keeping the liveliness of the original, but I did not want to produce a book rife with misspelt words. So I have corrected spelling but not otherwise changed the originals.

A contentious issue is whether it should be "Bitcoin" or "bitcoin". A common approach is to use Bitcoin for the system and bitcoins for currency amounts. However, for simplicity I have used Bitcoin throughout.

Bitcoin addresses are generally given in full the first time and then abbreviated to several initial characters. Some less important addresses only appear in abbreviated form.

CONTENTS

Note on text v
Introduction 1

1. Bitcoin 10
2. Satoshi Advent 22
3. Genesis 37
4. Saint Satoshi? 57
5. Satoshi Exit 72
6. Satoshi's Greed Loop 89
7. Patoshi 104
8. K5 116
9. Dave and Craig 124
10. Satoshi revealed 139
11. The Bonded Courier 158
12. The Rich Foreign Guy 170
13. The Satoshi Profile 184
14. Paul Le Roux 197
15. TrueCrypt 214
16. Rx Limited 226
17. Goldfinger 242
18. Empire 248
19. Bond Villain 259
20. The Sting 268

21. A perfect match 280
22. Satoshi Nakamoto 297
23. Bitcoin addresses................................. 300
24. The Third Man 318
25. Craig Wright is shot............................ 330
26. X invents Bitcoin 346
27. X and Entropy.................................... 361
28. Conclusion 372

Appendix A: Timing of the Malmi emails..... 383
Appendix B: The Wright-Kleiman email total 384
Appendix C: Rx Limited early websites......... 387
References and notes..................................... 391
Acknowledgments 393

INTRODUCTION

Bitcoin went live on 9 Jan 2009 when Satoshi Nakamoto set the world's first cryptocurrency in motion by mining the first Bitcoin block. The previous day, he had published the software with an announcement to the metzdowd Cryptography Mailing List. Hal Finney, an early enthusiast, downloaded the software and ran it when he had some spare time. To Satoshi's chagrin, it crashed.

It was an inauspicious beginning to what was to become a phenomenon. But Bitcoin has always had extraordinary highs and lows. One Bitcoin was valueless in 2009. By the end of 2010, it was worth cents. The record high is now over $100,000. The increase has not been in a straight line. There have been appalling price crashes, exchange hacks, bankruptcies, and government bans. Many still doubt whether cryptocurrency has a future. Bitcoin has survived fifteen years—but will the world celebrate its fiftieth anniversary?

The world's financial system was on the brink that January. Banks in the US, Britain and Europe were in deep trouble. What a time to introduce an entirely new currency that did not depend upon banks, regulators or governments! Satoshi included a reference to the crisis in the so-called Genesis block. It quoted a headline in the Times of London about the UK chancellor having to bail out the banks.

Cryptocurrencies were not a new idea. The concept has been around since the 1990s, spurred on by the development of public key cryptography. It promised a new form of currency, a digital gold that did not depend upon any government or central authority. Individuals could receive payments by publishing their public key and use their private key to authorise spending. But early experiments failed. The fundamental flaw was the double spending problem. If you buy something with a banknote, you hand over your paper and cannot spend it twice. But when you transact with a virtual coin, there is nothing physical to transfer. You retain the private key and can spend it again and again. Solving this double spending problem required a trusted third party, a record keeper, who would sit in the middle and keep a score of all transactions. This third-party intermediary would credit and debit accounts, keeping tabs on balances. They would essentially be a bank, the very thing that cryptocurrency was supposed to eliminate.

In 2008, Satoshi Nakamoto circulated a white paper proposing a solution to the double spending problem using the "proof of work" concept. He sent his paper first to some individuals for comments before publishing it on the Cryptography Mailing List. A few group members engaged in a lively discussion, but only one, Hal Finney, appreciated its significance.

This lukewarm reception was understandable. There were many such proposals, and they never resulted in anything usable. Most people who scanned the paper did not understand the principle or how it could solve the problem. The idea appeared to have obvious flaws. Even Finney concluded that a lot of work and development would be required to turn Bitcoin into a working system.

Putting Satoshi's ground-breaking idea into action should have required a group project. The closest analogue, Nick Szabo's bit gold, had been published as far back as 1998. There was talk about a development project for bit gold, but no results.

To come up with the software for a working cryptocurrency was much more complicated than just writing a paper. But not for Satoshi. He had written the code before the paper, and published the alpha software just a few months after the paper.

People could install the software, carry out transactions, and mine Bitcoin for themselves. Satoshi quickly sorted out the bug that had caused the software to crash, and on 12 Jan, the first transaction occurred when Satoshi gifted some coins to Hal Finney. Other people began to mine Bitcoin, but progress in those early days was painfully slow. It took time for people to get used to the concept and for the real enthusiasts to discover Bitcoin and push the currency forward. But eventually, the enthusiasts came.

The world has seen nothing like the fantastic growth of the Bitcoin price. In the early days, it was worth nothing—in one famous early transaction, two pizzas were bought for 10,000 Bitcoins. An early exchange offered 1,578 Bitcoin for $1 in Dec 2009. These prices were artificial because there was no real market. But they illustrate how easy it was to mine Bitcoin in the Satoshi era. With the establishment of the MtGox trading site, prices became a little more realistic, at $0.28 per Bitcoin in Nov 2010 and reaching almost $1 per Bitcoin in Jan 2011. In 2011, the price surged briefly to $30 before collapsing. Wild fluctuations in the Bitcoin price have been a feature ever since. Projections of the future price vary hugely; some predict that it will ultimately revert to its intrinsic value of zero, others that it will grow to $500,000 or $1,000,000 or beyond. These high values come from the idea that Bitcoin will become the new world currency or at least a universal store of value, the new digital gold.

Satoshi would have been disappointed by the reception of Bitcoin. He was strangely silent for much of 2009 but recovered his enthusiasm by October. He set up the Bitcoin forum and worked with volunteers to improve the software. He led the Bitcoin development effort for a year, posting regularly and offering insights that would come to be treasured by Bitcoin aficionados. His style was always brief, intelligent and to the point. Then, in Dec 2010, Satoshi stopped posting in the forum. He continued with some private email conversations which quickly tailed off. His last communication was on 26 Apr 2011. Satoshi gave the software administrator rights to Gavin Andresen and withdrew. It was not so much that he appointed Andresen as his successor, more that he dumped Bitcoin into his lap and fled.

Satoshi Nakamoto was a most unusual person. He solved a knotty theoretical puzzle that had defeated many of the best minds in cryptography and put his solution into practical action by writing the software. Satoshi combines the talents of an expert coder with the ability to think outside the box with unusual economic insight. But who was he?

Satoshi Nakamoto first appeared in Aug 2008 when he sent an email to Adam Back. All Satoshi's communications were over the internet. No one ever met him or spoke to him on the phone. He was careful never to divulge any personal details. The name is Japanese, and he claimed to be a Japanese man on his profile, but he is clearly a native English speaker. He wrote in British-flavoured English with a sprinkling of American spellings. He never published a Japanese version of the software even though he encouraged translation to other languages. Satoshi Nakamoto is undoubtedly a pseudonym, and it is doubtful that he has any Japanese connection.

There is something very mysterious, even suspicious, about Satoshi. He was obsessive in protecting his true identity and very good at it. He used an anonymous service to disguise the origin of his emails and register the Bitcoin.org address. Many people use an alias on the internet, but it is very unusual for an alias to be constructed so securely that it has defied all attempts to uncover the owner.

Satoshi has left behind many questions. Why has he never re-emerged to claim the adulation of Bitcoin's many supporters? Why did he not give Bitcoin the leadership it needed at times of crisis? And why has he never spent any of the Bitcoin he mined in the early days?

With the surge in the Bitcoin price, interest in its mysterious genius creator increased. There was speculation over his Bitcoin wealth. Satoshi was the most enthusiastic early miner. The best study puts his mined Bitcoin at 1.1 million. If Satoshi is still alive and still has his keys, he is a billionaire many times over.

Those most involved with Bitcoin have generally been reluctant to probe Satoshi's identity too closely. This might be out of a genuine respect for his privacy. More cynically, Satoshi as an enigma is good for Bitcoin. If you pull away the mask, you destroy the mystery. And you never know what you are going to find underneath.

Such sentiments have not stopped the search to uncover his true identity, and many suspects have been advanced. Suspicion naturally fell on the cypherpunks involved in the earlier ideas for cryptocurrencies. Adam Back employed the concept of the proof of work in Hashcash, which was aimed at controlling spam. Nick Szabo created the bit gold concept and, by 2008, had initiated a project to put bit gold into action. Hal Finney had developed a reusable proof of work system to help implement bit gold. He was also the most enthusiastic early promoter of the new currency. All three have been put forward as Satoshi either individually or as a group. They have all denied being Satoshi, but that has not stopped others from continuing to speculate about their involvement.

In 2014, an enterprising Newsweek reporter had the bright idea of looking the name up in a phone directory. He discovered a Japanese-American computer engineer called Dorian Satoshi Nakamoto. Dorian had even lived in the same town as Hal Finney at one time, although there is no evidence that they knew each other. Nakamoto spent a suspiciously large amount of time in his basement—self-evident proof that he was the Bitcoin creator. In an initial conversation with the reporter, Dorian appeared to admit that he had moved on from Bitcoin. But it was all a misunderstanding: he had thought the reporter was asking him about a former work project and had never heard of Bitcoin. His basement hobby turned out to be model trains. Dorian Nakamoto vehemently denied being Satoshi, saying that he was so impoverished he could not even afford an internet connection. The last message from Satoshi's account says that he is not Dorian, but the account is believed to have been hacked.

While most Satoshi candidates have been doxed by others, one man has gone out of his way to claim the mantle of Bitcoin creator. Craig Wright, an Australian computer security expert, claimed to have created Bitcoin with his American business associate, Dave Kleiman. As Kleiman was dead, he could neither contradict nor corroborate this story. Wright convinced Gavin Andresen that he was Satoshi by signing a message with one of Satoshi's keys. But the supposed proof was flawed—the verification of the message took place on a computer under Wright's control. And Wright has never released the signed message to be independently verified. When he did attempt a public signing, the Bitcoin community soon established that Wright had cut-and-pasted a historical Satoshi transaction. Wright's claim to be Satoshi was widely derided and he became known as Faketoshi.

Wright was financed by the former online gambling entrepreneur and one time billionaire Calvin Ayre. Together they had set up a company, nChain, in London that applied for a vast number of crypto related patents. Wright and Ayre had also sponsored a Bitcoin fork called BSV—Bitcoin Satoshi Vision. According to Wright, BSV was the true Bitcoin designed according to Satoshi's, that is Wright's, original intentions before Bitcoin was taken over and manipulated in a different direction by the supposedly malevolent developers. These developers were essentially volunteers, but Wright was determined to ruin them.

Backed by Ayre's money, Wright embarked on a torrent of legal cases. He laid claim to the copyright on the Bitcoin white paper and won a default judgement in the UK which made the paper officially unavailable to browsers from the UK. He successfully sued English Bitcoin influencer McCormack who had maintained that Wright was not Satoshi. McCormack withdrew his defence when confronted with the legal costs that would be required to contest the mountain of evidence that Wright submitted.

However, when cases did come to court, they went badly for Wright. He was sued by Dave Kleiman's brother Ira in Florida in a fascinating case which put a vast amount of information in the public domain. Wright was shown to have forged the emails and other documents that were the basis of his claim to be Satoshi. Wright even managed to snatch defeat from the jaws of victory in the McCormack case. Although he had won, he then submitted false evidence about the harm done to his academic reputation (actually non-existent) in an attempt to get a large payout. Because of his dishonesty, the judge gave him a derisory £1 in damages. Wright had sued the Norwegian "space cat" tweeter, Hodlonaut for defamation in the UK, but Hodlonaut counter-sued in Norway. Wright submitted his evidence to the Norwegian court, but hundreds of these documents were proved to have been forged. Hodlonaut won the case, although Wright appealed and continued to sue Hodlonaut in the UK.

The final showdown came in Wright's favourite venue, the UK. Wright had sued both the developers and the exchanges in an attempt to gain control of the Bitcoin IP which would have given him enormous power over Bitcoin. He had been sued in turn by COPA, an alliance for the patent-free development of crypto currencies. And separately, Wright had sued the Bitcoin developers in an attempt to "recover" billions of dollars of Bitcoin that he claimed he owned through his trust, the so-called Tulip Trust, but which were lost in a supposed hack. The initial trial was held in London in early 2024. For the first time a court would determine whether or not Wright was Satoshi. Wright got busy manufacturing evidence with his usual lack of skill. He submitted an incredible 500 documents that the opposition expert showed were forged. Most unusually, Wright's own expert largely agreed with this conclusion. Wright even continued to forge evidence while the trial was in progress.

The decision of the court was emphatic: Wright was not Satoshi and had no claim to the white paper or any other Satoshi related IP. "We are all Satoshi" was a popular saying. The joke now was to add "except for Wright", who was literally the only person to have been legally declared not Satoshi.

Ironically, Wright is probably one of the very few people who knows Satoshi's identity. Wright has always been confident in coming forward as Satoshi at a time when the real Satoshi would have been expected to appear to contradict him. He initially maintained that Satoshi was three people; along with himself and Kleiman there was a mysterious third man. And the real Satoshi has never made any move to contradict Wright's nonsense, not even when Wright was attempting to take over and destroy Bitcoin.

We are not all Satoshi—only one person is the real Satoshi Nakamoto and it is certainly not Wright. Has the search come to a dead end? There are a few clues. When Bitcoin was launched, Satoshi may have revealed his IP address which is traceable to an internet provider in Los Angeles, California. The white paper incudes metadata which records Satoshi's time zone as US Mountain Time, or perhaps Pacific Time. An analysis of his posts suggests that he tended not to post in the early morning hours on the West Coast. So, an open and shut case that Satoshi was somewhere in the US, perhaps California, the tech centre of the world?

In fact, the IP address evidence is far from conclusive and the time zone data on the white paper is inconsistent. And Satoshi used UK time on some emails and for his code commits. He wrote in British English, used colloquial British phrases, and referenced the Times of London. All of which points to him either being British or coming from some place under British influence. Another clue comes from a mysterious individual posting as X, who may be the "young Satoshi". He proposed an idea that sounded suspiciously like Bitcoin years before Satoshi appeared. And he posted it to a very odd place for a Californian—the Usenet UK finance group.

Or perhaps Satoshi is Dutch. Some early Bitcoin modules show a time zone of +1 hour, corresponding to Western Europe, excluding the UK. And the poster X was not based in the UK. He used an internet connection from the Netherlands and claimed to be Dutch. Also, the white paper's keystone reference was to an obscure paper presented at a small conference in the Benelux countries which include the Netherlands.

The clues are contradictory, and it is no surprise that many consider Satoshi to be a group of people. But reading and studying the large number of posts and emails from Satoshi belies this idea of a group. They were surely all written by one person. And would a group be able to keep such a secret for over a decade? Would they all be prepared to sit on a fortune of billions of dollars? Not in real life. Only a single person with strong reasons could keep the secret for so long.

The quest for the real Satoshi may seem futile, but Satoshi was only human and made mistakes. Most significant was his choice of pseudonym. He could have used something completely random. But like most of us, Satoshi could not help being clever. The name "Satoshi Nakamoto" gives the game away. It is not obvious, though. Satoshi thinks outside the box. He would not use anything easily penetrated, like an anagram. We need a clue to have any hope of decoding the Satoshi enigma. Pure chance has given us that clue.

It comes from an unlikely source: a diplomatic passport issued by the Democratic Republic of the Congo and uncovered by investigative journalist Evan Ratliff while on the trail of a notorious drug lord and arms dealer. When Ratliff published a picture of that passport in a magazine article, some internet posters noticed a strange coincidence. The passport used an alias, "Solotshi", very similar to "Satoshi". And the passport was issued in the same month, Aug 2008, that Satoshi Nakamoto first appeared.

The coincidences did not stop there. The passport was issued by a corrupt official to Paul "Solotshi" Calder Le Roux in return for a large bribe. Le Roux was not just a criminal mastermind, a real-life James Bond villain, but also a computer genius. He had worked for years as a professional programmer specialising in cryptography. He was the author of a remarkable open source program called E4M that encrypted a user's hard disk. He had worked on other encryption products, including software that met GCHQ standards for British government and military use. And E4M served as the basis for TrueCrypt, the number one disk encryption tool of its time. We will see that it was Le Roux who had the idea for TrueCrypt and who was the moving force behind the revolutionary software.

Le Roux was a citizen of South Africa and Australia and had connections to Britain and the Netherlands. He would communicate in an odd mixture of British and American English. His writing style was brief, intelligent and to the point, just like Satoshi's. And like Satoshi, Le Roux specialised in Windows programming in C++.

It would be an unbelievable coincidence to have a passport issued using a very similar name in the exact same month to a person who was such a perfect match with Satoshi. And yet, strangely, this coincidence has been mostly ignored. Those who have put forward Le Roux as a candidate are routinely labelled as conspiracy theorists. Good, sensible, clever people know Satoshi is Nick Szabo who created Bitcoin along with some others. Much better to have a philosopher king of Bitcoin than a crime lord of Bitcoin.

Conformist views are often wrong. This book is not about conspiracy theories but evidence. We will follow the trail of Satoshi, his posts, his emails, his white paper, the design of Bitcoin and his remarkable mining activity. We will look at Le Roux, not just the criminal mastermind with his Rx Limited pill business pumping out hundreds of millions of dollars, his illegal arms and hard drugs trading, his cruise missile development program, his mercenary force, his sex harem and his multiple murders. We will look at the very different Le Roux the programmer—largely self-taught, focused, painstaking and brilliant. We will look at Faketoshi, the fantasist, narcissistic forger Craig Wright whose lies always seem to start with something genuine, and his friend Dave Kleiman, Satoshi's helper and perhaps the first person to know his true identity.

The truth is out there and we will find it. We will construct a case that points unerringly at Le Roux. And we will find the evidence that proves the case: a Bitcoin address, Le Roux posting as X, the third man, a forged email that reveals too much of the truth. And most significant of all, the name.

So what about all those Bitcoins that Satoshi mined? At least 1.1 million which have never been touched. We will see that he mined more, perhaps many more, that cannot be linked back to his Satoshi identity. These other Bitcoins have been moved and perhaps spent. But why has Satoshi never touched his main cache of 1.1 million Bitcoins and never reappeared? Why is Craig Wright so confident in coming out as Satoshi? Paul Le Roux was captured by the US in 2012 and has been in prison ever since.

ONE

BITCOIN

What is Bitcoin, and how does it work? It is a type of money that is backed by nothing and issued by no one. It exists on the blockchain—which is to say it exists nowhere and yet in many different places. The integrity of the blockchain is ensured by miners who do not dig or delve. The miners carry out a vast number of entirely useless calculations that consume an enormous amount of energy and result in globally significant carbon dioxide emissions. Although the calculations have absolutely no value in themselves, the proof of work they represent makes the blockchain un-hackable. And the Bitcoin price goes up faster than anything in human experience or history. Except on those quite frequent occasions when it collapses 80% or so. Bitcoin is magic.

Let's start again. Bitcoin is a digital cryptocurrency implemented over a peer-to-peer network. The "peer-to-peer" part of that definition means there is no central authority or register of Bitcoin holdings. Instead, the blockchain exists in the form of many copies stored around the network. The blockchain records every Bitcoin transaction ever made, so it is now quite large. This is necessary so that a node can work back through transactions to check the amount of Bitcoin at an address and prevent double-spending.

The blockchain consists, not surprisingly, of a chain of blocks. Each block will wrap up a large number of transactions which have been transmitted over the network. Transactions will include a fee to the miner, incentivising miners to include that transaction in their generated blocks. New blocks are generated by the Bitcoin miners on average every ten minutes and are added onto the end of the blockchain. The blocks are chained together mathematically because each successive block contains a "hash", a mathematical representation, of the previous block.

There is no master copy of the blockchain, no central authority, nothing which can be called "The Blockchain". Instead, there are many, many copies held all over the world. As these copies may differ, how can everyone agree on which version is the "truth"? This is where the proof of work comes in. Any new block must include a valid proof of work. If it does not, it will be rejected by miners. Each new block carries a reward of a certain number of new Bitcoins. The miner who finds a valid proof of work allocates those Bitcoins to their own address which, of course, is the whole point. The reward was set initially at 50 Bitcoins for each new block, but it halves every four years, and from April 2024, it is only 3.125 Bitcoins per block.

Just because a miner has found a valid proof of work does not mean that the Bitcoins are theirs quite yet. Their block has to be accepted and become embedded into the blockchain. It is possible for two miners to come up with a valid proof of work more or less simultaneously. So there could be two, or even more, versions of the "truth" that are equally valid yet differ. Does this not cause a fundamental difficulty? No, because the situation is quickly resolved.

All the other miners will select one or the other version as the base for finding the next new block. Eventually, a miner will come up with this next valid block, making one blockchain version longer than the other. This breaks the tie as the proof of work method strongly incentivises miners to use the longest valid blockchain.

Can the miner who mined the losing block refuse to accept the longer blockchain and keep trying to make their version longer? Yes, but they have a crucial disadvantage because all the other miners will adopt the longer blockchain. They will be fighting against the combined power of all these other miners, who are likely to generate the next block quicker than a single miner. Our miner would then be two blocks behind. This assumes that the miner has less than 50% of the total network power, the "hash rate." If a miner has more than 50%, then it is theoretically possible for them to catch up with the others and make their version of the blockchain the longest. Which is why it is essential that no single miner or pool of miners can command more than 50% of the hash rate.

How about changing a historical record? Suppose a miner spent some Bitcoin yesterday. Could they redo the block that records the spending to remove the transaction? If so, they can spend the Bitcoin again. This is where the chain part of the blockchain comes in. As each block contains a hash, a mathematical representation, of the previous block, you can't just change one block in the past. You would have to rework the entire blockchain after that point. To change a transaction one day ago would involve changing about 150 blocks, each of which would require a proof of work. Let us suppose our miner has 25% of the network hash rate. By the time the miner has regenerated the 150 blocks, the remainder of the network would have added about 450 new blocks. So, the miner now has to generate all those blocks also. But by the time they have done this, the remainder of the network would have added another 1,350 blocks. The miner is running an impossible race, getting ever further behind.

If you can't change a transaction one day in the past, how about 30 minutes? This would only require reworking three blocks on average. Assuming our miner has 25% of the network hash rate, they might succeed—if they were very lucky or tried many times. Which is why Satoshi advised people to wait an hour or longer before trusting a transaction.

Theoretically, Bitcoin only works if no single miner, or pool of miners, can command more than 50% of the hash rate. A miner with more than 50% could reverse historical transactions. In reality, a single miner or pool has come close to, or even exceeded, 50% on some occasions but has always continued to play fair. Miners have a strong incentive for Bitcoin to work. And rules can always be changed by consensus. Others would spot any malfeasance and reject the false blocks.

So what is a "hash"? It is a mathematical function that takes one big number as input and outputs another big number. The inputs and outputs of the hash function are usually represented as a string of numbers and letters, but mathematically such a string can be thought of as a number. A mathematical hash is a chopping up and mixing type of function. Imagine a cook chopping up and mixing some ingredients. The process is quite simple starting with the whole ingredients and making a hash. But it is impossible to reverse—you can't begin with the hash and end up with the ingredients all separated and whole. Similarly, a hash function is straightforward to calculate one way but impossible to reverse. There are various hash functions that have been found to be secure. Bitcoin uses the SHA-256 function for the proof of work.

The proof of work is often described as solving a mathematical puzzle, but this is slightly misleading. There is no puzzle. The whole process is mechanical. The miner has to calculate the hash value of their block combined with a random element called the nonce. When they find a hash within a specific range, they have discovered the proof of work. Because the hash function is irreversible, there is no shortcut. The miner has to try a vast number of random values and calculate an enormous number of hashes, which requires expensive hardware and a great deal of energy.

The narrower the target range, the harder it is to find the proof of work, which is where the difficulty level comes in. The software automatically adjusts the target range to keep new block production at an average of one every ten minutes. As more and ever better hardware is dedicated to mining, the difficulty level increases, and the target range gets narrower and narrower. The hash rate is the total number of trial hashes the network carries out, which is currently around 500 million trillion hashes per second.

Initially, Satoshi set the range wide enough for someone using a desktop computer to find a new block within a few hours. This represented a difficulty level of one. The difficulty level has increased quite a lot since then—it is now over seventy trillion. Nowadays, corporations do the mining with specialist hardware, often located in some cold place (to reduce cooling costs) with access to cheap renewable power. It is also common for miners to operate in mining pools, with rewards shared proportionally to the hash rate regardless of which pool member actually found the proof of work. There is nothing to stop any individual mining, but such is the competition that they are unlikely ever to earn any Bitcoin.

A Bitcoin is an amount recorded on the blockchain associated with a Bitcoin address. Effectively, it is a credit balance. Transactions are not generally in whole Bitcoins. A Bitcoin is stored in eight decimals, making very small transactions possible.

Bitcoin uses public-key cryptography to safeguard Bitcoin transactions and balances. The principle behind this well-known cryptographic method is that one key, the public key, is published while the other, the private key, is kept secret. Anyone can encode a message with the public key, but that message can only be read by someone with the private key.

In Bitcoin, the public key is used to generate the Bitcoin address—technically, the address is a hash of the public key. Each address is a seemingly random sequence of letters and numbers. Addresses were originally 34 characters long, but innovations after Satoshi's time have lengthened possible addresses to potentially 62 characters.

Only a person with the associated private key can generate a valid transaction to spend the Bitcoin credited to an address. The use of private keys is both the strength and weakness of the Bitcoin system. No one can steal Bitcoin without a private key. However, a hacker who obtains a copy of the private key can transfer the whole Bitcoin balance to another address, and the actual owner has no recourse or means of reversing the transaction. And if the private key is lost, all the Bitcoins stored at the address are in limbo. They are stranded, and no one can move or use them. This has happened to many early users, and millions of Bitcoins are currently stranded.

Although Bitcoin can only be spent by someone with the private key for an address, anyone can transfer Bitcoins to that address. Some addresses known to be associated with Satoshi have received a large number of transactions of small amounts, known as "dust". These are people thanking Satoshi by sending him a small amount of Bitcoin. As Bitcoin prices have increased, this activity has become less common.

There is no way of working out the private key from the public address. An attacker would have to use the brute-force method, which involves generating a vast number of random combinations of the private key until the one that produces the address is found. But the private key is too long for this process to be feasible on any existing computer: it would take billions of years, which is a long time to wait.

Most people now hold Bitcoin via Bitcoin wallets, which can be software or hardware devices. Encrypting the keys gives another level of security. And a prudent person will keep their keys in "cold storage"—offline, out of the reach of hackers.

New transactions are transmitted over the network to a central pool either by the wallet software or an individual. Anyone can submit a transaction, and they all have to be validated. This validation involves checking that the correct private key has signed the transaction and that the Bitcoins exist at that address by tracking all previous transactions. Full nodes conduct this validation. All miners are nodes, but not all nodes are miners. The non-miners check things for altruistic reasons and keep watch over the miners. The miners take care to incorporate only valid transactions into their new blocks. If a single transaction is invalid, the whole block will be rejected, and the miner will not earn the new Bitcoins.

In the early days, if you wanted some Bitcoin, you had to mine it. This made adoption difficult or impossible for people who were not tech geeks. Gavin Andresen had the idea of operating a "Bitcoin faucet" so anyone could obtain a supply of the currency. Yes, Andresen was giving Bitcoin away for free! Satoshi was delighted, but you do have to wonder about Andresen. The Bitcoin faucet was not a long-term fix, and the development of an exchange infrastructure, most significantly the notorious MtGox, was crucial for Bitcoin adoption.

Another issue was getting retailers to accept the new digital currency. Most people in the crypto-sphere see digital currency as a way of conducting transactions, but in reality, this has always been a very minor aspect. Occasionally, a retailer will announce the radical news that they are accepting Bitcoin, proving they are a go-ahead corporation with their finger on the technological pulse. This is all public relations. No one really buys anything with Bitcoin as it is far more convenient to transact in dollars, euros and pounds. There is one major exception to this rule: criminals collect ransoms in Bitcoins and use the currency to trade illicit goods, such as drugs and guns. But they have to be careful: all transactions are fully visible on the blockchain, as some paedophiles who used Bitcoin to buy child porn have found out to their cost.

Bitcoin is the global currency of the future, or so its supporters would have us believe. It will replace the so-called "fiat currencies" because the total ultimate supply is fixed. Governments will always be pushed to print more and more of their fiat currencies because electorates want more public services and less taxation. But although Bitcoin supply is limited, the supply of cryptocurrencies is not. There is nothing to prevent anyone from starting a new crypto, and there are currently about 10,000 different cryptocurrencies.

Bitcoin does have the crucial advantage of being the first working cryptocurrency. Network effects are important in crypto—the more people use a currency, the more useful it is to own. An existing network creates an almost impenetrable barrier for new entrants unless they bring something radically new.

The most significant competitor to Bitcoin is Ethereum, the brainchild of the then nineteen-year-old Vitalik Buterin. He was the co-founder of Bitcoin magazine when he presented his white paper for a new cryptocurrency. Ethereum would not just have its own currency, Ether, it would also be a virtual machine capable of running decentralised applications, including smart contracts. This idea can be traced back to Satoshi, who included a coding language in Bitcoin. But Ethereum does it better: unlike Bitcoin, it is Turing complete, meaning it can, in principle, run any program.

Ethereum became a reality in 2015 which opened the floodgates to the "alt-coins". Starting a new cryptocurrency piggybacking the Ethereum blockchain was simple. The new currencies are powered by "gas" bought in Ether, enabling Ether to become the most significant competitor to Bitcoin.

The low barrier to entry resulted in the launch of a vast number of new cryptocurrencies. Most of them were Ponzi-type scams. The only reason for buying the currency was the expectation of selling it to a greater fool at a much higher price. Unfortunately, fools are in finite supply. All Ponzi schemes must eventually crash and burn; the only ones to make money are the devisers, backers and very early adopters.

Ethereum brought in another innovation—NFTs, which stands for Non-Fungible Tokens. That beautiful word "fungible" means interchangeable and replaceable by something identical. A Bitcoin is fungible because one Bitcoin is just like another. And so is Ether, the currency of the Ethereum blockchain. A non-fungible object exists as a unique individual thing. You and I are non-fungible, as is an original Van Gogh painting. Mass-produced prints of the same artwork are fungible.

An NFT exists in the ether, is uniquely identifiable and represents something else. Although an NFT can represent anything, most often they are associated with digital works of art or documents. The idea is to create an indelible record of "ownership" of that digital artwork. It is an interesting concept, but the thinking behind it is confused in a very un-Satoshi like way. The ownership represented by the NFT is nebulous and undefined. It is not legal ownership, as an NFT does not usually carry the copyright to the underlying work. Others can copy and enjoy the same digital artwork. And if the NFT has copyright, that would have to be enforced through the courts, which is an expensive, tedious and non-digital process. Anyone can issue an NFT for an artwork even if they don't own it. So, an NFT looks pretty much like another scam.

If NFTs are scams, they have been highly profitable for some artists, promoters and traders. In 2021, the market exploded with 17 billion dollars of trades. Major auction houses like Christie's wanted to get a cut of the action. A digital work by the artist known as Beeple, "Everydays: the First 5000 Days", was auctioned at Christie's for $69m. Predictably, the market collapsed in 2022, and many NFTs are now worthless.

Perhaps the most significant development is the move of Ethereum from a proof of work to a proof of stake consensus mechanism. At a stroke, this has eliminated the massive energy consumption associated with Bitcoin. But it has not helped Ethereum to catch up; the "market-cap" of Ether is only one-third that of Bitcoin. However, Ethereum has an ecological advantage which may enable it to win in the long term. Whether a proof of stake is as inherently robust as a proof of work or more liable to political interference is another matter.

Vitalik Buterin is a high-minded, altruistic individual, and Ethereum has, in many ways, been a tremendous success, permitting thousands of projects to ride its coattails. Yet little of any significant economic value has been achieved. The net result has been to enable a small group of scammers and traders to get rich at the expense of a multitude who have been all too eager to jump into the latest thing. That is pretty much the case for crypto as a whole. For all the hype around the blockchain, there has been no significant application beyond cryptocurrencies. And the growth of these currencies has been driven by speculation rather than economic usefulness. In a developed country there is little benefit in using crypto for transactions unless you are a criminal. Existing networks such as Visa and Mastercard are amazingly efficient, safer, and more convenient. That is not the case everywhere, and crypto has become essential in some lawless territories and marginal economies.

It is a general observation that cryptocurrencies work well in trustless, lawless environments. However, the benefits are dubious where there is a strong rule of law and sophisticated financial and social systems. In developed countries, trust exists because it is backed and enforced by law. In such a trustful environment, cryptocurrencies function only as a means of speculation.

How about the libertarian argument that trusting mainstream finance is naïve? Western governments are increasingly able to track every transaction using the justification of taking action against money laundering or imaginary terrorist financing. There is a war against cash as governments take control over the financial lives of their all-too compliant populations. Often this goes in hand with an abandonment of freedom of speech as many Western governments impose censorship under the guise of hate speech laws. A frightening development is the use of "unbanking" to silence people with views that deviate from standards deemed acceptable by the establishment. When all cash is electronic, you can ruin a person's life by denying them banking services.

So is Bitcoin a beacon of safety from the assault against personal liberties in our increasingly conformist societies? This is the libertarian justification, but in reality, Bitcoin is of little help. All transactions are public on the blockchain. Governments can trace the owners of the addresses through the exchanges. You need to convert your Bitcoin into the despised fiat currencies before you can buy things. Governments know they can tame Bitcoin by forcing the exchanges to report all transactions between fiat and crypto. Control the entry and exit ramps, and you control Bitcoin.

Our brief survey of Bitcoin would not be complete without covering the extraordinary increase in the price of Bitcoin, which is unprecedented in the world's financial history. It is based on the notion that Bitcoin would become a world currency. Satoshi thought this from the very beginning, but others were slow to catch on. They saw Bitcoin as a means for transactions and nothing else. Since there were no transactions in the early days—there was practically nothing to buy with Bitcoin and no way to exchange it for real money, the so-called fiat currencies—it had no value. Bitcoin cannot exist in a vacuum. The existence of an exchange mechanism is crucial.

The first Bitcoin exchange was NewLibertyStandard, which began as early as October 2009. Martti Malmi, who did the first transaction with NewLibertyStandard, also started an exchange, as did the poster BitcoinFX. But the first significant exchange was MtGox. The odd name stands for "Magic: The Gathering Online eXchange". Yes, the MtGox.com site was set up for trading game cards! The card-trading business was not profitable for its creator, Jed McCaleb, and was discontinued after just three months. After McCaleb read about Bitcoin, he decided to reuse the site and software to trade Bitcoin. The exchange went live in July 2010 and quickly became the primary market for buying and selling Bitcoin. There was now a liquid market and a dollar price.

As the infrastructure developed, that price increased exponentially. The table below shows the highs and lows year by year. The all-time high (at the time of writing) is over $100,000. As late as 2011, you could buy Bitcoin for less than $1.

Year	Low	High
2009	$0	$0
2010	$0	$0.4
2011	$0.3	$32
2012	$4	$16
2013	$13	$1,163
2014	$310	$936
2015	$172	$465
2016	$351	$981
2017	$784	$19,892
2018	$3,217	$18,343
2019	$3,401	$13,017
2020	$3,850	$29,096
2021	$29,796	68,789
2022	$18,490	$47,835
2023	$16,547	$44,705

Mt. Gox went bust in 2014 after suffering a hack that went unnoticed for years. This is the kind of thing that happens when your currency exchange was designed for trading cards. McCaleb had sold the exchange to Mark Karpeles, a French programmer living in Japan. It suffered repeated hacks and has been called the worst-managed company in the world. The bankruptcy of MtGox meant that many Bitcoin holders lost their money, resulting in a crisis of confidence and a collapse in the Bitcoin price.

The price recovered after a few years and rose to new highs, reaching almost $20,000 in 2017. Those buying at the high, though, would lose 84% of their money as Bitcoin fell to just over $3,000. This fall was eventually reversed to a new high of $68,000 in November 2021. From this high it plummeted again, this time by 73% to below $20,000. The price has since recovered and broken the previous high

Bitcoin has always been subject to crashes in value, a sure sign that speculation is driving the currency. But the trend has undoubtedly been upwards. A vastly increased price has brought in more and more miners and dedicated hardware, all of which consume power. In a competitive market, mining activities will adjust so that power consumption is proportional to the rewards the miners can derive. It will increase with the increase in the Bitcoin price and reduce with the halving every four years. Miners also earn revenues from transaction fees, which have increased along with the price. The introduction of ordinals and inscriptions in 2023 has brought the benefit, or curse, of NFTs to Bitcoin. This brings greater competition for the limited space on the blockchain, further increasing transaction fees. The balance of these effects, all driven ultimately by the Bitcoin price, is a tremendous increase in power consumption, giving an enormous CO2 footprint for Bitcoin, as much as many small countries. Although there is a trend for miners to use renewable energy, this can still be seen as diverting power away from other, more useful purposes. A counter-argument is that Bitcoin mining, making use of surplus energy at times of glut, can subsidise renewable power investments.

Bitcoin's current power consumption may be nothing compared to the future. If the price were to reach the more optimistic forecasts, such as $1 million or more, then the power consumption would increase by a factor of 20 (which would be reduced by the impact of future halving). Would the world really tolerate such a waste of power?

The power use of Bitcoin is sometimes compared favourably to the existing banking system, which consumes even more power. However, this is a faulty comparison because banking involves millions of deals, loans, mortgages, and investments. Bitcoin is not some magic bullet that can solve all financial needs. Individuals would still need mortgages, loans, pensions and investments. Companies would still need financing and credit arrangements. It is irrelevant whether you are dealing in dollars, euros or Bitcoins. Someone would still have to perform all these activities, either banks or their high-tech equivalent.

A better comparison is with gold, which, like Bitcoin, is a store of value. Like Bitcoin mining, gold mining is wasteful and environmentally damaging. But the comparison ends there. Bitcoin depends upon ongoing mining to operate, whereas gold does not. Most extractable gold has already been mined, and if gold mining were banned tomorrow, gold would be a better store of value than it is now. The reason is that gold mining contributes a moderate inflation to the existing supply of about 1-2% per annum. Gold, once mined and processed, consumes zero energy. It will sit passively in a vault for centuries; it does not need to be kept warm or cool, and it does not rust or tarnish. Nature has already supplied us with the ideal store of value. So why invent Bitcoin? To get rich, of course.

TWO

SATOSHI ADVENT

> "I'm getting ready to release a paper that references your Hashcash paper and I wanted to make sure I have the citation right. Here's what I have: [...] (20 Aug 2008)

Thus started the first known communication from Satoshi Nakamoto. The email was sent to Adam Back and came from Satoshi@AnonymousSpeech.com. It continued:

> "I think you would find it interesting, since it finds a new use for hash-based proof-of-work as a way to make e-cash work. You can download a pre-release draft at http://www.upload.ae/file/6157/ecash- pdf.html Feel free to forward it to anyone else you think would be interested. I'm also nearly finished with a C++ implementation to release as open source." (20 Aug 2008)

Back replied briefly the next day:

> "Yes citation looks fine, I'll take a look at your paper. You maybe aware of the "B-money" proposal, I guess google can find it for you, by Wei Dai which sounds to be somewhat related to your paper. (The b-money idea is just described concisely on his web page, he didn't write up a paper)." (21 Aug 2008)

Back downloaded the paper but didn't read it straight away. He returned to Satoshi with another recommended paper by Revest et al. called "micromint". And that was it as far as Back was concerned. When Hal Finney gave Bitcoin his enthusiastic backing, Back looked at it more carefully.

He was not impressed. Bitcoin suffered from a major privacy flaw: it exposed all transactions to public view. It was not anonymous but only pseudonymous.

It was clear to Back that Satoshi was unaware of developments in cryptocurrencies. The only previous scheme that Satoshi had referenced was Back's own Hashcash, a method for discouraging spam emails. Hashcash validated emails with a simple proof of work. This would cause the sender's computer's fan to whir for a minute while it completed the computationally intensive task. It would be a minor inconvenience for anyone sending genuine emails, but it would impose a significant cost on spammers who send thousands or millions of emails. Any email without a proof of work would be rejected.

The Hashcash idea did not catch on. It was only useful if everyone else was already using it. Otherwise, you would reject genuine emails from the non-users. There was no incentive for early adopters, so it remained a theoretical concept.

Satoshi did contact Wei Dai:

> "I was very interested to read your b-money page. I'm getting ready to release a paper that expands on your ideas into a complete working system. Adam Back (hashcash.org) noticed the similarities and pointed me to your site.
>
> I need to find out the year of publication of your b-money page for the citation in my paper. It'll look like: [1] W. Dai, "b-money," http://www.weidai.com/bmoney.txt, (2006?)." (22 Aug 2008)

Satoshi also included the abstract of his paper "Electronic Cash Without a Trusted Third Party." Dei replied with the link to the b-money paper, which was released on the Cypherpunks list in 1998, not 2006, as Satoshi had thought, and promised to read Satoshi's paper. Then, on 10 Jan 2009, Satoshi sent another email giving Dai an update on the software's release.

This early correspondence shows that Satoshi knew surprisingly little about prior cryptocurrency attempts. He was unaware of Dai's work on B-money and of the previous idea closest to Bitcoin, Nick Szabo's bit gold. Back did not mention bit gold, so the final Bitcoin paper does not refer to

Szabo or his work. Some have seen this as perverse evidence that Szabo was Satoshi. However, Szabo knew about Dai's concept and would certainly have included a reference to Dai in his paper. And Dai was convinced by his own limited interaction that Satoshi was not Szabo.

Satoshi was no cypherpunk. As we will see, his ignorance of existing ideas ties in with the mysterious poster X, who was also ignorant of previous attempts. Satoshi was someone who liked to work things out from scratch and who did not need to read every paper on a subject before coming up with his ideas.

The references he included in the draft Bitcoin paper give us more clues. There were not many, another sign that Satoshi was no academic. Modern academics include endless references and citations which serve as an academic "proof of work". And the references that Satoshi did include are odd. Apart from Back's Hashcash and Dai's paper, which came from Back, there was a 1957 probability textbook, a reference to a classic paper by Merkel, and four other papers concerned with time-stamping documents. Three of the four references were by the same joint authors, Haber and Stornetta.

Time-stamping documents and building a cryptocurrency may seem very different, but are closely related. The time stamping problem involved determining what documents existed at a particular time, either without recourse to a trusted party or using a minimal trust model. Similarly, a cryptocurrency had to determine the order of transactions without a trusted intermediary. If someone attempted to spend their Bitcoins multiple times, only the first transaction would be valid. The Bitcoin blockchain is a development of the method used by Haber and Stornetta, which also used a blockchain approach incorporating Merkel trees to construct a reliable timestamp.

The most intriguing reference is "Design of a secure timestamping service with minimal trust requirements" by Massias, Avila and Quisquater. It describes a Belgium time-stamping project called "TIMESEC" and is the first paper Satoshi referenced after Dai's so it would have stood first in his draft paper. Its short list of references starts with the same three Haber and Stornetta papers that Satoshi included. Most likely, this Belgian paper was Satoshi's starting point for his journey to the blockchain.

As one of the joint authors, J.J. Quisquater, has pointed out, it is an obscure paper for Satoshi to reference. It was presented at a small conference, the 20th Symposium on Information Theory in the Benelux, in Belgium on May 27-28, 1999. There were about fifty attendees at this academic conference, which would have been of mainly local interest to the Benelux countries—Belgium, the Netherlands, and Luxembourg. Quisquater speculated that Satoshi may have been at this conference although that does not necessarily follow. He could have come across the paper in the published conference proceedings. The session after the timestamp paper included a paper on anonymous systems for electronic cash, but Satoshi did not reference this.

Satoshi's new e-cash system did not have a proper name in the version of the paper he sent to Back and Dei. But he had already come up with a name: "Netcoin". Satoshi registered the domain netcoin.org on 18 Aug 2008 using a specialist service AnonymousSpeech dot com. The next day, he changed his mind and registered bitcoin.org.

AnonymousSpeech, which Satoshi also employed for his first email communications, was established by a developer named Michael Weber. Its primary use was for sending emails in an untraceable way. An email sent through AnonymousSpeech's servers could not be traced back to the sender because the sender's IP address or other identifying information would not be revealed in the header text. Satoshi would also use another email address, satoshi@vistomail, which went through AnonymousSpeech.

A user establishing an account at AnonymousSpeech did not have to provide their real name, email address or contact details—just a username and a password. The account could be funded by various methods, including e-gold, bank transfers to a Swiss account, or, for the ultimate anonymity, posting cash to the AnonymousSpeech bank account in Switzerland.

The fact that Satoshi had considered calling his new currency Netcoin was only discovered in 2022. Or Weinberger had the idea of searching for names registered through AnonymousSpeech when bitcoin.org was registered and came across netcoin.org.

The dates of these early actions by Satoshi are interesting. He registered a domain name on 18 Aug and another on 19 Aug. He emailed Back on 20 Aug and Dai on 22 Aug. Satoshi typically does things in a burst of activity and then goes quiet for a while. The next we hear from Satoshi is 31 Oct 2008, Halloween, when he announced his new currency to the world by posting his paper to the Cryptography mailing list:

> "I've been working on a new electronic cash system that's fully peer-to-peer, with no trusted third party.
>
> The paper is available at:
> http://www.Bitcoin.org/Bitcoin.pdf
>
> The main properties:
> Double-spending is prevented with a peer-to-peer network.
> No mint or other trusted parties
> Participants can be anonymous.
> New coins are made from Hashcash style proof-of-work.
> The proof-of-work for new coin generation also powers the network to prevent double-spending."

The paper abstract differs slightly from the version sent to Dai. Satoshi has corrected a typo and smoothed some of the language. Most significantly, e-cash has become Bitcoin, and the paper is titled "Bitcoin: a Peer to Peer Electronic Cash System".

In November, Satoshi's paper was the main topic of discussion on the list. James A. Donald took the idea seriously but was sceptical. His very first comment, on 3 Nov, hit the nail on the head. "We very, very much need such a system, but the way I understand your proposal, it does not seem to scale to the required size." The main flaw in Bitcoin, as originally conceived, was that it could not handle the enormous volume of transactions required of a world currency. For Satoshi, this was a detail to be addressed if the network grew large:

> "Long before the network gets anywhere near as large as that, it would be safe for users to use Simplified Payment Verification (section 8) to check for double spending, which only requires having the chain of block headers, or about 12KB per day. Only people trying to

> create new coins would need to run network nodes. At first, most users would run network nodes, but as the network grows beyond a certain point, it would be left more and more to specialists with server farms of specialized hardware. A server farm would only need to have one node on the network and the rest of the LAN connects with that one node." (2 Nov 2008)

He continues "the bandwidth might not be as prohibitive as you think". He calculates that the number of transactions that Visa processes daily would amount to two HD quality movies. "If the network were to get that big, it would take several years, and by then, sending 2 HD movies over the Internet would probably not seem like a big deal."

Another poster, John Levine, thought it would be easy for the bad guys to take over the network. He pointed out the alarming growth of zombie farms, networks of hacked computers, some involving 100,000 computers. Satoshi replied that such an attacker would have to gain more than 50% of the total processing power on the network and that it made more sense for the criminals to become "honest miners":

> "There would be many smaller zombie farms that are not big enough to overpower the network, and they could still make money by generating Bitcoins. The smaller farms are then the "honest nodes". (I need a better term than "honest") The more smaller farms resort to generating Bitcoins, the higher the bar gets to overpower the network, making larger farms also too small to overpower it so that they may as well generate Bitcoins too. According to the "long tail" theory, the small, medium and merely large farms put together should add up to a lot more than the biggest zombie farm." (3 Nov 2008)

He also points out that if someone succeeded in overpowering the network, it would still be more profitable for them to mine Bitcoin: "With a zombie farm that big, he could generate more Bitcoins than everyone else combined."

Satoshi was correct in his prediction that hackers would take over computers to mine Bitcoin. In fact, it would have been easy for an attacker to overwhelm Bitcoin in the early years. But Satoshi designed the system with a strong incentive for criminals to mine Bitcoin rather than attack the network.

Another poster, "Bear", made the point that Bitcoin is bound to fail because it had no value: "Computing proofs-of-work have no intrinsic value. We can have a limited supply curve (although the "currency" is inflationary at about 35% as that's how much faster computers get annually), but there is no demand curve that intersects it at a positive price point." Bear is using classic economics in this critique. As Bitcoin has no intrinsic value, people will not want to hold it. But Satoshi is cleverer than classical economists.

In his reply, he addresses the issue of inflation. He points out that the difficulty will increase to compensate for computer power applied to mining, to keep "total new production constant". He comments: "Coins have to get initially distributed somehow, and a constant rate seems like the best formula" (8 Nov 2008). The paper also implied a constant rate of new coin production. However, the final design had a rate of coin creation that was anything but constant. The schedule of new coin creation was not included in the paper. Is this because Satoshi had not thought it through, or was unwilling to disclose it at this stage?

Other posters also believed that Bitcoin would be inherently inflationary and that no one would want to hold it for long. With hindsight, this view seems incredible. Bitcoin has been the most deflationary token in history—deflationary in the sense that the price keeps increasing. It shows how far Satoshi was ahead of the knowledgeable posters to this list in understanding the economic consequences of Bitcoin.

One poster pointed out that the government would inevitably attempt to gain control of the new currency in one way or another. When someone commented, "You will not find a solution to political problems in cryptography", Satoshi disagreed:

> "Yes, but we can win a major battle in the arms race and gain a new territory of freedom for several years. Governments are good at cutting off the heads of a centrally controlled networks like Napster,

> but pure P2P networks like Gnutella and Tor seem to be holding their own." (6 Nov 2008)

It is a splendid illustration of Satoshi's libertarian beliefs. Unfortunately, the moderator quickly closed this thread, or we might have learned more.

The discussion only involved a few posters, and they were pretty negative. Only one respondent, Hal Finney, thought that Bitcoin had the potential to succeed:

> "Bitcoin seems to be a very promising idea. I like the idea of basing security on the assumption that the CPU power of honest participants outweighs that of the attacker. It is a very modern notion that exploits the power of the long tail. When Wikipedia started I never thought it would work, but it has proven to be a great success for some of the same reasons.
>
> I also do think that there is potential value in a form of unforgeable token whose production rate is predictable and can't be influenced by corrupt parties. This would be more analogous to gold than to fiat currencies." (7 Nov 2008)

The idea that Bitcoin is more similar to gold than fiat currencies is very insightful. He goes on to compare it with Szabo's bit gold concept. Finney was the only one who properly understood the principles behind Bitcoin. He was highly respected by the cryptographic community, and his advocacy for Bitcoin helped it win some acceptance.

Finney had shown early mathematical talent. He studied at Caltech, where he became interested in computers. After college, he took a job coding computer games. In 1991 Finney discovered the cypherpunks and found his life-long interest. He was particularly inspired by the foundational work of American cryptographer David Chaum, who proposed many of the principles used today for anonymous communications. Chaum even came up with the idea of an anonymous payment system as early as 1983. Chaum's system depended upon a bank acting as the trusted third party maintaining the account balance dominated in dollars or some other conventional currency. He set up a company, DigiCash, in

1989 to implement his system, which was now called eCash. However, the uptake was poor, and DigiCash went bankrupt in 1998.

Finney was a hands-on programmer and became an active cypherpunk coding in his spare time. Phil Zimmermann had written a system, PGP or "Pretty Good Privacy," to encrypt communications such as emails and to prove identity over the internet. Finney was heavily involved in contributing to the second version of this software, PGP v2.0, which became the internet's most widely used encryption tool. Finney never received much credit due to Zimmermann's legal problems. The US government investigated him for breaking restrictions on the export of weapons. Whether a cryptographic method could be characterised as a weapon was controversial. Zimmermann wanted to protect Finney and kept his involvement out of the public eye.

Finney had long been interested in electronic cash and was fascinated by the bit gold concept. He even implemented a variant of bit gold in 2004 called Reusable Proofs of Work. Finney has the perfect CV to be Satoshi. He had the practical programming ability, a deep understanding of cryptography and an interest in electronic currencies. And when Newsweek named Dorian Nakamoto as the Bitcoin creator, an amazing coincidence was uncovered. The two had grown up close to each other in Los Angeles; Dorian came from Temple City, and Finney from neighbouring Arcadia. And for ten years Hal Finney had lived with his wife in Temple City, just two miles from the Nakamoto family home.

It seemed that Finney and Dorian Nakamoto, who was born Satoshi Nakamoto, had developed Bitcoin together. Or perhaps the young Finney had known Dorian and used the name later as his alias for Bitcoin. Finney strongly repudiated both scenarios and denied ever knowing Dorian.

In truth, the coincidence is not that surprising. Satoshi and Nakamoto are common Japanese names, and many ethnically Japanese people live in California. Dorian was several years older than Finney, and they did not attend the same schools. Although the Finneys moved to Temple City, two miles is still quite a distance. It was all long before Bitcoin, and Dorian was not even living in Temple City at the same time as the Finneys.

It is what cryptographs call a collision. When you have lots of things that could be connected, a coincidence somewhere or other is more likely than you would think. To find two people who can be linked to Bitcoin to be connected in some random aspect (such as location at some point in the past) is not that improbable.

We can rule out Finney as Satoshi by reading his posts. He obviously did not know about Bitcoin before Satoshi posted the paper: "Unfortunately I am having trouble fully understanding the system". Finney goes on to ask detailed questions about the operation of Bitcoin and ends with a suggestion:

> "Sorry about all the questions, but as I said this does seem to be a very promising and original idea, and I am looking forward to seeing how the concept is further developed. It would be helpful to see a more process oriented description of the idea, with concrete details of the data structures for the various objects (coins, blocks, transactions), the data which is included in messages, and algorithmic descriptions of the procedures for handling the various events which would occur in this system." (7 Nov 2008)

It would indeed have been helpful to see a specification, but Satoshi did not have one. His reply addresses Finney's points briefly and intelligently, before making an admission:

> "I appreciate your questions. I actually did this kind of backwards. I had to write all the code before I could convince myself that I could solve every problem, then I wrote the paper. I think I will be able to release the code sooner than I could write a detailed spec." (9 Nov 2008)

Nothing could tell us more plainly that Satoshi was a programmer, not an academic. Programmers write code, academics write papers. Satoshi thought in code and wrote the program before the paper. Programmers are notorious for their general unwillingness to document, and scholars are notorious for their software's often poor quality and general user unfriendliness.

It has to be said that Satoshi's coding is quite untidy in some ways. It is also dense and difficult for other programmers to follow. Programmers in professional corporate environments are taught to document. It is not that Satoshi's code is careless—it functions well. But he does things like leave redundant modules in the code, which is typical of us amateurs. Some have suggested this shows that Satoshi was not a professional programmer. But this takes no account of his undoubted expertise in programming C++ in Windows, his excellent knowledge of technical issues, and his ease at handling support queries and updates. Satoshi is no amateur. But he has not been trained in his craft by working in a high-level professional environment. Satoshi comes over as a highly capable loner, a coder who has only worked for smaller organisations or as a one-man band.

The email exchange with Finney shows he was not part of some Satoshi team. His questions are not those that someone with prior knowledge would ask. Or is it an elaborate deception, with Finney acting a part and pretending ignorance? If so, why would he ask Satoshi to come up with a bunch of specifications? Finney would have known nothing would be forthcoming. He would have asked questions that Satoshi could answer convincingly.

There is another coincidence concerning Hal Finney. On 27 Dec 2008, a fortnight before the launch of Bitcoin, Nick Szabo made two posts on his blog. One titled "Bit gold" was a repost of an article he had posted initially three years previously, in December 2005:

> "A long time ago I hit upon the idea of bit gold. The problem, in a nutshell, is that our money currently depends on trust in a third party for its value. As many inflationary and hyperinflationary episodes during the 20th century demonstrated, this is not an ideal state of affairs." (27 Dec 2008)

This post mentions Finney: "Hal Finney has implemented a variant of bit gold called RPOW (Reusable Proofs of Work). This relies on publishing the computer code for the "mint," which runs on a remote tamper-evident computer."

The start of Szabo's second post, "Bit gold markets", might be taken as a description of Bitcoin:

> "The basic idea of bit gold is for "bit gold miners" to set their computers to solving computationally intensive mathematical puzzles, then to publish the solutions to these puzzles in secure public registries, giving them unique title to these provably scarce and securely timestamped bits. These titles to timestamped bits will be more secure and provably scarce than precious metals, collectibles, and any other objects that have ever been used as money." (27 Dec 2008)

Are Szabo and Finney acting together as Satoshi? Does this explain Finney's enthusiastic response to Bitcoin? But why would Szabo post about a failed old idea if he has a better new one?

In truth, bit gold is nothing like Bitcoin. They both use the proof of work concept, but in radically different ways. For Bitcoin, the proof of work validates the blockchain, which records transactions. The Bitcoins themselves have nothing to do with the proof of work. Szabo's idea was to use proof of work solutions as the tradable currency. Users would solve computationally intensive puzzles and timestamp their solutions using an external service while setting a new puzzle for others to solve.

Szabo believed the solutions could be combined into pools with a currency unit giving ownership rights to a fraction of a pool. If I have read his post correctly (it is quite confusing), he argues that equal value would be attributed to pools produced at different times. If more solutions were produced next year than this year, the value of each solution would be lower, but the total value of the pool would be the same. Supposedly, this would be the result of market forces. However, the post is unclear on what market mechanism would produce such an outcome.

Szabo's idea is conceptually fascinating but impracticable. His solution does not envisage a single currency, like Bitcoin, but a whole sequence of currencies, each representing a share in a pool of collectables—proof of work solutions produced in a given time frame. So, the solutions produced year to year, month to month, or even day to day (Szabo does not define the interval) would form different tranches, which are effectively different currencies.

As the number of solutions solved in the past would be fixed and known, Szabo believed that this would give those past pools scarcity value. What about future pools though? Increasing computing power would produce an ever-increasing number of new solutions year by year. Why would this not result in high inflation?

Unsurprisingly, bit gold never gave rise to a workable system. But did Szabo evolve bit gold into Bitcoin? There is absolutely nothing about his post to suggest he did. If Szabo had invented Bitcoin, why post an article considering how to get the cumbersome bit gold concept to work? In his new post, Szabo talks about making the proof of work solutions fungible in pools and how a market could value proof of work solutions generated at different times, allowing for the increase in computing power. It is all horribly complex and nothing like the practical, elegant simplicity of Bitcoin. Satoshi had already solved the problem in a much better way.

Nor should Finney's enthusiastic response to Satoshi's paper be a surprise. Finney had attempted to implement bit gold. He would have understood the problems and been receptive to a better solution. As for the coincidence in timing, the discussion about Bitcoin on the Cryptography Mailing List in November touched on the prior bit gold idea, which could have resulted in Szabo's renewed interest.

Satoshi's launch of the white paper on the Cryptography list did have some useful results. Two list members, Ray Dillinger and Finney, helped him with testing. Finney was even listed as a developer on the SourceForge project site at the start of January. Ray Dillinger gave a brief account of his own contribution:

> "In November of 2008, I did a code review and security audit for the block chain portion of the Bitcoin source code. The late Hal Finney did code review and audit for the scripting language, and we both looked at the accounting code. Satoshi Nakamoto, the pseudonymous architect and author of the code, alternated between answering questions and asking them." (20 Sep 2017)

An email recovered from Hal Finney's computer confirms that Satoshi sent him the source code in Nov 2008. The two had also been discussing Bitcoin privately. Finney thanks Satoshi "for the corrections" on some points. He then asks some good questions about how Satoshi sees the network developing:

> "Some of the discussion and concern over performance may be related to the eventual size of the P2P node network. How large do you envisage it becoming? Tens of nodes? Thousands? Millions?
>
> And for clients, do you think this could scale to be usable for close to 100% of world financial transactions? Or would you see it as mostly being used for some "core" subset of transactions that have special requirements, with other transactions using a different payment system that perhaps is based on Bitcoin?" (19 Nov 2008)

We would love to know Satoshi's replies, but we only have a small part of the email exchange. The failure of the posters on the Cryptography List to appreciate Bitcoin may seem obtuse. But then Bitcoin was not what the cypherpunks were expecting. They were looking for an anonymous mechanism to carry out a large volume of transactions equal to existing payment systems such as Visa. The libertarian dream was to transact outside the banking system, out of the sight and mind of Big Brother government.

Bitcoin failed to meet these expectations. For a start, it was not truly anonymous but only pseudonymous. Every Bitcoin transaction is glaringly visible on the blockchain. Although you can only see the public addresses, being able to track transactions provides a great deal of information for law enforcement, the government, and random snoopers.

Nor was Bitcoin equipped to handle a large volume of transactions. Satoshi set the cycle length at ten minutes, and it could take several cycles before a person could be confident that their transaction had made it to the longest blockchain. So perhaps an hour before a transaction can be confirmed. Given ubiquitous and instantaneous modern cash transmission, this seems like an age.

The other problem was that the block size of 1 MB was insufficient if Bitcoin took off in a big way. This limitation was well known from the beginning, but Satoshi never included any mechanism to increase the file size if the demand for transactions increased. In Bitcoin's short history, there have been many arguments over the block size leading to a damaging civil war.

It was Hal Finney who put his finger on it. Bitcoin was never designed as a mechanism for a large volume of transactions. It was a store of value. It was digital gold.

Satoshi must have been frustrated by the general tone of the discussion but remained remarkably patient: "It's very attractive to the libertarian viewpoint if we can explain it properly. I'm better with code than with words though." It is another revealing comment. We can't imagine the articulate, legally trained Nick Szabo ever saying that. It confirms that Satoshi saw himself first and foremost as a programmer. However, Satoshi's comment is not actually true. He is very good at explaining himself, although he always uses the minimum number of words. It was hard for people to get their heads around what he was saying because the concept was so new.

By the end of November, the discussion had died down, and there were no posts on the Bitcoin list in Dec 2008. People had either lost interest or were waiting for Satoshi's code. Many would have thought they would never hear of Bitcoin again.

On 10 Dec 2008, Satoshi established the Bitcoin-list on SourceForge. It was not a great success. The person who had engaged the most with Satoshi, James A. Donald, posted to this list in mid-2010. He had always been ambivalent about Bitcoin, both dismissive and yet also intrigued. Now he replied to someone who asked why there had been no posts for months (Satoshi had actually moved the discussion to the new Bitcoin Forum):

> "Yes - Bitcoin kind of went dead. [...] Long ago, I had an argument with the guy who designed it about scaling. I heard no more of it - of course with no one using it, scaling is not a problem. I do not know if the software is in useable condition, or has been tested for scalability." (30 Jun 2010)

Later that day, Donald had second thoughts:

> "I did not mean to sound so negative. If we manage to get there from here, this is a huge win for liberty - but it is a long trek [...]" (30 Jun 2010)

THREE

GENESIS

Bitcoin went live on 9 Jan 2009. The start is often incorrectly dated from 3 Jan, when Satoshi established block zero, the so-called Genesis block. Satoshi included within this block a message, an ironic headline from the Times of London of that day: "Chancellor on brink of second bailout for banks". We should not trust the date because the Genesis block was not mined. Each Bitcoin block has to include a coded representation, a hash, of the previous block. To avoid an infinite regression, Satoshi had to hardcode a dummy block into the software as block zero. As he explained later on the forum:

> "Technically, yes, the genesis block is a block. It's a hardcoded block that you start out with. You can't *not* have the genesis block." (16 Aug 2010)

The Genesis block Bitcoins can never be spent, but it is able to receive transfers. Over the years people have transferred Bitcoin to the block, thinking they are rewarding Satoshi. Most significantly, in Jan 2024 just after the fifteenth anniversary of the Genesis block, someone transferred 26.91 Bitcoin worth $1.17 million. These Bitcoins moved to Genesis are lost forever.

What about that message? Are we to imagine the Bitcoin developer picking up his daily paper on 3 Jan, reading the headline with a smile, and deciding to incorporate it into the Bitcoin software? Does it mean that Satoshi was someone who read the London Times and lived in the UK? Or is it all an illusion by that magician, Satoshi? New Bitcoin blocks are mined every 10 minutes or so. Yet, the next Bitcoin block was not created until six days after the Genesis block timestamp.

Why the delay? The standard explanation is that Satoshi spent the time rigorously testing Bitcoin and then deleted all the blocks he mined in this period before posting the software. But this is not how solo software developers work. The natural cycle is to write something, test it, write a bit more and test that. Get something to work and then refine it. Satoshi had been working on Bitcoin for two years, and it is unbelievable that he would have run it for the first time a few days before he issued it. We can expect Satoshi to have created several Genesis blocks to test the system. His final checks that everything worked would only have taken a few hours. So, most likely, the Genesis block was created a day or two before he issued the software. The timestamp is deceptive. Genesis was backdated

Satoshi could choose whatever date he wanted. As the headline is relevant, we can deduce that Satoshi dated the block to match the newspaper. By making it look like he had read the headline on the 3rd, he was leading us to think he was in the UK. So we can be confident that he was not in the UK. He could have been living on an island on the other side of the world, some place where it took a day or two for the Times to reach.

And yet, we learn something about Satoshi from the Genesis block. He read the London Times. An American would have referenced the New York Times, the Wall Street Journal or the Washington Post. It is one of many hints that Satoshi came from somewhere in the world under British influence. Unless it is all a deliberate attempt to deceive us.

On Thursday, 8 Jan, Satoshi posted a link to the Cryptography mailing list.

> "Announcing the first release of Bitcoin, a new electronic cash system that uses a peer-to-peer network to prevent double-spending. It's completely decentralized with no server or central authority."

The Windows-only software was published to SourceForge with the open source C++ code included. The software not only operated as a primitive Bitcoin "wallet" but could also mine Bitcoin.

> "I made the proof-of-work difficulty ridiculously easy to start with, so for a little while in the beginning a typical PC will be able to generate

> coins in just a few hours. It'll get a lot harder when competition makes the automatic adjustment drive up the difficulty."

Hal Finney replied on Saturday, 10 Jan: "Congratulations to Satoshi on this first alpha release. I am looking forward to trying it out." But when he ran it that same day, the software crashed.

To help Satoshi resolve the issue, Hal Finney published his debug log on the Bitcoin list. Satoshi sorted out the problem and posted an updated version of the software on 11 Jan:

> "All the problems I've been finding are in the code that automatically finds and connects to other nodes, since I wasn't able to test it in the wild until now. There are many more ways for connections to get screwed up on the real Internet.
>
> Bugs fixed:
>
> - Fixed various problems that were making it hard for new nodes to see other nodes to connect to.
> - If you're behind a firewall, it could only receive one connection, and the second connection would constantly disconnect and reconnect.
>
> These problems are kind of screwing up the network and will get worse as more users arrive, so please make sure to upgrade." (11 Jan 2009)

Satoshi fixed the problem, but did he leak his IP address? The evidence lies in the debug log that Hal Finney uploaded. It reveals three people connected to the Bitcoin IRC channel. One is Finney, and one is the Admin, Satoshi, who connected through Tor. But there is also the IP address of a third person, who, it is argued, is Satoshi signed on as a user. The address resolves to an internet provider, Covid Communications, in Van Nuys, Los Angeles, California. And it was not a Tor node.

Is it Satoshi's IP address? This is based on the assumption that Finney and Satoshi were the only two people running the Bitcoin software at that time. But the Bitcoin software had been published to a public mailing list two days earlier. We know that some people downloaded and ran the software in early January, so it is possible that the Van Nuys IP address belonged to another user.

Who was the first person other than Satoshi to mine Bitcoin? It is usually taken for granted that it was Finney. However, he only attempted to run the software on 10 Jan, and his first mined block, 78, is timed at 1:00 UTC on 11 Jan (it was still 10 Jan in California). Satoshi was using special software which enables us to allocate mined blocks to him with a reasonably high certainty. The analysis shows that someone else was mining on 9 Jan.

The Bitcoin software would only commence mining once it found another node on the network. Satoshi's first mined block is timed at 2:54 on 9 Jan, so if his software was waiting for someone else to connect, that happened shortly before 2:54. However, as Satoshi was not using the standard software, he could have commenced mining with no one else connected. This is unlikely because someone else did mine block 12 at 4:21, and this miner had been operational from the start when block one was mined. (I am indebted here to an analysis of the first 1,000 blocks by Wolfgang Wester.)

The 9 Jan mining ceased after only two hours and did not restart for twenty-four hours. Mining then continued for two hours before stopping again, with regular mining only starting at 15:30 on 10 Jan. The next block that was not mined by Satoshi's setup was block 64 at 21:48. Nor was it mined by Finney, who had posted his debug log a few hours before. The block 64 miner could be the Van Nuys IP address, although this is not certain as the block 64 miner started their software after Finney posted his log. The miner's software could have been running earlier, but we can't be sure.

Who was the mystery miner of Block 12? It is possible that some unknown person downloaded the software and succeeded in getting it to run shortly before 3:54 on 9 Jan. This would trigger Satoshi's machine to start mining. The unknown user would have succeeded in mining block 12 before switching off their computer, perhaps because they wanted to go to bed.

However, Wester's analysis suggests a different story. His method allocates both block 12 and block 64 to a miner he designates as K5. This miner ran the standard software and used a fast machine or machines. In total, K5 mined 35 of the first 1000 blocks. Who was this mystery person? Wester believes it was Satoshi because K5 was mining from the very beginning. It is also significant that most of the K5 Bitcoins have never been moved.

So the first person other than Satoshi to mine Bitcoin was K5—who was probably Satoshi. We can conclude that Satoshi ran a second computer using the standard software to start the network. After all, he would want to test whether other people could connect. The first person apart from Satoshi or K5 to mine Bitcoin was indeed Hal Finney on 11 Jan. (We will look closer at that mystery IP address when we consider Satoshi's mining activities.)

Another very early user was Dustin D. Trammell, a Texas security researcher and cypherpunk with a taste for wearing luminous green. He became interested in Bitcoin after reading the paper on the Cryptography mailing list. Then he downloaded the very first version of the software and began running it on 9 Jan. However, Trammell was unaware for a few days that he had to turn on the software mining feature. He emailed Satoshi on 11 Jan and received a gift of 25 Bitcoin on 14 Jan in the second transaction. Trammell's crucial contribution was keeping his computers running 24/7 at Satoshi's request to stabilise the network.

Although most Bitcoiners were programmers and libertarians, Nicholas Bohm was quite different. He was a retired English solicitor (lawyer) with an interest in cryptography. Long fascinated with open key cryptography, he had been involved in legal issues around digital signatures and other computer issues and subscribed to the Cryptography list. He had previously lent his computer's processing power to a collaborative project to factor large numbers. Reading about Bitcoin on the list, he saw it as a similar kind of experiment. So towards the end of January, he downloaded the software but couldn't get it to run because of a bug. He posted on the Bitcoin-list on 25 Jan, and Satoshi took the discussion offline. The bug was fixed, and the two continued to exchange emails.

On 1 Feb, Satoshi sent Bohm a gift of 100 Bitcoins and then another 50 the next day. When he posted the update with the bug fix (v0.1.5) on 4 Feb, he thanked both Bohm and Trammell for their help. Unlike most other Bitcoiners, Bohm not only used his real name but also gave his full home address and phone number in all his communications. Clearly, pseudonymity was not important to him. He had only a hazy view of what Bitcoin was about and was less technically savvy than most early Bitcoin users.

Satoshi was very helpful and found Bohm useful precisely because he was less experienced. When Bohm remarked, "Please treat my comments with caution, as my grasp of Bitcoin is pretty superficial, to put it mildly; but I hope naive comments may still be useful", Satoshi replied:

> "No, that's exactly what I need, it's very helpful. I don't know how someone who doesn't already know all about Bitcoin will interpret things. You only get one chance to see how something looks for the first time, and I already spent all of mine." (3 Feb 2009)

By the end of February, Bohm had mined 8,550 Bitcoins. He continued mining for a few years and accumulated a remarkable stack of Bitcoins, although he had no appreciation of its value. His correspondence with Satoshi lasted until July 2009.

Another early known miner is Jeff Kane who posted on the Bitcoin-list on 30 Jan that he was running v.0.1.3 fine. He mined for just a few weeks from 21 Jan to 2 Feb. James Howells from Wales started mining a few weeks later on 15 Feb 2009 and continued until late April by which time he had mined several thousand Bitcoins. Unfortunately, his keys literally ended up on a rubbish dump. These are the known miners in the first few months—Finney, Trammell, Bohm, Kane and Howells. There were others we can trace but not identify.

These unknown miners can be distinguished using a variety of analytical techniques to determine that a set of Bitcoin blocks have been mined by same miner. If a large number of mined blocks are consolidated into a single address, which happened with almost every early miner, it is a giveaway that they all belong to the same person. We will use the designations Wester has given to these anonymous miners, although a single person may be responsible for multiple designations.

M2809/M3654 began mining on 27 Jan 2009 using as many as

four computers. They soon reduced to a single computer (M2809) and continued for eighteen months, mining in excess of 70,000 Bitcoins, only a small proportion of which remain under their control. They have periodically moved some of their Bitcoin including some very early Bitcoins recently, creating speculation that Satoshi had returned. But the miner is not Satoshi. Wester knows his identity although he has withheld it for obvious reasons.

Another miner M1928 started on 28 Jan 2009 and continued for only two months, mining a total of around 10,000 Bitcoins. They appear to have retained their mined Bitcoins. The Bitcoins were consolidated in 2011, and this was followed by a huge number of repeated transactions, continuing to the present day, slicing off Bitcoins and recombining them in different combinations. The motivation is, presumably, to confuse the trail.

Satoshi made the case for mining Bitcoin in a reply to Dustin Trammell:

> "I would be surprised if 10 years from now we're not using electronic currency in some way, now that we know a way to do it that won't inevitably get dumbed down when the trusted third party gets cold feet.
>
> It might make sense just to get some in case it catches on. If enough people think the same way, that becomes a self fulfilling prophecy." (16 Jan 2009)

Elsewhere, in the post announcing the software to p2p lists, Satoshi had made clear his distaste for systems that relied on trust:

> "The root problem with conventional currency is all the trust that's required to make it work. The central bank must be trusted not to debase the currency, but the history of fiat currencies is full of breaches of that trust. Banks must be trusted to hold our money and transfer it electronically, but they lend it out in waves of credit bubbles with barely a fraction in reserve. We have to trust them with our privacy, trust them not to let identity thieves drain our accounts."

This is a typical libertarian tirade. Most people attracted to the currency were libertarians of one sort or another. It is important to remember that libertarians can skew to the left or right—Satoshi is pretty obviously the right-leaning type.

Satoshi understood that Bitcoin has a built-in mechanism for price increases and is keen to start the process: "It might make sense just to get some in case it catches on" turned out to be the understatement of the century. But no one else, apart from Hal Finney, seemed to see it this way. There was some discussion on the Cryptography list, mostly negative. Jonathan Thornburg raised the obvious problem of money laundering considerations:

> "In the modern world, no major government wants to allow untraceable international financial transactions above some fairly modest size thresholds. (The usual catch-phrases are things like "laundering drug money", "tax evasion", and/or "financing terrorist groups".) To this end, electronic financial transactions are currently monitored by various governments & their agencies, and any but the smallest of transactions now come with various ID requirements for the humans on each end." (17 Jan 2009)

Governments have indeed attempted to tame Bitcoin. But Finney pointed out that Bitcoin had some inherent advantages that made it robust against government interference:

> "Bitcoin has a couple of things going for it: one is that it is distributed, with no single point of failure, no "mint", no company with officers that can be subpoenaed and arrested and shut down. It is more like a P2P network, and as we have seen, despite degrees of at least governmental distaste, those are still around." (24 Jan 2009)

Another poster drew attention to the potential wasteful CO2 generation for proof of work systems. Finney's response speculated whether it was possible to compute a proof of work without power usage. The power requirement of a computation actually comes from deleting bits of information. Was it possible to design a proof of work that preserved bits and did not require power-hungry deletion? The answer seems to be no, but the post illustrates Finney's depth of thought.

Through the recent release of the Malmi emails, we have Satoshi's response to the power issue, although it was not recorded on the archive (perhaps Satoshi never posted it):

> "Ironic if we end up having to choose between economic liberty and conservation. Unfortunately, proof of work is the only solution I've found to make p2p e-cash work without a trusted third party. Even if I wasn't using it secondarily as a way to allocate the initial distribution of currency, PoW is fundamental to coordinating the network and preventing double-spending. If it did grow to consume significant energy, I think it would still be less wasteful than the labour and resource intensive conventional banking activity it would replace. The cost would be an order of magnitude less than the billions in banking fees that pay for all those brick and mortar buildings, skyscrapers and junk mail credit card offers." (3 May 2009)

Satoshi disliked the banking system. However, his assumption that banking would somehow disappear if the world adopted Bitcoin is surely wrong.

There were other discussions going on at the same time on the list, and one of these is intriguing. Stefan Kelm posted on 19 Jan 2009 about the "myth" that it was necessary to overwrite data several times on a hard disk to securely delete it: "Craig Wright, a forensics expert, claims to have put this legend finally to rest." Yes, that is the same Craig Wright who later claimed to have invented Bitcoin together with his friend Dave Kleiman. Kelm is referring to a paper that Wright wrote in conjunction with Kleiman. Wright was not a member of the Cryptography mailing list, but Kleiman was. He replied on 20 Jan with a technical post about deletion software, which ended with the comment: "And yes, I am the same Dave Kleiman from the paper."

So Kleiman was an active participant on the list, reading and posting at the same time that Satoshi was posting about Bitcoin. Did he also download and run the Bitcoin software?

Bitcoin was a flop. That would be the conclusion of an unbiased observer in 2009. For most of the year, there was little activity and not much mining. We can see this in the email exchange between Satoshi and Bohm. On 12 Feb, Bohm reported that his system showed four other nodes (miners) connected. By July, he reported problems finding any other miner to connect to. He told Satoshi on 19 Jul that he typically saw three to five other nodes running Bitcoin but had had problems finding nodes recently. On 20 Jul, Bohm could only connect to two nodes. At that time, Satoshi was connected to IP 70.113.114.209 which resolves to Texas—probably Dustin Trammell. It seems that the system was completely dependent upon just a few people running open ports.

The lack of activity is confirmed by the very low volume of transactions, only 219 for the whole year. This was one transaction for every 150 blocks. Most of these would have been trial transactions of the type that Bohm did with Satoshi. The only real activity was mining, and even that was less than expected. The difficulty level was set at 1, which was supposed to be ridiculously low, but it was still too high to mine the target of one block every ten minutes. The average block time for 2009 was over 15 minutes.

Finney had been mining Bitcoin for a few months using a desktop machine. Satoshi proposed in February that the next update, v0.1.6, would include multiple processor support. Finney replied enthusiastically about the potential for running multiple mining machines using Satoshi's proposed multi-threading update. He was also keen to explore the possibilities of using Bitcoin as a time-stamping system. But v0.1.6 never appeared, and Finney's mining machine began to overheat from too much hashing. He turned it off at the end of March and wrote the keys to his 8,600 Bitcoins to a CD Rom which remained, forgotten, on his desk. This was a typical pattern. Bitcoin was an exciting idea; people began enthusiastically mining, but there was nothing to do with the Bitcoin they generated, and they soon lost interest.

Bitcoin was coming to a halt before it had even properly started. The problem was partly due to Satoshi's own diminished activity. At the end of February, he was keen to progress the software, but by April he had gone quiet. He continued mining, but had become preoccupied with something else.

Bitcoin could have failed in the summer of 2009. That it did not was mainly due to the participation of a young computer science student from Finland, Martti Malmi. It is a familiar story: he was finishing his course and could only find boring work below his capabilities. Malmi wanted to work on something more interesting, and in April he came across Satoshi's white paper in a Google search. As an idealistic libertarian, he was immediately attracted to the idea, downloaded the software and mined his first block on 9 Apr 2009.

Malmi posted about Bitcoin to a free-market anarchist site called anti-state.com under the name Trickstern. Then, in early May, he mailed Satoshi, offering to help. Satoshi eagerly took him up on his offer.

It was Malmi who established the Bitcoin forum (he posted under the name Sirius) and who was responsible for the majority of new features of the software release, v0.2, in Dec 2009, including a Linux version. Satoshi's contribution was support for Tor and multiple cores as well as "laying the groundworks for future functionality". Satoshi had probably already made the multiple-core upgrade in his private software version before the Bitcoin launch. So he did little coding in 2009 after the initial debugging in January.

For years, Malmi kept his correspondence with Satoshi confidential. The 2024 Wright court case in London changed his mind. Wright has shown animosity towards almost everyone involved in the early days of Bitcoin. In a US court deposition, he made accusations against Malmi—he misspelt his name and called him a Norwegian—most significantly claiming that Malmi had set up the Silk Road crime site along with another early Bitcoin enthusiast, Theymos. Malmi submitted his private email correspondence to the court to set the record straight and simultaneously placed the emails online. This release has given us hundreds more Satoshi emails.

The emails give valuable insight into Satoshi during 2009 when he was otherwise silent. They confirm that Satoshi saw himself, first and foremost, as a programmer: "My writing is not that great, I'm a much better coder" (3 May 2009). In fact, Satoshi's writing style was excellent.

Malmi was attracted to Bitcoin for its potential to increase human freedom. He did not envisage getting rich himself and was not particularly focused on mining. But Satoshi wanted him to maintain a node that accepted incoming requests to give new users something to connect to. Malmi agreed: "I'm running a Bitcoin node always when my PC is powered on, which means about 24/7. Bitcoin is a great project, and it's really cool to participate!" Operating a node meant continued mining, and Malmi ended up with 55,000 Bitcoins.

Apart from mining, Satoshi's first tasks for Malmi were writing a FAQ and setting up a website on SourceForge. Satoshi wanted it "clean and professional looking". He explained that the existing bitcoin.org site "was designed in a more professorial style when I was presenting the design paper on the Cryptography list, but we're moving on from that phase." Satoshi was no academic and was ready to move on from his faux "professorial" style.

Even though Malmi was an inexperienced young graduate previously unknown to Satoshi, the Bitcoin creator gave him admin rights to SourceForge and let him implement a new website. He also allowed Malmi to begin coding his own ideas for improvements to the software. Satoshi may have been a loner but was undoubtedly a good delegator.

Satoshi's emails to Malmi are to the point and focused on what needs to be done. He sounds like a successful businessperson who delegates ruthlessly and aims to get action going rather than for everything to be perfect from day one. Most technical people are poor delegators because they are fixated on the detail which they want to get right. Satoshi could also be very technical at times. This mix of ferocious delegation and attention to technical detail is typical of the high-tech entrepreneur.

In June, Satoshi suggested to Malmi a new word for Bitcoin:

> "Someone came up with the word "cryptocurrency"... maybe it's a word we should use when describing Bitcoin, do you like it?" (11 Jun 2009)

So we have "cryptocurrency," which is now used not just for Bitcoin but for any electronic currency that relies on cryptography. This email is the first recorded mention of the word. Satoshi got it from some unknown person.

Malmi was also involved in programming, including a "minimise to tray" feature and getting the program to automatically start when Windows started. These were his ideas and Satoshi loved them—particularly the auto start: "Now that I think about it, you've put your finger on the most important missing feature right now that would make an order of magnitude difference in the number of nodes. Without auto-run, we'll almost never retain nodes after an initial try out interest." (29 Aug 2009)

The emails show that Malmi was leading the Bitcoin development in these crucial months. Satoshi did no coding until well into the autumn. And Finney was no longer involved:

> "Hal isn't currently actively involved. He helped me a lot defending the design on the Cryptography list, and with initial testing when it was first released. He carried this torch years ago with his Reusable Proof Of Work (RPOW)." (21 Jul 2009)

Finney was not part of some Satoshi team. He became involved when he read the white paper on the Cryptography mailing list and then helped win some acceptance of the idea. At a practical level, he helped Satoshi with code review and debugging. But Finney had other things to think about that summer.

He was worried about his health; he was experiencing unexplained fatigue along with strange tingling sensations and a lack of coordination. His doctor diagnosed him with a progressive terminal disease, Amyotrophic Lateral Sclerosis, in August 2009. Hal explained the implications in an article in LessWrong:

> "Unfortunately I have been diagnosed with a fatal disease, Amyotrophic Lateral Sclerosis or ALS, sometimes called Lou Gehrig's disease. ALS causes nerve damage, progressive muscle weakness and paralysis, and ultimately death. Patients lose the ability to talk, walk, move, eventually even to breathe, which is usually the end of life. This process generally takes about 2 to 5 years. {…} ALS normally does not affect higher brain functions. I will retain my abilities to think and reason as usual. Even as my body is dying outside, I will remain alive inside." (5 Oct 2009)

Within a few years, Finney was almost completely paralysed and could only communicate through eye movements. That did not stop him coding. Finney returned to Bitcoin at the end of 2009. He made some valuable contributions to Bitcoin code, most significantly improving its elliptic-curve cryptography.

As for Satoshi, he did very little on Bitcoin in 2009 between April and October beyond sending the odd reply to Malmi and keeping his own mining going. He was occupied with something else that summer: "I've been really busy lately" he told Malmi on 14 Jun 2009. He repeated this message in July:

> "I'm not going to be much help right now either, pretty busy with work, and need a break from it after 18 months development." (21 Jul 2009)

An 18-month development period is consistent with Satoshi's statements that he started working on Bitcoin in 2007. (In a later post on the forum, he also said that "The design and coding started in 2007".) Satoshi is a busy person with something important to do other than Bitcoin. He is also suffering from Bitcoin burnout. The lack of progress would have been disheartening and Satoshi is even struggling to keep people mining. Malmi's open connection was vital to give newbies something to connect to.

Satoshi was searching for an application to get people interested in Bitcoin, a valid use case that would start things going. He asked if Malmi had any ideas and offered to arrange funding: "There are donors I can tap if we come up with something that needs funding, but they want to be anonymous, which makes it hard to actually do anything with it" (21 Jul 2009). Malmi came back with the concept of an exchange. He had the idea of setting a minimum guaranteed price for Bitcoin to establish confidence in the digital currency. He was concerned that Satoshi might be alarmed by the financial exposure of this guarantee and did a calculation. He set the target price so low that Satoshi should have been able to buy up the entire supply for 1000 euros!

Malmi offered to set up this exchange himself if Satoshi wanted to avoid taking it on. It took Satoshi a whole month to reply, but when he did, he was enthusiastic:

> "That's great, I could probably get a donor to send currency to you which you convert to euros and pay out through methods that are convenient for users. I don't want to do an exchange business myself, but it can be done independently of me. Like you say, there is more software development to be done first, and also I'd like to keep trying for a while to think of a bootstrap application to use Bitcoins for. I've had some ideas that could only be done before an exchange exists." (Satoshi, 24 Aug 2009)

Who were these mysterious donors who wanted to contribute to Bitcoin through Satoshi yet needed to remain anonymous? Satoshi said anonymity "makes it hard to actually do anything with it". Which is odd because the many charities accepting anonymous donations have no trouble spending the money. But Satoshi seems to be anticipating complete secrecy. Transferring significant funds through unidentifiable channels is difficult due to money laundering rules. It is surely Satoshi himself who is providing this money. His overwhelming concern is that it should not be traceable back to him. But he is willing, in principle, to fund Malmi's service to drive the Bitcoin price up.

But not quite yet. Although Satoshi likes the idea, he wants to put off the exchange while he continues to look for a bootstrapping application. What does he mean by that odd comment: "I've had some ideas that could only be done before an exchange exists." What idea could possibly require that an exchange does not exist? Satoshi is up to something and we will see later the evidence of what it was.

Satoshi never did find his bootstrapping application for Bitcoin. But by October, the Bitcoin magic was starting to work anyway. A new user named NewLibertyStandard beat Malmi to setting up a Bitcoin exchange. Satoshi liked the appearance of new people: "It's encouraging to see more people taking an interest such as that NewLibertyStandard site." (16 Oct 2009)

At this time, Satoshi's involvement revived. Whatever he had been doing in the summer of 2009, the pressure must have abated by October. He had recovered his mojo and was actively contributing again:

> "I'm still merging in some changes I had that need to go in before any next release. Some things based on questions and feedback I've received that'll reduce confusion. I'll probably enable multi-proc generating support, and hopefully make it safe to just backup wallet.dat to backup your money. It's good to be coding again!" (MM emails, 16 Oct 2009)

The Malmi emails show extensive back-and-forth with Satoshi over several months. Satoshi was once more fully committed. Malmi had persuaded him to do a Linux port, and he was soon engrossed by the details of testing the new version.

Meanwhile, Oct 2009 marked the very first Bitcoin/fiat transaction. Malmi sold 5,050 Bitcoins to NewLibertyStandard for $5.02, which was around 1000 Bitcoins per dollar. Presumably, the transaction was intended to give NewLibertyStandard some Bitcoins to work with. But the absurdly low price shows how little Bitcoin was valued at this time. Malmi went on to establish his own exchange with Satoshi's blessing.

NewLibertyStandard also tested the Linux version. In one session, he saw the new software mine six blocks to give him 300 new Bitcoins. But when he restarted the software, all the blocks disappeared! He was alarmed. Had they somehow been deleted from the blockchain? But Satoshi explained that his computer ports had gone dead, so his software had been working as an island disconnected from the network. Without any competition, his computer had been able to find the proof of work for six successive blocks. But these blocks were a mirage—his computer had not transmitted them to the blockchain.

Satoshi was also working on the capability to connect through Tor:

> "Do you think anonymous people are looking to be completely stealth, as in never connect once without TOR so nobody knows they use Bitcoin, or just want to switch to TOR before doing any transactions?" (5 Nov 2009)

It was not a question that Malmi could answer. He replied that the people who wanted complete anonymity tended to know what they were doing.

The other big topic was a new forum. Malmi had established a forum on SourceForge that was attracting users. Satoshi recognised the importance of developing this further:

> "I've seen projects that have major following just from forum talk and pie-in-the-sky planning without even having any code yet. Having a lot of forum talk gives a project more presence on the net, more search hits, makes it look big, draws new users in, helps solve support questions, hashes out what features are most of wanted." (5 Nov 2009)

SourceForge was slow, and its forum tools were primitive. Satoshi also hated that it logged all interactions. He wanted something better, including SSL encryption to make it more secure for people (like Satoshi himself) who wanted to achieve complete anonymity by connecting through Tor. Malmi put forward some suggestions and even set up a trial site. But Satoshi had his own ideas:

> "I'm not really a fan of that type of forum layout. [...] It's more of a social networking site, not really conducive to technical discussion. I'm thinking phpBB or IPB or similar. One line of text per thread, small fonts, efficient use of vertical space. Most people are already familiar with the interface." (8 Nov 2009)

Satoshi mocked up a design on a free forum site, but they decided that was no better. Eventually, they used the Drupal web content management program using SMF software. This had to be hosted on a paid site. Satoshi had been very keen on using free services. Could he not afford even a modest hosting fee? Or was this because he wanted to avoid making any payment traceable back to himself? Criminal investigators are taught to "follow the money", a concept Satoshi appreciated from the start. He was obsessive about not leaving a money trail.

The Bitcoin forum was established on the bitcoin.org site, which moved to Malmi's server alongside his exchange. Eventually, the forum was ported to bitcointalk.org to make it seem less official, which is why it is often known as BitcoinTalk. But this only happened after Satoshi had become inactive.

Malmi was now funding the Bitcoin server site. As he was a student/new graduate, the monthly cost was onerous, and Satoshi had to find some way to get funds to him. Satoshi addressed the problem in June:

> "BTW, it's looking like I may be able to get us some money soon to cover web host costs, back your exchange service, etc, in the form of cash in the mail. Can you receive it and act as the project's treasurer?" (22 Jun 2010)

And:

> "I got a donation offer for $2000 USD. I need to get your postal mailing address to have him send to. And yes, he wants to remain anonymous, so please keep the envelope's origin private." (23 Jun 2010)

For a month, nothing happened, perhaps because Satoshi had been too busy. But then he mentions it again:

> "I take it you haven't received anything from that donor yet? He seemed pretty certain he was going to send it, maybe more. (if you get anything, we need to keep private for him the fact that we got a donation)." (15 Jul 2010)

Two days later Malmi emailed Satoshi to propose moving the site to another provider who charged $10 per month rather than the current $30. It reduced Satoshi to despair:

> "Please promise me you won't make a switch now. The last thing we need is switchover hassle on top of the slashdot flood of work we've got now. I'm losing my mind there are so many things that need to be done.
>
> Also, it would suck to be on a smaller, less reliable host just to save a measly $20. I will try to think of a polite way to ask the donor if

> he sent it, but right now there are other higher priority things that are going to bump even that for a few days. Would a donation of Bitcoins help in the short term?" (MM emails, 18 Jul 2010)

Malmi gave Satoshi his Bitcoin address but it was not used because three days later he received the money: "Good news: I received the donation of $3600. At least the hosting costs are no problem anymore." When he counted the bills again, he found it was actually $3,500 packed in two bundles of $100 notes. Satoshi replied:

> "That's great! I'll let him know it was received and thank him.
>
> It might be a long time before we get another donation like that, we should save a lot of it. Spend what you need on hosting. Email me a simple accounting when you take out money for expenses, like:
>
> -$60 rackspace monthly
> $2540 balance" (21 Jul 2010)

Note how obsessive Satoshi was in protecting the donor's identity who undoubtedly was Satoshi himself. We would love to know where that envelope was posted from. The idea that someone else was sending it may have been a deliberate tactic to avoid Malmi thinking it was from Satoshi's home location. Alternatively, he may have used an intermediary or some indirect route to get the money to Malmi. That could explain the delay.

After a year of disappointingly slow progress, Satoshi began to be pleasantly surprised: "The forum sure is taking off. I didn't expect to have so much activity so fast" (7 Feb 2010). Other people were becoming engaged, including two experienced developers, Laszlo Hanyecz and Gavin Andresen.

Would Satoshi have given up in 2009 if it had not been for Malmi? It was the young student's enthusiasm that kept the momentum going in that crucial but frustrating year. He was the perfect foil to Satoshi—helpful, eager, competent, and full of ideas. He was just the type of person you would love to have working for you. But Malmi had his career to think of. In mid-2010, he got his first proper job and began to disengage. After Satoshi's withdrawal, he was left to control the Bitcoin sites, bitcoin.org and the BitcoinTalk forum. However, as Bitcoin grew, the heat attached to this role increased, and he passed them on around 2013.

The Malmi emails give us a fascinating viewpoint on the very early development of Bitcoin. And they leave us with some unanswered questions. Most significantly, what was it that Satoshi was doing in the summer of 2009?

FOUR

SAINT SATOSHI?

Satoshi's second period of engagement lasted just over a year, from Oct 2009 to Dec 2010. He did what might have been expected of him in 2009 by leading the development of the currency and posting frequently. Satoshi handles everything thrown at him with intelligent, to-the-point replies that are just as long as they need to be and no longer.

In 2010, Bitcoin really began to take off—at least in the sense of engaging a significant number of enthusiasts. At the end of the year, Satoshi credited five developers on the website, including himself and Malmi. Laszlo Hanyecz was very important in 2010 but has become best known for ordering the world's most expensive pizzas. Coming a few months later was Gavin Andresen, whom Satoshi trusted to carry the project forward. The fifth developer was Nils Schneider.

Not that Satoshi had much time to spare. He was swamped, as he told Malmi:

> "I've also been busy with other things for the last month and a half. I just now downloaded my e-mail since the beginning of April. I mostly have things sorted and should be back to Bitcoin shortly. Glad that you've been handling things in my absence. Congrats on your first transaction!" (16 May 2010)

He was still busy in August, as he posted to the forum: "Sorry, I've been so busy lately I've been skimming messages and I still can't keep up" (27 Aug 2010).

There was a major software update in June 2010, including the first version for the Mac, which was the work of Laszlo. The update should have been 0.3 in sequence, but Satoshi thought it time to move the software out of beta:

> "But 1.0 sounds like the first release. For some things, newness is a virtue, but for this type of software, maturity and stability are important. I don't want to put my money in something that's 1.0. 1.0 might be more interesting for a moment, but after that we're still 1.0 and everyone who comes along thinks we just started. This is the third major release and 1.3 reflects that development history. (0.1, 0.2, 1.3)" (27 Jun 2010)

Others replied that the release of version 1.0 of software was seen as a significant milestone by the open source community and could attract publicity. Renumbering the software as 1.3 would be confusing and odd. Ultimately, the release stayed as 0.3:

> "BTW, I did come to my senses after that brief bout with 1.3, this release is still going to be 0.3 beta not 1.0. I really appreciate the effort, but there are a lot of problems." (5 Jul 2010)

It became a tradition for all versions of the software to be prefixed by 0, reaching 0.21.0 in 2021. Only then was the 0 finally dropped.

In July 2010, a Bitcoiner using the name Olipro carried out experiments to improve the hash rate of the software. He managed to produce blisteringly fast versions. Some of these improvements involved optimising the implementation of the SHA-256 hash algorithm. Satoshi arranged for the upgrades to be included in v0.3.6 of the official software, which ran 2.4x faster than the previous hash rate. Ironically, this would not have benefited an individual miner. The net impact was to increase mining competition as the mining difficulty adjusted to the performance level of the new software. Faster software was only valuable if you had it but the competition did not.

One amusing episode—in hindsight—was the removal of the project's Wikipedia page. On 14 Jul, Giulio Prisco posted that the Wikipedia page was up for removal for not being notable enough. Satoshi was annoyed but calm:

"The timing is strange, just as we are getting a rapid increase in 3rd party coverage after getting slashdotted. I hope there's not a big hurry to wrap the discussion and decide." (20 Jul 2010)

NewLibertyStandard pointed out that Wikipedia often deleted something just as it became important: "Article gets written, and nobody notices it, even to delete it. Then it starts to get some publicity, and the editors notice it just enough to say it's not notable enough. And then they delete it until it really becomes notable."

And true to form, on the 30 Jul, the Bitcoin Wikipedia article was deleted. It was reinstated less than six months later, in December, when Bitcoin was obviously notable. It just shows the weakness of Wikipedia, that it reinforces the stasis quo conformist view. Anything new is labelled "fringe" unless it is endorsed by the "experts", who are often the very people with the most to lose if the consensus view is overturned. With the growth of so-called "fact-checking", this is a concern as most fact-checkers know nothing about the subject and will start with Wikipedia.

Cypherpunk Zooko Wilcox-O'Hearn had decided that Bitcoin was notable very early and wrote the first blog post about the currency. In August, he joined the forum and Satoshi thanked him: "Hey Zooko! I wanted to thank you for posting about Bitcoin on your blog a year or two ago, back when I announced it on the Cryptography mailing list."

That summer of 2010 was an eventful time. In August, what everyone had been dreading actually happened: a hacker successfully attacked Bitcoin. They had discovered a bug in Bitcoin's transaction testing and devised an exploit by triggering an integer variable overflow. With a transaction input of 0.5 BTC, the attacker generated two outputs of 92,233,720,368 BTC, which is over four thousand times greater than the supposed ultimate Bitcoin supply. This got through the software because the sum of the two very large numbers overflowed to give a small negative, typical of a transaction fee.

The strange transaction in block 74638 was noticed and highlighted in the forum within 90 minutes by Jeff Garzik. Within three hours, "lfm" gave the correct explanation. Gavin Andresen made a first stab at a patch, and when Satoshi was alerted, he made his own code adjustments. The patch was released five hours after the faulty transaction.

In the meantime, mining had continued almost as normal. Many miners would not have known about the bug, and the blockchain had advanced with the corrupt transaction embedded within it. Miners now had to download the patch and start verifying blocks again. The patched software would reject the faulty block and every block after it on the corrupt blockchain. However, miners running the old software would be unaware of the issue. So some miners would be working on a new blockchain while others would still be adding to the corrupt chain which was already quite a bit longer. There were two competing blockchains. Which one would win?

Within a day, the new chain had more hash power than the old chain. Twelve hours later, Satoshi announced victory, that the new chain was longer than the old. The issue had been resolved thirty-six hours after the transaction that had caused the problem. Bitcoin had survived its most significant crisis to date. The episode showed the software was still immature, yet the protocol proved resilient. The main losers were the miners who, in all good faith, had mined blocks after the corrupt transaction only to find their Bitcoin taken away by the new chain. This did not create a big issue in 2010, as Bitcoin was still relatively worthless.

The year was one of great progress for Bitcoin. Compared to 219 transactions in 2009, there were 400 transactions per day by August 2010. Bitcoin might still be small, but the compound rate of growth was astronomical. The growth in mining difficulty illustrates this. Throughout 2009, it was 1, only increasing to 1.18 on 30 Dec. But in 2010 it increased rapidly: 1.34 in January, 3.78 in February, 4.57 in March, and 11.46 in April. In the summer, the rate of increase accelerated; by the end of August, it was over 623. Mining was beginning to get hard, at least for those mining on ordinary desktop computers.

Two miners had started using GPU mining rigs. The first generally accredited GPU miner is Laszlo, while Artforz started GPU mining in July 2010. Graphics Processing Units were designed to carry out the huge number of parallel calculations necessary to display and update images on computers. This characteristic made them ideal for mining Bitcoin and they were much faster than CPUs.

Artforz mined an incredible amount of Bitcoin with his Artfarm, mostly in the second half of 2010. Wolfgang Wester estimates 300,000-400,000

Bitcoins including his earlier CPU mining. This would make him one of the most successful miners ever. It was the beginning of the end for the CPU miners.

Bitcoin was in transition, and its potential was becoming visible to more people. Satoshi was leading the charge, and the Bitcoin community has greatly treasured his words. They have become part of the Saint Satoshi myth. So let's look at his views on some important topics.

Anonymity

Satoshi's views on Bitcoin's anonymity evolved over time. At the Bitcoin launch, he had written, "Participants can be anonymous". However, in the next year, he understood that it was too easy for a third party to track transactions and potentially even uncover a participant's identity. Satoshi began emphasising the importance of not connecting your real identity with your Bitcoin addresses in any way: "For greater privacy, it's best to use a new Bitcoin address each time." (25 Nov 2009)

In July 2010, he went further and edited the website to remove anonymity, as he discussed with Malmi:

> "I think we should de-emphasise the anonymous angle. [...] It's possible to be pseudonymous, but you have to be careful. If someone digs through the transaction history and starts exposing information people thought was anonymous, the backlash will be much worse if we haven't prepared expectations by warning in advance that you have to take precautions if you really want to make that work." (6 Jul 2010)

This also relates to Satoshi's own Bitcoin. He must have realised the problems with spending this Bitcoin if he was to remain anonymous.

The future of Bitcoin

In the myth, Satoshi always knew that Bitcoin would succeed. His true position was more nuanced: "I am sure that in twenty years there will either be very large transaction volume or no volume." (14 Feb 2010)

People tend to forget the qualification "or no volume". Satoshi regarded Bitcoin as a long shot and was certainly working on other things that took priority for his time.

The Bitcoin price

From the very start, Satoshi recognised the potential of Bitcoin to go to a very high value, such as $1 million. This was based on calculating the world money supply and dividing it by the ultimate total number of Bitcoins. Most others did not share this view. Another approach was to take the price as equal to the cost of the electricity required to mine a Bitcoin. Because the difficulty was low in 2009/10, this gave a very low valuation of a fraction of a dollar. NewLibertyStandard preferred this method, and Satoshi was content to go along with it:

> "I like his approach to estimating the value based on electricity. It's educational to see what explanations people adopt. They may help discover a simplified way of understanding it that makes it more accessible to the masses. Many complex concepts in the world have a simplistic explanation that satisfies 80% of people, and a complete explanation that satisfies the other 20% who see the flaws in the simplistic explanation." (16 Oct 2009)

Note that phrase "more accessible to the masses." Earlier, he talked about the time when "encryption became available to the masses." We will meet someone else who loved to talk about "the masses" in this way.

In early 2010, the price of Bitcoin was equal to the generation costs. But Satoshi recognised this would not always be the case: "A rational market price for something that is expected to increase in value will already reflect the present value of the potential price increases. In your head, you do a probability estimate balancing the odds that it keeps increasing." (21 Feb 2010)

The issue came up when some Bitcoiners wrote a description of Bitcoin for Slapdash. It shows that the predominant view was that the Bitcoin price was fixed by the cost of the electricity to mine it. Satoshi was not happy:

> "'The developers expect that this will result in a stable-with-respect-to-energy currency outside the reach of any government.' -- I am definitely not making any such taunt or assertion.
>
> It's not stable-with-respect-to-energy. There was a discussion on this. It's not tied to the cost of energy. NLS's [NewLibertyStandard's] estimate based on energy was a good estimated starting point, but market forces will increasingly dominate.
>
> Sorry to be a wet blanket. Writing a description for this thing for general audiences is bloody hard. There's nothing to relate it to." (5 Jul 2010)

Satoshi had always seen that the relation between mining and price was the reverse of the majority view. The Bitcoin price was not determined by Bitcoin mining; it was the intensity of mining that was determined by the Bitcoin price.

One poster raised the question of someone taking advantage of the low price by buying up all the Bitcoin—and perhaps destroying it! Satoshi replied with an economic argument:

> "What the OP [original poster] described is called "cornering the market". When someone tries to buy all the world's supply of a scarce asset, the more they buy the higher the price goes. At some point, it gets too expensive for them to buy any more. It's great for the people who owned it beforehand because they get to sell it to the corner at crazy high prices. As the price keeps going up and up, some people keep holding out for yet higher prices and refuse to sell." (9 Jul 2010)

He referenced the Hunt brothers' notorious attempt to corner the silver market, which bankrupted them. Satoshi was certainly an economically aware individual, unlike most of the other posters.

Giving Bitcoin away

Satoshi was keen to spread Bitcoin ownership to as many people as possible. In June 2010, Gavin Anderson wrote his first Bitcoin program: "For my first Bitcoin coding project, I decided to do something that sounds really dumb: I created a web site that gives away Bitcoins" (11 Jun 2010). The website would allow anyone to withdraw 5 Bitcoins, and Satoshi was delighted:

> "Excellent choice of a first project, nice work. I had planned to do this exact thing if someone else didn't do it, so when it gets too hard for mortals to generate 50BTC, new users could get some coins to play with right away. Donations should be able to keep it filled." (18 Jun 2010)

On 23 Jun, Andresen announced that some users were abusing the Bitcoin faucet with multiple requests. He was forced to impose limitations and would soon stop the service altogether. As Xunie pointed out: "I think the "5 BTC for FREE!" thing, is kinda... Flawed…"

Satoshi expressed his support and made a donation of 100 Bitcoins. It was a trivial amount compared to his total Bitcoin wealth. And his interest in distributed ownership was not altruism. He wanted to draw in more users and grow the price.

Scripting and the avoidance of forks

The philosophy behind the open source movement was that the software was available for anyone to examine, modify, create their own versions, or incorporate into their own products. For a cryptocurrency, this freedom was troublesome. Satoshi knew that Bitcoin should not fork. The philosophy is that there should be a fixed maximum number of coins. But if Bitcoin forked, then the total supply of Bitcoin would increase by splitting the currency in two. Multiple forks could flood the market.

Splits would also weaken the security of the blockchain. The proof of work method relied upon no player commanding more than 50% of the hash rate. But suppose there were ten equal blockchains instead of one. If an attacker concentrated all their hash power on one chain, they could carry out a successful attack with only 5% of the total hash power. Once the attacker had overwhelmed the first target, they could switch their firepower to another blockchain. To maximise security, the network hash rate should be devoted to a single blockchain.

Satoshi thought all this through before Bitcoin was even launched. He recognised that the design needed to be flexible to allow for new functionality without triggering a fork. His solution was a scripting language built into Bitcoin.

Satoshi explained the thinking behind the scripting language. "The nature of Bitcoin is such that once version 0.1 was released, the core design was set in stone for the rest of its lifetime". The scripting language would allow for new functionality, such as smart contracts. Transacting parties could encode the contract in the scripting language, which would then be evaluated as "true" or "false" by the network. "The design supports a tremendous variety of possible transaction types that I designed years ago. Escrow transactions, bonded contracts, third party arbitration, multi-party signature, etc.." Although they were not operative, all these things had to be designed to ensure that they could be implemented at some time in the future. Satoshi's concern was to avoid forks. "I don't believe a second, compatible implementation of Bitcoin will ever be a good idea."

Eventually, what Satoshi had wanted to avoid happened. Bitcoin forked over the civil war between the small blockers and big blockers, not helped by the toxic presence of Craig Wright and his backer Calvin Ayre. First, Bitcoin Cash forked from Bitcoin core. Then, the Ayre/Wright currency, the so-called "Bitcoin Satoshi Vision" or BSV, forked from Bitcoin Cash. In both cases, almost all the value remained with the main fork.

Bitcoin Cash was not even the biggest problem. Satoshi envisaged a single cryptocurrency—Bitcoin. This ideal was destroyed by Vitalik Buterin and the launch of Ethereum in 2015. Perhaps it was inevitable that there would be competition. Ironically, Satoshi himself paved the way for Ethereum. His scripting language introduced the concept of smart contracts, but it was never fully developed. This created an opening for someone else to do it better.

Scalability

The most controversial issue is Satoshi's view on scalability. The problem arose because Bitcoin, as launched by Satoshi, was completely inadequate to handle a large volume of transactions. It had a small block size and transactions could take an hour or more to be secure. These failings were evident from the start. The earliest criticism of Bitcoin was that it could never handle anything like the volume of transactions of the Visa and Mastercard networks.

There are two interpretations of Satoshi's words. The first is that Satoshi saw Bitcoin as a store of value, as digital gold. The second is that he saw Bitcoin primarily as a means of carrying out transactions, as digital cash. You can find support for both views in Satoshi's writings. Satoshi himself did not distinguish between the two. He saw Bitcoin as a way to accumulate enormous wealth analogous to gold. But he also regarded its ability to conduct transactions as the foundation for its value.

In a forum post, Satoshi gave a thought experiment about a base metal that could be transmitted over a communication network:

> "If it somehow acquired any value at all for whatever reason, then anyone wanting to transfer wealth over a long distance could buy some, transmit it, and have the recipient sell it.
>
> Maybe it could get an initial value circularly as you've suggested, by people foreseeing its potential usefulness for exchange. (I would definitely want some) Maybe collectors, any random reason could spark it." (27 Aug 2010)

So he saw Bitcoin's role in cash transmission as pump-priming its general use as money. If it were used for cash transmission, it would acquire a value, which would start a feedback loop of people wanting it because its value was increasing. Satoshi saw Bitcoin as taking on the historical role of gold in its widest sense. In the modern world, gold is used only as a store of value, but for most of human history gold was the means of exchange, particularly for large transactions. If you wanted to buy something valuable, such as a house or a set of fine clothes, you would pay in gold. You would use silver or bronze for everyday transactions, such as buying food. Bitcoin has the magic ability to function for both very large and very small transactions. Satoshi certainly appreciated this.

In reality, there were few transactions during the Satoshi era. But he knew that at some point the original Bitcoin software would prove inadequate as transaction volume grew:

> "The design outlines a lightweight client that does not need the full block chain. In the design PDF it's called Simplified Payment Verification. The lightweight client can send and receive transactions, it just can't generate blocks. It does not need to trust a node to verify payments, it can still verify them itself.
>
> The lightweight client is not implemented yet, but the plan is to implement it when it's needed. For now, everyone just runs a full network node.
>
> I anticipate there will never be more than 100K nodes, probably less. It will reach an equilibrium where it's not worth it for more nodes to join in. The rest will be lightweight clients, which could be millions.
>
> At equilibrium size, many nodes will be server farms with one or two network nodes that feed the rest of the farm over a LAN." (14 Jul 2010)

Currently there are less than 20,000 nodes so his prediction that there will "never be more than 100k nodes" looks to be correct. In the early days everyone was running a node, but that is now a specialist task.

In Sep 2010, Satoshi actually advocated reducing the block size because there were so few transactions:

> "The threshold can easily be changed in the future. We can decide to increase it when the time comes. It's a good idea to keep it lower as a circuit breaker and increase it as needed." (Forum, 8 Sep 2010)

This is typical of Satoshi. He talked about money transmission quite a lot but designed the software to handle only a very low volume of transactions. He always left the details for money transmission and micro-payments to future Bitcoin developers.

Technical threats to Bitcoin

Even in the early days, posters were very alive to potential threats to Bitcoin. Satoshi showed depth in his thinking when designing resilience to these threats.

One concern was the growing size of the blockchain. Someone feared that downloading the blockchain would take a lifetime when there are "millions of blocks". Satoshi replied that the maximum download time would be reached after just eight months because the speed increase of computers from Moore's law would more than offset the increase in the blockchain (10/12/2009). His reply does not consider the increase in the average block size from increased transaction volume, but the blockchain size has remained manageable even as it has grown.

Another concern was whether the cryptography underlying Bitcoin would remain secure. Previous hash functions had been broken in about a decade. If someone hacked the SHA-256 hash function would this not invalidate the whole Bitcoin system? Satoshi had thought this through:

> "SHA-256 is very strong. It's not like the incremental step from MD5 to SHA1. It can last several decades unless there's some massive breakthrough attack.
>
> If SHA-256 became completely broken, I think we could come to some agreement about what the honest block chain was before the trouble started, lock that in and continue from there with a new hash function.

If the hash breakdown came gradually, we could transition to a new hash in an orderly way. The software would be programmed to start using a new hash after a certain block number. Everyone would have to upgrade by that time. The software could save the new hash of all the old blocks to make sure a different block with the same old hash can't be used." (14 Jun 2010)

Even in 2010, posters were alert to the possibility of a quantum computer being able to break the keys. Satoshi was relaxed about this risk also:

> "If it happens gradually, we can still transition to something stronger. When you run the upgraded software for the first time, it would re-sign all your money with the new stronger signature algorithm. (by creating a transaction sending the money to yourself with the stronger sig)" (14 Jul 2010)

Someone worried that lost Bitcoins—where the owner has lost their keys—could gradually destroy the currency by reducing the amount in circulation. Satoshi pointed out this was no problem: "Lost coins only make everyone else's coins worth slightly more. Think of it as a donation to everyone." When Laszlo asked if people might direct more attention to breaking the keys of lost coins than mining new coins, Satoshi replied in the negative:

> "Computers have to get about 2^200 times faster before that starts to be a problem. Someone with lots of compute power could make more money by generating than by trying to steal." (21 Jun 2010)

Satoshi's initial development of the Bitcoin concept

The scripting language shows the depth of design that Satoshi built into Bitcoin. As Laszlo remarked: "How long have you been working on this design Satoshi? It seems very well thought out [...]". Satoshi replied: "Since 2007. At some point I became convinced that there was a way to do this without any trust required at all and I couldn't resist to keep thinking about it. Much more of the work was designing than coding."

Satoshi told Malmi that the Bitcoin development took him eighteen months. On another occasion, he said two years. Satoshi announced the concept in the summer of 2008 and launched Bitcoin at the start of 2009, so he must have commenced development in the first half of 2007. But the idea of an electronic currency would have occupied him much earlier. Satoshi says he could not stop thinking about the problem after he worked out how to do it without trust, which is the proof of work. He could only start development when he had the proof of work concept, which must have been no later than early 2007. But Satoshi implies that he had been engaged on the problem for a long time: "at some point I became convinced that there was a way to do this without any trust required…". Which is where the mysterious person "X" comes in. He posted an idea very like Bitcoin, but without a proof of work, at Christmas 2002. If X is Satoshi, then the gestation of that early idea took four and a half years before he could begin development.

Secret Satoshi

There is one other remarkable thing about Satoshi—his obsession with secrecy. This obsession was present from the start. He registered the Bitcoin.org site using AnonymousSpeech because the site anonymised his communications, and he could pay by mailing cash with no proof of identity required. Satoshi used three email addresses: satoshi@anonymousspeech.com, satoshi@vistomail and satoshin@gmx.com. The first two were operated and paid through AnonymousSpeech. The third was a free service. None of the emails sent from these addresses can be traced back to the individual behind Satoshi.

When Satoshi connected to the Bitcoin forum, he used the Tor browser. We know this little nugget from Theymos, the administrator who once proposed releasing Satoshi's private messages and logged IP addresses. He changed his mind due to privacy concerns with other individuals. In any case, Theymos did not believe that it was possible to trace Satoshi's identity from this information because he was paranoid about secrecy.

When the Bitcoin site was hosted on its own server, Martti Malmi paid the bills until he received cash in the post from a mysterious donor who wished to be completely anonymous. This donor was surely Satoshi, either directly or through an intermediary.

Satoshi went to great lengths to safeguard his identity, even when he started by showing his idea to a few people. He always knew that Bitcoin had a probability of becoming very big. And he set out to ensure that no one could ever trace it back to him. Why?

FIVE

SATOSHI EXIT

"I'm looking for the best and brightest IT pro in the Bitcoin community to be the lead developer in a venture backed Bitcoin startup company." (11 Oct 2011)

This forum post by Altoid sounded like an exciting opportunity for a young developer interested in Bitcoin. It did not give any details about the new company but promised that "we can talk about things like compensation and references and I can answer your questions as well". Altoid's venture was on a roll: a global business that would dominate its niche, becoming one of the fastest-growing enterprises in the world. There was just one catch—it was highly illegal.

We can trace the genesis of Altoid's venture to a Bitcoin forum post from "teppy" under the title of "A Heroin Store":

"As a Libertarian, the thing I love most about the Bitcoin project is the chance that it could be truly disruptive.

I think that drug prohibition is one of the most socially harmful things that the US has ever done, and so I would like to do a thought experiment about how a heroin store might operate, accepting Bitcoins, and ending drug prohibition in the process. We'll assume that the drug store is very high profile, and that law enforcement makes discovering the operator a high priority. [...]" (9 Jun 2010)

So started one of the most fascinating and shocking threads in Bitcoin history. The post is actually rather naive—teppy comes up with a rather complex idea that for each package mailed to a client, another would be sent to a random address. The aim is to confuse law enforcement and give those who order from the service plausible deniability. We can imagine the chaos such a random mailing would cause. It is illuminating that neither teppy nor anyone else considers the psychological and legal impact on people who receive large shipments of hard drugs they have not ordered.

Laszlo was the first person to respond with a common-sense objection:

> "Sounds interesting.. but the US government has endless resources and nothing to stop them from doing things they're not supposed to.. I think if it's high profile enough you would still get busted somehow, something you didn't think of." (9 Jun 2010)

Later, he became more positive: "So when/where can I place an order?". Malmi, as Sirius, also contributed to the discussion:

> "You'd need some kind of a reputation system before sending money to an anonymous merchant. Maybe something PGP based to verify he's the same guy people have successfully traded with previously. But even that is difficult, because in this case his customers want to remain anonymous too, and anonymous recommendations are next to nothing." (10 Jun 2010)

The other person who ran the forum, Theymos, came up with an idea to use "trust coins" to build confidence in suppliers. While some posters pointed out that the whole idea was crazy, most were keen to consider how it could be done. When someone objected that heroin users, being addicts, would not have any money to buy Bitcoin, bitcoinex replied: "Using it for four years. Without addiction. Recommend." Which drew the response: "Congrats for being the first recreational heroin user. I don't know where you live, but if they have test centers there, I would let them test your heroin."

It took a new user, ploum, to point out how ridiculous the concept was:

> "Sending heroin to random people? This is insane. If you are caught, you will end up with spending the rest of your life in prison (just imagine that some kids find your package). I've always said that drugs

> kill your brain. It seems I'm mostly right in your case. The fact that you seem proud of it says it all. As a side note, being brand new on this forum, I'm kind of uncomfortable with topics discussing how to use Bitcoins to bypass the law." (26 Oct 2010)

Naturally, his common-sense view drew antagonistic comments from the libertarians.

Altoid joined the forum on 29 Jan and posted six minutes later:

> "What an awesome thread! You guys have a ton of great ideas. Has anyone seen Silk Road yet? It's kind of like an anonymous amazon.com. I don't think they have heroin on there, but they are selling other stuff. They basically use Bitcoin and Tor to broker anonymous transactions. It's at http://tydgccykixpbu6uz.onion. Those not familiar with Tor can go to silkroad420.wordpress.com for instructions on how to access the .onion site.
>
> Let me know what you guys think." (29 Jan 2010)

Malmi thought the Silk Road was a great idea:

> "This has big publicity potential and could increase the user base. It's just a bit difficult for them to build reputation as most people don't want to publicly admit they bought from there. Maybe private recommendations will do. Or people can say 'I know somebody who successfully bought from them'." (31 Jan 2010)

ShadowofHarbringer was more insightful:

> "So here we go, first Bitcoin drug store. We're going into deep water faster than I thought then. I wonder how long will it take for govs to start investigating Bitcoin." (30 Jan 2010)

Altoid's original idea was to grow magic mushrooms and distribute them himself. Since he must have extensively researched Bitcoin before starting the Silk Road two days before his Bitcoin post, we can conclude that this thread gave him the idea. The concept soon moved to a virtual store with other people as suppliers, which avoided the inevitable small risk of Altoid posting products.

The Silk Road offered drugs and other items supplied by merchants to customers around the world. Everything was paid for by Bitcoin and sent through the post. The marketplace existed on the dark web and was accessed through the Tor browser. As the Amazon of illegal drugs, it quickly rose to prominence and notoriety. Merchants were reviewed and rated by their customers, which gave a degree of reliability. And it was not just drugs. You could also buy forged identity documents, guns, and, most notoriously, murder-for-hire services. Altoid, the founder and owner of the Silk Road, was initially known on the site as just "Silk Road". Later, he took his famous moniker, Dread Pirate Roberts or DPR. The name comes from the film The Princess Bride. In the film, Dread Pirate Roberts retires, but several other characters in succession take his identity. Altoid intended to suggest that DPR was not one person but many. However, he was the only Dread Pirate Roberts in the original Silk Road.

It was a priority for the FBI to close the site down, but the technological obstacles were daunting. The anonymity provided by the Tor browser seemed impossible to crack. They did not have any lead about the real identity of DPR or his associates. Identifying and closing down individual merchants had minimal impact on the site as a whole. None of the merchants knew any more about DPR and his organisation than the FBI.

But Dread Pirate Roberts had made a fatal slip. In that October Bitcoin forum post, Altoid included an email address for responses: "rossulbricht at gmail dot com". Ross Ulbricht must have thought his Altoid identity would not be connected to the Silk Road. Later, he became more cautious and returned to his Forum history to delete any Altoid posts that referred to the Silk Road. But he couldn't delete the snippets included in other people's replies. And Ulbricht missed the incriminating email address in the October post.

An enterprising IRS officer, Gary Alford, searching Google on his own time, cracked the case. His job was to trace Silk Road Bitcoin transactions, but DPR used mixers to obscure the trail. A mixer is a transaction with inputs from multiple random parties and several outputs, making it impossible to trace an output to a particular input. If you wanted to obscure the origins of your Bitcoins, you could put them through a mixer several times, completely jumbling up the transaction history. One weekend, Alford had the idea of searching for the earliest mentions of the Silk Road using Google. He located two very early posts. One was by "Altoid" on 27 Jan 2011 to a site www.shroomery.org catering to users of magic mushrooms. The other was his post on the Bitcoin Forum heroin store thread two days later. Altoid claimed he had come across the Silk Road and wanted to know other people's views. But Alford knew that such posts were often disguised marketing. He strongly suspected that Altoid was DPR.

Looking at Altoid's other contributions to the Bitcoin forum, Alford found the October recruitment post and its compromising email address. This tied Altoid to Ross Ulbricht. The FBI agents were not impressed when Alford told them about his discovery. How could a lowly tax official using Google do what the best brains and technical experts at the FBI had failed to achieve? They did not follow up on the lead. To be fair, there was no proof that Altoid was DPR.

Alford was undeterred and continued to investigate Ulbricht. He found he used another username, "frosty", and was able to track him to an address in San Francisco. Meanwhile, the FBI was making progress. They had infiltrated the Silk Road with multiple informers and were learning a great deal about DPR—everything apart from who he was.

Ross Ulbricht gained a physics degree from the University of Texas in 2006 and studied at graduate school at the University School of Material Science and Engineering. There, he became interested in libertarian economic theory, spurred on by the writings of the Austrian economist von Mises. Taking a brave decision to practice what he preached, Ulbricht left university to live according to libertarian principles. In 2009, he took up day trading without success and attempted to develop a computer game but had to give up the project. A friend had started an online bookstore for second-hand books, and Ulbricht ran it as his partner. His heart was not in the business, and this was not the life he had dreamed of.

Everyone liked Ross Ulbricht—the word most often used to describe him was "nice". Women were attracted by his good looks, amiable personality and intelligence. But in Ross' own eyes, he was a failure. The reality of trying to forge a path on your own was disheartening. He had given up his academic career for nothing. When his online books store project literally collapsed—he had put up the stock shelves himself, and they gave way one day, spilling fifty thousand books—he knew it was time for a change. So began his transformation into Dread Pirate Roberts.

Ulbricht was a self-taught programmer who struggled to make his systems airtight. And he was stressed out trying to run the Silk Road while knowing law enforcement was on his tail. A Redditor warned him that a Silk Road server was leaking the site's IP address. Yet Ulbricht, trusting to Tor, failed to close the leak. The FBI read the Reddit post, and one of their experts identified the leaking IP address. They traced it back to a server in a state-of-the-art data centre in Iceland. The Icelandic authorities cooperated and gave them a disk image of the server. From this, they uncovered an IP address for the last person to log on. It resolved to the Cafe Luna in San Francisco, just a few hundred yards from the address where Ulbricht was staying. DPR also used the same username, frosty, as Ulbricht. It was clear now that Alford had got the right man.

The FBI put Ulbricht under surveillance. He lived a modest lifestyle, renting a room in a shared house. No one suspected that the nice guy who spent a lot of time on his computer was living a double life as a ruthless crime boss with many millions of dollars of Bitcoin at his disposal. But how to arrest him? Ulbricht's computers were encrypted. From his conversations online, the FBI knew that if he had just a few seconds warning he could press a single key to secure the hard disk. The FBI needed that computer. A raid on his house was too risky. They had to seize the open laptop.

The takedown took place on 1 Oct 2013 in the unglamorous setting of San Francisco's Glen Park Library, one of the several locations used by Ulbricht to connect through public WIFI. Ulbricht settled down to work, while a deadbeat couple shuffled by and began arguing with each other. As he momentarily turned to look, the well-dressed, petite Asian woman sitting opposite deftly seized the open laptop and passed it on to a technical expert who was waiting nearby. The woman, the couple and everyone else around Ulbricht were FBI agents. He had been caught red-handed.

His laptop showed him signed on to the Silk Road site as DPR. The FBI expert also found the addresses and keys of 144,000 Bitcoins associated with the Silk Road. They would be confiscated by the government and eventually auctioned.

The FBI had been reading DPR's messages and already knew that he had contracted several hit jobs on people he wanted eliminated. The first had been taken out on an employee, ChronicPain, who had been busted. DPR correctly suspected that the employee had done a deal with the DEA. He also believed that ChronicPain had been stealing from him as a large number of Bitcoins were missing. DPR contacted an associate to beat up ChronicPain and then hired the same person to eliminate him. Ironically, this associate was the same undercover DEA agent who was running ChronicPain as an informer. DPR knew this agent as "Nob" and paid $80,000 to have ChronicPain killed. He was told the job had been completed, while the supposed victim hid out of sight under DEA protection.

Another target was a Canadian hacker, FriendlyChemist, who was blackmailing DPR by threatening to release customers' contact details. Ulbricht arranged a bounty of $150,000, which he thought a bit steep, with a Hell's Angel, redandwhite. The hit was supposedly executed. As proof, redandwhite sent DPR a photo of the body with a number supplied by DPR written on a piece of paper. DPR paid the promised bounty, but no murder had taken place. The victim and hired assassin knew each other, and the photo was faked.

This was the fundamental weakness of murder-for-hire contracts between anonymous parties on the Internet. It was much less risky for the hired killer to fake the assassination or simply disappear with the money rather than commit murder. The customer could hardly complain to the police.

Ulbricht was found guilty of drug dealing and money laundering and sentenced to life imprisonment without parole and a fine of $183 million. None of the assassinations he had ordered had been carried out—he had been duped repeatedly. Although Ulbricht was indicted on one charge of attempted murder, this was never prosecuted. There was a complication. The same DEA agent whom Ulbricht had contracted to kill his own informer was himself arrested for stealing the missing Bitcoins.

Ross Ulbricht's sentence was surely unduly harsh. He was only 31, and the US government was going to lock him up for the remainder of his life even though he had not actually killed anyone. In reaction, many libertarians viewed Ulbricht as a hero, and a movement to get him pardoned gained momentum. But Ulbricht was undoubtedly guilty of serious crimes including fumbled attempts to arrange multiple murders.

Was the Silk Road the cause of Satoshi leaving Bitcoin for good? Was he concerned about the legal risk of his currency being used for money laundering and drug crime? This is one theory, but the timing is all wrong. Satoshi had already essentially withdrawn several weeks before Altoid posted about the Silk Road. And the early Silk Road, with its sales of home-grown magic mushrooms, was hardly sufficient cause for Satoshi's withdrawal.

The last definite communication from Satoshi was on 26 Apr 2011. (A brief email from his satoshi@gmx.com account in 2014 said, "I am not Dorian Nakamoto." But the account was likely hacked, which may have been as simple as re-registering an address that Satoshi had abandoned.) On 27 Apr, Gavin Andresen announced that he was giving a talk at a CIA conference. Bitcoiners, being libertarians, hated the CIA, and many saw this as a betrayal by Andresen. A popular theory grew that Anderson's CIA assignation caused Satoshi's withdrawal.

But Satoshi had already left the community months before, although he continued to send a few private emails. His penultimate communication was a direct reply to an email sent by Mike Hearn a few days earlier. In this reply he said he had moved on to other things. This message was repeated in his final email to Andresen on 26 Apr 2010 when he gave Andresen the alert code and key. At the time he sent this email, Satoshi did not know about the proposed CIA visit. The timing is coincidental.

The key to this mystery lies not with the CIA or the Silk Road. In Dec 2010, Satoshi was active in the forum with 21 posts in the first eleven days. He was fully engaged in the project and gave no warning signs of an impending withdrawal. Hal Finney had joined the forum at the end of November, and his contributions would have stimulated Satoshi. In fact, Hal even started mining again, this time with a GPU with which he mined around 2,000 Bitcoins.

On 8 Dec, Satoshi published an update of the software, v0.3.18, featuring some bug fixes and enhancements, but mainly implementing Andresen's work on JSON-RPC accounting commands, a vital step in facilitating Bitcoin's use in online commerce. Everything appeared normal. But just four days later, Satoshi issued a surprise new release, v0.3.19, which wrapped up all his own work in progress. It included improved resistance to DoS (Denial of Service) attacks and removed a "safe-mode" alert feature:

> "There's more work to do on DoS, but I'm doing a quick build of what I have so far in case it's needed, before venturing into more complex ideas." (12 Dec 2010)

This was Satoshi's last post to the Bitcoin forum. On SourceForge he amended the copyright notice for this release from the previous "Satoshi Nakamoto" to "Bitcoin Developers". What did he mean by "before venturing into more complex ideas"? Clearly, he was intending to withdraw, at least temporarily. If he had been planning his withdrawal in advance of the release on 8 Dec, he would have included his DoS work in that release. So, something happened between 8 and 12 Dec to make Satoshi withdraw.

Satoshi continued to exchange private emails with a few individuals for a while. He told Andresen that he intending to withdraw from day-to-day involvement. The Malmi emails give us a window into this period. On 3 Dec, Malmi asked Satoshi who should be the third server admin after Malmi and Satoshi. Xunie had volunteered, but Malmi was unsure. Satoshi's reply shows his high opinion of Gavin Andresen:

> "It should be Gavin. I trust him, he's responsible, professional, and technically much more linux capable than me. (I don't know Xunie, but he hasn't posted for months and he was a goofball)" (3 Dec 2010)

After 12 Dec, Satoshi's replies to Malmi become infrequent and brief. On 20 Dec, he stressed the importance of keeping the user database backed up and safe. On 6 Jan 2011, he replied to Andresen's question, "Satoshi, I assume you don't want to deal with press/PR/interviews?" with one word, "true". He told Andresen to take over Bitcoin's PR. On 25 Jan, he gave Malmi the correct date of the Bitcoin paper to pass on to a student researcher. On 22 Feb, he referred Gavin to Malmi for a password query. And that was it.

Satoshi had a more substantive discussion with Google employee Mike Hearn, who was working on a Java implementation of a simplified Bitcoin client for the Android phone. Hearn began his first email on 27 Dec 2010 with "Happy Christmas Satoshi, assuming you celebrate it wherever you are in the world :-)". Satoshi did not respond to this friendly greeting, but he appreciated the importance of Hearn's project and gave him a long reply, including some code. The two exchanged emails until 10 Jan when Hearne mentioned a thread started by "Hal" about the security of the elliptical curve method that Bitcoin used for its private/public key cryptography. Satoshi confirmed that Hal was Finney: "Yes, it's him. He was supportive on the Cryptography list and ran one of the first nodes." Satoshi then gave an account of how he came to choose the curve:

> "I must admit, this project was 2 years of development before release, and I could only spend so much time on each of the many issues. I found guidance on the recommended size for SHA and RSA, but nothing on ECDSA which was relatively new. I took the recommended key size for RSA and converted to equivalent key size for ECDSA, but then increased it so the whole app could be said to be 256-bit security. I didn't find anything recommend a curve type so I just...picked one. Hopefully there is enough key size to make up for any deficiency." (10 Jan 2011)

It is a revealing answer. No academic would have said, "I just...picked one." Satoshi does not understand the deep mathematics behind the tools he uses, but he is brilliant at applying cryptography to real-world problems.

Satoshi says it took two years of development, which gives a programming start date of the beginning of 2007. Elsewhere, he says the development took eighteen months, but perhaps that was to the point where he was ready to contact Adam Back with the paper rather than the final release date.

Hearn made contact again in early March: "Hope you can find the time/energy to rejoin us soon!" (7 Mar 2011). Satoshi replied to Hearn's email but did not answer this particular hope. Finally, in April, they had their last conversation. Hearn sent Satoshi an email on 20 Apr including a question:

> "I had a few other things on my mind (as always). One is, are you planning on rejoining the community at some point (eg for code reviews), or is your plan to permanently step back from the limelight? One reason I'm peppering you with questions is I worry that much of BitCoins potential lies in careful use of currently inactive features, but there's little guidance on how to do it. And frankly, I don't think I'm smart enough to figure it all out on my own. Maybe theymos is, he seems to understand it well. But if one day you leave entirely, parts of the protocol might fall into disuse, which would be a shame." (20 Apr 2011)

Satoshi made his famous short reply three days later:

> "I've moved on to other things. It's in good hands with Gavin and everyone." (23 Apr 2011)

He added his wishes for Hearn to continue with his Java version. A few days later he sent his last known message to Gavin Andresen:

> "I wish you wouldn't keep talking about me as a mysterious shadowy figure, the press just turns that into a pirate currency angle. Maybe instead make it about the open source project and give more credit to your dev contributors; it helps motivate them.
>
> I've moved on to other things and will probably be unavailable. Here's the CAlert key and broadcast code in case you need it. You should probably give it to at least one or two other people. There are a few long time users who are always around all the time." (26 Apr 2011)

And that was it. Satoshi had always been busy, and it is clear that he was involved in more than just Bitcoin. The above email text was published by Andresen who also gave his reply in which he informs Satoshi about the CIA talk:

> "On a completely different subject: I did something that I hope turns out to be smart, but might be stupid. I was contacted by http://www.iqt.org/ – they're a US-govt-funded 'strategic investment' company, and part of what they do is holding an annual conference on emerging technologies for US intelligence agencies. This year the theme is 'Mobility of Money'. They asked if I'd be willing to talk about Bitcoin, and I committed to giving a 50-minute presentation and participating in a panel discussion."

He continues with a prescient comment:

> "I plan on posting about this on the forums soon, because "Gavin secretly visits the CIA" would spin all sorts of conspiracy theories. "Gavin openly visits the CIA" will create enough conspiracy theories as it is."

He was certainly right about the conspiracy theories! But the correspondence is proof that it was not the CIA visit that caused Satoshi to leave—providing we accept, as I do, that the emails as released by Andresen are genuine. They show that Satoshi announced his withdrawal before Andresen told him about the proposed talk. And Satoshi is very concerned with directing attention away from himself and on to the developers.

To find out why Satoshi left, we need to go back to that crucial four-day period between 8 and 12 Dec. What happened to cause Satoshi's abrupt departure from the forum? Most obviously, there was a long thread on Wikileaks which was in the news due to the release of the huge cache of US Army intelligence papers from Bradley, later Chelsea, Manning. The US was trying to eliminate Wikileaks' sources of funding, and some Bitcoiners suggested contacting Wikileaks to persuade them to use Bitcoin. Almost all the contributors on the thread were positive about Wikileaks, but Satoshi did not participate until one poster suggested "Bring it on":

> "No, don't 'bring it on'.
>
> The project needs to grow gradually so the software can be strengthened along the way.
>
> I make this appeal to WikiLeaks not to try to use Bitcoin. Bitcoin is a small beta community in its infancy. You would not stand to get more than pocket change, and the heat you would bring would likely destroy us at this stage." (4 Dec 2010)

Satoshi did not feel the need to defend Wikileaks—he is no left-winger—but was concerned only with the potential negative effect on Bitcoin. The issue led to Bitcoin's first mention in a mainstream publication when PC World published an article titled "Could the Wikileaks Scandal Lead to New Virtual Currency?" The title was the most controversial thing about the piece, which gave a balanced, non-sensational account of Bitcoin as the invention of a Japanese man called Satoshi Nakamoto. Satoshi was not pleased:

> "It would have been nice to get this attention in any other context. WikiLeaks has kicked the hornet's nest, and the swarm is headed towards us." (11 Dec 2010)

Is this why Satoshi left the forum? It was posted only eighteen hours before his final post. Would that have given him enough time to make his decision and produce his final software update? Perhaps, but it would have been an overreaction. It was only PC World and just one article.

The publicity from Wikileaks may have contributed to Satoshi's withdrawal, but something else could have been the immediate trigger. Another active thread had turned into a discussion about Satoshi's code. Satoshi was not the sensitive type, but one poster made a comment that may have caused him more anxiety than Wikileaks ever did. To understand this comment, we must consider the contentious issue of Satoshi's programming style.

Was Satoshi a good or poor programmer, an amateur or professional? In one sense, the question is absurd. The original Bitcoin code is an incredible production for any solitary coder. Not only did Satoshi get almost everything right, he also added many features, most significantly the script language, that, although not used initially, would lead to rich directions for future development. Satoshi was always intent on future-proofing to avoid forks. As early as 4 Dec 2010, Hal Finney considered uses for "the mysterious and extravagant 'scripting' system" in a thread about implementing a domain system through Bitcoin. Mike Hearne was also impressed. He was trying to puzzle out an obscure technical complication when Satoshi enlightened him, "It's for contracts":

> "Ah ha. A whole unexplored area of the system opens up before my eyes:-) the concept of forming distributed contracts and escrow transactions without needing to trust an intermediary is a concept nearly as novel as Bitcoin itself, I think" (9 Mar 2010)

Satoshi's scripting idea would add an extra dimension of functionality to Bitcoin and was the predecessor of Ethereum's virtual machine.

Quite apart from the excellence of the feature-rich program, there is also the evidence of the forum. Satoshi's attention to detail and the rapid way he understood and dealt with bugs and issues are very evident. You do not get that good working on a few hobby applications. It is inconceivable that Satoshi was not a highly experienced programmer.

And yet, many professional programmers have criticised Satoshi's style. He is undoubtedly guilty of a lack of documentation and general untidiness. He wrote terse code that was often difficult for others to follow. Mike Hearn spent months working on Bitcoin and had to admit that he still found it hard to understand the program. A good description of Satoshi's style comes from Dam Kaminsky's assessment, as reported by expert witness Kevin Madura in the Kleiman trial:

> "Dan Kaminsky, a leading Internet-security researcher, is famous among hackers for discovering, in 2008, a fundamental flaw in the Internet Domain Name System which would have allowed a skilled coder to take over any Web site. He is also regarded as one of the world's best experts for testing software errors and weaknesses. In

> July 2011 he dug deeply into the Bitcoin software in an attempt to uncover its weaknesses.
>
> Kaminsky found none he could exploit. This attempt is recounted in a New Yorker article, in which he was interviewed on the subject by the author, Joshua Davis. In this same article, Kaminsky, after noting that the programming style was dense and inscrutable is quoted as claiming, "the way the whole thing was formatted was insane. Only the most paranoid, painstaking coder in the world could avoid making mistakes." He then went on to proclaim, "He's a world-class programmer, with a deep understanding of the C++ programming language. He understands economics, cryptography, and peer-to-peer networking."

This sums it up well. The code was remarkable, and it worked. Yet the style was idiosyncratic and would not have gone down well in a corporate environment.

What is not in doubt is that Satoshi preferred Windows programming in C++. He was by no means a Linux man. In response to a volunteer who described himself as a "Linux/BSD guy", Satoshi replied, "That's great because that's where I have less expertise" (10 Dec 2009). This preference for Windows marks Satoshi as a commercial programmer rather than an academic. Nor did Satoshi program on the Mac. It was Laszlo who produced the first Bitcoin Mac version.

Satoshi's preference for a dense coding style is illustrated by his response when a new developer, Andrew Buck, commented on the lack of internal function documentation. He volunteered to correct this, but Satoshi disagreed:

> "I like that in libraries for the external API's, but you can probably tell from the code that I'm not a fan of it for interior functions. Big obligatory comment headers for each function space out the code and make you hesitate about creating a small little function where the comment header would be bigger than the function. They're some trouble for maintenance, as changes to the function then require duplicate changes in the comment header. I like to keep

> code compact so you can see more code on the screen at once. [...] Sorry to be a wet blanket." (16 Jul 2010)

Satoshi wanted to keep things compact. He liked to read the code rather than an English description of what the code did. This might be fine for him but not always for other, less talented, coders. Developers working in a team do not typically get to exercise such style choices. Corporate departments have a house style so that code can be understood and maintained by others. Satoshi has coded in a different environment. He is a loner.

At times, Satoshi seemed to actively discourage documentation. Andrew Buck was very keen to help and documented the user commands. Satoshi became alarmed because the documentation included commands that were not actively used: "They're only intended for intrepid programmers who read the sourcecode" (18 Jul 2010). Satoshi respected programmers who read source code and did not need real language descriptions.

Experienced programmers working on the project had great admiration for Satoshi. When Dorian Nakamoto was put forward as Satoshi, Finney sent an email to reporter Andy Greenburg:

> "The reason I was skeptical about Dorian Nakamoto is that he didn't match the picture in my mind that I had of Satoshi. I pictured him younger, as he was giving the impression of youthful vigor. Then there is the language Bitcoin was written in, C++. Satoshi was a master of the intricacies, and I've only seen this in young programmers. It seems hard to master C++ if you didn't learn it while you're young. [...] I program in C, which is compatible with C++, but I don't understand the tricks that Satoshi used." (Hal Finney email, quoted by Forbes 25 Mar 2014)

Finney had a vast experience of programming, so this is very revealing. Satoshi was a complete C++ expert, but his code was hard for others to follow. Most famously, Hal Finney gave his appreciation on a thread in which someone offered to write a minimalistic Bitcoin client. A new poster called farmer_boy made a comment that raised everyone's hackles:

"Another client is useful, especially since the current Bitcoin client is a big mess. I was *shocked* that cryptography code looked like this." (10 Dec 2010)

Among those who posted back supporting Satoshi was Finney:

"I'd like to hear some specific criticisms of the code. To me it looks like an impressive job, although I'd wish for more comments. Now I've mostly studied the init, main, script and a bit of net modules. This is some powerful machinery." (11 Dec 2010)

Satoshi gave his thanks to Finney: "That means a lot coming from you, Hal. Thanks." (11 Dec 2010)

This is the exchange that people remember. But it may have been another post on this thread that caused Satoshi to leave Bitcoin. The poster farmer_boy was not popular—he accumulated a merit score of zero—and continued to criticise Satoshi's code:

"The cryptography code that competent people use, doesn't look like a mess, btw. That 99% of the world uses this kind of obfuscated cryptography only shows that users don't know what they use. Have you ever looked at TrueCrypt for example? It's the exact same kind of mess." (10 Dec 2010)

TrueCrypt was heavily based on Paul Le Roux's E4M product. Some 80%-90% of the TrueCrypt code was Le Roux's work, including all of the cryptography elements that farmer_boy is criticising. farmer_boy claims that Bitcoin is the "exact same kind of mess" as code that Le Roux wrote.

Two days after farmer_boy's post Satoshi published his unexpected software update and departed the forum for good without any farewell or explanation.

SIX

SATOSHI'S GREED LOOP

What accounts for Bitcoin's incredible increase in value and its equally remarkable price volatility with repeated crashes? Bitcoin's price surge is no accident. Satoshi programmed in a greed loop to Bitcoin. And he knew exactly what he was doing.

Satoshi intended for Bitcoin to grow really big, as large as the gold market and perhaps even bigger than that, maybe to replace the dollar as the world's currency. Given this enormous ambition, how should new Bitcoins have been created? There should have been some mechanism to increase the Bitcoin money supply to allow for the vast growth. As the use of Bitcoins increased exponentially, the number of Bitcoins in existence should have increased exponentially as well. Initially, only a limited volume would be needed because only a few people were interested in the currency. But if Bitcoin secured wide adoption, the world would need billions of Bitcoins to meet demand.

So we would expect an exponentially expanding schedule of new coin creation. However, Satoshi programmed the exact opposite: an exponentially decreasing supply of new coins. The ultimate number of Bitcoins would be fixed at 21 million. A full 50% of these would be created in the first four years. The new supply would then halve every four years.

New coin creation:
Years 1-4: 10.5 million (50%)
Years 5-8: 5.25 million (25%)
Years 8-12: 2.625 million (12.5%)
Years 12-15: 1.312 million (6.25%)
Years 16-20: 0.656 million (3.125%)

The increase in Bitcoin supply was very high in the early years, with a 100% annual increase in 2010. In 2009 and 2010, there were few users, yet the market was flooded with Bitcoin. The value was close to zero, and the mining difficulty was very low, so vast amounts of Bitcoin could be mined very easily. But as demand grew, supply was gradually choked off. The new shortage of Bitcoin drove up the price, and the mining difficulty increased in tandem.

Everything that has happened to the Bitcoin price can be explained by Satoshi's perverse schedule of new Bitcoin creations. The very high price volatility shows that the underlying demand is speculative rather than genuine. The supply of Bitcoin is limited not by the laws of mathematics but by some arbitrary numbers that Satoshi hardcoded into his program.

Satoshi always envisaged a fixed total supply, but the numbers were not in the original white paper:

> "The steady addition of a constant of [sic] amount of new coins is analogous to gold miners expending resources to add gold to circulation. [...] Once a predetermined number of coins have entered circulation, the incentive can transition entirely to transaction fees and be completely inflation-free."

In a post to the Cryptography list, Satoshi confirmed the constant rate: "Coins have to get initially distributed somehow, and a constant rate seems like the best formula" (9 Nov 2008). The actual schedule was not specified, but we could get to the total of 21 million with 20 coins every block for twenty years or 10 coins every block for forty years. If Bitcoin caught on, then the expansion in users would be much greater than the increase in coin supply, and the new currency would still experience very high deflation, meaning huge price appreciation.

This was not good enough for Satoshi. In the software he launched in January, he encoded an exponentially decreasing pattern of new coin creation. Did he come up with this idea in the two months between his November post and the launch? It would take time to code and test it. We know that Satoshi gave Ray Dillinger and Hal Finney the source code in November, although they may not have seen the whole programme.

Or did he already have this idea but decided not to mention it to the "professorial" readership of the Cryptography mailing list?

Satoshi designed Bitcoin primarily as money, as digital gold, rather than as a cash transmission mechanism. However, he was always aware that most people expected an electronic currency to be a means of carrying out transactions. He would pay lip service to Bitcoin as digital cash, while leaving the details vague for future developers to work out. The white paper emphasised this cash aspect, reflecting the interests of its intended audience. But actions speak louder than words, and Bitcoin, as implemented by Satoshi, was not efficient at managing transactions.

We also have many posts from Satoshi showing how he was focused on increasing Bitcoin's value from the start:

> "Historically, people have taken up scarce commodities as money, if necessary taking up whatever is at hand, such as shells or stones. Each has a kernel of usefulness that helped bootstrap the process, but the monetary value ends up being much more than the functional value alone. Most of the value comes from the value that others place in it. Gold, for instance, is pretty, non-corrosive and easily malleable, but most of its value is clearly not from that. Brass is shiny and similar in colour. The vast majority of gold sits unused in vaults, owned by governments that could [not] care less about its prettiness.
>
> Until now, no scarce commodity that can be traded over a communications channel without a trusted third party has been available. If there is a desire to take up a form of money that can be traded over the Internet without a TTP [Trusted Third Party], then now that is possible." (3 May 2009)

This comes from the "dump" of information Satoshi gave Malmi, and it must have been originally drafted earlier than May. It shows how he intended Bitcoin as money analogous to gold.

If Bitcoin were intended as money, the supply should increase with demand. The fairest and most economically efficient form of money has zero inflation or deflation. The need for an increasing supply to meet increasing demand was raised very early after launch. But this was not in

Satoshi's interest. In a post to the P2P Foundation, he said that he could not think of any mechanism to manage the Bitcoin money supply without something like a central bank, before adding a revealing comment:

> "In this sense, it's more typical of a precious metal. Instead of the supply changing to keep the value the same, the supply is predetermined and the value changes. As the number of users grows, the value per coin increases. It has the potential for a positive feedback loop; as users increase, the value goes up, which could attract more users to take advantage of the increasing value." (18 Feb 2009)

Here is the key to Satoshi's thinking: Bitcoin is like a "precious metal"—it is digital gold. Satoshi's concept of the price changing rather than supply will be very familiar to anyone who knows the gold market. To understand why, it may help to have a brief primer on the nature of money.

Money is a necessary evil. In a modern economy, when people work, they specialise in something, be it growing crops, cooking meals, or writing software. As Adam Smith pointed out, specialisation is far more productive than attempting to do a bit of everything. Money is the mechanism by which we can exchange our specialised work for the vast range of goods and services we need and which are available on the market. Money is a bookkeeping device, a way of keeping score. We produce goods or services for others, get paid for our work, and spend our money on things others produce for us. It is a perfect cycle. We can also save some of our money, enabling us to work now and consume later. Money also functions as a store of value.

The ideal money would be boring; it would be 100% reliable, in the sense that its value when we spend it should be exactly the same as when we earn it. (We can, of course, invest our money, but an investment is not money.) If we had perfect money, there would be no leakage between earning and spending. But the world is not perfect; banks, conmen, and governments attempt to siphon some of that monetary value into their own pockets.

All sorts of things can be used as money as long as they are rare enough to act as a store of value. However, historically, most societies have ultimately come to precious metals, silver and gold. Gold is an unreactive metal which does not tarnish or rust. It is malleable with a conveniently low melting point so that it can be shaped, cast, and divided. It is attractive to humans. And it is rare, so a small amount of gold has high value. The alchemists tried long and hard to manufacture new gold but failed. Science now understands that gold is an element and cannot be made or destroyed through chemical processes: the gold in the earth's crust was forged in the nuclear furnace of a supernova. The only practical way to get new gold is to mine it. And mining is a high-cost enterprise; nasty, dangerous and difficult.

In many ways, gold was the perfect form of money, but it suffered from the disadvantages of its perfection. Because it was physical it could be stolen. A thief could melt down a gold object and make it untraceable: gold coins could become a cup, and a gold cup could become bracelets for the ladies. The security problems with gold were particularly trying for merchants who needed to send substantial amounts long distances. Soldiers to guard the gold were expensive and corruptible. Was there a better form of gold that could be transmitted over a network, a form of gold that was non-physical, that existed in the realm of information?

The invention of "info-gold" revolutionised society. Instead of moving gold, merchants would exchange tokenised gold or digital gold. The tokenised gold was banknotes, and digital gold was a number in a bank balance. The shrewd bankers of Florence made these innovations. The idea was that the bank would hold the gold in their vaults and issue a piece of paper representing that gold. International trade was facilitated by developing a branch network across Europe's major cities. A merchant could deposit their gold in a bank in Italy with their holdings recorded in a note, take the note to a merchant in England, and exchange it for a consignment of wool cloth. The English merchant would then take the note to a bank in London and obtain the gold. But merchants soon found leaving the gold in the bank easier and safer. What could go wrong with that?

Initially, the banks ensured that they kept all the notes they issued fully backed with gold in their vaults. However, as the banknotes were rarely redeemed, it soon occurred to some financial genius that the cover ratio did not need to be 100%. They just had to hold enough gold to meet all the withdrawal requests that were likely to occur. Fractional reserve banking had been invented. The honest banks leant out the gold for interest and then kept that interest for themselves. Dishonest bankers simply spent the gold. The reputable bankers got rich, the conmen even richer. But all banks were subject to runs when redemptions were far higher than expected because the customers suddenly realised there was insufficient gold to pay everyone.

Many people, including nice middle-class families, were ruined when banks failed. Governments could not let this situation continue, so they nationalised the racket. Only government-owned and controlled banks would be able to issue bank notes. These notes would be backed by gold—to some extent. Theoretically, you could go to the central bank and swap your notes for gold. But because people knew they could do this, they did not need to.

The most fortunate nations were those that could aspire to reserve currency status. In the nineteenth and early twentieth centuries, the reserve currency was the British pound and, after that, the mighty US dollar. The great thing about a reserve currency was that foreigners had to hold it for bank reserves and international trade. Those foreigners would exchange precious assets of real value for your beautifully printed but inherently worthless bits of paper.

These banknotes could theoretically be exchanged for gold. However, when enough citizens and foreigners attempted to do this, governments changed the rules. The British pound lurched on and off the gold standard in the early decades of the twentieth century. In the US, citizens were even prohibited from holding gold in 1934, shortly before the dollar was devalued. Although dollars could be exchanged for gold by foreigners, if you were a US citizen, you would commit a crime by owning the gold.

The Second World War marked the final eclipse of one superpower and the rise of another. The 1944 Bretton Woods agreement firmly established the dollar as the world's reserve currency. Britain, with enormous wartime debts to the US, was in a poor negotiating position and had to suffer the humiliation of having the pound pegged to the dollar—just like everyone else. A pseudo-gold standard was maintained because foreign banks could exchange their dollars for gold at a fixed rate. However, Nixon removed the link entirely in 1971, bringing in our familiar floating exchange rate system.

The dollar, along with most other currencies, was now fiat, backed only by the order of Uncle Sam who declared it legal tender. But the dollar had a far greater reach than just America. By building a security alliance with Saudi Arabia and the other Gulf states, the US was able to get all oil contracts settled in dollars; the petrodollar was born out of the ashes of the fractionally backed gold dollar. The dollar became the currency of international trade and the world's banking system.

Not everyone thought this was a good idea. Some investors clung to gold as the only real money. These so-called "gold bugs" looked down on fiat money as nothing more than paper. They pointed out that without the gold standard, there was nothing to stop governments from printing more and more paper to cover their ever-increasing spending. And this was precisely what happened. The result was predictable: persistent high inflation worldwide that took decades to control.

In the 1970s, the goldbugs did very well. Gold was seen as protection against inflation, and the price surged. But as governments slowly and painfully tamed the inflation dragon, the gold price fell and languished in a two-decade-long bear market. It looked as if the precious metals had no future as money or even as an investment. To most economists, gold was nothing more than a "pet rock" and a "barbarous relic."

Gold's nadir came when the British Chancellor, Gordon Brown, decided to sell 50% of the Bank of England's gold between 1999 and 2002 at an average price of $275 per ounce. This event is now known as "Brown's Bottom" because it precisely marked the low point. What followed in the next decade was a remarkable surge in the gold price, which maxed out at over $1,800 per ounce in 2011. Bitcoin came into existence amid this raging bull gold market when it looked as if conventional finance was collapsing. When Satoshi mined the Genesis block, he included a message about Brown's government (he was now Prime Minister) having to bail out Britain's banks again.

Like the gold bugs, the crypto crowd denounce fiat currencies as being backed by nothing other than the whim of the government. This is odd because crypto is not backed by anything, not even the word of a government. But then money has this magic quality that once enough people accept something as money, it becomes money. It was an alchemy that Satoshi entirely appreciated. He engineered Bitcoin to be the new gold—a type of money that did away entirely with physical metal and the power of nations, which consisted of nothing but digits. It would start on a mailing list of geek enthusiasts and end up as the world's currency. It was the dream of a madman, a genius or a megalomaniac. Or someone who was all three.

Let's go back to Satoshi's explanation about the Bitcoin supply. He said that "it's more typical of a precious metal" and that "instead of the supply changing to keep the value the same, the supply is predetermined and the value changes". This is a very revealing comment.

Goldbugs have always dreamed of a return to the gold standard. Mainstream economists would regard this dream as a nightmare. They see the restriction of the money supply caused by the gold standard as one of the causes of the great depression. And they make the point that there is insufficient gold in existence to back the world's currencies. Almost all the gold that has ever been mined in the past is still above ground, and there is not enough gold in remaining underground deposits to significantly increase the supply. Newly mined gold increases existing stocks by less than 2% a year.

The gold bugs argue in reply that it is the value of gold, not the amount, that matters. The price of gold would increase until the value of gold in existence was sufficient to supply the world's money needs. That is why those holding gold are so keen on returning to the gold standard. If the world used gold as money again, then the price would need to increase, perhaps by 10x and maybe even more. They would make a fortune.

Satoshi is using the same reasoning for Bitcoin. By keeping supply fixed, the Bitcoin price must adjust to meet the demand for Bitcoin money. This means that the price could go to very high levels.

How far could the Bitcoin price go? The value of all gold in the world is approximately $10 trillion. If Bitcoin were to take over from gold completely, then the total value of Bitcoins could be $10 trillion. While this is unlikely, suppose the world's fiat monetary system broke down.

People would then have to turn to alternative forms of money, such as gold and Bitcoin, so both could increase in value. The total amount of money in the world depends on how you measure it, but it is approximately $100 trillion. Suppose that 20% of this was held in Bitcoin. The price calculation is then:

Value of Bitcoin = $20,000,000,000,000

Maximum number of Bitcoin (allowing for some lost coins) = 20,000,000

Price per Bitcoin = $1,000,000

Even now, it may seem absurd to think that the price of Bitcoin will be $1 million. Surely no one would have considered this in 2009/10 when you could mine 50 Bitcoin using a desktop computer and cents of electricity?

In fact, someone came up with a similar calculation the day after the Bitcoin launch and came to a price of $10 million. This was Hal Finney, who made some comments on the potential price:

> "As an amusing thought experiment, imagine that Bitcoin is successful and becomes the dominant payment system in use throughout the world. Then the total value of the currency should be equal to the total value of all the wealth in the world. Current estimates of total worldwide household wealth that I have found range from $100 trillion to $300 trillion. With 20 million coins, that gives each coin a value of about $10 million.
>
> So the possibility of generating coins today with a few cents of compute time may be quite a good bet, with a payoff of something like 100 million to 1! Even if the odds of Bitcoin succeeding to this degree are slim, are they really 100 million to one against? Something to think about..." (10 Jan 2009)

Finney was actively helping Satoshi test the code and was listed as a developer on SourceForge. Satoshi announced the number of coins and the halving schedule publicly for the first time on 8 Jan, but Finney would have had advanced knowledge from the source code. He must have discussed this with Satoshi so we can see Finney's words as reflecting Satoshi's views. The post may even have been agreed in advance because Satoshi said that Finney "…helped me a lot defending the design on the Cryptography list…". Satoshi must have done a similar calculation because of the number of decimal places he allowed for in his software.

Satoshi was well aware of the potential for the Bitcoin price to go to very high levels. He designed Bitcoin with a supply crunch that would inevitably drive up the price. Not only was the total supply of Bitcoin limited to an artificially low level, but new Bitcoin would be created disproportionately in the early years. Satoshi never explained the reason for the exponentially decreasing Bitcoin creation. In his paper, he does not mention the ultimate number of Bitcoin or the creation schedule. Why did he not justify such an essential part of the design? It seems that Satoshi did not want to draw attention to these features in the early stages.

The schedule of Bitcoin creations appears for the first time hardcoded into his program and made explicit in his email of 8 Jan 2009. Some early users queried the basis of these numbers. In an email of 12 Apr 2009, Mike Hearn, a Google researcher interested in cryptocurrency, asked, "How did you decide on the inflation schedule for v1? Where did 24 [sic] million coins come from?" In his reply, Satoshi says it was an "educated guess". If Bitcoin remains small, it will not be worth much, but it has the potential to be huge. "If you imagine it being used for some fraction of world commerce, then there's only going to be 21 million coins for the whole world." The implication is that the price will appreciate hugely. Satoshi has allowed for an enormous price increase by including 8 decimal places for a fraction of a Bitcoin.

Satoshi made the same points in a forum post: "Eventually at most only 21 million coins for 6.8 billion people in the world if it really gets huge" (6 Feb 2010). He again mentions the eight decimal places and adds: "If there's massive deflation in the future, the software could show more decimal places." Deflation would mean that the Bitcoin price increases. The implication is staggering. If we assume the lowest denomination is one cent, then eight decimal places imply a Bitcoin price of $999,999.99 or one million dollars.

Satoshi designed Bitcoin from the beginning to be a world currency and allowed for a price increase to $1 million. The way that the Bitcoin amount is stored in the data records actually allows for more than 8 decimal places should they be necessary. This would enable a price of more than $1 million with the smallest transaction valued at one cent or allow for smaller microtransactions at a Bitcoin price of $1 million.

A person trained in conventional economics would not think this way. Satoshi's reasoning comes straight from the gold bugs and the gold market. He has just applied it to a new digital gold rather than the old physical gold.

Did Satoshi hold substantial gold himself? A forum post gives an intriguing clue:

> "As a thought experiment, imagine there was a base metal as scarce as gold but with the following properties:
> - boring grey in colour
> - not a good conductor of electricity
> - not particularly strong, but not ductile or easily malleable either
> - not useful for any practical or ornamental purpose
>
> and one special, magical property:
> - can be transported over a communications channel
>
> If it somehow acquired any value at all for whatever reason, then anyone wanting to transfer wealth over a long distance could buy some, transmit it, and have the recipient sell it.
>
> Maybe it could get an initial value circularly as you've suggested, by people foreseeing its potential usefulness for exchange. (I would definitely want some.) Maybe collectors, any random reason could spark it.
>
> I think the traditional qualifications for money were written with the assumption that there are so many competing objects in the world that are scarce, an object with the automatic bootstrap of intrinsic value will surely win out over those without intrinsic value. But if there were nothing in the world with intrinsic value that could be used as money, only scarce but no intrinsic value, I think people would still take up something." (27 Aug 2010)

Note that comment, "I would definitely want some". Satoshi had some personal need for something like gold but which, unlike gold, could be easily moved around over a communication network. One gets the impression that Satoshi is wealthy and has some special financial requirements. Most of us are happy with the system of international bank transfers using the Swift network. And if we want to invest in physical gold, many services are available that will hold it in a vault for us at a fee. But Satoshi needs to conduct his finances outside the financial system. Why is that?

Satoshi's emails and postings show that he deliberately kept the supply of Bitcoin limited to increase the price to extraordinary levels. But what really matters is how the coins come into circulation. The most striking feature of Satoshi's schedule is the exponentially decreasing supply of new coins. In the Feb 2009 post, he explained his thinking: "As the number of users grows, the value per coin increases. It has the potential for a positive feedback loop; as users increase, the value goes up, which could attract more users to take advantage of the increasing value." This is the greed loop that Satoshi programmed into Bitcoin.

Satoshi's idea that price increases would incentivise new users has proved accurate. The remarkable price action has been the only genuine reason to hold Bitcoin. The idea of using Bitcoin for everyday transactions is fiction. It is far too chunky for that. Satoshi programmed a 10-minute cycle, and it takes several cycles to be sure that a transaction has been accepted on the blockchain. Waiting thirty minutes or more to confirm your payment for a cup of coffee or grocery shopping is not practical. And Bitcoin could never cope with the vast number of transactions of a network like Visa or Mastercard.

The exponentially decreasing supply of new coins has turbocharged the Bitcoin price increase, which has driven a vast increase in demand. The Bitcoin halving has resulted in remarkable price increases as new supply is choked back. The four-yearly cycle has become part of Bitcoin lore. The halving in 2012, 2016 and 2020 all resulted in a bull run over the following year, with the price reaching extraordinary new highs. Satoshi's greed loop was working. (The halving effect will inevitably wear off over time as the supply reduction becomes an insignificant percentage of the total Bitcoin in existence.)

It is not that a decreasing supply was necessary to drive a rapid price increase; only that the supply increased by less than demand. As the potential ultimate demand was huge, this was almost inevitable. Satoshi said there was no simple method to increase the Bitcoin supply with demand. But this is not true. He could have used the mining difficulty as a proxy signal for increasing price and, hence, increasing demand. If the difficulty increased much faster than the expected improvement in processing power from Moore's Law, this would show that the price was increasing and could trigger additional coin production. Satoshi was well aware of the connection between mining difficulty and price:

> "In later years, when new coin generation is a small percentage of the existing supply, market price will dictate the cost of production more than the other way around." (21 Feb 2010)

The increase in the Bitcoin price and associated mining difficulty has given rise to an enormous energy demand by Bitcoin miners, which has environmental implications. This was raised as an issue with Satoshi. His response was a comparison with gold:

> "It's the same situation as gold and gold mining. The marginal cost of gold mining tends to stay near the price of gold. Gold mining is a waste, but that waste is far less than the utility of having gold available as a medium of exchange. I think the case will be the same for Bitcoin."

The evidence shows that Satoshi deliberately limited supply to increase the ultimate price and was well aware of the economic consequences of the design. The purpose of money is to act as a store of value between working and consuming. The ideal form of money would have no gains or losses between these two. Such a form of money would be inherently fair, and fairness produces the best result for society as a whole. Now, suppose that Bitcoin became the world currency as Satoshi intended. He pointed out that it would be used by 6.8 billion people. Yet, he placed 50% of the total money supply in the hands of the few who had mined Bitcoin in the early years.

Satoshi designed Bitcoin to be massively unfair and knew what he was doing. But is it not well known that Satoshi was altruistic? He certainly said some altruistic things. Such as being pleased that the mining seigniorage would go to the poor:

> "The overhead of doing an exchange doesn't make sense if you just need a small bit of pocket change for incidental micropayments. I think this is a nice advantage vs fiat currency, instead of all the seigniorage going to one big entity, let it go in convenience amounts to people who need to scrape up a small amount of change." (Forum, 15 Aug 2010)

This sounds so nice that instead of the seigniorage going to the big evil government, it goes to the little people. But in democratic countries the government represents the people and so the seigniorage belongs to the whole population. Bitcoin, however, was designed so that a tiny number of Bitcoin barons could accumulate vast holdings while the Bitcoin peasants, the 99.999% of the population who came later, would grab around for a few satoshis. (A satoshi is 100 millionth of a Bitcoin.)

Satoshi talks altruism but does not act it. He paid lip service to micropayments but never designed the software to allow for them. An altruistic person would have considered the 6.8 billion, not just the handful. Never in the course of human history has so much money come from doing so very little. And, human nature being what it is, few have ever felt a greater sense of entitlement. Bitcoin has become a quasi-religion, and the semi-mythical Satoshi is its prophet.

Why did Satoshi flood the market with 50% of Bitcoin creation in the first four years? To make the Bitcoin bros who chanced upon Bitcoin in the early years ridiculously rich? And why did he create 12.5% of the ultimate supply in 2009 when virtually no one was interested? We must ask, "Who profits?"

It is, of course, the early miners who profited enormously from Satoshi's schedule of coin creation—providing that they continued to hold their

Bitcoin. And most of the very early users did not hold; they gave their Bitcoin away or sold it at low, low prices. There was, however, one exception. This person realised the potential from day one. He started mining early, used specialised software that was much faster than the standard version, mined far more than anyone else, and never sold his Bitcoin. Who was this person? Meet Patoshi.

SEVEN

PATOSHI

The early adopters of Bitcoin were reluctant to probe Satoshi's activities too closely. They believed that if Satoshi wanted to remain private, that was his right. But in 2011, an independent security researcher from Argentina called Sergio Lerner began researching Bitcoin. Although he was a trained computer scientist with a deep interest in cryptography, he only heard about Bitcoin late in 2011 when a friend introduced him to the new digital currency. He read the Bitcoin paper, was intrigued by the concept and rushed to examine the source code. Almost immediately, he found some areas for improvement, which he posted to the mailing list and soon found himself part of the Bitcoin community. Despite his fascination with Bitcoin, Lerner never bought or mined any. He loved the idea but was doubtful of the implementation, regarding it as a step towards something bigger and greater rather than something that would be huge in its own right. So he missed out on the tremendous appreciation of the Bitcoin price.

With a more sceptical attitude than most Bitcoin enthusiasts, Lerner turned his attention to the blockchain and began examining the early transitions. With his deep knowledge of the code, he found a minor security flaw that might give useful information on miners. In the Bitcoin blocks there were two fields called the "nonce" and the "extra nonce" that added a random element to each attempt to find the proof of work. The nonce and the extra nonce acted as counters. The nonce would increase by one with every attempt at the proof of work puzzle until it overflowed when it would go back to zero, and then the extra nonce would increment by one. We can think of the nonce as the second hand on a clock and the extra nonce as the minute hand. Lerner had noticed that the program did not reset the extra nonce, the minute hand, when a miner had successfully found a new block, but instead advanced it by one. It continued to increase until the miner restarted the program. Lerner saw that this could be used to identify blocks mined by the same person.

It was not a very promising idea. At most, you might link several Bitcoin blocks as probably coming from the same miner without knowing the identity of that miner or what other blocks they may have mined. Still, Lerner thought it worth a try. So he graphed the extra nonce in each successive Bitcoin block and immediately made a surprising discovery.

A strange, unexpected pattern jumped out. The graph showed many low-sloping lines, but one miner stood out from all the others. The slope of his lines was much steeper, and the extra nonce went to much higher values. Lerner could tell it was one miner because the nonce would periodically reset to zero, and a new steep slope would commence. This meant that the miner had stopped and restarted his program, probably because he was backing up his system.

As this miner had commenced with block 1, it was clearly Satoshi, but Lerner, with typical caution, labelled him "Patoshi"; a play on "pattern" and "Satoshi". We will keep this name for the mining setup that generated the identifiable Satoshi Bitcoins.

The Patoshi pattern started very regular, reverting to zero every five days. Later, it would become less regular. However, Lerner believed that it was one miner who had been active throughout 2009 and up to May 2010. He estimated by eye that Patoshi had mined about 1 million Bitcoins, which was considerably more than anyone had thought. His blog post caused a sensation among the Bitcoin community but also a degree of scepticism. The initial pattern was obvious, but it then varied in strange ways. Others suggested that this indicated that Lerner had conflated different miners as Patoshi and that Satoshi had bowed out quite early. A more reasonable estimate of Satoshi's mining activities might be 300,000 Bitcoins—or so the critics claimed.

Lerner, however, was convinced that all the million Bitcoins had been mined by one person. He doubled down on his work, addressing some valid criticisms, and probed more deeply. He confirmed his intuition that there was something strange and unique about the Patoshi miner. Put simply, the minute hand of Patoshi's extra nonce "clock" was going about four times faster than it should. This was puzzling, but it gave a definite signal that enabled Lerner to identify the Patoshi Bitcoins rigorously. His more detailed work showed that Patoshi had mined 1.1 million Bitcoins.

Lerner had already identified another odd characteristic of the Patoshi Bitcoins; very few had been moved since their creation. He was able to quantify this: 90% of the Bitcoins mined by other miners in the early years were subsequently transferred to other addresses, probably meaning they were spent. However, 99.9% of the Patoshi Bitcoins had never been moved from their original addresses.

This left the mystery of why Patoshi's extra nonce was running so fast. A friend of Lerner's suggested he should look at the nonce (the second hand of the metaphorical clock) to try and gain information about the type of machine that Patoshi was using. More specifically, Lerner looked at the least significant byte of the nonce, which could take values from 0 to 255. It should have been more or less evenly distributed over all the possible values. But when Lerner graphed the values for the early Bitcoin blocks, he found that they were anything but random. There were two plateaus of high values and two valleys of low values. Further investigation showed that this pattern was entirely due to Patoshi and that the other miners had the expected random distribution.

Allowing for a degree of noise arising from the method used to identify Patoshi's Bitcoins, his least significant nonce byte was only taking certain values:

0-9 Used
10-18 Not used
19-58 Used
59-255 Not used

Patoshi only used 50 of the 256 possible values distributed in two blocks. Using the clock analogy, the second hand skipped over 80% of the seconds, which explained why the minute hand was moving so fast. This solved one mystery but raised another greater mystery. What could account for the strange distribution of the nonce byte?

One theory was that Patoshi had 50 networked machines for his mining and used the least significant byte of the nonce to distinguish between machines. Why the gap at 10-18? Perhaps he had planned on 59 machines but, for some reason, had not used 9. It was a nice theory, but Lerner accumulated evidence against it. On one occasion, the tell-tale Patoshi line changed into two interweaving lines, each increasing at half the normal rate. It strongly implied that Patoshi was using a single machine and had mistakenly started two instances of his mining program.

Lerner's findings got others interested in Patoshi. A blog poster, "organofcorti", decided to look at Patoshi's hash rate. It exhibited another strange step pattern. The following table is derived from the information in his blog post:

Patoshi normalised hash rate (100%=4350 khps)

Jan 2009 to May 2009:	100%
June 2009 to Sept 2009:	60%
Oct 2009 to Nov 2009:	23%
Nov 2009 to May 2010:	36%, reducing by 2% per month
May 2010 onwards:	0%

Patoshi's hash rate was stable for the first five months but declined abruptly in June 2009. After another five months, in early October, there was a second considerable reduction, partially reversed a month later. The hash rate then appears to decline steadily for several months until Patoshi switched off his mining setup in early May 2010. (It is possible that the steady decline after November is an artefact caused by a rise in orphan blocks due to the rapidly increasing network hash rate.)

It looked to organofcorti that Patoshi was mining to ensure network stability and had unselfishly cut back his activity as others became interested in Bitcoin. In fact, the hash rate for the entire network dipped in mid-2009 as a result of Patoshi's reduction. However, other miners gradually came in, and mining took off in 2010.

It was not until 2020 that Lerner made real progress with the problem of the least significant byte of the nonce. He found that it was not, in fact, the byte that was important. Patoshi had divided the nonce range into nice round hexadecimal sub-ranges and used five in his program. This disproved the idea of 50 computers, although it left the possibility of five linked computers. Lerner, however, concluded that Patoshi was using a single machine and that his software ran five threads to take advantage of his computer's multiple cores.

Using multiple cores would have made Patoshi's software something like four times faster than the standard program. But that was not all. The Bitcoin v0.1 software that Satoshi had provided online was actually very inefficient. For a start, it used an outdated version of the SHA256 hash function for the proof of work, even though the software incorporated a more efficient version of the very similar SHA512 function. Also, the way the program looped through the proof of work hashes required manipulation of the large header for every hash. A more efficient algorithm would only manipulate the header once before it started hashing. Satoshi corrected these issues in an update released in 2010. However, Lerner's analysis convinced him that Patoshi had fixed these issues in his own specialised software from the start.

Taking all these changes together, Patoshi's optimised software would have run around 10 times faster than the v0.1 Bitcoin software everyone else was using.

Lerner conducted an experiment re-mining the early coins to determine what computer power would have been needed. He concluded that a single powerful computer server available in 2009 would have been capable of mining all of Patoshi's coins if the software had already incorporated the 2010 improvements.

How realistic is Lerner's contention that Satoshi had made all these improvements from the start? We can be sure he scanned the nonce range more efficiently than others. And an early email to Nicolas Bohm provides evidence about the multi-threading. Satoshi had discussed with Bohm why his dual-core CPU only used 50% of its power for Bitcoin mining. When Bohm asked Satoshi "what's next" for development, he promised to address the multi-threading problem and copied his answer to the Bitcoin-list:

> "The next thing for v0.1.6 is to take advantage of multiple processors to generate blocks. Currently, it only starts one thread. If you have

a multicore processor like a Core Duo or Quad this will double or quadruple your production." (22 Feb 2009)

As early as Feb 2009, Satoshi considered using multiple cores as a trivial update. We can go further. Wolfgang Wester has drawn attention to what appears to be a high hash rate miner testing the new version as early as Apr 2009. It seems that Satoshi had largely completed the work on a fast-mining client by that spring. Which supports Lerner's assumption that he had already implemented it for his own system. When Satoshi finally produced the multiple processor support, the software update was released only two months after he restarted coding. This at a time when he was very busy with other Bitcoin enhancements as well as non-Bitcoin related work. The long-anticipated v0.2 was released at the end of December 2009. Because of the late release, Satoshi had the field more or less to himself throughout 2009. And he mined a lot of Bitcoin.

What was Satoshi trying to accomplish with his mining? One theory was that his sole goal was to support and stabilise the network. We might see the "altruistic" reining back of his mining activities in 2009/10 supporting this theory. Satoshi could have mined even more coins had he kept his rig operating at full power into 2010.

The Patoshi miner ran continuously except for a few glitches. The longest happened in August when it stopped for ten days. The network was very dependent on Patoshi in this period to secure the blockchain, so it seems unlikely that the miner was stopped deliberately. Did Satoshi take his eye off the ball? Was he simply too busy? Or was there some technical problem? We will see the significance of this gap later.

It is remarkable that Satoshi moved very few Bitcoins. We can list the Bitcoins he did move:

12 Jan 2009, 10 to Hal Finney
(4 other transactions were associated with the block 9 address 12cbQL moving coins to other addresses controlled by Satoshi.)
15 Jan 2009, 25 to Dustin Trammel
1 Feb 2009, 100 to Nicholas Bohm
2 Feb 2009, 50 to Nicholas Bohm

18 Apr 2009, 50 to Mike Hearne
17 May 2010, 500 to 1PYYjU95wUM9XDz8mhkuC1ZcYrn4tB3vXe
18 May 2010, 100 to 1H5wBiJGX43FLHWz4nzAhLfyENNmYj8uA1
and then…
…11 July 2010, on to Gavin Andresen's Bitcoin Faucet
23 Jul 2010, 50 to 1LzLve1uY7hmq71AimBEeRuHf7qEtnP4Xr (not moved)

The early transactions are all made direct to people who expressed an interest in Bitcoin. Transactions then stop for a year until recommencing with the transfer of 500 Bitcoins to address 1PYYjU. (The owner of this address is known to Wester who is the source of the above information.) This is the era of the famous first pizza purchase. Laszlo posted his offer of 10,000 Bitcoins for pizza just a few hours after Satoshi's transfer.

A further transfer of 100 Bitcoins was made an hour after the 500 to 1H5wBi where it stayed for several weeks before being transferred to Gavin's Bitcoin faucet. Finally, 50 Bitcoins were transferred to 1LzLve and have never been moved. Note that the last two transactions were made to an intermediary address whereas all the previous transfers were direct from coinbase.

Apart from this short list, the 1.1 million Patoshi Bitcoins have never been moved. Why not? Lerner suggested that Satoshi had destroyed his keys. Here we encounter the Saint Satoshi myth at its extreme. He was so removed from the sin of material desire that even after putting so much effort into Bitcoin, he resolved not to accept the merest reward. It was enough for him to give the tremendous gift of Bitcoin to the world and make others ridiculously rich. Perhaps we see an aspect of Lerner's altruistic personality projected onto Satoshi here.

From Satoshi's posts and emails, we discern an economically aware individual who is very different from the Saint Satoshi of myth. When Satoshi discusses digital gold, he says he would like some. His comments about gold are those of an investor. I do not doubt that Satoshi had a significant gold holding before he even thought of Bitcoin, and his experience of the economics of gold was a significant factor in Bitcoin's design. Satoshi, more than anyone else in the early years, was very aware of the potential of Bitcoin to generate enormous wealth. He is not going to destroy his keys.

Then there is the fact that Satoshi had optimised his own software to perform far better than the standard software. Or, to put it another way, Satoshi had provided a slow version of the software to others while keeping the much faster, improved version for himself. Not only that but he had tested a fast version of the public software in the spring but did not release it until the end of the year. Does that suggest an altruistic individual? However, the standard software was good enough to mine significant amounts of Bitcoin in the early days. Anyone who used that software in 2009 and retained their Bitcoin would also have become very rich.

Here we uncover Satoshi's real motivation: he was 'rationally greedy'. He aimed to maximise his own Bitcoin wealth, a goal that could only be achieved by making others rich at the same time. Satoshi could have hoarded Bitcoin entirely for himself and mined 100% of the coins, but such a private currency would have been utterly valueless! The worth of Bitcoin hinged on its widespread adoption, a feat that required others to have a strong incentive. The potential early adopters were pivotal to this process.

Satoshi was concerned with getting as many people as possible into using and mining Bitcoin. He tried to discourage Laszlo Hanyecz from mining too much and made an early comment in the BitcoinTalk forum about avoiding an arms race:

> "We should have a gentleman's agreement to postpone the GPU arms race as long as we can for the good of the network. It's much easier to get new users up to speed if they don't have to worry about GPU drivers and compatibility. It's nice how anyone with just a CPU can compete right now." (12 Dec 2009)

And yet Satoshi was secretly playing with dice loaded in his favour. Why did he not simply allocate a load of coins to himself? This was what later crypto promoters did. But things were different in 2009. The philosophy of the open source movement was altruistic. No one was in it to get rich. Satoshi needed others to buy into Bitcoin and could not appear greedy. Bitcoin mining had to be fair—or at least, it had to appear to be fair.

What about the other very early miners? Did they become billionaires? If we look at the motivation of the first Bitcoiners, we see the same repeated pattern. They were not focused on getting rich. They just wanted to be involved with something cool and exciting from a technical viewpoint.

The most famous example is the early developer Laszlo Hanyecz. He spent the famous 10,000 Bitcoin on two pizzas. He had an expensive taste for pizza, and his purchases eventually totalled 100,000 Bitcoins, which would have been worth $10 billion at the latest high.

The retired English solicitor Nicholas Bohm eventually mined more than 100,000 Bitcoins. He continued mining for years but never thought that it had any value, so he was amazed when someone set up a site offering Amazon tokens for Bitcoin. In 2011, he moved his files to a new machine, wiped the old machine, and gave it to a charity. In this process, he lost access to his Bitcoin wallet. That did not bother him because he had sold or transferred all his Bitcoin by then.

Dustin Trammell explained what happened to his Bitcoin in an interview with Coin Telegraph:

> "I wish I still had most of the Bitcoin I mined. I had a lot. I gave a lot of it away to promote Bitcoin. I bought a lot of Casascius coins and Bitbills, and gave them out at hacker and computer security conventions, renaissance fairs, parties, left them as tips at restaurants, etc. I gave it literally to anyone that would take Bitcoin. I also bought a lot of things with Bitcoin, from real estate and a car to Bitcoin miners to random electronics. I own one of the Bitcoin nerd merit badges that cost me... 1 BTC." (Coin Telegraph, 28 Mar 2021)

Trammell did retain enough Bitcoin to make him rich even if it was just a fraction of his original holdings. James Howells was the unluckiest of all. He kept the hard disk with the keys to his 8,000 Bitcoins in a black plastic bag. His partner thought it was rubbish and threw it away. The disk is now buried in a rubbish tip in Newport, Wales. Howells got venture capital backing and proposed to use AI in the search for the keys, but Newport council has consistently refused permission.

The anonymous miner M2809/M3654 who had started in Jan 2009

accumulated over 70,000 Bitcoin. On 13 Jul 2010, a forum poster NghtRppr offered to buy Bitcoin at a rate of 5000 Bitcoins for $1.00 USD in cash by mail. Malmi pointed out that the rate was ridiculously low and NghtRppr improved the deal: "We've lowered our rate to 100 Bitcoins per $1 USD. We will keep adjusting our prices until we find something sustainable." In September, the 70,000 Bitcoins were transferred to NghtRppr's address. M2809 would have received around $700 for Bitcoins that would later be worth over $7 billion. It was a low price even for the time. The Bitcoins were sold on by NghtRppr who offered them for $0.04 per Bitcoin, four times what he had paid. M2809/M3654 did retain the other Bitcoins he mined early and became rich, but not the billionaire he could have been.

As for Martti Malmi, he received only 0.1 cents per Bitcoin in his first transaction with NewLibertyStandard in 2009. Two years later, he sold over 10,000 Bitcoins at a rate of $15-30. He used the proceeds to achieve every young person's dream—a place of his own. The twenty-two-year-old bought a nice studio flat in Helsinki. The remainder of his 55,000 Bitcoins were sold off by 2012. Had he kept his Bitcoin, he would have been a billionaire. But equally, he made more money than he would have thought possible when he first contacted Satoshi. An older and wiser Malmi tweeted his lessons learned:

> "1) Money matters: more is always better than less. 2) Still, you don't need to be rich to lead a perfectly good life. It's about the basic things. 3) You don't live forever. Pursuing something greater than yourself brings meaning in life."

The person who was most aware of the potential value of Bitcoin after Satoshi himself was Hal Finney. But he had an urgent need for money. His ALS had progressed until he was almost completely paralysed. He could not breathe, was on a ventilator and was only able to communicate through eye movements, which activated voice synthesis software. Even so, he continued to program. But the medical bills were mounting up. He and his wife Fran decided to sell most of the Bitcoin, which they did at a price of $100. As Fran told reporter Andy Greenberg:

"[Our son] Jason is always saying 'what if, what if'. It's fine with me if it means we have enough money to keep Hal alive, at home and comfortable." (Forbes, 25 Mar 2014)

Hal himself wrote in 2013: "I'm pretty lucky overall. Even with the ALS, my life is very satisfying. But my life expectancy is limited. I'm comfortable with my legacy."

In Aug 2014, Finney passed away. His body was prepared for cryonic preservation according to his wishes.

We will return to the question: who profited most from Satoshi flooding the market with Bitcoin in the early years? It was Satoshi himself.

If our analysis is correct, Satoshi was a wolf among lambs. He would have aimed at mining the maximum number of Bitcoin subject to the constraint of leaving a significant amount on the table for other miners to start the greed feedback loop. This would suggest a target of no more than about 50% of Bitcoin in the first few years. Satoshi did not know how quickly Bitcoin would be adopted and had to be ready for a rapid escalation of mining activity. But like most radical innovations, adoption was disappointingly slow. Given the effort Satoshi must have put into optimising his software, it was ironic that his main problem was mining too much Bitcoin. Patoshi accounted for some 75% of Bitcoin production in the first five months. This was far too high, which explains the substantial reduction in his hash rate in June 2009. However, other early miners were losing interest, and Patoshi was still mining 60% of all Bitcoin after this reduction. Patoshi's proportion only began to seriously decline after the further October reduction. His share for the entire year averaged out at 60% or almost a million Bitcoins.

Few very early Bitcoiners saw it as a way of making money, but as the price increased, it drew in profit-focused individuals. Those who have made a fortune from Bitcoin have ridden on Satoshi's coattails and jumped onto the speculative machine he created. But he wasn't doing it for their benefit. Satoshi was rationally greedy. The fact that he had to make others rich was a side effect of making himself rich. He needed to start the positive feedback loop of greed that would propel Bitcoin to dizzy heights. To do this, he had to secure the support of the early adopters to make them rich and so attract others. But Satoshi always had his long-term objective in mind. Unlike most others, Satoshi held onto his Bitcoin.

So, what was Satoshi's objective? To secure a significant proportion of the world's money supply. That is the conclusion from his actions and emails. Most likely, he was aiming at something like 10%. If Bitcoin achieved the price of $1 million that he thought possible, then his share would be worth $1,000 billion ($1 trillion), which would make him by far the wealthiest man in history. Satoshi was no altruist—he was a megalomaniac.

To achieve 10%, Satoshi would have to mine 20% of all Bitcoin in the first four years or 40% in the first two years. Patoshi achieved 60% in 2009, although the total Bitcoin mined that year was lower than expected. He could have done even better had he not curtailed his mining activities. And he stopped entirely in May. Patoshi ended up mining 5.7% of the ultimate Bitcoin supply, short of 10% if that were Satoshi's target.

The Patoshi Bitcoins have never moved. But we must remember that Patoshi is not Satoshi. At some point Satoshi would have realised that he was leaving his digital fingerprints all over the Patoshi Bitcoins. Attempting to spend any would create a trail leading right back to him. The most logical solution was for Satoshi to start a second mining operation using standard software and mining in a way that was untraceable back to his Satoshi identity. If he mined enough with this second operation, he could keep the Patoshi coins in reserve without moving them. In support of this idea is the fact that Satoshi had been running other miners from the beginning.

EIGHT

K5

Satoshi's non-Patoshi mining most likely started on day one. Although the Genesis block was dated 3 Jan 2009, the first mined block was at 2:45 UTC on 9 Jan. It was generated by the Patoshi machine, which then took one minute and nineteen seconds to mine block 2. Patoshi mined for just two hours before stopping for almost exactly twenty-four hours. This is the first little mystery. Another mystery concerns the second miner, who was operating at the same time as Patoshi. The most significant question is whether Satoshi inadvertently revealed his IP address and location.

Techniques to track miners and transactions have greatly increased in sophistication since Lerner's ground breaking work. Modern analysts are now using AI to investigate the massive amount of information available on the blockchain. However, as Bitcoin is pseudonymous, how can we deduce much about the early mining activity?

Two key pieces of information recorded on the blockchain are the nonce and the extra nonce. We have already seen their value in identifying the Patoshi pattern. They are equally helpful at analysing the activities of other miners. The standard software incremented the extra nonce by 1 with every new block added to the blockchain. It would also increment once a miner scanned the whole nonce range, but this rarely happened with the slow early mining machines. So the extra nonce acts like a counter telling us how many blocks had elapsed since the miner started their software. It can link together a series of blocks that were likely mined by a single miner and tell us which blocks were definitely not mined by that miner.

The nonce also provides valuable information. The speed at which the nonce space is scanned depends upon the computer's hash rate. So, using the nonce, we can estimate this hash rate and distinguish between miners.

Transactions are another source of information. Spending or transferring

Bitcoins enables different blocks mined by the same person to be linked. And if Bitcoins are not transferred or spent that is also significant as almost all Bitcoins apart from Satoshi's were moved at some point.

Finally, we know of some individuals who were mining Bitcoin and can often identify some of the Bitcoin they mined. For example, an early article about Finney included a screenshot from his software that identifies his first twelve blocks of mined Bitcoin.

Wolfgang Wester has published an analysis of the first 1,000 blocks using tools such as these. (I have combined the conclusions from his report with some of my own analysis, so any mistakes are mine.)

To illustrate the method, consider the first non-Patoshi block 12. The extra-nonce for this block was also 12, which is not a coincidence. The extra-nonce is incremented by one with every mined block, so this miner had been running from the very beginning when block 1 was mined.

Wester identifies eight different miners active in the first 1,000 blocks mined between 9 Jan and 19 Jan 2009:

Patoshi	858
Hal Finney & Dustin Trammell	74
K1	3
K2	4
K3	16
K4	10
K5	35

Each of these blocks was worth 50 Bitcoin. The identities of K2 to K4 are unknown. As for K5, that is almost certainly Satoshi. We can use the analysis to work out a timeline (UTC) for mining in the early days:

9 Jan, 02:45 - approx. time that Patoshi and K5 both start mining
9 Jan, 02:54 - Patoshi mines block 1
9 Jan, 04:21 - K5 mines block 12
9 Jan, 04:33 - Patoshi mines block 14 and stops

10 Jan, 04:45 - Restarted Patoshi mines block 15
10 Jan, 06:56 - Patoshi mines block 27 and stops

10 Jan, 15:30 - Restarted Patoshi mines block 28
10 Jan, 19:13 - Finney posts debug log
10 Jan, 20:40 - approx. time for K5 restarted
10 Jan, 21:48 - K5 mines block 64
10 Jan, 22:32 - Satoshi posts v0.1.2 correcting bugs
11 Jan, 00:19 – Patoshi mines block 77 and stops
11 Jan, 01:00 - Hal Finney mines block 78
11 Jan, 03:46 – Patoshi restarts and mines block 79
11 Jan, 13:52 - K4 mines block 127
12 Jan, 07:01 - K1 mines block 106
12 Jan, 10:37 - K2 mines block 204
12 Jan, 17:25 - K3 mines block 236

The timeline raises questions. Why did Satoshi mine for only two hours on 9 Jan and then stop for twenty-four hours? Does it have anything to do with the fact that K5 had just mined its first block? Was it a test, or had Satoshi run into connection problems?

We know he was hard at work on 10 Jan fixing connection bugs. That presumably is why he stopped a second time, on 10 Jan after only two hours. It was not until 15:30 that day that Patoshi began running more or less full-time. K5 was started at around 20:40—presumably because Satoshi used it to test v0.1.2 of the standard software before he published it on the Bitcoin-list.

Note how Patoshi stops for three and a half hours while Finney is mining block 78. Is this to allow Finney, who was using an old IBM computer, to mine a block?

It was not the end of communication problems. Finney encountered a "select failed: 10038 bug" which took several hours for Satoshi to fix with v0.1.3. In the meantime, there were several "zombie nodes" that confused things.

Six individuals, including Trammell and Finney, successfully mined within two days of the bug fix. Trammell was using two fast machines.

The K5 machine was also particularly fast, with over 250,000 hashes per second, compared to less than 25,000 per second for the slowest machine, K1. However, all these miners were tortoises compared to the Patoshi hare. And unlike the hare of the fable, Patoshi kept running. Patoshi accounted for 86% of the first 1,000 Bitcoin blocks. If we assign K5 to Satoshi, he mined 44,650 Bitcoins in those ten days, which is 89% of the total.

K5 was fast, but its contribution is almost insignificant compared to Patoshi. So why run it? We must consider Satoshi's technical difficulties in establishing the Bitcoin network.

The original Bitcoin software connected through IP addresses and needed a seeding mechanism by which new users could see who was available to connect to. In the early years, it used the IRC messaging service. The software would log on to the IRC Bitcoin channel, revealing its IP address. It could then see who else was logged on and attempt to connect to their IP addresses. If at least one user had an open port able to receive incoming communications, then the software could connect to the network.

Once a network connection had been established, a miner did not need to be logged on to IRC. Anyone connecting through IRC would reveal their IP address. As Satoshi was obsessive about secrecy, how could he avoid this? Either by not connecting through IRC or connecting via Tor which Satoshi used extensively. Satoshi used customised software, so his connection may have worked differently from the standard software. While trying to remedy the communication problems with Hal Finney he made a revealing comment:

> "Unfortunately, I can't receive incoming connections from where I am, which has made things more difficult. Your node receiving incoming connections was the main thing keeping the network going the first day or two." (12 Jan 2009)

It is a fair assumption that Satoshi programmed Patoshi to never reveal its IP address. But this left him with a problem. Users could only connect to a computer which had an open incoming port. However, most users did not run a port allowing incoming connections because of security concerns. Which is why Satoshi was keen, right from the start, on getting people to run their setup to accept incoming connections. He emphasised this at the first release: "If you can keep a node running that accepts incoming connections, you'll really be helping the network a lot. Port 8333 on your firewall needs to be open to receive incoming connections" (Cryptography mailing list, 8 Jan 2009). Satoshi asked Trammell and Malmi to run open connections, as well as Bohm: "You should set your router to forward port 8333 so you can receive incoming connections." (5 Jun 2009). Naturally, Satoshi was not running an open port himself: "I run a node but I can't accept incoming connections and if your IP address changed then I would have lost contact with you" (10 Jul 2009). Running an incoming connection would have given away his IP address.

However, at the start, there were no other users. Unless Satoshi was prepared to take a chance that someone would connect with an open incoming port, he had to arrange a computer to receive incoming connections. The IP address of that computer would be inevitably compromised. So he would have to take precautions.

How could Satoshi provide for such an open connection? The easiest method was to get someone else to run an open node. The obvious candidate was Hal Finney, the only person other than Satoshi able to log into SourceForge as a developer. But we know Finney was not running the Bitcoin software on 9/10 Jan because he encountered a bug when he tried to run it on 10 Jan.

Satoshi would have had to provide that open connection himself. The K5 miner provides the evidence that he did. There was no purpose in running that miner other than to give a port to which others could connect. And we know that K5 was operating from the very start. Either Patoshi or K5 had to run an open port, or the network could not have started. This is where Finney's debug log becomes interesting. It showed three Bitcoin users logged into IRC on 10 Jan. Finney was connected through his IP address 207.71.226.132. The admin, Satoshi, connected through Tor. The IP address of the third user was 68.164.57.219, which resolves to Covad Communications in Van Nuys, Los Angeles, California. It was not a Tor exit node. Whoever connected from Van Nuys used a standard ADSL connection that assigned a new IP address each session.

Finney was able to connect to 68.164.57.219 and download the block-chain. So the Van Nuys computer was running port 8333 open. We know that K5 mined block 64 a few hours later, but we cannot be sure it was running at the time of the log. The extra nonce tells us that the Van Nuys miner started, or perhaps restarted, the K5 miner after Finney posted his log. Assuming the Patoshi software did not commence mining until it found a node, another computer must have connected at around 16:30 on 10 Jan. We would expect that Satoshi would have run K5 to start the mining process. However, we can't rule out the possibility of another user. One potential candidate, Dustin Trammell, ran the Bitcoin software from 9 Jan and emailed Satoshi on 11 Jan about his attempts to mine Bitcoin. However, Trammell was based in Texas and was using an IP address of 24.28.79.95 so he can be eliminated.

To summarise, it is very likely, although not certain, that the Van Nuys IP address belonged to K5 and hence Satoshi. Does this mean that Satoshi was living in Los Angeles? Probably not, as he would have been aware that he was revealing this location. So, how could he have arranged an open connection that did not lead back to him?

Running the standard software on this secondary setup gave some protection as it cannot be definitely tied to Satoshi. And using a temporary rather than permanently assigned IP address makes it all but impossible to trace the connection to a particular individual.

However, using an IP address that gave away Satoshi's geographical location would still be dangerous. There were not many cryptographers in the world, so even an approximate area could pinpoint him.

One possibility is that Satoshi deliberately launched Bitcoin while he was travelling. The main Patoshi setup could remain at his home base and be operated remotely. He would then use a travelling laptop as the open port connection, running the standard software over a public internet connection. This would have been virtually untraceable. And K5 did not have to stay in one place. It could have been moved around, further confusing any snoopers.

We should note that Van Nuys has one of the largest General Aviation airports in the US. If Satoshi was the type of person with his own private jet (and we will see that he was) then he could have parked his plane at Van Nuys for a few days while launching Bitcoin.

One factor that supports the travelling scenario is the strange 24-hour break in mining on Jan 9/10. Was Satoshi unable to connect because he was in transit? Running a connection while travelling would only have been a temporary solution, but it would not have been needed for long. Satoshi was keen for others to supply the open port. And just because K5 was mining does not mean that it was always running an open port.

There are other ways that Satoshi could have arranged an open node in Van Nuys that did not involve travelling. If he had access to a computer run by an associate or an employee, he could have connected remotely, loaded the software, and operated it without the associate knowing what he was doing. Afterwards, he could delete the software, leaving no trace.

Or he could have rented a server in a server farm, loaded the software remotely and ran the open node from there. In fact, the Van Nuys IP address area included a Covad server farm. The main problem would be payment, which could be traced back to Satoshi. However, the risk would have been minor. An observer could not tie the IP address to the server farm, let alone a specific server, without access to Covad's records. And internet providers did not tend to keep such records for long.

Finally, he could have used a remote VPN connection. The Wayback Machine capture for the Covad website shows that it did offer a remote VPN service for business users at this time. Again, the weakness of this method is that it would be traceable by Covad, assuming that they kept records of who was connected through a particular IP address.

Of course, he may have been lazy and taken the chance of running K5 from his home in Van Nuys. But that would be very unlike Satoshi.

Although K5 enabled Satoshi to mine extra Bitcoin, it would not have been the primary motivation as it was far slower than Patoshi. If Satoshi had wanted to mine more Bitcoin, he could have run a second Patoshi setup. But that would have been gross overkill. In 2009, he was mining too much Bitcoin, leaving too little for everyone else. The existence of K5 shows that Satoshi was aware of the advantage of the standard software, that it was hard to trace back to him. And if our analysis is correct, he was running K5 from a remote location. Running standard software on a remote machine was the key to untraceable mining.

Patoshi and K5 were not the only miners that Satoshi was operating in the first month. Wester has identified a miner, M254, that was running the standard software from 13 Jan to 21 Jan. It was probably a laptop and mined 21 blocks. Interestingly, all the Bitcoin were moved to five different addresses, but not moved on any further. It seems that Satoshi was testing out an ordinary miner and checking that transactions were working. We know M254 was Satoshi because the Bitcoins mined in block 360 were combined with Bitcoins from block 9 which was used in the Finney transaction.

At the beginning of 2009, the standard software was too slow: Patoshi had a 10 times speed advantage. However, the updated software in late 2009 and 2010 incorporated most of the Patoshi improvements, dramatically reducing the speed difference. With his intimate knowledge of his own software, Satoshi would have become aware of the digital fingerprints he was leaving all over the Patoshi Bitcoins. By mid-2010, there was no advantage in running Patoshi. Unsurprisingly, Satoshi turned off the setup in May 2010. Was this to switch to mining by other, non-detectable, means?

The K5 experiment may have led Satoshi to think about mining in locations remote from his home base, perhaps using an intermediary or intermediaries to assist him. This would remove any danger of leaking his IP address. However, an intermediary would introduce a human risk point. Which brings us to the person who may have been that intermediary, and the unusual circumstances of their death.

NINE

DAVE AND CRAIG

In April 2013, forty-six-year-old Dave Kleiman was found dead at his home in Riviera Beach, Florida. His nearest relatives were his elderly father, Lou, and his brother, Ira, a self-employed web designer. Under Dave's will, Ira was the sole beneficiary, but the two brothers were not close. Ira had not seen Dave for years and had little knowledge of his work in computer security. As Ira wrapped up Dave's affairs, he found that there was no estate. The deceased had debts, and his house was worth less than the mortgage. Ira found some computers, several hard disks, and USB drives. But as Dave encrypted almost everything, Ira could not access the contents. A couple of the drives appeared unformatted: when he put them into a computer, it asked if he wanted to reformat them, and he pressed 'Y'. Later, Ira would install new operating systems on them. One drive appeared not to work, so he threw it away.

Ira did not have Dave's passwords, and the encryption was unbreakable. Nor could he get into Dave's mobile phone. He gave it to one of Dave's business partners to see if he could gain access. Ira never saw the phone again—it broke and was thrown away. Ira sorted through Dave's papers but found little of importance and trashed most of them. He took Dave's certificates, some books and mementoes, leaving everything else behind. And that was that—or so Ira thought.

The few boxes that Ira took from Dave's small house were the scant remains of a life that had been promising but ultimately tragic. Dave Kleiman was born in 1967 and adopted from birth. The Kleimans had two other sons, Leonard and the youngest, Ira. Dave excluded Leonard from his will, but in the event, he predeceased Dave from a drug overdose. After high school, Dave joined the US Army as a helicopter technician. He had a good army record and was even named US Army Soldier of the Year in 1987. After leaving the army, he occupied his time with his main interests in life—computers, motorbikes and women. Kleiman was a likeable person who was attractive to the opposite sex. His job as a bouncer at a strip club gave him a string of exotic girlfriends wistfully remembered by his male friends years later.

Kleiman wanted to be more than just a security guard and joined the training program to become an officer with the Palm Beach County Sheriff's Office. One of his supervisors was Patrick Paige, who would become a lifetime friend and business partner. Kleiman became a traffic cop and was training to be a police helicopter pilot. He was active and energetic, but in Apr 1995, his life changed forever when his motorbike was involved in a collision with a car. He survived but suffered spinal damage and was paralysed from the waist down. Dave would spend the rest of his life in a wheelchair. It was a cruel fate for a man still in his twenties.

Kleiman started in computer security work in 1990 while still working at the strip club at night. His disability moved him further into the newly developing fields of computer crime detection and computer forensics. Taking and passing courses, he eventually ended up with such an impressive list of letters after his name that colleagues jokingly called him Dave Mississippi.

Dave moved on from the police to a series of jobs at high-tech companies. He was a Vice President of Technical Operations at Intelliswitch, supervising an international telecommunications and ISP network. Then, in early 2001, he joined a new start-up called Security-e-Doc (also called S-Doc), where he was Chief Information Security Officer. The company was involved in cryptography, developing an on-the-fly system for communicating and storing documents. He joined the Cryptography mailing list and made some posts.

After leaving S-Doc, Kleiman drifted into freelance work and later formed a Florida partnership called Computer Forensics LLC with Paige and another friend, Carter Conrad. Kleiman was becoming well known in the industry: he was a sought-after trainer with a reputation as a technical author and editor. He wrote several guides about Microsoft technologies for security professionals and was the Technical Editor for a book on Winternals, a suite of technical tools to troubleshoot Windows. With his likeable personality, he was in demand as a speaker at industry events. He even appeared on television a few times.

Kleiman was an extroverted risk-taker who would never stop talking. But he had a different side to his personality. More than one friend remarked that he would keep secrets. As the old family lawyer and friend said, "there were parts of Dave that were very closed and private." He did not tell others about his relationships with women. He had a secret affinity with wolves. A long-term ambition, never realised, was to take a degree in astrophysics.

Kleiman married two or perhaps three times, but none of the marriages lasted long. His first marriage was to a woman at the Sheriff's office. It ended in a public scandal when his wife had an affair with another police officer. Kleiman reported it to the news, and the story even appeared on a news report.

A work colleague at S-Doc, Kimon Andreou, became a very close friend. They worked together and had a shared interest in guns and gun shows. The friendship continued after they both left S-Doc, and Andreou was as close as anyone to Kleiman in his last decade:

> "I believe he was married three times and after that his philosophy was to date strippers. According to him it was a lot simpler. It was much more transactional, a lot easier for him to manage." (Andreou Deposition, p. 29)

Kleiman had an off-and-on relationship with one stripper whom he lived with for a while. Then, he had a more serious relationship with another woman who was not a stripper. This would have been Kursten Karr, who became his fiancé. Kleiman lived with her and her son for several years. Andreou said that Kleiman had an odd work pattern after S-Doc shut down. He would work for three months, earn a lot of money, not work for the rest of the year, and have trouble with his mortgage payments.

At S-Doc, Kleiman worked with Andreou on developing a product to lock down servers. Kleiman was the expert on server security, and Andreou did the programming. Andreou was quite sure that Kleiman could not program. He had to regularly help him by writing small programs and scripts for Kleiman's publications. As for Kleiman's own computers and drives, "he was paranoid about security" and very secretive:

> "So he would use software called TrueCrypt and what that does is it has the option of either encrypting the entire drive whatever that drive may be or create a container..." Asked about Dave's password, he continued: "All I know is that it was very long and would take a while to type it. [...] 64 characters. So what I would do is when he was done typing a password, I would just throw out random numbers to confuse him, and then he would have to restart." (Andreou Deposition, p. 51-3)

Kleiman seems to have come to TrueCrypt quite late. Even in 2010, he still used two older products, DriveCrypt and DriveCrypt Plus Pack. Kleiman had to type in a password before the computer loaded the operating system, which indicates whole disk encryption, either TrueCrypt or DCPP. (Both products were substantially the work of Paul Le Roux.) He never wrote down his passwords but memorised them, so his files were unrecoverable after his death.

Andreou remembered Kleiman talking about another friend, Australian security expert Craig Wright. Living on opposite sides of the world, the two hardly ever met in person, but they communicated frequently by email and phone. They had much in common—both worked in the same field of computer security and forensics, loved to collect qualifications, and were technical authors and editors. They collaborated on a paper investigating whether it was sufficient to overwrite a hard disk once to wipe any data on the disk completely. This involved examining hard disks under an electron microscope. Their conclusions were controversial and bucked conventional belief by maintaining that a single overwrite was sufficient. (Doubts have been raised as to the reliability of Craig Wright's supposed experimental results in this paper.) The paper was discussed on the Cryptography list at the same time Satoshi was launching Bitcoin.

The relationship may not always have been smooth. Wright faced repeated accusations of plagiarism. On one occasion, Wright wrote a blog post about his disappointment with an American friend who failed to defend him when others doubted Wright's claims: "This person I called my friend said they doubted my qualifications as well." It sounds like Kleiman.

Mostly, though, the two got on very well. They would have long telephone conversations, even though it was the middle of the night for Wright in Australia. They even attempted to become business partners by setting up a jointly owned Florida corporation to pursue some tenders with the US Department of Homeland Security. The tenders were all rejected. By that time, Kleiman was very ill.

Like many other paraplegics, Kleiman had a problem with sores, which became infected with bacteria, including the MSRA bacteria. Because he was paralysed in the infected area, he felt no pain to warn him that the sores were getting bad. He passed out in the shower and was there for two days before he was found by a friend, Jody

After being found in the shower, Kleiman was admitted to hospital in 2010. He would spend most of the remainder of his life in hospitals, the West Palm Beach Veterans' Administration Medical Center, and then the Miami Veterans' Administration Medical Center, to which he was admitted on 28 Sep 2010. He suffered from a long series of operations and complications, including a bodged attempt to remove his left hip joint. The sores had penetrated his bones, requiring surgery. During physical therapy, old wounds reopened, and he even suffered bone fractures.

It was very difficult for Kleiman in hospital:

> "I am really starting to hate this place...Not actually this place itself, just the concept of being confined to a room and having to rely on everyone else for everything. I do not think this is good for my type of personality. It may start manifesting into inappropriate behaviour and misplaced anger." (Kleiman to Andreou, 25 Apr 2011)

In the hospital, Dave became socially withdrawn. The medical report records no family visits or social visits, but this is not the whole story. The old family lawyer and his wife visited Dave a few times in the beginning. Once, when the wife visited on her own, she was so upset that she crashed and wrote off her car on the way home. Later, Dave told them he did not want them to continue their visits.

The one regular visitor was Kimon Andreou, who would call in to see Dave every evening on his way home from work, typically picking up a Hooter's order for Dave on his way. His visits had to become less frequent when his wife became pregnant. She had a baby girl towards the end of 2012, and Andreou's visits more or less stopped at that time. Dave also had regular long phone calls from Kursten Karr. Although the couple had split up, she continued to care about him. As for Ira, he never visited Dave even once.

The medical records show that Kleiman worked on his computers while in bed. He was frequently busy and also had phone calls and occasional conference calls. He was certainly still conducting training sessions while in the hospital, but this could not have taken much of his time. Whatever he was doing, he was not earning much money.

Kleiman was not only ill but getting ever deeper into debt. He had never been a saver and had always spent whatever he earned. His friends remembered his instinctive generosity—he would give his last dollar to someone in need. As a veteran, his medical bills were paid for. But he could no longer meet his mortgage repayments and stopped paying them. At the time of his death, he owed twenty-four months' payments. He even had to ask a friend to pay his phone bill.

It was in March that Kleiman left hospital. The myth developed that he went home to die, but there is nothing at the time to suggest that. On 12 Mar 2013, Kleiman sent Andreu a message that he had a meeting at the FBI and that, by a strange coincidence, the female agent's name was Mulder. (There is nothing suspicious about an FBI meeting as Kleiman was a sector chief of the FBI's InfraGard program.) Kleiman and Andreu had a habit of wishing each other a happy day for some imaginary cause. On the 14 Mar, Kleiman outdid himself with a series of texts:

Happy 3.14159265259 (Pi) Day!
Happy Learn About Butterflies Day!
Happy Popcorn Lover's Day!
And Happy Potato Chip Day!

On 22 Mar 2013, Dave left the hospital and went home. When a friend asked if the hospital had discharged him, he replied, "No...I told the doctors to go fuck themselves". The record shows that it was more complex. The hospital ran on military principles, and an inmate had to apply for a timed leave of absence pass. According to the medical report, Kleiman never applied for a pass until 16 Jan 2013. (In fact, we know that Kleiman did leave the hospital on a few occasions over the years.) Starting on 16 Jan, he was granted no less than twelve passes. The final leave was to arrange for a home lift, but Kleiman never returned. He was given an "irregular discharge".

There is a mystery about Kleiman's last month. His business partner and close friend, Carter Conrad, called on him at home sometime after he left the hospital. Kleiman told him that he had simply removed his computers and other things from hospital and taken them home. He talked to Conrad enthusiastically about his plans for the future and developing their joint business. Conrad had no reason to be concerned. Kleiman appeared fine and had been able to look after himself in the past.

In truth, the infection had not gone away, and Kleiman could not look after himself. He needed care, and he was not receiving it. He was also in danger of having his home repossessed. After finding his bed empty at the hospital, Andreou texted him: "Alive?" He received no answer to that nor the other messages he sent over the next month. Finally, on 18 Apr, he got a reply:

Andreou: "Still Alive?"
Kleiman: "Yes"
Andreou: ":) are you accepting calls?"
Kleiman: "No"
Andreou: "ok, still at home?"
Kleiman: "Yes"

This is the last known contact with Kleiman. He attempted to secure financing at an exorbitant interest rate—a loan company ran a credit check on 22 Apr. The application was declined. Patrick Paige was becoming increasingly concerned and arranged for another friend who lived on Kleiman's estate, a young woman called Lineda, to check his home. She found his body.

The scene was distressing. Kleiman was slumped over in his wheelchair. The body was decomposing, and there was blood and shit all over the floor and in the wheelchair tracks. In front of Kleiman, on the bed, was a loaded gun. There was a bullet hole in the mattress. The police said it was old and had nothing to do with Dave's death. But when Ira was cleaning the room, he found a discharged cartridge the police had missed.

Kleiman had been dead for several days, and there is a question concerning the timing of that credit check, just four days before the body was discovered. Kleiman would have had to authorise that check, but perhaps it was only performed after his death. Or maybe the body decomposed faster than expected in the warmth.

Kleiman had not been shot. The autopsy showed that the cause of death was myocardial infarction, a heart attack. A plaque build-up is a common result of the type of infection Dave suffered from. Kleiman was not drugged up when he died. There were some traces of cocaine, but not much, and only a small amount of alcohol, which may have been produced post-mortem.

His friends were surprised by the cocaine, for Kleiman was against drugs. They attributed it to "his crazy girlfriends". Later, Wright was to spread the story that Kleiman was heavily into drugs sourced from the Silk Road. This is not the man his Florida friends remembered. The Silk Road story makes no sense because Kleiman was in hospital receiving regular blood tests almost the entire time the Silk Road was operational.

The natural conclusion is that Kleiman died from lack of care, with an untreated infection eventually causing the heart attack. He must have contemplated suicide. The bullet hole is suspicious but could have been caused by Dave firing his gun in a state of disturbed mind. At the time Ira found the cartridge, there was no reason to doubt that his brother died from natural causes. Later, he would suspect that Dave was murdered.

As Ira finalised Dave's affairs, he little guessed that his life would become entangled in a strange, frustrating legal case that would go on for years and involve tens of thousands of documents. At stake were billions of dollars of supposed Bitcoins.

It began ten months later, in Feb 2014, when Lou Kleiman, Dave's father, received an email from Craig Wright telling him that Dave had been part of a group that had developed Bitcoin. He was one-third of Satoshi Nakamoto, alongside Wright and a third man. Lou was pleased but had no idea what Bitcoin was and took it no further. Craig Wright persisted and contacted Dave's business partners, who alerted Ira. Wright told Ira that he and Dave had invented Bitcoin—no more mention of a third man. Craig painted a picture of two friends and computer geniuses on opposite sides of the world working together on Bitcoin while keeping it secret from everyone around them. He sent Ira copies of emails to prove his story. He told Ira that the two had established a business, W&K Info Defence Research LLC, in Florida to exploit the new technology and mine Bitcoin.

Ira, initially deferential and awestruck by Wright, soon found himself in a web of confusion. He was eager to understand Dave's share of the famous Satoshi Bitcoins, but Wright's answers only deepened the mystery. The Bitcoins, it seemed, had all been placed in an overseas trust, a decision Ira couldn't comprehend. As he probed further, Wright's explanations became more convoluted, leaving Ira feeling like he was trapped in a Kafka novel.

Things got worse when Ira was contacted by the Australian Tax Office (ATO). They sent him copies of two documents that Dave had apparently signed electronically, one of them just a few weeks before he died. They showed that W&K was worth many millions of dollars. And the effect was to transfer full ownership of W&K Info to Craig Wright. Ira could not see why Dave would have agreed to these contracts and suspected that Wright had forged them. And that was not all. Craig had also submitted a claim to the Australian Courts alleging that Dave had failed to fulfil his side of an agreement. The Florida company had been served papers but did not respond, which is not surprising as Dave had died several months before. Wright received a court order giving him all the assets of W&K Info.

It looked as if Craig was defrauding Dave's estate of billions of dollars of Bitcoin. As the sole beneficiary of Dave's will, those Bitcoins should have belonged to Ira. He continued to push for his fair share and Craig stopped responding to his emails. Eventually, Ira would get litigation financing and sue Wright for the Bitcoins. But in 2014/5 he was powerless against Wright.

That Craig Wright was one part of Satoshi had remained a close-kept secret. But that was to change. In Dec 2015, Wright was outed. There was no longer much talk about Kleiman, let alone a third man. Wright alone was Satoshi Nakamoto.

Who was Craig Wright? He was born in 1970 and studied engineering at the University of Queensland but left in 1992 without a degree. After college, he worked for three to four years as a chef. During this period, he began a side hustle as a technician maintaining computer networks. He soon gave up his chef career to become a full-time network manager. This was followed by a year as a corporate accounts manager at an Australian email provider before he landed a job at the Australian Stock Exchange working on computer security and firewalls. It was largely an administrative role, with Wright helping with things like job descriptions. This job would only last for a year but enabled him to pivot to the emerging field of computer security.

In 1997, Wright set up his first company, DeMorgan, which specialised in offering computer security services. Wright's LinkedIn profile claimed that DeMorgan employed over twenty staff. He left the company in acrimonious circumstances in 2003 when he and his wife Lyn resigned their directorships in favour of an investor. They had previously signed a shareholder agreement that if they left, they would not carry out a competing business or approach a customer of DeMorgan for three years. As was his right, the investor gained a court order to enforce this agreement. Wright broke the court order by approaching DeMorgan's customers for work. He was found guilty of contempt of court in Jul 2004 and sentenced to 28 days imprisonment, suspended for 250 hours of community service.

Following DeMorgan, Wright became "Chief Research Officer" at another of his companies, Ridges Estates. Despite his grandiose title, he seems to have been involved mainly in conducting risk assessments, documentation and staff training. Then, in Oct 2004, Wright joined accountancy firm BDO in Sydney as a computer security specialist. He was a mid-level employee with the job titles of "Manager of Information Systems" and "Manager, Risk Advisory Services". It was the most settled period of Wright's professional life.

While at BDO, he made a post to the IT Security discussion group about computer auditing in which he claimed to have conducted an amazing number of audits:

> "My current tally on audits is 1761 audits for 363 organisations over 22 years (I am a statistician as well as auditor)." (27 Feb 2008)

Wright had only worked as an auditor for three years and could not have carried out a tenth of the number of audits he claimed. Such exaggeration is very typical of Wright. His BDO employment ended when he was made redundant in Dec 2008. His redundancy payout would not have been immense as he had only been at BDO for four years.

Wright was exaggerating his importance in more ways than one. As early as Mar 2007, he styled himself as "Dr Wright" in computer security Usenet posts. After he was made redundant, he changed his email tagline to "Dr Craig S Wright" and displayed the title prominently on his website. But Wright did not possess a doctorate—at least not an identifiable one.

He did have many other qualifications. Collecting certificates had become a hobby. It started with a Masters in Network and Systems Administration from Charles Sturt, a middling Australian university, in 2004 when he was already in his mid-thirties. Other master's degrees rapidly followed at a rate of one or sometimes even two a year. The subjects studied were Management, IT Security, Commercial Law, and Statistics. (At the London trial, it was shown that his Law dissertation was extensively plagiarised.) In addition to these masters, he sat and gained an enormous number of lesser "certificate level" qualifications from the computer security institute GIAC. Wright achieved so many of these certificates that he would style himself as the globally most qualified security professional. And he did study for a PhD in Computer Science at Charles Sturt between 2009 and 2012. Although his CV from 2015 shows him as having this qualification, it was not awarded until 2017, when Wright was forty-seven. He had been calling himself "Dr" for at least a decade.

To justify his earlier use of the title, Wright would claim that he had studied for another doctorate between 1998 and 2003, but not in computer science. He was a "Doctor of Theology, Comparative Religious and Classical Studies"! This is amazing on many levels. An obvious objection is that a doctoral-level course would demand a prior qualification in a relevant subject such as Classics or Religious Studies. But in 1998, Wright had nothing but an abandoned attempt at an engineering degree.

As the worth of a qualification depends on the body granting it, Wright's Theology doctorate is worthless because he has refused even to name the institution. No college or university has ever acknowledged giving Wright this doctorate or enrolling him as a student. There is not a shred of evidence that Wright has actually studied Theology or Classical Studies on a formal basis. There is no record of the doctorate, and no academic has come forward to say they supervised Wright.

What about Wright's supposed coding abilities? According to his own account, he started programming in C++ at seven and was writing games by age eleven. This is remarkable in many ways, not least because the computer language C++ had not even been invented at that time. (We may also wonder how a seven-year-old gained access to a computer in the 1970s.)

If we look at Wright's verifiable qualifications, none involved any significant programming element before 2009. His PhD did not involve coding, and was not hard computer science. The subject was risk assessment applied to the quantification of systems risk. It was primarily concerned with statistics and economics. And none of his jobs involved software development. Wright was employed at different times in installing and maintaining computer networks, administration, management, risk assessments, and security audits. He attended a computer programming course, but only in 2009-10. In this Masters in Systems Development from Charles Sturt, Wright learnt to program in "Java, C#, C, C++". Why would a highly accomplished C++ programmer like Satoshi, who developed the Bitcoin software in 2007/8, attend a beginner's software course to study C++ in 2009?

Nor can we point to a single piece of software that Wright wrote. He claimed to have written some highly sophisticated programs, but these claims are always shadowy, vague and unsubstantiated. Supposedly, he developed this software for "grey zone" or even criminal operations, making the claims inherently unverifiable. In an email to Ira, he described the online Casino software and other projects that he and Dave had supposedly developed:

> "Dave took the 2 million lines of code that [I] had in 2010 and transformed these into a documented set of over 6 million lines of code. I have sent the software analysis to you already." (23 Apr 2014)

The numbers are absurd. A good software developer can produce up to 50 lines of thoroughly tested and documented code daily, or about 10,000 lines a year. Many produce much less. The idea of anyone writing 2 million lines of code, let alone 6 million, is ridiculous. It would take a large team of dedicated programmers to create such a monster. Dave Kleiman was in hospital at the time and could not even code.

One actual project that Wright has claimed was his work in 1998 for Lasseter's, a very early Australian online casino. He often advances his involvement in designing the "architecture" of the Lasseter's casino as evidence of his technical capabilities. However, his descriptions of the work show that he was not involved in coding. In a 2021 interview, he said that he was contacted by Lasseter's to provide advice on regulatory requirements and security systems. This rings true, but it is a world away from writing the software.

Overall, there is no evidence that Wright could program at anything like Satoshi's level in 2008 and probably not at all. He had certainly never worked as a professional programmer.

The period from 2009 to early 2013 can be characterised as Wright's "wilderness years". He and his first wife, Lynn, had enjoyed an enviable lifestyle with a large house in Sydney and a hobby farm up the coast for the weekends. After his redundancy from BDO, they soon had financial difficulties and had to give up the Sydney house and move full-time to the farm. Lynn was much older than Craig, and their relationship was on the rocks after Wright had an affair with a younger woman, Ramona Watts. His marriage with Lynn was dissolved in late 2010, and they parted in early 2011.

Wright married Ramona, who had children from a previous marriage. Their finances could have been healthier. In a blog post, Wright said he had come down from a large house and a farm to living in a rented apartment. Ramona complained in an email that they were struggling to put food on the table for the children. Then, in 2013, everything changed. Wright set up a group of companies to exploit crypto technologies. He opened offices and recruited staff. Wright and Ramona suddenly had money and were not shy about spending it.

In April 2013, Wright converted to Bitcoin almost overnight. There is an odd coincidence in timing here. He wrote nothing in his blog about Bitcoin until 27-29 Apr 2013, when he made four long pro-Bitcoin posts. Dave's body was discovered on 26 Apr, but Wright was not informed until 29/30 Apr. Wright wrote these first Bitcoin posts after Kleiman died but before he was told. That same day, 30 Apr, Wright wrote a post about Kleiman, starting "Last night a good friend of mine passed away." So Wright did not know that Kleiman had already been dead for several days.

In Wright's memorial blog post, he told how they had "long-distance… talks that would go on for hours. We discussed anonymity and ways to both forensically recover data as well as means to ensure non-recovery." He mentions two specific projects they did together: the disk rewriting project "that ate 18 months of my life" and "DoD research contracts" in which Dave was Wright's "person on the ground". This is a reference to the failed Department of Homeland Security tenders. He said nothing about Bitcoin but did claim to know some of Dave's secrets:

> "Dave was my sounding board and in some ways my muse. Whenever I became stuck Dave would help me step through the issues until we came up with a solution. […] Dave shared many of my secrets and I some of his." (30 Apr 2013)

It is difficult to work out Dave's state of mind from the scraps of evidence available to us. But there is nothing that points to him being in a state of despair throughout his final months. His house was being repossessed, but that had been going on for a long time. He had not lived there for years and could have continued in the hospital being fed and cared for. The fact that Kleiman took twelve leave passes starting in mid-January suggests a determination to put his life back together.

During this period, he gave at least one online training session. A woman posted a link on a Usenet group (the poster did not know that Kleiman had died):

> "Windows Log File Analysis in depth by Dave Kleiman.
>
> Back by popular demand (and this time not from hospital) Dave took us through the various log files on Microsoft Windows systems (you did know there was more than just the event logs didn't you?) […]" (31 May 2013)

Dave could have given this talk in one of his absences from hospital—one pass was for Dave to give a lecture—or it may have come from the time after he left hospital.

Kleiman was a mentally capable, tough and determined person, not the type to be self-delusional. His financial situation was desperate, but he may have had an unexpected opportunity. Did Kleiman involve Wright in some plan? If this plan involved Bitcoin, it would explain Wright's sudden conversion. Indeed, Wright's behaviour changed dramatically at this time.

Dave Kleiman ran out of road. His illness defeated him. The infections got worse, and he sank into a black hole. He was unable to care for himself and was unwilling to return to the hospital. His death was tragic. But he had already set in motion a strange and remarkable series of events.

TEN

SATOSHI REVEALED

On 10 Dec 2015, the world was disappointed to learn that Satoshi Nakamoto was Craig Wright. An anonymous whistle-blower, claiming to be a former employee of Wright's, had emailed several news outlets a package of incriminating documents. Although the press mostly ignored the email, Gizmodo and Wired took it up.

At the time, Wright was on the run. The day before, police raided his Sydney home on behalf of the Australian Taxation Office (ATO), searching for evidence of tax fraud. He and his wife Ramona were not living in the house but were staying at a deluxe apartment in central Sydney. Now, the apartment building was besieged by journalists, and the police had also turned up.

Writer and journalist Andrew O'Hagan tells the story in the "Satoshi Affair". Wright and Ramona had to flee separately from the building, with Wright hiding from the police in the cubicle of a lavatory. Ramona booked him on a flight to New Zealand, and he went from there to the Philippines, where he met Stefan Matthews, who was now organising his life. Wright and Ramona flew from the Philippines to London, where they moved permanently. Whether Wright would really have been arrested had the police caught up with him is uncertain.

Who was the secret whistle-blower who informed the press about Wright? There is no proof, but the package sent to the press outfits included documents forged by Wright. Realistically, they must have come from Wright. He had doxed himself.

Wright's financial and legal position in 2015 was precarious. His companies were facing bankruptcy. He had financed his organisation with tax credits. The ATO was now challenging these payments, alleging that they were based on fraudulent information. Wright had already stopped paying his people. But he had a white knight in the form of a Canadian venture capitalist, Rob MacGregor. We need to go back to the months after Kleiman died to understand the circumstances.

Ira Kleiman's court case against Wright in Florida placed a vast amount of information in the public domain. One witness who had personal knowledge of the events of 2013 was Jamie Wilson, an accountant who had known Wright since early 2012. Wilson was setting up a new security solution for documents called Cryptoloc and contacted cybersecurity experts including Wright who had impressed him. Wilson paid Wright to review his patent concept, which he later saw as a waste of money. Wilson had already got someone to develop code, but Wright insisted on having his name on the patent – it would be the first of many for Wright.

In 2013, they were close business buddies, and Wright invited Wilson to be the Chief Financial Officer for the new companies he was setting up. Wilson was unpaid but granted a large amount of stock. He was excited to be working with Wright but also disturbed by a strange change in his behaviour:

> "But, where I didn't feel comfortable is Craig's change of attitude from a developer that would be in hoodies and, you know, very low key and working with, to one that, that is it, I've got to be the man, I've got to be the CEO, new flash suits, ties, and it was just a massive change from where he was conservative to right out there." (Wilson Deposition, p. 22)

The change started after Kleiman's death:

> "Craig said to me a good mate of his just passed away, and I believe he came over to Florida. Or he did fly to the States." (Wilson Deposition pp.35-6)

After travelling to the US, Wright began spending money:

> "... when I would have meetings down in Sydney, he would turn up and we'd go to a little cafe shop and things like that where the train station was.
>
> Once Dave had passed away and things started to get kicked off with these new companies, there was a matter of all of a sudden he had to dress in flash suits, you know, wear the best watches, shoes, fascination with socks. Even down to vehicles. He moved from his normal Subaru which was beaten up and went and got a brand new car. It was just a massive change in lifestyle. It wasn't the Craig I originally met." (Wilson Deposition pp.36-7)

Wright's self-confidence "went through the roof", and Wilson remembered this all happening by June/July. He gave an example of Wright's extravagance —he had given a team Christmas dinner for ten people when Wright and Ramona turned up, began ordering the best champagne and picked up a tab for $15,000. This was "absolutely not" how Wright would have behaved before:

> "I mean, prior to Dave's passing, I was the one buying the coffees and spending the money travelling back and forward."
>
> "Q. And then thereafter?"
>
> "It was a matter of he would even fly his team up to Brisbane. We would all go out together. Craig would actually pay for everyone who came along." (Wilson Deposition p.40)

Wright was suddenly rich:

> "Q: Did it appear to you that after Dave died, Craig had access to massive amounts of assets that he did not previously have before?"
>
> "The money came from somewhere. I believe that there was a change, and overnight he had a lot of wealth." (Wilson Deposition pp.35-6)

Wilson saw this change as somehow connected with Dave Kleiman's death. Wilson knew that Wright had taken a flight to the US and had the impression that he was visiting Florida. This was probably because Wilson assumed he was going to meet Dave's family or attend his funeral. But Wright never met the Kleimans, and there is no reason to believe he went to Florida.

In an email, Wright had written that Dave was "an essential part of this project". Wilson was asked if he knew what this meant:

> "Yes. In that they worked together. Now, I believed that Dave was the original start. He started looking on the Blockchain. And then later on Craig joined it; it was a joint thing together, though."
>
> Q. "And did you form that belief through statements Craig made to you?"
>
> "Yes."
>
> Q. "Okay. When he refers to "this project," did you take that to mean the mining of all of this Bitcoin?"
>
> A. "Yes."
>
> (Wilson Deposition pp.49-50)

Wilson's recollections give us insight into what Wright was saying in the months after Kleiman's death. Kleiman was involved in mining before Wright, and there was also a mysterious third man, who Wright began to identify as David Rees.

Wright opened an account on MtGox in April 2013, around the time he posted his Bitcoin blog articles. After the hack, his account details were leaked, showing that he was trading Bitcoin in relatively small amounts, investing a few thousand dollars. This is typical of a neophyte trying to understand the mechanics of Bitcoin transactions.

In contrast to his small-time trading on MtGox, Wright claimed to control an enormous amount of Bitcoin. He talked of "5% of the global Bitcoin market" and having over 1 million Bitcoins. Wilson fully believed these claims, as Wright showed him wallets with addresses containing the Bitcoin. But he never witnessed a single transaction.

It is all consistent with Wright having no genuine involvement with Bitcoin until Kleiman brought him into some scheme in early 2013. An unknown third party was also involved, but the plan had not come to fruition before Kleiman's death. Wright knew enough to continue on his own, but without the benefit of his friend's common sense, he went seriously off-course. And this brings us to an email from Wright to the ATO. He said the Bitcoin was "in my control now as a matter of fate and other circumstances". The wording is odd. "Fate" would be the death of Kleiman, but what does "other circumstances" mean?

Just two days after he was informed of Kleiman's death, Wright issued a manifesto on his blog. It started, "I AM going to innovate and CREATE like it or not", as if the world were trying to stop him. The manifesto promised "I will produce" and "not live off or accept welfare". It continued:

> "I am producer. I build, I create and I trade. I do not take handouts. I do not beg. I learn, I contract and I do all I can to better the society I am in." (2 May 2013)

Fine sentiments. However, Wright was actually concocting a scam to get his companies funded by the Australian taxpayer. He planned to take advantage of a scheme by which the government would give a 45% tax credit for R&D expenditure. Crucially, these credits could be paid in cash by the ATO. He also intended to take advantage of Australian Sales tax "GST" refunds by constructing transactions in which his companies had supposedly paid GST, which he could reclaim from the ATO. We know about Wright's alleged fraudulent tax claims because some ATO reports were put in the public domain in the Kleiman trial.

Wright's idea was to claim for fictitious expenditure supposedly financed by Bitcoin. He began by establishing several companies under a holding company, DeMorgan. There were no external customers. Wright's companies only traded with each other.

The Florida corporation W&K Info Research, founded by Dave and Craig, was key to Wright's scheme. Wright produced two contracts as evidence that it was engaged in Bitcoin mining. Under the first, dated 22 Apr 2011, Craig supposedly supplied W&K with a supercomputer, a 1024-core GPU-based system, to mine Bitcoin in a data centre. He also transferred more than 200,000 Bitcoins into the company. The value of the contract was assessed at 40 million Australian dollars.

The second contract was dated 2 Apr 2013, supposedly signed by Kleiman shortly before his death. Under the agreement, Kleiman sold his 50% holding in W&K to Wright, including all equipment and IP. Kleiman would have to pay 250,050 Bitcoin to Wright for the privilege of granting his shares to him, and then give his remaining 323,000 Bitcoin for a 49.5% share in Wright's new Australian company, Coin-Exch. Ira disputed this contract and that the signature was Dave's.

It looked as if Wright was defrauding Kleiman. But it was really all about tax. W&K Info Defence had no value. At the start of 2011, it was registered to submit tenders to the US Department of Homeland Security. Craig produced the tenders, but only Kleiman was listed as a corporation member so that he could front the applications as a US vet. However, all four tenders were rejected. W&K was nothing but an empty shell.

Wright had written the sales contract to only become binding after Kleiman's date of death. On 25 Jul and 13 Aug 2013, Craig applied to the New South Wales court for two judgments against W&K and Kleiman. He claimed that he had given W&K a bond of $20 million backed by Bitcoin and gold and that W&K had not fulfilled its mining contract. Both judgements were granted for a total of $57 million.

Neither claim had been contested. Uyen Nguyen, a Director of W&K, represented that company in the settlement negotiations. As a young intern in Wright's organisation, she was a surprising choice for such a senior role. An email from Kleiman approving her appointment was later shown to have been forged. Wright took advantage of Uyen's lack of experience, and her name would appear in many of his schemes.

The amount of $57 million would not be paid in cash. Instead, W&K's supposed IP and equipment, valued at $57 million, would be allocated to Wright. But there was no IP. W&K had never done any business, and its registration had lapsed—Uyen had to get it reinstated. Wright was not defrauding the Kleimans, but getting paperwork to back his tax claims. The court papers showed he had $57 million worth of IP, which he now sold to his other companies. Those companies would reclaim tax refunds on those purchases, both sales tax and R&D credit. He even said so much in emails to Ira:

> "I did the court action to ensure that the value was accepted. Not to force you, the estate etc into giving me anything, but to ensure I had a value against the software that I had received already."
>
> "The sale of the software and its use leads to a Research & Development refund into the company. Coin-Exch receives the moved software and uses it for an R&D claim. That is why it was done. This is 45% of the expense.
>
> That is what is obtained from this. That is what the ATO do not like." (23 Apr 2014)

The amounts are huge: 45% of the claimed $57m value of the W&K IP would be over $25 million of refunds. It was not enough for Wright. He began inventing other fictitious expenditure. He claimed to have paid over $2 million to an English mathematician, David Rees, who had conveniently died in Aug 2013. Supposedly, Rees was the "third man" who had supplied unpublished mathematical work to Wright that he claimed was critical to Bitcoin. The ATO determined that Wright had no connection to Rees, who had been in a nursing home suffering from senile dementia for years.

Wright also claimed to have purchased banking software. Supposedly, he had bought the source code for a core banking package from Siemens. He also purchased banking software from a Turkish bank, Al Baraka. Wright used a very odd intermediary for these purchases: an Australian entrepreneur in the gold mining industry called Mark Ferrier, who operated through his company MFM. Ferrier was a high-profile individual in Australia who had been accused of unrelated fraud in Sep 2013. Wright was counting on no one believing Ferrier's denials of a business relationship. He claimed two invoices from Mark Ferrier for these software packages, one for $38 million, including $18 million in "gold options", and the other for $18 million.

Why would anyone buy sophisticated and complex banking software from a dodgy mining entrepreneur based on a conversation at a conference and a few emails? Like most things that Wright did, it defied common sense. The ATO were naturally suspicious. But Wright gave them a demonstration in which he had access to the Siemens support website and showed them what appeared to be the Al Baraka source code. This was critical in the ATO's agreement to release a tax refund payment to Wright. But they continued to investigate. Siemens told them that they had not sold any software to Wright and that he did not possess a valid licence to use the software. As for Al Baraka, not only did they deny supplying any software to Wright, but there was no software to supply—they were not in that business.

Wright had given the ATO copies of support emails from Al Baraka's virtual office. The ATO discovered that the email domain was only registered in Jan 2014, after the face date of the emails, with Wright's credit card showing a payment to the virtual office provider. Wright had set up the supposed Al Baraka virtual office himself.

Wright also claimed to have acquired an SGI supercomputer, supposedly one of the most powerful in Australia. He named it C01N, and it was owned by his company of that name. SGI denied selling him such a computer, but Wright maintained it was operating in 2012/3. The ATO asked for a demonstration and sent along two computer scientists who noticed several discrepancies. They discovered a serial number and other parameters consistent with an ordinary Hewlett-Packard server. They even determined that the serial number belonged to a machine that HP had exported to Australia. Such a server would have cost a few thousand dollars new, but Wright was not the original purchaser—he had obtained it second-hand.

The amounts claimed by Wright's companies were substantial. The GSV refunds alone were $2.8 million for Cloudcroft, $3.7 million for Coin-Exch, $4.1 million for Denariuz and $3.4 million for Hotwire, a total of $14 million. This did not include the R&D credits. For the supposed supercomputer company C01N, he claimed $7 million for the 2012/13 tax year. He made tax refund claims for the following tax year, ultimately disallowed, of $30 million.

Wright intended to notionally fund his companies with supposed Bitcoin transfers until the ATO ruled these would be taxable. So he invented the Seychelles trust, later called the Tulip Trust, that would become such a feature of his story. Supposedly, Bitcoin was assigned from the Tulip Trust to the Australian companies, which avoided a GST liability.

Things did not go according to plan. The ATO queried these refunds, causing Wright to run up a legal bill of over $1 million. He contacted the Kleimans in early 2014 because the ATO intended to talk to them, and he needed support for his story. At this time, he began forging an email chain to show how he and Kleiman had invented Bitcoin.

While arguing with the ATO, Wright was building his business. He recruited expensive staff in 2013 and ultimately had around 50 people in the group. A recruiting blog post for one of his companies, Hotwire PE, is typical:

> "Independent, creative and innovative thinking should be celebrated and encouraged.
>
> To this end, we have devoted:
>
> Fifteen years of planning;
>
> Four years of development;
>
> Ten companies in a consolidated group;
>
> A five year, $x million development budget.
>
> And so far... It is still secret.
>
> In the next nine months, secrets will start to come out." (15 Sep 2013)

But before the nine months were up, Hotwire would be placed in administration due to delays in refund payments. By 2015, the ATO ruled that all the transactions were a sham. Wright ran out of money and was unable to pay his people. As for Jamie Wilson, he left before the end of 2013 when he discovered that Wright was using him as a director of a company without his permission or knowledge. Like many others, he came to regret his association with Wright. The ATO hounded him for years for his apparent involvement in Wright's schemes.

Did Wright fund all his businesses with tax refunds? In Aug 2014, the ATO calculated that 94% of Wright's income from the previous two years had come from tax refunds. There is, however, a question of timing. Wright began claiming GST refunds from the third quarter ending 30 Sep 2013. However, the ATO refused payment pending an investigation and did not release the refunds until mid-2014. So where did Wright get the money for his business expansion in 2013? He did get a refund of $157,000 early in 2013 for his security company, Panopticrypt. Was this sufficient to start his spending spree in 2013? It would only cover the salary of one of his highly-paid staff.

The ATO investigations ended with penalty notices clawing back any refunds. An ATO letter for just one of his companies, Coin-Exch, shows a claim for $5.6 million, including a $1.9m penalty. Wright had to find a lot of money very quickly. Why would anyone finance a business failure accused of serious tax fraud? Because he was Satoshi Nakamoto.

Wright had been introduced to MacGregor through a former business associate, fellow Australian Stefan Matthews. Wright had known Matthews since his time at BDO when Matthews was CIO of a client, an online gambling company called Centrebet. In 2011, Matthews moved from Australia to the UK to work for another online gambling technology company called Tyche Consulting, which belonged to Calvin Ayre's Bodog group. He moved on to Manilla in the Philippines the following year. When Matthews visited Australia in early Jan 2014, he connected again with Wright. They discussed an investment in Wright's companies, which was followed up by an email introduction to MacGregor. Nothing came of it at that time.

In Apr 2015, a desperate Wright contacted Matthews again. On a trip back to Australia, Matthews visited Wright's offices:

> "When I arrived in Sydney, that trip, there was no staff in the office at all. The office looked like somebody had blown a whistle, everyone had dropped what they were working on and walked out." (Matthews cross-examination, London trial)

On this visit, Wright dropped a bombshell—he told Matthews he was Satoshi Nakamoto. With this disclosure, Matthews arranged a meeting on 27 Apr 2015 between Wright, Matthews, and Matthews' ultimate boss, Calvin Ayre. They met on the roof deck of Ayre's Vancouver penthouse. It was the pivotal moment when Ayre decided to invest in Wright.

However, the money was supposedly not coming from Ayre but from Rob MacGregor's venture capital company, nTrust. Which is odd because MacGregor was always sceptical about Wright. Both Matthews and Wright have denied in court that Ayre was the ultimate backer. But the emails from the time show Calvin, signing himself C., making all the decisions. Ayre operates his businesses through a thicket of interlinked companies, which makes the truth hard to verify. As for MacGregor, he was a loyal lieutenant who had worked for Ayre for years.

MacGregor now became involved in negotiating and organising the deal. They had to move fast because Wright owed his legal advisers, Clayton Utz, millions of dollars. Heads of agreement were reached before the end of June. In the event, Clayton Utz resigned from representing Wright when they discovered he had forged emails supposedly from the ATO.

Although MacGregor was uncertain about Wright, he did take comfort from Matthews' story that Wright had given him a copy of the draft Bitcoin white paper in 2008 before it was published. Matthews' account of how Wright gave him a USB stick containing the paper became more elaborate with each retelling. In the London court case, Matthews claimed that he had discussed the ideas behind Bitcoin with Wright numerous times in the years leading up to the paper. The judge concluded that Matthews was lying.

Matthews' story is contradicted by contemporaneous emails. When he first introduced Wright by email to MacGregor in Jan 2014, he omitted the vital fact that Wright was the inventor of cryptocurrency. He just said that he had discussed cryptocurrencies with Wright "in my last year at Centrebet", which was 2010. In another email, Wright said that Matthews had been familiar with his involvement in cryptocurrencies since "Mar 2009". That is probably too early, but confirms that Matthews had no knowledge dating from 2008 or earlier.

There were other inconsistencies. The version of the story Matthews told O'Hagan in 2015 differed in some vital details from his later version. And Wright said he gave Matthews a hard copy of the paper rather than a USB stick. When the 2024 London trial judge asked Matthews how he could remember the timing to be confident that he had seen the paper before Oct 2008, his reply was unconvincing.

MacGregor was now spending $15 million rescuing Wright's failed businesses with only Matthews' story as independent evidence. The plan was to buy up Wright's companies, settle the debts and move Wright away from Australia and the wrath of the ATO. Wright and his second wife Ramona would relocate to the UK. A new company, nCrypt, later renamed nChain, would take over the many patents that Wright was working on. They did not trust Wright to run the new company, so he would be appointed Chief Scientist. The whole rationale of nChain was to sell Wright as Satoshi.

MacGregor was open with O'Hagan about his plans for the company—add some noughts and sell it to a group such as Google with a target price of $1bn+. As the blockchain was widely seen as revolutionising finance and society, such a price for Satoshi's company was not unrealistic.

Ayre's London operation, Tyche Consulting, initially employed Wright so that he could get a work permit. He signed a contract giving Tyche rights over his life story and virtually over his whole life, which is where O'Hagan came in. He was a highly respected author and journalist who had written an account of Wikileaks' Julian Assange. MacGregor offered him a contract to tell the world about Wright as Satoshi Nakamoto. O'Hagan was given unrivalled access to Wright, and his book gives us a fascinating eyewitness account of Wright's disastrous coming-out.

MacGregor planned the formal announcement and demonstration for May 2016. By that time, press interest in Wright had died down. The Bitcoin community had rejected him as Satoshi, and a number of instances of dishonesty were coming to light. The manufacturer of Wright's claimed C01N supercomputer publicly denied selling him such a computer. Questions were also raised about his qualifications. Wright claimed to have a PhD in computer science and to be a lecturer at Charles Sturt. That university released a statement that they had not awarded him a doctorate, and he was only a part-time, unpaid adjunct lecturer. Wright responded that he had completed the work for the PhD—it was finally granted in 2017. We have seen that Wright used the title "Dr" for at least a decade, years before he even started working on a PhD.

Most significant was the issue of Wright's blog, which contained several early entries about Bitcoin. For example, the blog entry for 10 Jan 2009:

> "Well.. e-gold is down the toilet. Good idea, but again centralised authority.
>
> The Beta of Bitcoin is live tomorrow. This is decentralized... We try until it works.
>
> Some good coders on this. The paper rocks."

Proof that Wright is Satoshi? And yet it reads oddly, too good to be true and too brief. The language is nothing like Satoshi's style, and there are some serious errors. It says the beta version of Bitcoin will be released, but Satoshi's announcement said, "The software is still alpha…". The most significant error is the date. Satoshi posted the Bitcoin software on 8 Jan and began mining Bitcoin on 9 Jan. So why does the blog post, dated 10 Jan, say that the software will go live the next day? Perhaps because the first transaction to Hal Finney took place on 12 Jan, leading Wright to think that Bitcoin had started the day before.

The Wayback Machine records the state of websites on different dates in the past and shows that Wright had backdated the post. It was in the blog sweep for 2 Jun 2014, but an earlier capture shows no entry for 10 Jan 2009. It has been shown that all of Wright's apparent early Bitcoin mentions on his blog were backdated. The first genuine mention of Bitcoin in the blog was in Apr 2013. Why would Satoshi edit his blog to provide fake proof? It did not make sense.

Wright had mentioned Bitcoin earlier in the comments to a 2011 online article he wrote. He suggested that Wikileaks could have used Bitcoin and spelt it "BitCoin" and "bit coins", even though Satoshi had settled on the spelling "Bitcoin".

So Wright's coming-out was made in the face of considerable scepticism in the Bitcoin world. To overcome the doubters, MacGregor was determined that Wright would publicly sign a message with Satoshi's keys. Wright was resistant to this idea. Even as early as 2015, he claimed that the keys were actually under the control of the so-called Tulip Trust. Wright had to ask the trustees permission to even use the keys. MacGregor, however, was determined that Wright must provide proof.

The first link in the chain was Jon Matonis, a director of the Bitcoin Foundation. Wright was already friendly with Matonis who was invited to attend a private session in London. There, he witnessed Wright sign a message with one of Satoshi's keys and became a strong supporter of Wright's claims. Wright made two similar signings for O'Hagan. As the signing and verification for all these demonstrations took place on Wright's own computer, they have no value as proof.

Matonis introduced the biggest catch to Wright, Gavin Andresen, who was the public face of Bitcoin. They had a lengthy exchange of emails, and despite his initial scepticism, Andresen accepted that Wright seemed to be Satoshi. He admitted later that this was not based on hard evidence, something that only Satoshi could know, but on Wright's general tone and his knowledge about the early days of Bitcoin. It seems not to have occurred to Andresen that an imposter would have carefully studied Satoshi's many publicly available communications.

Andresen may have been gullible, but he was not naive enough to accept Wright without proof that he possessed the private keys. Verifying that someone has a private key is easy. The person simply has to encode a message such as "Wright is Satoshi" with the key and post the digital signature to the internet or send it in an email. Anyone can then use Satoshi's public key to verify that the message has been correctly signed. The process takes minutes and is foolproof. Such a signing does not compromise the private key. But instead of this simple process, Andresen was invited to London to witness a signing similar to that done for Matonis.

The best account of what happened comes from Andresen's court deposition in 2020. He flew to London early on the morning of 7 Apr 2016 on the red-eye flight and arrived at the London hotel where the demonstration would take place at 11:00 am. There, he was greeted by the money men, one of whom told him he had known Craig Wright for a long time and was convinced that he was Satoshi. Andresen was then introduced to Wright.

Andresen placed a brand-new USB stick on the table and asked Wright to sign a message with one of Satoshi's keys, which he would then verify on his own laptop. Wright objected. He pointed out that Andresen could then release the signed message early, disrupting the planned reveal of Wright as Satoshi. So, it was agreed that an nCrypt employee would go out and buy a new computer. Wright would sign the message—"Gavin's favourite number is 11"— and it would be verified using Electrum software that had been downloaded and installed upon the new computer using the hotel wi-fi. It may be significant that Wright added his initials, "-CSW", to the end of the message.

At the time of the deposition, several years after events, Andresen was vague on the details but gave the general sense of what happened:

> "Craig and I waited in the room while the laptop was purchased. It was then unpacked and booted up for the first time in front of me. And the proof then was Craig downloaded and installed software. And then, after some -- many hours, I don't recall how many hours, but it took much longer than -- than expected, at the end of that, I was convinced that he had taken one of the early blocks and signed a message using its private key."

Andresen should not have been convinced. He was jet-lagged and had hardly slept the previous night. The whole process took several hours, a long time to concentrate on what was done on the new laptop. Editing the Electrum software to verify a message falsely is a trivial matter. This can be as simple as adding two lines of code to the start of the program. The software would continue to work perfectly, except that it would incorrectly verify a message encoded with the scammer's private key as if it came from Satoshi. Andresen did not verify that the Electrum software was downloaded from the genuine site or that the installed software had not been tampered with. And we know from Wright's dealings with the ATO what Andresen didn't—that Wright had forged other sites and computer demonstrations.

That addition by Wright of "-CSW" may be significant. There was no valid reason to add it to Gavin's original message. The first attempt at verification actually failed. Then Wright remembered the "-CSW" and the message was verified. Modifying the Electrum code to verify any message ending in "-CSW" would have been trivial.

Andresen should never have accepted verification of the message on a computer not under his control. Wright's smoke-and-mirrors demonstration was a red flag when he only had to sign a message privately and pass it to Andresen to verify. The excuse that this might reveal the private key was nonsense.

In Andresen's defence, the demonstration was supposedly preliminary to the official release of a signed message. He never expected his private signing to be the main event. But Andresen had been skilfully played. He was backed into a corner, and his endorsement gave Wright much-needed credibility. The PR team invited the BBC and the Economist to witness a similar signing. It occurred entirely on Wright's computer, and the BBC filmed it. A third signing was planned for a lifestyle magazine, but the journalist had brought along a university cryptographer who argued with Wright and was thrown out. The hilarious soundtrack of Wright's expletive-filled rant against the cryptographer was posted online.

Wright wanted to stop there, but MacGregor was insistent. He wanted a high-profile signing run by his PR agency. Matthews would later talk about MacGregor's supposed bullying behaviour and his "aggression." Despite Wright's best efforts to deflect the signing, MacGregor would not let him off the hook.

The plan was for Wright to digitally sign a message about Jean-Paul Sartre refusing the Nobel prize. He would use the private key associated with block 9, which Satoshi had used to transfer Bitcoins to Hal Finney. Unlike the other demonstrations, there was no possibility of tampering. On 2 May 2016 at 8:00 am London time, Andresen and Matonis posted that they were convinced that Wright was Satoshi.

> "During our meeting, I saw the brilliant, opinionated, focused, generous—and privacy-seeking—person that matches the Satoshi I worked with six years ago. And he cleared up a lot of mysteries, including why he disappeared when he did and what he's been busy with since 2011." (Gavin Andresen, 2 May 2016)

The other developers' response was instant: Andresen's commit access to the Bitcoin code repository was revoked on the grounds that he must have been hacked. They could not believe that a person of Andresen's intelligence had been fooled by Faketoshi. In reality, Andresen had been unpopular with them for almost a year.

Satoshi's unexploded bomb of the inadequate block size had finally detonated. The block-size wars started in Aug 2015 when Mike Hearne proposed a new version of the Bitcoin client, Bitcoin XT featuring a rapidly increasing block size. If implemented, Bitcoin XT would result in a "hard fork", with potentially two active blockchains and two Bitcoin currencies. Andresen backed Hearne and Bitcoin XT, but it was an extreme solution that did not win widespread support from the community. The two lost moral authority by attempting to implement Bitcoin XT dictatorially. Andresen believed that he had the authority, derived ultimately from Satoshi, to make key decisions. The other developers resented this; some even questioned whether Satoshi had appointed him as lead developer and whether Satoshi's final emails to Hearne and Andresen were genuine. Andresen had also made the tactical mistake of surrendering control of the Bitcoin repository to another developer, Wladimir Van Der Laan.

Wright inserted his toxic presence into this argument and favoured the big blockers against the developers who belonged to the small block camp. Eventually, the developers were able to get an agreement for a very complex solution called SegWit that implemented a larger block, notionally 4 MB, without a hard fork. But the big-blockers split from Bitcoin by implementing their own fork, Bitcoin Cash, from which Wright's and Ayre's BSV (supposedly Bitcoin Satoshi's Vision) subsequently split. Many big blockers lost credibility by supporting Wright's claims. On that morning of 2 May after Andresen published his blog post, the embargo on the reporter's stories was lifted, and Wright digitally signed the message on his blog. Andresen was vindicated. The Bitcoin world was finally convinced that Wright was Satoshi—for a few hours.

Many were suspicious from the start. Wright should have posted both the message and the signature. But he did not include the message, claiming it would be revealed in the future. Wright had certainly posted cryptographic proof of a signed message using Satoshi's key. However, without knowing the content, no one could verify that the digital signature was for Wright's message. It was quickly discovered that Wright had used an existing signature from the transfer of Bitcoins to Hal Finney. He had changed the signature format to make it look different, but it was mathematically identical. The supposed proof was a crude forgery.

MacGregor was furious. Wright claimed that the wrong blog post had been uploaded by mistake. Another demonstration was planned. It would take place in his own London home to reduce the stress on Wright. He would digitally sign a message. Andresen, Matonis and a British TV reporter, Rory Cellan-Jones, sent small amounts of Bitcoin to a Satoshi address. Wright would return the payments as proof that he controlled the keys. They never saw their Bitcoin again. Wright disappeared into the bathroom with a razor and came out bleeding from the neck. He was taken to hospital, but the wound was superficial, and he was discharged after a few hours. After this supposed "suicide" attempt, no one could pressurise Wright for more signings.

It was a humiliation for Wright and everyone else involved in the project. For Gavin Andresen, it was a disaster that ended his career as a Bitcoin developer. We can sympathise with the difficult position he had been placed in, but he was his own worst enemy by refusing to admit that he had been fooled. Whatever mistakes Andresen may have made, he was a selfless person who had worked hard for Bitcoin without any reward in the early days. And he was undoubtedly Satoshi's chosen successor, as the newly released Malmi emails have confirmed.

Possessing Satoshi's keys would not necessarily prove that you were Satoshi. But the lack of the keys proved you were not Satoshi—unless you had a good explanation. Wright's explanations changed all the time.

First, it was a mistake; the wrong signature had been cut and pasted into the blog. Then, people had misunderstood him: he had never intended to sign the Sartre message even though everyone had expected him to provide cryptographic proof, including Matthews, Calvin Ayre and Rob MacGregor. Wright next claimed that MacGregor's hostility had so upset him that he destroyed the hard disks containing the keys by stomping on one and throwing another at a piece of furniture. Finally, he came to the Tulip Trust—the trustees would not allow him to sign. All these explanations, offered at different times, are mutually inconsistent. But that is very typical of Wright.

The Tulip Trust served Wright for years as a catch-all excuse for why he could not sign. The trustees would not allow him until the allotted time. All of Wright's schemes were based on a fundamental absurdity. None of

Satoshi's identifiable Bitcoins had ever been moved. So how could the Tulip Trust, a separate legal entity, hold them? And how could Wright buy things, such as banking software, with a paper, off-chain transfer of Bitcoin? Bitcoin worked on cryptographic principles. The seller would transfer coins to the buyer's address. You would never buy Bitcoins and leave them at the old address because the previous owner would retain the keys.

A furious MacGregor wanted to pack Wright and his wife Ramona back to Australia to face the ATO. But this never happened. It was MacGregor who was removed from the project and shuffled to one side. Here we encounter another mystery. Despite the obvious signs that Wright was a conman, Ayre decided to double down on him. He would invest perhaps a hundred million in Wright and the new company nChain. Matthews was appointed as executive chairman and Wright as Chief Scientist. They no longer attempted to convince people that Wright was Satoshi through cryptographic proof. In the future, they would use lawyers.

ELEVEN

THE BONDED COURIER

After the fiasco of the Sartre signing, no sensible person could believe that Wright was Satoshi. That left Wright a large potential market for his claims. He was backed by something more powerful than truth—money, which attracts both prostitutes and lawyers. London lawyers were falling over themselves to represent such a fine person as Wright, backed as he was by Calvin. But the ladies and gentlemen of the law play both sides. In the US, Wright's obvious access to cash had attracted litigation financing. Kleiman could now sue Wright for his supposed Bitcoins.

It was not just Wright who Ira sued. In his final years, Dave had been supported by his close friends Paige, Conrad and Andreou. In contrast, he had no contact with Ira and the two stepbrothers were more or less estranged. This did not stop all three of Dave's friends from generously helping Ira in his doomed attempt to gain access to Dave's devices. Now Ira sued them all. As Andreou put it to Paige: "Ira was always a bit… odd" (27 Feb 2018). The suits were eventually withdrawn, and Ira concentrated on his case against Wright.

And so, in Florida, one of the most surreal cases to come to any courtroom in the world commenced in 2018. Ira Kleiman, as the executor of Dave Kleiman's estate, and W&K Info Defence sued Craig Wright for hundreds of millions of Bitcoin worth billions of dollars. The case was never about whether Wright was Satoshi. Both sides agreed that he was, and the whole giddy edifice of the court case was built upon this essential falsehood.

Almost all the evidence for Wright and Kleiman's Bitcoin collaboration came from documents on Wright's computer. These included the email in which Craig first asked for Dave's involvement:

"From: Craig S Wright
Sent: Wednesday, 12 Mar 2008 6:37 PM
To: dave kleiman
Subject: FW: Defamation and the difficulties of law on the internet

I need your help editing a paper I am going to release later this year. I have been working on a new form of electronic money. Bit cash, Bitcoin…
You are always there for me Dave. I want you to be a part of it all. I cannot release it as me. GMX, vistomail and Tor. I need your help and I need a version of me to make this work that is better than me.

Craig"

Things have moved on since Wright told Wilson that Kleiman was involved in Bitcoin before him. The emails Wright now put forward show him as having done most of the work on Bitcoin before Kleiman's involvement. Note how the subject heading, which has been taken from a genuine email, has nothing to do with the content.

A later email showed how the two of them were writing Satoshi's posts and emails:

"From: Craig S Wright
Sent: Monday, 25 Jan 2010 2:15 PM
To: 'Craig Wright'
Subject: Bond Villains

Craig,

How does the following sound?

I very much wanted to find some way to include a short message, but the problem is, the whole world would be able to see the message. As much as you may keep reminding people that the message is completely non-private, it would be an accident waiting to happen.

Look up Wotty - it is not a mistake.

Are you really sure you want to know nothing of the Panama fund? I know you are having tax problems, but Bitcoins are not worth enough to be a bother. They are a wonderful idea, but you need to get some others involved and actually accept help from somebody other than me one day. I am not going to be here for you forever you know.

Worse, if you send yourself bankrupt it will not help anyone. I know you are a stubborn bastard mate (I can be an Ozzie too), I have helped you in many of the fights you get into online and more, but you need to know when to stop. Leave the government for now. Stop or they will really do some damage to you.

Dave"

The paragraph "I very much wanted…" matches exactly a paragraph that Satoshi posted to the forum on 28 Jan 2010. So the email is apparent proof that Wright and Kleiman were composing Satoshi's communications together. (If you are wondering what "Wotty" means, it comes from a children's program, the Wot Wots.)

There are some odd features about the email, not least that it was sent from Craig Wright to Craig Wright, although he claimed it was forwarded to another of his accounts. Note the odd subject heading, "Bond Villains", which does not have a "Re:". Why would Dave start a new thread called "Bond Villains" with a post that contains nothing about a Bond villain? The same subject line appears in a later email:

"From: Dave Kleiman <dave@davekleiman.com>
Sent: 2012-10-31 14:27:41
To: 'Craig Wright'
Subject: Re: Bond Villains

Craig,

You need to use the FB picture of yours for a corporate profile. Then with a UK group you can be Bond and the villain all at the same time.

Right now, the trust holds the following keys:

[List of 17 Bitcoin addresses]

They are all in one wallet, so we need to be careful of backups and also loss.

I have created a paper wallet for a couple of the holdings (as an offline backup and in case). These are:

[List of 4 Bitcoin addresses]

Most of these go back to 2010 and 2011 when you first transferred them, but I have moved a few of the online ones. There are only single copies of the paper wallets and there is no backup.

The rest are with you.

The keys are setup in the TrueCrypt Drive on the main server [...]

Respectfully,

Dave Kleiman"

This email provides evidence for the Trust's existence in 2012. The four Bitcoin address keys supposedly stored on a single paper wallet include the infamous 1Feex address, which would become the subject of a separate billion-dollar court case in London. The paper wallet for this address was handed over to MacGregor's team to be held in a vault as supposed security for the deal. Needless to say, Wright has never given any cryptographic proof that he actually controlled this address or any of the others.

Supposedly, this email is from the "Bond Villains" thread that started with the January 2010 email, even though one is two years and nine months after the other. The Facebook picture in the first line is the one that Wright used on his blog, showing him in a dinner jacket and looking a bit like James Bond. The UK company is Design by Human, an off-the-shelf company that the ATO discovered was transferred to Wright in early

2014, several months after Kleiman died. So the text of this email was definitely forged.

Wright's technique is to take something genuine, like an existing email, and modify it to suit his purpose. The odd "Bond Villains" subject line was probably taken from an authentic email exchange between Dave and Craig. The date of 31 Oct 2012 may well relate to this original exchange (the earlier Jan 2010 email is an obvious forgery that was backdated). Why were Dave and Craig discussing Bond villains? Did they have someone in mind?

Interestingly, the October date is about a month after the US captured Le Roux. His imprisonment was kept secret, but he had means of communication with the outside world.

Ira's team commissioned an expert witness to examine Wright's email and documentary evidence. He found they were a mass of forgeries. The above 31 Oct email was signed by Kleiman's PGP key as "proof" that the email was genuine. Wright had actually manufactured the key and placed it on a public registry but did not realise that a PGP signature included the date of signing. The expert determined that this date was 2 Mar 2014, a week before Wright forwarded the email to his financial guy, John Chesher, as proof of the existence of the trust. This would be a typical pattern. Wright made many of the forgeries in early 2014 to support his story to the ATO.

Many other emails and communications were exposed as forgeries. Wright had made numerous errors. The PGP signing date was a key indicator. PDF documents included fonts that were not released until after the purported date of the document. A Bitmessage conversation between Wright and Kleiman was dated before the Bitmessage software was released. The metadata of some documents indicated that they were edited or created long after the face date. Emails were sent from domains which did not exist at the time of the email.

Among the forgeries were the emails that showed Kleiman offering Uyen the role of Director at W&K and then thanking her for her acceptance. One of these emails contained a signature created on 12 Mar 2014, a year after Kleiman died. The emails were saved as PDFs and modified on 17 Apr 2014 to change the From, To and Date fields in the header. Wright would have sent the original signed email to himself, saved it as a PDF and then edited the PDF to change the email headers. Another technique was to take a genuine email from Kleiman and edit it in PDF format. So on 13 Oct 2012, Kleiman apparently nominated Uyen as COO of Design by Human, a company not actually purchased by Wright until early 2014. This forgery was based on an email Kleiman sent to a mailing list nominating a new member—nothing to do with Wright, Uyen or Design by Human.

As Wright claimed to be a security expert, the degree of incompetence in the forgeries is breathtaking. But this is typical of Wright. He can absorb a massive amount of information on a subject but does not fully comprehend what he absorbs. He makes fundamental errors. He talks technobabble, which sounds great to those with a little knowledge but does not fool the experts.

Many of Wright's forgeries date from early 2014 when he was dealing with the ATO and contacting the Kleimans. He even sent emails from Satoshi's address, satoshi@vistomail.com, to his tax advisor, Andrew Sommer, to convince Sommer he was Satoshi. It is easy to edit the email "from" field to anything, a simple trick regularly used by scammers. The trial expert determined that the email was sent from a user identified as "cwright".

If Craig Wright were a performance artist, the Tulip Trust would be his masterpiece. Invented as a last-minute addition to a tax claim, it developed over the years into an arrangement of astonishing complexity. The unknown trustees of this enigmatic trust controlled over 300,000 Bitcoins. No living soul knew their identity, for the trust had been established by a dead person. That individual had arranged for the key slices to unlock this Bitcoin treasure to arrive at preordained dates in the hands of a mysterious "bonded courier".

The name Tulip Trust came from an aged shelf company that Wright purchased in 2014. He altered the invoice to make it look like the company was bought in 2011. As early as 2015, Wright told Matthews and MacGregor that the trust controlled the keys and needed the trustees' approval to use them for a signing demonstration.

At his first court deposition, Wright denied that Kleiman had anything to do with the trust. The keys were split using Shamir's Secret Sharing Scheme, a cryptographic method by which several individuals could hold part keys to a file without any of them having access on their own. Wright claimed he had never put Bitcoin into the trust and denied that the Trust controlled any Bitcoin keys. This changed when Judge Reinhart ordered Wright to detail all the Bitcoin he controlled.

Wright now said that he had transferred all his Bitcoin into the Tulip Trust in 2011 as a blind trust over which he had no control or knowledge. He did not even possess the Bitcoin addresses, as they were generated by an algorithm and could not be accessed without the Shamir scheme key slices. The judge was not impressed and demanded that he disclose the details of the trust. So Wright changed his story again. The trustees were now David Kleiman, Coin Ltd, Uyen Nguyen, Craig Wright, Panopticrypt, Savannah, and the holders of Satoshi's PGP keys, supposedly Wright himself. Almost all these trustees are either Wright or companies he controlled. Yet he maintained he had no access to the addresses or keys, which were in a file encrypted by a Shamir scheme.

Wright now produced the documents and emails from Kleiman showing the establishment of the Tulip Trust. The expert showed they were all forged, including that backdated invoice. With his documents exposed as forgeries, Wright claimed that the trust was just a legal wrapper and that Dave Kleiman had stored all the addresses and keys in the Shamir scheme. Kleiman had distributed the keys to persons unknown but arranged for the keys to be returned at preset dates. How many key slices were necessary to unencrypt the Shamir scheme? It was either 8 of 15, 12 of 15, or 3 of 5: Wright gave all these variations at different times.

It raised the question of why Wright set up such an absurd arrangement. At a hearing before the judge, he claimed it was all due to Martti Malmi and Theymos (Michael Marquardt). He made some vile accusations against the pair:

> "Both of them, together with Ross Ulbricht, set up Silk Road, Hydra and a number of other darker websites. I protested this to them. […] Silk Road was designed to sell heroin, MDMA, Fentanyl, weapons,

> et cetera. Martti also started working on a reputation system to allow assassination markets. [...] Hydra was worse than Silk Road. The nature of Hydra that Theymos wanted was as a mechanism to have children exchange hard drugs for pornographic photographs. They sought to alter Bitcoin to allow the distribution of encrypted child pornography that would be exchanged in schools for Fentanyl and other such drugs." (Court transcript 28 Jun 2019, pp. 15-16)

Needless to say, this characterisation is entirely false. Wright starts with something true and elaborates it into a complete falsehood. The nugget of truth is that Malmi did comment on the need for a reputation system on the notorious Heroin Store thread, and Theymos talked about reviews. Their posts were nothing more than a few lines discussing purely theoretical issues. Although Wright has been seen as an amusing, comical figure, this quote, and many like it, shows the true nature of his character.

Wright said he gave up on his Bitcoin mining in Aug 2010 and now maintained that he only brought in Kleiman at this point. Wright wanted to destroy his keys in disgust, but Kleiman devised a scheme to remove the keys and addresses from him until 2020. So, Wright could not give the court a complete list of addresses. Instead, Wright offered the court a "Probabilistic list", which would be essentially correct but not 100% accurate.

Wright brought in the nChain Chief Technology Officer, fellow Australian Steve Shadders, to produce this list from the public blockchain based on criteria to determine what Bitcoin Satoshi had mined. The criteria were mostly simple, such as only including addresses if the Bitcoin had never been moved. One criterion, the least significant byte of the nonce, was taken from Lerner's analysis.

A popular theory to explain Lerner's findings was that Satoshi had used 59 machines. Wright seized on this theory. He came up with the story that he had used 69 machines set up in Australia with a large electricity bill. (It is typical of Wright's carelessness that he got the number wrong.) But now, he told Shadders that he had used 59 machines and marked this first byte by the numbers 0 through 58 to identify the machine that mined the block. So Shadders should eliminate those blocks which did not have 0 to 58 in this byte. Shadders attempted to do this but later discovered an error in his program (which became known as "the Shadders bug"), so his list included some nonce values that should have been excluded. In total, the list had 27,000 addresses, or 1.35 million Bitcoins. This is more than the 1.1 million mined by Patoshi, both because of the Shadders bug and because Wright's criteria were too crude.

In fact, Lerner's later work disproved the theory of 59 machines. He showed that Patoshi was scanning over four hexadecimal ranges and using no more than four machines, perhaps only one. Wright had no actual knowledge of early Bitcoin mining.

Wright had claimed that Kleiman had arranged to send him the key slices from the Shamir scheme by "bonded courier":

> "The access [...] was given to Dave to distribute, and so that I wouldn't be in trouble, was set so that after a period, in January of next year, a bonded courier is meant to return key slices." (Court transcript 28 Jun 2019, pp. 23-4)

So the bonded courier would return the key slices and access to the Bitcoin keys to Wright in Jan 2020. Judge Reinhart was scathing about Wright's story:

> "Apparently, dead men tell no tales, but perhaps they send bonded couriers. I completely reject Dr Wright's testimony about the alleged Tulip Trust, the alleged encrypted file and his alleged inability to identify his Bitcoin holdings. Quite simply, Dr Wright's story not only was not supported by other evidence in the record, it defies common sense and real life experience." (Bruce E. Reinhart, Court transcript 26 Aug 2019, pp. 78-9)

The judge concluded that Weight had committed perjury by forging numerous documents and that the Tulip Trust did not exist. As a sanction, he threw out much of Wright's defence, which would have handed Ira victory by default. Wright appealed to the more senior trial judge, Beth Bloom. She agreed with Reinhard's conclusions but vacated the sanction:

> "Given the Defendant's many inconsistencies and misstatements, the Court questions whether it is remotely plausible that the mysterious "bonded courier" is going to arrive, yet alone that he will arrive in January 2020..." (Beth Bloom, Court judgement 19 Jan 2020, p.22)

Nonetheless, she decided to give Wright until the end of the month. The internet was agog for the arrival of the bonded courier. Who was he? And what bizarre means of transport would he use to bring the key slices to Wright? Some claimed to have seen the bonded courier on his way and posted pictures. One woman posted a photo of a dominatrix dressed in stockings and holding a whip. Perhaps Wright had misheard Kleiman, who had really promised to send him a "bondage courier". Calvin Ayre had a sense of humour failure and blocked her.

The bonded courier never arrived. Instead, Wright claimed that someone had mysteriously emailed him a list of his Bitcoin addresses, even though he had previously said they were impossible to derive except by cracking open the Shamir scheme. Ira's team showed that Wright's supposed Bitcoin addresses were a subset of the Shadders list, which had been sorted, cut and pasted. Wright had even mistakenly included addresses that were subject to the Shadders bug. When some of the addresses were inadvertently revealed in a court document, the actual owner of 145 of those addresses responded by encoding a message with the private keys: "Craig Wright is a liar and a fraud" (24 May 2020).

After over three years of gruelling discovery proceedings, the case finally came to a jury trial in Nov 2021. Ira's legal team, led by Val Freedman and Kyle Roche, had demolished the evidence that Wright had put forward, proving that he was a liar and forger. So, game set and match for Ira? Not so. The headlines read that Satoshi had "won" and was allowed to keep his Bitcoin.

The jury dismissed all of Ira's claims to Wright's Bitcoins. It did grant an award of $143 million (mere pocket money for Satoshi) to W&K Info Defence. The jury must have thought they were giving this money to Ira. But no one knew who owned W&K Info Defence. Was it 100% Kleiman, the only member listed on the registration documents? Or was it 50/50, probably the initial intention? Or perhaps one-third each for Kleiman, Wright and his first wife Lynn, as she and Wright maintained? So this most surreal of court cases ended with another court case in a different Florida court to determine ownership of W&K Info Defence.

The ownership dispute would eventually be decided in Ira's favour. But needless to say, his legal team has never seen any of the $143 million owed by Wright. He has persistently used tactics to delay proceedings and when forced by the court to submit a form listing his assets, he served it to his current and previous wives rather than Ira! Wright was found in contempt of court once again and his revised asset form was made public as a sanction. It showed essentially zero net worth and $135,000 of annual income. Not much chance of collecting $143 million from that.

Calvin Ayre has financially supported Wright in all his legal cases, supposedly through loans. The details are murky, with a web of companies making the flow of money impossible to trace. It is unclear what assets Wright has squirrelled away out of reach of the court through trusts and other such legal devices.

So how did Wright get what Calvin Ayre's PR team and his Coingeek propaganda outfit characterised as a win? His lead attorney, Amanda McGovern, made an unconventional and brilliant defence. (Sadly, McGovern died not very long after the trial). She argued that the mass of forged documents and inconsistent statements showed that nothing her client said could be trusted. She frankly told the jury that these forgeries were all about Wright's tax dispute. And she pointed out that if you disregarded Wright's statements and these forged documents, there was virtually nothing left to suggest that Kleiman was part of Satoshi or had mined any Bitcoin.

By uncovering Wright's forgeries, Ira's legal team had sawn off the branch upon which they sat. They had discredited Wright but needed to prove that Kleiman was one part of Satoshi and had mined hundreds of thousands of Bitcoins in partnership with Wright. McGovern maintained that this was a fiction created by Wright in his dispute with the ATO. It was a brilliant argument and, like most brilliant arguments, was true up to a point. There was just one inconvenient loose end, one piece of evidence that did not come from Wright. It was testimony showing that Kleiman was involved with Satoshi and mining Bitcoin in 2009. It was crucial for McGovern to discredit this testimony. As the source was Ira himself, she could argue that his story was fabricated to advance his self-interest. And she seized upon a discrepancy to cast doubt upon the whole story. She also cleverly managed to let the jury know that Ira had never visited Dave once in his years in hospital, in blatant contradiction to the judge's instructions.

It was an emotional point that may have carried the day. Quite simply, Ira did not deserve the Bitcoins. But the jury could not ignore Wright's blatant dishonesty. It granted Ira the consolation prize of a sizeable award to W&K.

McGovern was a clever advocate, but clever advocates are concerned with winning cases and not with the truth. Had Ira come up with his story in his court deposition, it would have been suspicious. But the earliest version comes much earlier, from a time when he had no reason to lie. And if he had lied, he would have come up with something much better. Through Ira's story we get our first glimpse of Satoshi under his own identity.

TWELVE

THE RICH FOREIGN GUY

Ira first gave his story in an email he sent to Wright about three months after the two began talking. Ira had been trying to remember anything that supported what Wright had been claiming. He could not recall Dave ever saying the word "Bitcoin" but remembered a strange conversation they had at a family Thanksgiving dinner at their father's house. Ira dated it to 2009 because it was the first time Dave met his baby daughter. While everyone else was out in the kitchen, Ira asked Dave what he was up to:

> "We started talking about how successful Facebook had become and I asked him if he was working on anything interesting. He told me he was making his own money. I was like what? Are you making counterfeit money? I thought maybe he was up to something fishy. And then he said it was digital money and opened his wallet to show me something like a business card with a logo on it. But he couldn't find it so I think he just scribbled it on the back of a card, the B with lines through it."

This logo would be the main line of attack for Wright's lawyers. Ira continued:

> "He also said he was doing some work with a rich foreign guy. I asked him how rich is this guy? He said something like he's not super rich, but he owns some properties. Then he said some other stuff about the foreign guy that I don't remember. I replied to him saying why don't you partner with this guy. With your brains and his money you guys could create the next big thing like Facebook. He gave me a blank look and was silent, which I thought unusual for Dave to stop talking. Maybe he didn't want to directly come out and say you

> guys were already partners. Anyway, that's the only time I can recall where he mentioned this stuff to me.
>
> I was wondering if you were aware of any business cards ever being printed with the Bitcoin logo on it. I never found any in his belongings. I wasn't sure if he was opening his wallet to show me a Bitcoin business card or if he just wanted to grab an existing card to draw the logo on the back of it." (20 May 2014)

Ira assumed that the rich foreign guy must have been Wright, and the Australian went along with this:

> "We did partner ;)
>
> The properties were not magnificent, but I loved them. In total I had a few cattle ranches and farm. Up in Port Macquarie. Wonderful beaches, but underdeveloped unlike Florida. In total about 550 acres."

The discrepancy in Ira's account concerns the Bitcoin logo. In Nov 2009, the logo was actually the letters "BC" on a gold coin. The B with two lines through was only suggested in February 2010. Wright's team used this discrepancy to argue that Ira had made up the whole story to support his claim to Satoshi's Bitcoins.

Ira comes over as a truthful witness. It would have been very easy for him to say that Dave had admitted he was working on Bitcoin or that Dave had hinted at being one part of Satoshi. Instead, Ira bluntly says that Dave never mentioned the word Bitcoin to him. Ira is no liar.

And Ira had no motive to lie in May 2014. Although he was beginning to lose patience with Wright's bizarre explanations, the court case was years in the future. Wright kept insisting that Dave had been one part of Satoshi. Ira was trying to think of anything that might collaborate Wright's story. Had he made it up, he could have done much better than the "rich foreign guy" and a confused account of a card with the Bitcoin logo. It reads, in fact, just like a typical scrappy memory of something that happened years before.

So what about the wrong logo? Ira had been exposed to the Bitcoin logo for the previous three months. His memory substituted the logo as he knew it for something he could not remember. Ira was very doubtful about the logo in his conversation with Wright: "I think the logo he drew for me only had only one line going through the B, not two." And when shown a logo: "I guess the one he drew for me could have looked like that. Wish I kept the card." So Ira admitted at the time that he could not fully recall the logo. Such things are perfectly normal, indeed expected, with real memories.

And Dave may have shown Ira his idea for a new logo—a B with a single line—to get his opinion as a professional web designer. Ira was unsure if Dave had been looking for a printed business card or the back of a card to draw the logo on. No one is going to print a Bitcoin business card in 2009. It makes sense that Dave was drawing his idea, not actually adopted, on the back of a card.

Ira naturally assumed that Dave had meant Wright in this Thanksgiving conversation. Wright was very keen to reinforce that belief, but he does not fit the description of the rich foreign guy. Dave specifically identified him as someone who owned properties, a wealthy man with a property portfolio. Wright was neither wealthy nor did he own properties. He told Ira that he owned "a few cattle ranches and a farm" at Port Macquarie, which "were not magnificent" but had exaggerated even this. The most property the Wrights owned was a suburban house near Sydney and what Lynn called a "hobby farm" up the coast at Port Macquarie. By late 2009, the Wrights no longer had the Sydney house. Following Wright's redundancy in Dec 2008 they moved to the farm full time. So they only had a single residence.

Nor was Wright someone you would describe as "rich." He had only been a mid-level employee at BDO, not a partner. His salary was reported on his tax returns as 80k Australian dollars. By 2011, the Wrights had divorced, and the farm was sold. In a blog post of Oct 2011, Wright said he was poor due to the time spent on his research over a decade: "I have gone from a large 7 bedroom house and a farm to a small flat that I lease."

Dave's silence when Ira suggests he partner with the rich guy is also suspicious. There was nothing secret about his relationship with Wright. The two had been friends for years, and Dave talked openly with other friends about Wright and their joint disk overwriting paper, of which he was very proud. Had Dave been discussing Wright with Ira, he would surely have mentioned this project. The sudden silence is untypical of Kleiman, who must have thought he had already said too much about the "rich guy."

Making digital money at that time could only mean mining Bitcoin. Ira's story shows that Dave Kleiman was one of the tiny number of people mining Bitcoin at the end of 2009. Even more extraordinary, the association with the "rich guy" means that Dave was mining on someone else's behalf. This would be very strange in 2009. Bitcoin was worth nothing, so why would a rich guy pay someone to mine it? We know of only one person who was systematically acquiring large volumes of Bitcoin at that time—Satoshi.

He was leaving his digital fingerprints all over his Patoshi Bitcoins. Getting someone else to do the mining would ensure the Bitcoin could not be traced back to him. Satoshi could be confident that the miner fulfilled his end of the bargain because he would only pay him for coins transferred to his address. As he would be offering a price way above the market value (zero), there was no incentive to cheat.

Of course, this introduced the risk that the miner might come to know Satoshi's identity, which seems to have happened with Kleiman. But perhaps Kleiman had already been told or had worked it out for himself. A witness at the London trial recalled Wright asking around at BDO if anyone knew a person with a Japanese name, which the witness thought might have been Satoshi Nakamoto. He dated this to Nov or Dec 2008, just after the paper was published on the Cryptography mailing list. Wright was not a member of this list and must have heard about Satoshi through Kleiman. It indicates that as early as late 2008, Kleiman was keen to discover Satoshi's identity.

Kleiman would have been the ideal person to run a mining operation. Although he could not code, he was an expert at operating secure servers and was very keen on encryption. He could have begun mining on his own account in 2009 and contacted Satoshi. The mining arrangement with Satoshi would have come later.

We can even trace the email that most likely gave Satoshi the idea. On 22 Jul 2009, Martti Malmi suggested starting an exchange with a minimum price guarantee. Satoshi was intrigued: "I had imagined an auction, but it would be far simpler and more confidence inspiring to back it at a specific exchange rate." But he did not want to do it yet and made an odd comment: "I've had some ideas that could only be done before an exchange exists" (24 Aug 2009).

An idea that could only be done without an exchange? It sounds like Satoshi wanted to buy Bitcoin before an exchange pushed the price too high. We must recall Satoshi's objectives:

1. To secure his Bitcoin target (perhaps 10%) while avoiding the Patoshi problem of mining Bitcoin that could be connected to Satoshi.
2. To leave enough Bitcoin on the table for others (at least 50%) and get it widely distributed to start the greed loop.
3. To get the price increasing.

Malmi's exchange idea could help with the price. But any Bitcoin purchases Satoshi made to support the price would be all too visible. And exchange purchases would mop up the free float, failing objective (2).

So Satoshi had the idea of implementing Malmi's floor price as a private arrangement with one or more individual miners. He would offer them a generous price to mine Bitcoin on his behalf. Simultaneously, he would reduce his Patoshi mining to compensate, achieving (1) without compromising (2). If he were to subsidise multiple competing miners, that would increase the difficulty level and, hence, the price. We know about Kleiman—there may have been others.

The timing fits perfectly. In late August, Satoshi told Malmi he had "other ideas" he wanted to implement before a public exchange. In October, he reduced his Patoshi hash rate. Was this because he was putting other mining arrangements in place? Or did he just want to leave more Bitcoin on the table for everyone else to start the greed loop? It would be consistent with the Thanksgiving conversation if an alternative mining using Kleiman was in place around October. Satoshi increased his Patoshi rate again in November, which may indicate disappointment with the new mining output.

Kleiman's laptops were fast, top-of-the-range machines that could have been used for mining in 2009. Wright's forged contract for W&K said that Kleiman would mine Bitcoin on Satoshi's behalf through a server farm although, absurdly, Wright had a supercomputer doing the mining. During 2010 the difficulty increased a lot and multiple computers, perhaps in a server farm, would have been needed to mine volumes that would have been significant to Satoshi. And renting processing power in a server farm could have been managed from hospital. If Kleiman were working for Satoshi, it would explain why he had no money in 2012/13. He would have long ago transferred all his mined Bitcoin to Satoshi.

Ira's account is so significant that it is important to collaborate it from other evidence. Investigators use the principle of "triangulation" to build confidence in a witness's testimony. Is there independent evidence that validates at least part of what the witness is saying? In this way, investigators can cross-check to find out who is telling the truth and who is lying. Do we have anything that validates the story Ira gave in his email?

The circumstantial evidence certainly makes Ira's story plausible. We know that Kleiman posted to the Cryptography mailing list on 20 Jan 2009, less than two weeks after Satoshi had published the software and while the discussion about Bitcoin was ongoing. This gives credibility to the idea of Kleiman mining Bitcoin and contacting Satoshi. He was one of a small number of people (a few hundred?) exposed to Bitcoin at the very start.

Then, we have Wright's statements, forged emails, and forged documents. It is remarkable that Kleiman always does the Bitcoin mining and implements Bitcoin transactions according to Satoshi's (Wright's) instructions. Is there a nugget of truth behind all this, that Kleiman really was mining and moving Bitcoin for Satoshi?

We also have Jamie Wilson's eyewitness testimony when Wright first began claiming to be associated with Satoshi: "I believed that Dave was the original start. He started looking on the Blockchain" (Wilson Deposition pp.49-50). Wilson clarified that he meant that Kleiman was mining Bitcoin before Wright and that this had come directly from Wright. It is significant because this was from early 2013, before Wright had the chance to develop his story.

We would like to have evidence completely independent of Wright—and fortunately we do! BitcoinFX was a very early participant in the Bitcoin forum—number 30. His profile shows that he is from the UK and registered on 1 Feb 2010, a couple of months after the forum was established. He began enthusiastically mining Bitcoin and had the ambition of starting an exchange, also called BitcoinFX, which he announced on 26 May 2010. One of his early customers was "laszlo", of the famous Bitcoin pizza. Laszlo must have bought more pizza with the fiat currency he received from this exchange because BitcoinFX posted that he hoped Laszlo had enjoyed his pizza.

When he started mining, BitcoinFX was curious about who else was involved. So he ran special software to tell him what other addresses were running nodes. BitcoinFX was no fan of Wright and added a prominent statement in his forum footer that Wright was not Satoshi. But he felt compelled to post that one part of Wright's story was true—Kleiman had mined Bitcoin:

> "I, BitcoinFX hereby state that when I started mining Bitcoin in early 2010 I used the following windows program (Prio) - https://www.prnwatch.com/prio/ - to watch all incoming and outgoing TCP/IP connections to the Bitcoin network from my home PC, which was fully port forwarded on 8333.
>
> I distinctly recall resolving the website of said Dave Kleiman, as to this effect, the domain name was also acting as a Bitcoin P2P node. Either ... www.DigitalComputerForensicExpert.com or www.DaveKleiman.com or www. ComputerForensicExaminer.com
>
> The website had a distinct design that stuck in my memory coupled with the fact that, as an individual who had recently discovered Bitcoin, this reassured myself that other IT professionals were interested in the project (if only from a research/testing standpoint)." (Jul 2018)

Not surprisingly, he could not remember the exact domain name, but he recalls looking at the website associated with that domain. So we have an unbiased independent witness confirming that Kleiman was mining

Bitcoin in "early 2010". This is consistent with Ira's story that Dave said he was making digital money in Nov 2009. This crucial piece of evidence could have changed the Kleiman trial outcome, but it never came up at that trial.

A final piece of evidence comes from the forensic examination of Dave's hard drives and thumb drives for the court case. It was uncovered by Wright's expert witness, which may be why it also never came up at trial. The expert found three drives were encrypted with TrueCrypt and were essentially uncrackable. Three partitions on other drives also looked like they had been encrypted. If Dave had been working on Bitcoin, the evidence would be in those unreadable encrypted drives.

Dave was very hot on security and encryption, but no one is perfect. Did his attention ever lapse? The expert continued to search for anything unencrypted related to Bitcoin, looking through deleted files that could be read with special software. He drew a blank except for a single item, a text file "To do list" including a line "is this a satoshi address?" followed by a Bitcoin address.

This tiny clue has been preserved by chance from a deleted, unencrypted "to-do" list. It is not much, but it supports Ira's story. Dave was not only mining Bitcoin but doing something that required him to identify whether a Bitcoin address belonged to Satoshi. This was before Lerner published his analysis. Questioning whether an address belonged to Satoshi was an unusual occupation at that time. Apart from some very early blocks, it was impossible to identify Satoshi's mining until Lerner outlined the nonce method. Did Kleiman possess inside information?

It would greatly strengthen the case if we could identify Kleiman's mining on the block chain, but that is difficult without more information. On Wester's charts there are six unknown miners active around Thanksgiving 2009. One candidate looks particularly interesting: they started at just the right time and went on to mine a significant volume in 2010. But it would be foolish to point to this miner without hard evidence connecting them to Kleiman.

How are miners identified? Typically, through forum posts where they leave clues or addresses. It is notable that Kleiman appears to have never joined the forum, unless it was under an unidentified username. Kleiman loved to participate in mailing lists so this is unusual behaviour which supports the idea he was mining in partnership with Satoshi who was paranoid about revealing his identity. If Satoshi were using someone else to mine, he would have wanted the arrangement to be watertight, so it is unsurprising that that we do not find any obvious clues.

With Ira's account of his Thanksgiving conversation with Dave, we glimpse Satoshi under his own identity. The glimpse is uncertain, a recollection of a brief conversation Ira had years previously, but it tells us a few things.

First, Satoshi would have mined considerably more Bitcoin than previously thought. He reduced his Patoshi mining activity to protect his identity rather than for altruistic reasons. He implemented additional mining activity through Kleiman, and there is no reason to think this was his only arrangement. We know that mining activity took off at the end of 2009, but we do not know how much of this was due to Satoshi mining by other means.

We also learn some things about Satoshi. He is foreign, meaning not a US citizen, which is no surprise. More significantly, he is rich and owns some property. Although Dave said he was not "super rich", the context was a conversation about Mark Zuckerberg's enormous wealth. To be described as rich implies millions, at least, although Satoshi was not in the billionaire category. Dave is unlikely to have had perfect information about Satoshi's wealth. He knew was what was visible—that the rich guy owned properties. That implies a portfolio of properties, certainly more than a couple of houses.

The other thing is Dave's unusual silence when Ira suggested a partnership. He seems to have realised that he had already said too much. The rich foreign guy was not the type of person you talked to your family about.

We must ask one obvious question. Was Kleiman himself Satoshi? He can be ruled out very quickly. Kleiman was good at absorbing and passing on technical information and was fantastic as a practical computer guy. He would have been the ideal person to run a Bitcoin mining operation. But there is nothing to suggest that he had anything like Satoshi's depth of intellectual ability. We know from the testimony of Kimon Andreou that Dave did not code and had problems with even simple scripts. He could never have written or refined a complex program in C++.

That leaves the possibility that Kleiman assisted Satoshi in the development of Bitcoin. He could have been useful with testing. More significantly, Satoshi may have asked for assistance with the paper: he was not an academic and was better with code than words. In contrast, Kleiman had a reputation as an industry figure, technical author and editor.

It is more likely Kleiman only became involved after the launch. Many people interacted with Satoshi, but only Kleiman knew his identity, which suggests that Kleiman knew him before Bitcoin. There is that story about Wright asking if anyone knew of a Japanese name, perhaps Satoshi Nakamoto, just after the paper had been published on the Cryptography list. If, as we would expect, he got the name through Kleiman, then Dave was trying to find out who Satoshi was in Nov/Dec 2008. Kleiman may have had some early awareness of what Satoshi, under his own identity, had been working on. He put two and two together, deducing that Satoshi was…someone, let's call him X.

We must return to the events of early 2013. We have seen that Wright made four substantial posts about Bitcoin between 27 Apr and 29 Apr and established an account on MtGox around the same time. Jamie Wilson recalled that Wright went to America: "Craig said to me a good mate of his just passed away, and I believe he came over to Florida. Or he did fly to the States." After this trip, Wright began setting up his companies and suddenly had access to a lot of money.

Wilson connected Wright's US trip to Kleiman's death. But, in fact, it took place before he had died. On Saturday, 13 Apr 2013, Wright published a blog post with the heading "Location":

> "The next time somebody tells you that location data and social media are an effective way to analyze things...Try looking at my facebook, google, foursquare etc data for the day. Do you really think GPS is special?" (13 Apr 2013)

It suggests that Wright was on the move: he had gone somewhere. Ira looked up Wright's Foursquare travel page to find evidence for his suspicions. The page shows an entry for 13 Apr 2013 with the title "Evil" and the comment "Muhaha Evil grin and all". The entry is for a "Dive Bar" at Oak Ridge, US. Ira found that Wright's location for that day was Oak Ridge, NJ 07438, a wooded area 35 miles from central New York. Ira thought that as Wright had been in the US, he had opportunity to murder his stepbrother who died just over a week later. In reality, Wright had absolutely no reason to murder his friend: they were going into a Bitcoin business together.

"Muhahaha" means wicked laughter, such as by a comic book villain. It was a favourite expression of Dave Kleiman, one he used repeatedly in his texts to Andreou. As the zip code population is just 11,000, there are not many candidates for the "dive bar", and there is no evidence of a bar called "Evil". The best candidate is the long-established "The Daily Planet", which someone described in 2012 as a "dive bar" and "go-go" place. It started as a rough strip joint for rednecks but went upmarket over the years and now even caters for families on Sundays. In 2013, it would have featured scantily dressed, perhaps topless, female dancers and barmaids, which would explain Wight's comment, "Evil grin and all".

The Daily Planet is a log cabin in the woods. It is three miles off Route 23 and hard to find, located down some back roads. It would be a very odd place for an Australian to fetch up unless he had been taken there by a local or perhaps arranged to meet someone there.

On 10 Apr, Wright was in Australia having some cables installed. The air journey from Sydney to New York takes a little under twenty-four hours, but with the time difference, you can leave Sydney in the morning and arrive in New York in the early evening. So, the earliest he could have arrived in New York was the evening of 11 Apr. Turning up in a remote part of New Jersey shows that he was not on a stopover to Florida. But Wilson connected the trip to Kleiman.

Did Kleiman also travel to New Jersey? A physical trip may appear unlikely as he could have participated in a meeting by phone. But we can't entirely rule it out. Kleiman would not fly, and it was almost a day's journey by road, which was a very long way for a sick man. However, someone could have driven him, or he could even have driven himself. Kleiman drove a van that he had modified to enable him to travel independently. On one occasion in 2012, when he was quite ill, he got himself out of the hospital to a courthouse to testify on a case. But he was fearful about the after-effects of that trip.

Could Kleiman have left the hospital on 22 Mar in preparation for New Jersey? He may have known something important was coming up but not the precise date. He would not have gone to New York just to meet Wright, for the two communicated by phone and email all the time. If he did make that long journey north, it may have killed him. By 18 Apr, he was at home and seriously ill.

We can be confident that something happened on Wright's trip, for his behaviour changed dramatically on his return. Allowing for the time difference, he could not have returned to Australia before 16 Apr. And yet, as early as 17 Apr, he established the first of his new Bitcoin-related Australian companies, Coin-Exch Pty Ltd. The registration of this company is the very first evidence of Wright's involvement in Bitcoin. In the forged contracts produced in mid-2013, Wright represented Kleiman as having a 49.5% share in Coin-Exch. He told Ira it was intended as a joint venture:

> "Dave and I decided to start Coin-Exch so that we could lock in some of the value. When we started planning this, it was late 2012" (23 Apr 2014)

Some of this may be true. The original idea would have been a 50/50 joint venture, but Kleiman died just days after it was established and before it was properly capitalised or any shares could be assigned to him. If Kleiman and Wright began planning a venture in late 2012, it would explain Kleiman's many absences from the hospital starting in mid-January 2013.

The company name tells us the intended business. "Coin-Exch" was intended as a Bitcoin exchange. By mid-2013, Wright represented himself as one-third of Satoshi and as controlling an enormous amount of Bitcoin due to "fate and other circumstances". Initially, Wright told Wilson it was

Kleiman who was in Bitcoin first. Later, he changed his story and claimed to be the primary creator.

Would Wright have developed such an odd story on his own? It was unnecessary for his tax scheme—much better to represent himself as an early miner, which was inherently unverifiable, rather than Satoshi. And why has Satoshi never appeared to contradict Wright? We should remember that in April 2013, Satoshi had only been gone two years and was expected to reappear at any time. For all Wright knew, Satoshi could have remained in contact with his inner circle. Wright has said repeatedly over the years that three men were part of Satoshi. It suggests that he had some genuine knowledge, and that Satoshi was involved in the Coin-Exch plan.

We have seen that Kleiman worked for Satoshi in 2009/10 and knew his identity. We can deduce that Coin-Exch was a front. What better than a Bitcoin exchange to help Satoshi manage his Bitcoin wealth and convert some of it to usable cash? Especially if "other circumstances" meant that Satoshi couldn't manage his own Bitcoin. In that case it would be natural to turn to Kleiman who had managed Bitcoin transactions for him in the past. Were Kleiman and Wright even supposed to put themselves forward as part of a shadowy Satoshi collective to draw attention away from the man himself?

If this is correct, Wright must have met Satoshi or his representative in the New York area in Apr 2013. Satoshi would have wanted Kleiman, but because of his illness and death, had to make do with Wright. He would not have been impressed by Wright's performance. Coin-Exch never did operate as a Bitcoin exchange. Wright represented himself as acquiring "banking software", but it was fake. And anyway, such software would not have been necessary or useful for a Bitcoin exchange. The problem was that Wright was not up to the job of running a real business. In one forged email supposedly dated 16 Jan 2013, Kleiman makes a revealing comment:

> "Craig, I do recommend that you stick with Coin-Exch for now. The idea of automated smart systems controlling money is not something many people will get and that fewer will applaud you for."

Was this something that Kleiman wrote or, more likely, something that Wright wrote as reflecting Kleiman's concerns? Satoshi wanted a Bitcoin exchange, but Wright considered himself a genius who would build a crypto group far more complex than just an exchange.

Two other circumstances are of note. The first is that Paul Le Roux was in New York at this time. He was being held in prison in Brooklyn. He slept at prison overnight, but during the day, he was taken out to nearby locations to work with the DEA. Le Roux was closely monitored but had many opportunities to contact the outside world.

The second circumstance is a record in the US prison system. Le Roux's custody was supposed to be a closely guarded secret, but bureaucracy is hard to subvert. The prison service recorded Le Roux's name as an inmate on the publicly available database. While looking at this system, Evan Ratliff came across an odd entry which no one could explain. He concluded that it must have been an admin error. It recorded Le Roux as "Released" on 9 Apr 2013, a few days before Wright arrived in New York.

THIRTEEN

THE SATOSHI PROFILE

Satoshi left few objective clues to his identity. Time stamps are ambiguous. A version of the White Paper recorded Pacific Standard Time, indicating the US west coast and western Canada. This would be consistent with the Los Angeles IP address recorded in early Jan 2009, which may have belonged to Satoshi. However, we have seen that Satoshi needed to run a computer with an open port to start the network. He would have been well aware of the dangers in this, and we can expect him to have taken protective measures, such as running his K5 setup remotely.

Satoshi's time zone was not consistent. Another version of the white paper was set to Mountain Time. And his private emails to Malmi using satoshin@gmx.com are set to UK time, changing from UTC + 1hr in the summer to UTC in the winter. Some early Bitcoin software modules show a time zone of UTC+1 hour, corresponding to Western Europe but not the UK. It is more credible that the time zone on these old modules is a genuine oversight by Satoshi. That would mean that at some point before 2008, Satoshi was working from continental western Europe.

The actual timing of Satoshi's communications is more significant than the purported time zone. This is numerical objective evidence of the type that computer people love. Appendix A shows an analysis of the timing of Satoshi's emails from the newly released Malmi collection. These are a large set, and because the emails were private rather than forum posts, the timing may be less likely to be manipulated. Appendix A gives the analysis for three time zones: UTC, UTC -8 hours (California winter time), and UTC +8 hours (Japan and the Philippines). In line with other studies, there are virtually no communications between 11 pm and 7 am Pacific Time. Otherwise, emails are spread out over the working day, starting early and with a peak at 10:00 am - 12:00 pm. There is also a secondary peak at around 9 pm to 10 pm. It is consistent with California, where Nick Szabo and Hal Finney lived.

If Satoshi was in that time zone, he had a strikingly 9-to-5 pattern of activity. He is a good boy who gets up early, works hard in the morning, is always tucked up in bed by 11 pm, and never pulls an all-nighter. This doesn't sound much like the typical solo developer.

The problem with trying to work out Satoshi's time zone is that we have three unknowns:

Satoshi's time zone
Satoshi's sleep and waking pattern
The part of the waking day Satoshi devoted to Bitcoin

If we know two, we can deduce the other from the data. So if we assume that Satoshi has a regular wake/sleep pattern and attends to Bitcoin throughout his normal working day then the time zone must be California or somewhere with a similar longitude. But these assumptions may be false. And there is another problem. How do we know that Satoshi is not deliberately obfuscating his time zone by the simple stratagem of never sending communications in the hours of the night in California?

Can we rule out any locations? About the worst is Satoshi's claimed home country of Japan, which happens to be the same time zone as the Philippines where Le Roux was based. The period without emails is now between 3:00 pm and 11:00 pm. Activity then picks up through the night, peaking between 2:00 am and 4:00 am but continuing right through into the early daylight hours before tailing off, with a secondary peak around lunchtime.

We would have to imagine someone who sleeps all afternoon starting after lunch, perhaps the only period in which his main business is inactive. He wakes in the evening to attend to business, make calls, eat a large meal and visit his girlfriends. Then, as the night progresses and everyone around him goes to sleep, he turns his attention increasingly to Bitcoin, often working right through the night past dawn. His Bitcoin activity reduces in the morning because he needs to attend to his primary business and perhaps because he is napping before picking up as he takes lunch. And then another long sleep. Surely, no one could live such a crazy pattern?

Another favourite device is to look at Satoshi's writing style. Again, attention focuses on Szabo, who has a style that is not too dissimilar from Satoshi. In contrast, Craig Wright can be ruled out because his style is very different. Wright's blog posts are long and rambling, while Satoshi is always short and to the point. And yet Wright was able to convince Andresen that he was Satoshi. He did this by demonstrating that he could write like Satoshi when he chose to. This shows the great weakness of stylistic analysis: a person's style can be easily changed by putting on an act.

This brings us to the issue of Satoshi's spacing between sentences. He consistently uses a double space. This practice dates from the days of typewriters, which had fixed-width fonts. Using a double space made the start of a new sentence clearer. But with the introduction of word processing software and computer-printed documents, proportional fonts became the norm, and the double space became redundant. Almost everyone now uses single spacing. Satoshi appears to be old school as he still used double spacing in 2008, which suggests he was probably over forty.

But is this all a deception? Satoshi's communications show excellent grammar and spelling. This is odd because Satoshi said more than once that he was better with code than words. Few programmers exhibit excellent grammar. So how can Satoshi, someone who thought in code, write with such good flawless English? The answer is that he must be using a grammar and spelling checker. It is the little errors that give people away. Satoshi is careful to sanitise his communications to avoid all such errors. His style is Microsoft bland.

The desired spacing, double or single, could be set in the grammar and spelling checking software available at that time. The spacing would then be corrected automatically. So Satoshi may be using double spacing to confuse us, which means he would actually be a single spacer.

This shows our essential problem. We can never be sure whether to take any obvious clue at face value. And Satoshi has left plenty of evidence that he was paranoid and deceptive.

Most people who have studied Satoshi's communications have concluded that he comes from somewhere that speaks British English. Or is this another deception? Could Satoshi be an American who deliberately uses expressions such as "bloody" and "wet blanket" and uses British spellings to mislead us? Satoshi actually uses an odd mix of British and American spellings. We would expect an American pretending to be British to set their spell checker to British English. So, the mixture of spellings may give us a genuine insight into Satoshi unless he is spelling randomly to muddy the waters.

There is one final odd clue. Satoshi was often untidy in his programming style, leaving redundant modules which should have been deleted. One of these modules is a short piece of code for a casino game program. Satoshi must have reused an existing module intended to be used for an online gambling app. He has not noticed that the code has been left in. It is the type of error that gives us a little glimpse behind the carefully constructed facade. We do not know whether or not the app was ever written. But it appears that Satoshi was interested in online casinos.

We can now put together what we know about Satoshi into a profile.

1. Satoshi was a programmer with years of experience.

Satoshi was an experienced programmer. It is clear from his code and communications that Satoshi was in his element coding. Gavin Andresen rated him in the top 10% of C++ programmers, and Andresen was himself an elite programmer. No one becomes that good at coding by attending a course or two. Like playing a musical instrument, becoming a top programmer requires the archetypal 10,000 hours of practice. We can conclude that Satoshi has worked as a professional programmer for several years. It is possible to be self-taught, but you would still have to work full-time at coding something.

1a. Satoshi learnt his coding informally or by working for small outfits. He may have worked as a one-man band.

Although his skill as a programmer is evident, Satoshi has a very compact style that is difficult for others to follow. He does not document much or show the standard of discipline expected of a programmer trained in a professional IT environment. He does not clear up redundant modules and code. Indeed, some people thought his code looked like a mess. This indicates having learnt his craft in a more informal environment, such as a small outfit or even as a self-taught one-man band.

2. Satoshi programmed in C++ on a Windows computer.

Satoshi was an expert C++ Windows programmer, which was quite unusual for the open source brigade. They typically preferred Linux, but Satoshi freely admitted that he was not proficient with that operating system. Nor did he program on the Mac.

2 a. Satoshi most likely learnt his C++ programming when he was young.

This insight comes from Hal Finney:

> "Then there is the language Bitcoin was written in, C++. Satoshi was a master of the intricacies, and I've only seen this in young programmers. It seems hard to master C++ if you didn't learn it while you're young."

2 b. Satoshi was a painstaking coder who wrote dense, compact code. He may have worked close to the metal or on electronics products.

A lot of programmers have criticised Satoshi's style as out of keeping with modern (2000s) practice. When Kaminsky reviewed the Bitcoin code, he concluded that that the formatting was "insane" and that "only the most paranoid, painstaking coder in the world could avoid making mistakes".

Others have suggested that Satoshi was electronics engineer who was used to low-level programming.

3. Satoshi was not an academic.

Satoshi was a coder rather than an academic. Significantly, he built the software before writing the white paper. He even thought in code. Although Adam Back pointed him to additional references, the paper is still light on citations. If there is one thing that academics are good at, it is filling their papers with citations and references. And Satoshi included code, rather than formulae, in the paper, which is not something an academic would have done.

4. Satoshi was an expert in the practical application of cryptography but not an academic cryptographer.

Satoshi must have had previous cryptographic experience. He demonstrates a high level of competence in the technical aspects of cryptography in his program, his paper, and his responses to other people. Complex ideas like the hash function and Merkel trees were second nature.

Satoshi once told Gavin Andresen that he was no cryptographer. He would have meant that he was not an academic mathematician who understood the theoretical underpinnings of advanced cryptography. Satoshi was a practical programmer who used publicly available algorithms. However, he gives ample evidence of a thorough understanding of applying cryptography to real-world problems.

5. Satoshi was a revolutionary thinker with the viewpoint of a high-tech entrepreneur.

Satoshi was much more than just a programmer. He was a creative thinker of the highest order. Programming the Bitcoin software would have been technically challenging, but the principal difficulty was coming up with the idea and method. Satoshi had a helicopter view of the issues, which involved an appreciation of the economic aspects as much as the technological problems.

In many ways, Satoshi is more typical of a high-tech entrepreneur than an average programmer. An entrepreneur such as the late and lamented Steve Jobs sees both the potential and the problems. Understanding the problems inside out separates the entrepreneur from an ideas person like Craig Wright. However, it is not enough to see problems; you need creativity to find the solution.

Such skills are rare. They cannot be taught and are sometimes found in people who lack a high level of formal qualifications. Satoshi's combination of programming ability with revolutionary thinking is particularly unusual. Which is why many people think Satoshi is multiple individuals.

6. Satoshi was not a cypherpunk and was unfamiliar with most previous attempts at creating digital currencies.

The three most important previous attempts at digital currency were DigiCash (Chaum), B-money (Dai), and bit gold (Szabo). Yet none of these were referenced in the draft of the Bitcoin paper. The only previous work Satoshi was familiar with was Adam Back's Hashcash, a system to control spam email. The proof of work mechanism in Bitcoin has been taken from Hashcash.

Back alerted Satoshi to Dai's work, which resulted in the reference to Dai in the final paper. Back forgot to mention Szabo, so Satoshi did not reference the most important predecessor to Bitcoin. The other main references were concerned with time stamping documents, and they can all be traced back to a paper presented at a small conference in the Benelux countries in 1999.

So Satoshi appears to have approached the problem from an odd angle. He was no cypherpunk and had minimal knowledge of earlier attempts at digital currency, which rules out almost all of the favourite candidates such as Szabo and Finney.

7. Satoshi was familiar with the gold market and likely a gold investor.

Satoshi designed Bitcoin with the model of gold in mind. Aspects such as the limited supply, the mining of Bitcoin and the money supply increasing by price rather than supply all come from the precious metals market.

There are other clues that Satoshi was interested in the gold market. When asked if any commodity subject to supply inflation has ever been used as money, Satoshi replies: "There's gold for one. The supply of gold increases by about 2%-3% per year" (Malmi emails, 3 May 2009). The increase in the gold supply would be familiar to many gold investors but is not a statistic that would trip off most people's lips. When Satoshi comes up with the idea of putting an ad banner on the Bitcoin forum page, he immediately thinks of gold: "This would be much higher value traffic well targeted for high paying gold merchant keywords and VPN hosts." (Malmi emails, 17 Nov 2009)

Satoshi is familiar with the gold market and thinks like a goldbug. When discussing a thought experiment for a form of gold that could be easily transmitted over a network, he says he would like some. This suggests that his interest was not just theoretical but that he was a gold investor.

8. Satoshi was a native speaker of British English but used a mix of British and American spellings.

Satoshi gives evidence of being a native English speaker. He uses colloquial British expressions, such as "bloody" and "wet blanket", indicating that he came from an area of the world under British influence. This is confirmed by the headline from the London Times in the Genesis block: an American would not have been so interested in the condition of British banks. However, Satoshi's spellings are mixed, sometimes American and sometimes British.

There is nothing to suggest he was Japanese. Satoshi was keen on finding helpers to translate the Bitcoin software into other languages but never produced a Japanese version.

Satoshi wrote with excellent grammar and spelling and consistently used double spacing between sentences. However, all these characteristics could have come from using a grammar/spelling checker.

9. Satoshi was a libertarian.

Bitcoin is a libertarian concept. It aims to create a currency entirely independent of governments, banks, and other third parties. That was the whole ethos of the Bitcoin community. But Bitcoin was never altruistic. The design was engineered for massive personal profit. This combination of libertarian values with vast financial potential has always been the main attraction of Bitcoin.

Under the Saint Satoshi myth, he destroyed his keys to avoid personal profit. There is no evidence to support this myth other than the obvious fact that Satoshi's Bitcoins have never been moved. Nothing in Satoshi's writings implies that he was not personally motivated by profit.

10. Satoshi disliked the "copyleft" GPL license and was not against closed source code.

Satoshi disliked the open source GPL license, which compels any derivative product to use the GPL and hence be open source also. He preferred the more permissive open source licences, which allowed derivative works to be closed source:

> "If the only library is GPL then there is a project to make it a non-GPL one. If the best library is MIT, Boost, new-BSD or public domain, then we can stop re-writing it.

> I don't question that GPL is a good licence for operating systems, especially as non-GPL code is allowed to interface with the OS. For smaller projects, I think fear of closed source takeover is overdone." (12 Sep 2010)

This approach is consistent with Satoshi being a libertarian. The GPL appealed to left-wingers who opposed the profit motive. A libertarian would agree with the left-winger that there should be no restrictions on use arising from copyright, patents etc. But most libertarians favoured profit-making activities, considering them natural and honest. They would see the GPL as constraining individuals' freedom to make their own decisions by obliging them to adhere to socialist principles. So they preferred the more permissive licences such as the MIT under which the Bitcoin software was issued.

11. Satoshi was an established expert at hiding his identity, which suggests involvement in criminal activities.

Many people use a pseudonym on the internet, but to make such an identity impenetrable to determined attempts to uncover your identity is very difficult. In his emails and postings, Satoshi was obsessive at avoiding personal-level discussions and never gave away information about himself. You do not get so good at covering up all your digital traces without prior experience.

All of which indicates a darker side to Satoshi's nature. People not engaged in illicit activity would not have the same motivation or ability to hide their true identity.

12. Satoshi had megalomaniac ambitions and was deceptive in advancing his plans.

Satoshi was no ordinary person. He saw much further than others and did not merely want to become rich; he had a long-term plan to secure a significant percentage of the world's money supply. Satoshi kept his motives hidden from others and was deceptive when executing his plans. For example, his publicly supplied software for mining Bitcoin was far less powerful than his private version. He never let anyone know he was using different software from everyone else.

13. Satoshi was constantly busy with some other activity. In particular, he was doing something else that required all of his time and energy in the summer of 2009.

Satoshi's general busyness is clear from his interactions with the people who worked with him, such as Malmi. The Malmi emails show that he was doing something else in the summer of 2009 and this is supported by the fact that he went very quiet in his other communications.

14. Satoshi had an interest in online casinos.

This is an odd one, but it is indicated by the small section of code in the Bitcoin software that is evidently left over from another project.

15. Satoshi was not a US citizen.

If we accept that Ira Kleiman's memory of the Thanksgiving conversation with Dave is accurate, then Satoshi was not a US citizen but someone Kleiman called "a foreigner".

It may be significant that Kleiman did not pin down Satoshi's nationality, just calling him foreign. Why did he not say something like "British" or "Australian"? It suggests that Satoshi did not have a well-defined nationality but was someone who moved around.

16. Satoshi was rich (but not a super-rich billionaire) and owned multiple properties.

This also flows from Kleiman's recollections. Satoshi is not poor or a middle-class wage slave. He is not working out of a basement. He is someone who has made money and who has resources. In particular, he owns a portfolio of properties.

The detailed profile we have constructed considerably narrows down the field. We have triangulated several aspects, enabling us to eliminate most candidates. It would take a very unusual person to meet all the above characteristics. In fact, only one potential Satoshi satisfies all aspects of the profile. But before we meet him, we will look at the impressions of someone who knew Satoshi as well as anyone.

This person is Laszlo Hanyecz, who is famous for buying the two pizzas for 10,000 Bitcoins. Hanyecz enthusiastically mined Bitcoin in 2010 and offered to help Satoshi with the further development of the software. His main involvement as a developer came between Malmi and Andresen, and he was responsible for the Mac version. He exchanged hundreds of emails with Satoshi in this collaboration. In an interview with Business Insider, he gave his impressions of Satoshi.

It was a crucial time for Bitcoin before it won wider acceptance. The interest in Bitcoin was very much from hobbyists and enthusiasts. But Satoshi appeared to be a very different type of person. Hanyecz describes him as "paranoid". He was taken aback by how demanding Satoshi could be, and he was treated as a full-time employee even though he was a volunteer with a day job. Satoshi seemed to be a busy person who would not respond to emails immediately, but in a batch all at once, often at the end of the week. The strangest thing was how he would avoid giving away any personal information: "I asked a few questions, but he always dodged them. Those questions never got answered." For some reason, Satoshi was unusually secretive.

Hanyecz reports that Satoshi tried to push back on his mining activities:

> "He said, 'Well, I'd rather not have you do the mining too much,'" Hanyecz said. "He was trying to grow the community and get more commerce use cases. He fully recognized that mining would become a thing where a few people would get wealthy." (Business Insider)

This shows that Satoshi was fully aware of the value of mining and knew that the early miners would get rich.

Hanyecz found his dealings with Satoshi disturbing. There was something "off-base" about him, and he repelled attempts at friendship. Their interactions consistently gave him a "weird" feeling. Hanyecz ends the interview with some chilling words: "It's exciting because people love a man of mystery, but I try to steer people towards the fact that it doesn't matter who made it; he could be a psycho killer."

FOURTEEN

PAUL LE ROUX

Paul Calder Le Roux was born on 24 Dec 1972, in Zimbabwe, then called Rhodesia. He was given up for adoption at birth, although he never knew this until much later. His adoptive parents doted on him. A relative said that as a child and youth, he was "an utter delight" and "uncomplaining, undemanding, loving and affectionate" before adding, "I never knew what evil lay in him."

This quote comes from a book by investigative journalist Evan Ratliff: "The Mastermind: the hunt for the world's most prolific criminal". We are fortunate to have not just one but two excellent books on Le Roux, the other being "Hunting LeRoux" by Elaine Shannon. Both are recommended. But the two books are so different that it is hard to believe at times that they are covering the same events. The authors even spell their subject's name differently: Ratliff includes a space, "Le Roux", while Shannon has it "LeRoux". Ratliff follows Le Roux's own spelling, whereas Shannon spells it the way it appears in US legal documents (actually Leroux). This difference is telling: Ratliff has travelled the world and talked to many who knew Le Roux. Shannon had extraordinary access to the US team responsible for his capture.

Le Roux's adoptive father was a mining engineer, and when Paul was still a child, the family moved from Zimbabwe to the gold-mining town of Krugersdorp in South Africa. Krugersdorp was an Afrikaner town, and the white population mostly spoke Afrikaans, a variant of Dutch, with English as the minority language. Although Paul Le Roux's first language was English, his family claimed Dutch heritage and would have fitted into the milieux of Krugersdorp. Indeed, Le Roux would sometimes identify as Dutch. Race was at the forefront in South Africa, and it was the time of apartheid, which the Afrikaners very much led.

Le Roux was a reasonable student, but his real passion was computers, and he spent most of his time coding in his bedroom. The family's respectable suburban life was interrupted when the 16-year-old Paul was unexpectedly arrested at his home for selling pornography. It was the first sign of his unconventional business ambitions.

He gave his own account of how he learned to program in an ironic reply to posters on the scramdisk group. For them to get to his level would require:

> "...15 years to move from ZERO knowledge through BASIC programming on a Commodore 64, to serious programming on a modern machine..." (7 Jan 2002)

This is undoubtably a description from the perspective of the twenty-nine-year-old Le Roux of how he learned to program. It implies that he started at fourteen on the ubiquitous Commodore 64 computer.

Le Roux dropped out of college but successfully took a one-year computer course and was awarded a diploma for programming in C and COBOL. He left South Africa for London in 1992, getting his first computer job with Barratt Edwards International, a small company employing ten people. He was just nineteen. Most of his projects were programming in C or C++. He left this company in 1995 and moved to Australia after meeting an Australian woman called Michelle in London. He would marry her and become an Australian citizen while retaining South African citizenship.

Le Roux hated Australia. He started a series of anti-Australian posts on Australian Usenet forums, insulting his new nation. Some posters thought he was French because of his name, and Le Roux delighted in playing along and comparing their country negatively to France. He painted Australia as a "pussy country" which could not even defend itself. To give a few examples of his insults:

> "...what I was saying was that Australians are sufficiently different to be considered another "race", indeed one wonders, and one would need to debate, if Australians could even be called primates!" (6 Nov 1995)

> "As I recall, the genetic effects of human inbreeding are not as disastrous as those of breeding with animals. A lesson Australians have never learned." (6 Nov 1995)

And about Australia in the Second World War:

> "I would have loved to have fought for Germany, and killed you "digger" weaklings myself." (6 Nov 1995)

There was a hysterical reaction to Le Roux's posts. He received numerous threats, and one poster even tracked down his address. A typical response came from an enraged Australian who changed his posting name to fuck@you.paul:

> "Well from what you've just said here its pretty clear that your a bigoted racist and personally I hope one day you say it someone's face who pulls out a knife and slices you open and then you see your life slip away just as they slit your throat. Paul your the sort of scum that keeps racism alive in the world and its people like you that should be rounded up and thrown in jail.
>
> And also Australian wines are rated the best in the world..." (6 Nov 1995)

Le Roux was clearly enjoying himself. He was the matador tormenting the Australian bulls so he could place his barbs into them as he dodged aside their charge. Although we cannot take his insults against the Australians seriously, he also made racist comments about Asians and the effects of cross-breeding with them. The Asian-Australian gentleman this was aimed at seemed more amused than upset and gave as good as he got. And we should be cautious about taking these apparently racist remarks at face value. Le Roux would marry an Asian woman as his second wife and have his children with her.

Le Roux was only twenty-two when he made these posts, and they have a certain childish quality. But they do reveal an unsettling aspect of his character, a lurking anger and desire to antagonise. They show Le Roux playing a role, that of a villain, and loving it. He arouses fury in others but never appears to lose his own temper.

In these posts, he claimed he was about to leave Australia in December. This ties in with a CV dating a few months earlier in which he seeks a temporary position in the US as a contract programmer. If he was thinking about relocating to the US, it did not work out, and he was soon back in Australia again.

In this CV, at age twenty-two, Le Roux listed C++ as the first of his programming languages, followed by C. He would remain principally a C++ programmer on Windows throughout his programming career. His gigs in Australia included financial services experience, such as a project for an Australian bank to write software for the SWIFT system of international bank transfers. By the time he reached his mid-twenties, he was ready to take his programming to a whole new level. It would not be paid professional work but an open source project.

Le Roux was always an anti-government libertarian. He became interested in cryptography to secure information from prying eyes, particularly those of the authorities. Windows was appallingly bad at security, and one answer was encryption. Writing a high-level program in C++ or a similar language to encrypt a file was relatively easy. But there was an inherent flaw. Because the encryption took place above the operating system level, you could never be sure what backdoors might exist in the operating system itself. Suppose the operating system surreptitiously wrote your keys to the hard disk. Any encryption you did would be useless, as a snooper, such as a government agency, could retrieve your keys. It would not even need to be a malign backdoor. Windows did this type of thing all the time, dumping data all over the place.

Secure encryption must occur below the operating system at the disk read and write operations level. Once the user enters their password, the encryption is invisible and Windows works as usual. However, such on-the-fly encryption (OTFE) was very difficult to achieve. One existing Windows open source OTFE product called Scramdisk had been developed by an English programmer, Shaun Hollingworth. Le Roux set out to improve upon Scramdisk.

His product was called Abacus while under development and was published under the Latin name Caveo, "to guard, to be careful" in 1998. He changed the name to "E4M" for version 2.0—it stood for Encryption for the Masses. ("For the masses" was one of Le Roux's favourite phrases.) Le Roux had set himself an enormous task. Later, he would write about the time and difficulty of developing E4M:

> "Thousands of hours went into its development and testing, to those who believe that somehow a disk encryption product of this magnitude and scope, and which is stable and reliable can be slapped together quickly will soon find that their product exhibits strange bugs which result in data loss, crashes, and so on. E4M underwent exhaustive tests under the Windows hardware compatibility tests and various other stress tests to get it to its final stable state, this cannot be replicated without a major undertaking, this is the reason why this code is the foundation of so many popular products in use today..." (16 Jun 2004)

Because the encryption algorithm had to be below the Windows level, it was written in assembly code. Writing in assembly is perhaps the most difficult task a programmer can face. Few will ever need to. Assembly is often required for specialist, low-level programs such as hardware drivers. The tools available to Le Roux were relatively crude. Moreover, Le Roux was challenged to make the complex encryption algorithm ridiculously small. Because of the way Windows worked, it had to fit into less than 400 bytes. Le Roux wrote about the difficulty of programming these drivers:

> "... most of the low level code is hand coded assembler, sha1 for example took me 3 months to write, and in the end the full FIPS compliant SHA1 is about 400 bytes. Other bits of the low level code is self-decompressing using a 130 byte lempel ZIV 77 decompressor which also took months to write, and hand optimise the various parameters..."

Le Roux was the type of person who could disappear for months to focus on the bits and bytes of an encryption algorithm. By the time he finished, he had a working product, a separation from his Australian wife, and a detailed, practical knowledge of encryption.

Did the thousands of hours Le Roux devoted to E4M leave a mark on his programming style, making it dense and complex for others? Spending three months on 400 bytes of code is not usual. We may recall that quote from Kaminsky about Satoshi: "the way the whole thing was formatted was insane. Only the most paranoid, painstaking coder in the world could avoid making mistakes."

E4M was an extraordinary achievement for a twenty-five-year-old with minimal higher education and no relevant encryption experience. Is it too good to be true? Le Roux had no background in mathematics. His contracting jobs had typically been with legal firms and financial services outfits, working on projects like record management. So, how did he suddenly become a cryptography expert? We will see that Le Roux has never told the whole truth about E4M. Or rather, he told the truth, but in a way that no one understood.

Le Roux left Australia in 1998 and worked for a company called NEON in Hong Kong. There, he met Lilian Cheung Yuen Phi, who he married after his divorce the following year. Shannon says she was a Taiwanese expat. Ratliff makes the extraordinary statement that she was a Dutch citizen from Curacao in the Dutch Antilles, a Caribbean island offshore from Venezuela. Ratliff had talked to Le Roux's family and should know the truth. And the two did end up living in the Netherlands.

After Hong Kong, the couple moved back to London, where Le Roux returned to Barratt Edwards, including a six-month project in the US. That brings us to around the millennium and a startling claim that Le Roux made at his US sentencing hearing—that he had once worked for a British intelligence agency.

Le Roux said that if he were released, he intended to go into Bitcoin mining. He would use the expertise he had gained consulting for GCHQ to optimise the proof of work hash algorithm to mine Bitcoin more efficiently than other miners. This was an extraordinary statement in more ways than one.

GCHQ is the British intelligence agency concerned with electronic information gathering and cryptography. It is the UK equivalent of the NSA, and the two collaborate very closely. The story sounded doubtful because GCHQ had a policy of recruiting the best mathematics graduates and postgraduates from top British universities, such as Cambridge. Le Roux's higher education consisted of a programming certificate. Would GCHQ have taken on Le Roux even as a contract programmer?

Le Roux said he had gained expertise in the SHA2 algorithm used for Bitcoin mining. This family of algorithms, which includes SHA256, was only introduced by the NSA in 2001, which would push back any involvement with GCHQ to the period he was living in the Netherlands and had started work on another Windows encryption project. One possibility is that GCHQ was interested in Le Roux because of his Windows encryption software. The nightmare of the Scramdisk group was that intelligence agencies such as the NSA would install backdoors in their favourite software. Had this nightmare come true with Le Roux? There is no evidence that he put in any backdoors. And he specifically claimed to have obtained unpublished, in-depth knowledge of SHA2. GCHQ would never have shared this classified knowledge if they only used him to put backdoors into software.

So is it all a lie, a misguided attempt to impress the judge? The truth is that Le Roux did have an insider's relationship with GCHQ, just not quite the one he claimed.

The sentencing documents say that when Le Roux returned to London, he worked for Crypto-Solutions developing encryption software. Crypto-Solutions Ltd was a London-based company established by a computer security expert, Andrew Georgiou. The company was registered in 1999 and commenced business in May 2000. It produced "accredited security products for Computer Systems and Networks" and had a five-year partnership agreement with Novell, a network software provider. Novell, however, was in decline, and Crypto-Solutions did not last long; it went bankrupt in Nov 2003. Georgiou passed away in 2011.

Crypto-Solutions offered two products that involved Le Roux's speciality of disc encryption. CS-Data was on-the-fly transparent encryption of files and directories. Another product, CS-FDE, would "transparently encrypt all of the data on the disk drive, including the operating system".

They also provided software for use by the British government and military:

> "Crypto-Solutions are a specialist organisation developing accredited security solutions for commercial, financial, government, health, Internet, and military users. We are proud to be members in good standing with CESG and other security organisations." (www.crypto-solutions.net, 21 Jul 2001)

Their software was accredited under the government's encryption standards, which involved an audit by CESG: "Crypto-Solutions are proud to be participating members of the CAPS and CLAS schemes in partnership with CESG."

CESG was the division of GCHQ responsible for the British government's cryptographic security needs. It had a long and distinguished history: public key cryptography was actually first invented at CESG. The division did not produce software or hardware itself but worked in partnership with commercial partners, such as Crypto-Solutions.

Because of its close relationship with CESG/GCHQ, Crypto-Solutions could only employ people who had security clearance. It may seem ironic that Le Roux, the master criminal, was given such a clearance, but in 2000, there was no reason it should be declined. He was a citizen of Australia, part of the five-eyes group of nations, and had no criminal record.

Another product, CS-Authenticate, was issued in two versions; "controlled", intended for military and government use, and "commercial". The product page has a revealing comment:

> "The controlled version incorporates unpublished cryptographic algorithms provided by the UK government."

The relationship with CESG gave the company access to unpublished algorithms, which would have meant the SHA2 family, including SHA256, as used in Bitcoin. Le Roux would have collaborated with CESG while working at Crypto-Solutions. GCHQ would never have hired Le Roux for cryptographic work because he had no mathematical training. His skill was in programming, and a partner of GCHQ employed him to implement GCHQ algorithms in encryption software for the British military, the British government, and allied nations. This work would have required him to have access to detailed, unpublished information about these algorithms.

We see here Le Roux's habit of saying things that are literally true but misleading. He did work with GCHQ and had access to unpublished information on the hash algorithm, but as far as we can tell, he never worked directly for GCHQ. Could Le Roux really have improved the speed of the SHA256 algorithm through his special knowledge? It raises the fascinating possibility that the Patoshi software could have incorporated an enhanced SHA algorithm.

Le Roux must have been involved with Crypto-Solutions almost from the beginning of that company in May 2000. At the same time, he was establishing a new venture called Software Professionals in South Africa. The website was in operation by Sep 2000, and the selling point was "offshore programming and outsourcing services" at "up to 80% savings over Western rates". It was a good idea, anticipating the offshoring boom in which many companies would move their software development to countries with low labour costs. However, it did not take off. The website listed several staff members; Ratliff talked to one of them, a cousin of Le Roux in South Africa. He worked for the company for six months and saw Le Roux for about a week.

In 1997, twenty-four-year-old Wilfried Hafner was sentenced to three years in prison in one of the earliest cases of hacking in Germany. As the notorious hacker "Luzifer", he had "blue boxed" the telecom system to make long-distance phone calls for free. Luzifer had used this ability to set up sex lines, mostly recorded messages, for which he charged 30 to 50 cents per minute. A total of over 18,000 phone calls were logged, and Luzifer made over $250,000 profit.

Hafner was a computing prodigy, learning to program at the age of eight. He began hacking programs before moving on to the phone system. The phreakers go back to the 1980s when they would try and exploit weaknesses in the phone system to make free calls. An early phreaker would play correctly pitched sounds down the phone often using a "blue-box", a multi-frequency tone generator. Two early blue-boxers were Steve Wozniak and Steve Jobs, who went on to establish Apple. By the time of Luzifer, telecom networks were computer-controlled, and things had gotten more complex.

Hafner's sentence was perhaps not as severe as it sounds. It seems he was allowed out to work during the day. Hafner became a reformed character, a poacher turned gamekeeper. Working as a consultant for telecom companies, he helped them improve their security against people like his former self. Soon, Hafner would start a company called SecurStar to produce security products.

It is not certain when Le Roux met Hafner. Elaine Shannon had good access to Hafner and gave his version of events at length. She describes how a cosmopolitan and refined twenty-five-year-old Hafner met the scruffy, junk food-addicted twenty-four-year-old Le Roux in London in 1997. At this time, Hafner supposedly had several companies, rich investors, and major telecoms as his clients. He commissioned Le Roux to write some low-level assembly code, which Le Roux banged off impressively quickly.

The problem is that Hafner should have been in prison in 1997. He was sentenced in February to three years but had already served time since Jan 1996. Supposedly, he should not have been freed until early 1999. However, Hafner could continue working and may have been released early. We will see that it is credible that he did commission that code in 1997.

What is certain is that the two joined together in Hafner's new company, SecurStar, in 2001. By this time, Le Roux and his wife had moved from London to the Netherlands. They had a child and lived in a small, cramped apartment in Rotterdam. Le Roux drove a beat-up old car, and both of them worked hard. Lillian told a relative they were dirt poor and put their child in childcare for twelve hours a day.

Le Roux had introduced Shaun Hollingworth, author of Scramdisk, to Hafner. SecurStar was formed from Hollingworth's Scramdisk Inc., Le Roux's Software Professionals and Hafner's Telstar Industries. The SecurStar website declared rather grandly:

> "SecurStar was primarily established out of the special security needs of telephone companies like Global Telecom, manufacturing industries like Centurion Technologies, and state defence departments of several countries."

The team was predominantly Hafner, Le Roux and Hollingworth:

> "SecurStar's team is constituted of well known security experts as well as famous former Hackers. This mixture of former Hackers and Security experts gives to our company that extra knowledge and advantage over our competitors. To our core team we count the well known telecommunication security expert Mr. Wilfried Hafner, the programming genius and security guru Mr. Shaun Hollingworth, the well regarded cryptographer Mr. Paul Le Roux ..."

It was a dream team for the core business of encryption products. Hafner had secured the services of the two best programmers of Windows-based encryption systems. Both Scramdisk and E4M were open source, free products. Hafner planned to make the next generation of products proprietary and closed-source. This came to fruition with the launch of DriveCrypt in 2001. Hollingworth was the lead developer, but Le Roux contributed the all-important assembly-level drivers.

Hafner's plans did not go down well with the enthusiastic users of the open source products. The ability to review code was seen as essential to ensuring that government agencies like the NSA and GCHQ did not insert backdoors into the software. There were many arguments on this subject. Le Roux took the position that it did not matter, as no one actually reviewed the open source code anyway.

The problem with open source was that it worked very well for the users but not for the developers who gave their time for free. They could only make money if there was a commercial angle, such as providing paid services to corporate clients. Both Hollingworth and Le Roux considered that they had been exploited by the users of the open source software. Hollingworth responded to one user by suggesting he write his own encryption software:

> “Then when you write it, give it away and you then get loads of users complaining at you all the time, you will wonder what the point really was...... I presume even you have some method of making a living....
>
> When Scramdisk was being sold for NT, I would have made far more money cleaning the streets... In fact I LOST money on it....” (14 Apr 2002)

Le Roux agreed: “…any open source fanatics out there who know how to both make money and publish source? I’d like to hear from you” (13 Apr 2002). He never liked the open source movement’s favourite GPL licence: “It’s difficult to see a viable business model emerging from the GNU GPL stuff.” He continued:

> “Personally I think the entire open v’s [sic] closed source argument is the ‘open source religious zealot’s’ excuse for anti-business sentiment and has nothing to do with security.
>
> E4M was open source, I have not in all the time it was available anyone who actually looked at the code, most of the people in this group and elsewhere wouldn’t even understand the code -even though they’re the same people banging the open source drum. But I did get about 50 emails a day with time wasting questions... the whole point in the beginning of E4M was to publish the code to get peer review and help to enhance the product, in the end people climbed onto my back, did not help one bit, bitched all the time, stole the code for incorporation into their own products, and generally abused the whole situation.” (14 Apr 2002)

In April 2002, SecurStar had launched a new product written by Le Roux which was confusingly called DriveCrypt Plus Pack, or DCPP for short. It was, in fact, a completely separate, stand-alone product which encrypted a user’s entire hard drive. The user would enter a passphrase when starting a session, after which the computer would appear to work completely as normal. However, it would automatically encrypt any data written to the hard drive and unencrypt all data read from the drive. Without the password, no one could access anything on the drive. DCPP shared virtually no code with DriveCrypt and was entirely Le Roux's work, to the extent that Hollingworth was not even sure what was in the product.

There was much discussion about DCPP on the scramdisk group. It was received very favourably, with the only objections coming from those opposed to closed-source software who were worried that it could have a backdoor.

Although Le Roux liked to use Visual C++ for general programming, the hardest part of the disk encryption software was the drivers, which had to be written in assembly language. He explained why he had to use the old SHA1 cryptographic algorithm rather than the newer SHA2 (as used in Bitcoin):

> "it offers AES256 in CBC mode plus SHA1 is the crypto (SHA1 is iterated with salt to expand the key out to 256 bits); why not SHA2, well it took 3 months for me to hand tune the SHA1 implementation in 386 assembler and get the size down to about 500 bytes, that's right the code for a full SHA1 with padding the works is about 500 bytes, SHA2 would be too big code size wise." (6 Apr 2002)

Like E4M, it was encryption on the fly. Others had tried and failed at this task. As Le Roux put it, "Yeah, it's certainly not something you want to try without first telling your wife you will be in your room for a year...."

> Programmer and cryptography enthusiast Sam Simpson gave his verdict to Le Roux on DCPP: "I think you deserve great amounts of credit for single-handedly producing this solution. We may [not] agree on commercial aspects of SecurStar, but I certainly credit you and Shaun with being the best programmers I know!" (7 Apr 2002)

Le Roux always said that the most challenging part of writing the encryption software was getting it to work on the Windows operating system. Programmers hated Windows because the code was an absolute mess and had not been designed with security in mind. It did not help that Microsoft continually made changes, more for marketing reasons than to improve the product fundamentally. However, most computer users in the 2000s, including almost the entire business world, used Windows systems. Open source fans and academics might love Linux, but the general population used Windows.

SecurStar was on a roll. It might be a very small company, but it led in the Windows encryption space. One enthusiastic user of both DriveCrypt and DriveCrypt Plus Pack was Dave Kleiman:

> "I have been using DriveCrypt Plus (whole OS/Disk) and DriveCrypt (encrypted containers) for about 3 years now, and thus far have no negative feed back. [...] I do not even notice any performance degradation, although I am sure there is some." (23 Oct 2006)

He continued:

> "My forensic laptops are all DriveCrypted, I have let at least 50 different techs use them when working cases together, not one of them have ever said "your machine is slow", most of them comment that it is a screamer." (23 Oct 2006)

Did Kleiman know Le Roux? Kleiman was a prominent technical author and educator in the US with a wide interest in security matters. He was particularly keen on cryptography and disk encryption, so it is plausible that he would have reached out to the authors of his favourite encryption software.

Kleiman began working for S-Doc in early 2001. That start-up was in the business of developing on-the-fly encryption solutions for transmitting and storing information. Meanwhile, Le Roux was working for Crypto-Solutions, doing essentially the same thing on the other side of the Atlantic. Kleiman was an enthusiastic participant in mailing lists and knew many people in the industry. There is no smoking gun proving that Le Roux and Kleiman knew each other in the early 2000s, but their mutual involvement in the small world of disk encryption makes it likely.

Dave Kleiman was an example of a new class of "respectable" encryption users. When encryption began to emerge, there was a general perception that it only had value to criminals and paedophiles. The UK government even passed a law making it an offence to withhold an encryption key if asked for it by the police. This led to a wide discussion around "plausible deniability" in encryption products, which was replayed many times on the scramdisk group. The idea was that the user could deny that they were even using encryption. However, the software on a computer was a giveaway as its existence could not be hidden.

Today, encryption is completely mainstream. The market that would emerge for encryption products was quite different from the libertarians who frequented the Usenet groups in the early 2000s. Businesses and governments were becoming increasingly concerned about hackers, and encryption was seen as a vital tool to protect data. These new clients wanted their software supplier to be professional and respectable. SecurStar was well-positioned to take advantage of this corporate trend.

As for Le Roux, he seemed to have found his niche. Hollingworth called himself an employee of SecurStar, but Le Roux never did. In Shannon's book, she explains how Le Roux joined Hafner: "Two years later Hafner returned to Le Roux with an offer no budding entrepreneur could refuse—a big title—chief technical officer—more money, and most important, a place at the table, meaning a full partnership in the venture." We must put Hafner's offer to Le Roux in context: SecurStar was a very small enterprise, and Le Roux was often personally involved in supporting users of its products.

Hafner explained why he was keen to recruit Le Roux: "You can find programmers out there like sand on a beach but only a few—less than one percent—with the skills for developing full disk encryption." He continued, "Paul proved to be a brilliant programmer. He is one of the smartest and most consequential technical person I know. Many people have cool ideas, but Paul also knows or finds a way to transform those ideas into reality."

One idea was a device for encrypting phone calls "for the masses". Le Roux posted about this to various Usenet groups in 2001, asking for potential investors. It must have been a joint project with Hafner—Le Roux used the word "we" and was perfectly open about the idea. It got as far as a prototype but was never put into production, presumably because of doubts about its commercial viability. However, years later, Hafner's SecurStar produced just such a device.

Le Roux had made extraordinary progress as a programmer since leaving South Africa with that diploma in COBOL and C. Almost entirely self-taught, he had become a star programmer in everything from C++ to assembly code. Even though he had no background in mathematics, he was a cryptography expert. Yet there were disturbing signs about Le Roux's character.

Hafner said Le Roux would lie to a colleague when he did not need to and then brag about it: "He's a good actor, telling a story that is completely made up to achieve something else." This ability to put on an act, to assume another persona, was something that Le Roux would do whether he needed to or not.

A key experience seems to have been a trip with Hafner to his home in the south of France. Hafner had an apartment near the marina in Antibes, which is next to Nice and home to the Picasso Museum. Le Roux was not interested in Picasso but was amazed by the oligarchs' $100 million yachts and the girls sunbathing on them. He wanted it all for himself—the properties, the boats, the lifestyle, the women—but to get it all, he would need an awful lot of money.

Le Roux was dissatisfied at SecurStar. He told Hafner he wanted more money. But Hafner was unable to pay him more. The market for encryption software at that time was small. With hard work and persistence, Le Roux and Hafner could have made something out of the company. But Le Roux was impatient.

Hafner claimed that he advised Le Roux to enter the internet casino business if he wanted to make it big. He would introduce Le Roux to casino operators in Costa Rica, where he could find work as a programmer. However, he would have to relocate to that country. Le Roux replied that the South American women were pretty and that he would be happy to dump his wife and child. It was probably a joke, yet it would typify Le Roux's attitude to women in the years ahead.

Le Roux never did move to Costa Rica. Less than six months after launching DriveCrypt Plus Pack, he parted with Hafner on bad terms. On 4 Oct 2002, he posted a message on Usenet groups: "Hi Guys, I'm looking for crypto/or other contract programming work, anybody out there have anything available?". It seemed that he had blown his big chance. He was back where he started, a contract programmer with nothing to show for the fantastic encryption products he had developed.

Shannon's book gives Hafner's account of the breakup. He claimed Le Roux had stolen a proprietary piece of code for a "security device called a crypto-key" and sold it to a British company for $100,000. According to Hafner, this code was developed by other engineers working for SecurStar. When Hafner discovered the theft, he sacked Le Roux.

We do not have Le Roux's side of the story here. It is also difficult to understand what a "security device called a crypto-key" means—a crypto key is just a string of numbers and characters. Regardless of the details, Le Roux was evidently involved in some double-dealing.

Hafner retained his other star programmer, Shaun Hollingworth, who stayed loyal to SecurStar. The company's products were well received, and it looked like SecurStar would have a bright future. But everything was thrown upside down with the launch of a free, open source product that matched and exceeded DriveCrypt. The new software was called TrueCrypt and would become the most famous and infamous encryption software of its time.

FIFTEEN

TRUECRYPT

TrueCrypt ate DriveCrypt's lunch. Not all of it, but it took a big bite out of the sandwich. Unlike SecurStar's products, it was free and open source. It was as robust and stable as DriveCrypt. And it included some radical new features that took plausible deniability to a new level. No one ever found a backdoor or weakness in TrueCrypt. It became legendary and cool. If the exciting people with secrets to hide from the government used TrueCrypt, then so would many less exciting people who wanted to keep their internet browsing history private from their wives. It was Edward Snowden's favourite encryption product—which says it all.

Business users and corporations, however, were not concerned with plausible deniability or using the same product as Wikileaks. They preferred the more reputable options of DriveCrypt and DriveCrypt Plus Pack. Hafner eventually sold 4.5 million copies of his encryption products. That is not a bad return for his investment in Le Roux, but it would have been higher had it not been for TrueCrypt.

TrueCrypt was the evolution of Le Roux's E4M. It was announced on 2 Feb 2004 by a mysterious "TrueCrypt Team" and withdrawn the next day after protests from Hafner. The release notice described it as a sequel to E4M:

> "We are proud to announce that TrueCrypt 1.0 has been released today. […] On Windows XP/2000, it is also the only open source on-the-fly encryption system that offers plausible deniability. It can either encrypt entire partitions or devices, or it can create virtual encrypted disks within files. TrueCrypt is based on (and might be considered a sequel to) a discontinued product called Encryption for the Masses (E4M) by Paul Le Roux." (2 Feb 2004)

Although TrueCrypt looked like a revolutionary new product, it was very much E4M under the bonnet. Most of the code had come from Le Roux's earlier product. And it was due to Le Roux that TrueCrypt was quickly withdrawn:

> "In the last two days, we have been receiving e-mails from Wilfried Hafner, manager of SecurStar. In the e-mails he repeatedly accuses Paul Le Roux, the author of Encryption for the Masses (E4M), of the following:
>
> 1) Intellectual property theft, stealing the source code of E4M from SecurStar (as an employee of SecurStar)
>
> 2) Writing an illegal license that permits anyone to base his/her own work on E4M and distribute such modified work (while, according to W. Hafner, P. Le Roux did not have any right to do so).
>
> 3) Distributing E4M illegally (according to W. Hafner, all versions of E4M always belonged only to SecurStar)
>
> These statements have been made to make us stop developing and distributing TrueCrypt, which is based on E4M 2.02a. As we have a strong suspicion that these statements are false, we e-mailed Paul Le Roux and asked him to clear up this issue." (TrueCrypt Team, 4 Feb 2004)

Hafner's claim that SecurStar had the license to all versions of E4M is puzzling. This last public version of E4M was released in Nov 2000, and Le Roux only started working for SecurStar in 2001. The licence for E4M was very permissive, allowing other developers to use and modify the code for their own products. Even if Le Roux had transferred all the rights to SecurStar in 2001, this would not have invalidated that earlier licence. So how could Hafner stop TrueCrypt using E4M?

Hafner claimed that Le Roux had no right to issue that original permissive licence and that all versions of E4M belonged to SecurStar. This could only be true if Hafner owned the copyright to the code in E4M before the product was released. But how could this be true when the first release of E4M was years before Le Roux joined SecurStar? We should recall Hafner's story, that he commissioned assembly code from Le Roux in 1997. Is there more to the origins of E4M than Le Roux had admitted?

Before they fell out, Hafner had no problems with E4M, and SecurStar even continued distributing it for free. However, TrueCrypt was a direct competitor to DriveCrypt and DriveCrypt Plus Pack. If Hafner owned the rights to E4M, it is no wonder he was furious.

The only named member of the TrueCrypt team, David Tesarik, explained a bit more about the legal issues:

> "This is what W. Hafner told us. He claims, that E4M contains certain parts that Paul Le Roux had no rights to release (under the E4M license). He also said that SecurStar had all the necessary permissions and/or rights to the mentioned parts.
>
> Paul told us that his lawyer had advised him not to comment on any details regarding these issues - and unfortunately he hasn't. This is a difficult situation for us, because we need a confirmation that the E4M license is legal and valid. The only thing Paul told us was that there was (and still is) a legal dispute between him and SecurStar (intellectual property theft) and that he hadn't been involved with SecurStar since 2002. If we continued distributing TrueCrypt, Paul might someday have to pay consequent damages, caused by the allegedly illegal E4M license, to SecurStar. We would like to protect Paul from any negative consequences now. As soon as the E4M license is verified to be valid, TrueCrypt distribution will continue." (6 Feb 2004)

Paul Le Roux did not issue his own statement to the scramdisk group until June:

> "I do not follow this newsgroup. Having said that the pure speculation here (often stated as fact) is damaging and in some cases libellous.
>
> The E4M product was developed by me from scratch in Australia in 1997.

> [...]
>
> Regarding the controversy surrounding the licensing of E4M code. There are cases where permission has been granted to some parties to license the code under various commercial terms. There are also cases where various companies and individuals have used the code illegally because they failed to comply with the original License (even as generous as it is)." (16 Jun 2004)

This raises more questions than it answers. The first statement, "I do not follow this newsgroup", is untrue: we will show that Le Roux had actually been participating in scramdisk under two aliases. His statement that he had licensed the E4M code to some parties under commercial terms is odd. The E4M licence permitted full commercial use, so no additional licence was required. Le Roux's statement would only make sense if the parties he referred to had licensed the product before the open source version had been launched.

Strangest of all is the innocent looking statement that E4M "was developed by me from scratch in Australia in 1997". E4M was first released as a beta version under the name Caveo on 19 Dec 1998. We have the post announcing the release, and the date is confirmed by the E4M website, which also said that development commenced in Aug 1998. This is consistent with a post from Le Roux in Oct 1998 announcing that the "Abacus", as it was then called, was almost ready. By 1998, Le Roux had moved from Australia to Hong Kong, where he met his second wife. So E4M was not developed in 1997, nor was it developed in Australia.

But could Le Roux really have developed E4M from scratch in a little over four months in 1998? Recall that he said he had put thousands of hours into E4M, including three months to write a driver. There is something not right here, something Le Roux is not telling us.

The crucial clue to solving this mystery came from an unexpected place: the website of a London based company called Skygate Technologies. The company was started in late 1996 by a small group of Cambridge University computer science graduates. The majority shareholder and chief mover was Pete Chown, a cryptographer and libertarian. He was the same age as Le Roux, but unlike Le Roux, he had a good academic background and practical experience in cryptography. He participated in cryptography groups, including the Cryptography mailing list on which Satoshi announced Bitcoin. And he would become involved in defining a new standard for internet encryption.

As we will see later, I was led to Skygate while researching another company owned by Chown. While looking at the Skygate website with the Wayback Machine, I came across a surprising statement in a corporate overview of 1997. It mentioned three significant contracts in that year, one of which was:

> "The development of Caveo, a product that enables laptop users to secure data in case their computer is stolen."

So Skygate was contracted to produce an encryption product called "Caveo" in 1997! I soon found a much more direct connection between Le Roux and Skygate. When Le Roux first announced his Caveo, he had linked to the Skygate website:

> "The first beta version of my free disk encryption product for NT 4.0 is available (both source and binaries) at www.skygate.co.uk/caveo/caveo.html from 19 Dec 98."

Hafner claimed to have commissioned code from Le Roux in 1997 and that others had also contributed to that code. It was arranged in London when Le Roux was visiting from Australia. We can see now that Hafner must have commissioned Skygate to write that code, and they subcontracted to Le Roux.

So Le Roux's statement that he wrote the first version of E4M from scratch in 1997 in Australia was factually correct but disingenuous. He omitted to say that the first version of Caveo/E4M was proprietary software written for a client of Skygate—surely Hafner. The Skygate Caveo would have run on Windows 95, the operating system laptops used in 1997.

We can conclude that Le Roux did not produce E4M on his own. He learnt his cryptography by working for Skygate's Peter Chown, an expert in the field. Chown had the academic background and must have guided Le Roux in his cryptography programming. This explains why Le Roux's version of Caveo was written for the high-end Windows NT operating system, even though most potential users would be using Windows 95. He would not have been allowed to compete with the Skygate Caveo. Originally, Le Roux was going to call his product Abacus, but Skygate must have agreed that the open source product could be called Caveo and hosted it on their website as a complement to the laptop product.

Le Roux would never stick with agreements like this. In Jun 1999, he moved the website away from Skygate and renamed the product E4M. Then, in Sep 1999, he announced, "Windows 95/98 version of Encryption for the Masses is available now!"

Hafner would not have been happy. This new E4M, v2.01, competed directly with the original Caveo. But he admired Le Roux's technical ability and decided to recruit him rather than fight him. So they joined together to form SecurStar in 2001 and generate a new generation of proprietary products.

There is little doubt that what Hafner claimed was true and that he had the rights to the original Caveo, which would have involved contributions from Chown and others. This means that Hafner probably did have the rights to E4M and, hence, TrueCrypt. Le Roux never had the legal right to launch E4M under its permissive licence because it was based on an earlier proprietary product.

We can now read Le Roux's slippery Jun 2004 statement with this background in mind. His defence is that the first Caveo was all his own work and that he had granted licenses to "some parties", meaning Skygate and Hafner. It sounds very doubtful, given his inexperience with cryptography at that time. But the three parties, Le Roux, Chown and Hafner were all very young in 1997, no older than twenty-five. There may not even have been a legal contract. Perhaps it was a mates' agreement, allowing a wide variety of later interpretations.

What, if any, involvement did Le Roux have in the TrueCrypt project? David Tesarik gave what seemed to be a categorical denial:

> Paul Le Roux did not collaborate in the production of TrueCrypt. In my opinion, there isn't even any reason why he would want to. (6 Feb 2004)

There were good legal reasons for such a denial. If Le Roux had coded TrueCrypt he could hardly avoid being influenced by the work he had done for SecurStar and Hafner would have a very strong legal case. Tesarik's choice of words is revealing—Le Roux "did not collaborate in the production of TrueCrypt". The "production" would be the programming. So Le Roux did not code or collaborate on the coding. But that does not mean that he was not the mastermind behind TrueCrypt.

Several individuals told Ratliff that Le Roux was the main driving force behind TrueCrypt. Le Roux certainly required his employees to use TrueCrypt. Someone who knew Le Roux in captivity told Ratliff he had boasted of having launched TrueCrypt and handed it over to others. He then continued to fund the project over the years. The same source said that Le Roux had access to the outside world when he was cooperating with the DEA and had sent a message to the TrueCrypt team telling them he was in prison, which led to TrueCrypt's final withdrawal.

To confirm Le Roux's involvement, we can turn to two statements he made the year before the launch. The first was in Jan 2003, just months after his break with Hafner:

> "I have a new full disk encryption product under development which will support hibernation mode and among other things even SCSI and RAID disks using NTBOOTDD." (16 Jan 2003)

So in January, Le Roux is working on a revenge product, a successor to his own DCPP which he had released at SecurStar less than a year earlier. He does not say whether he intended this DCPP "killer" to be open source or closed source. Either option would have given Le Roux severe legal difficulties with Hafner. The product became more ambitious over the next few months, but by May, development had ceased:

> "...what is really needed is multiple o/s [operating systems] on the same disk without any ability to prove which o/s is the real one the user is using. The data on primary o/s and the shadow(s) o/s share the same disk; the pwd [password] selects between them; and there is no way of telling how many shadows there are, or if there are any shadows.
>
> Anyone smacking your head until you reveal your encrypted data is sent to one of the shadows and sees a complete working environment.
>
> This is the basis for a product I was developing, but now I don't have the time anymore.... "(26 May 2003)

Le Roux has come up with a great advance on plausible deniability. His idea was to have a secret, shadow operating system on the same disk as the primary operating system. The password would decide what operating system to load, and without the password, there would be no indication that the shadow operating system even existed. If the user puts in their first password, the decoy operating system loads, making some private, but not compromising, files visible. If the user puts in their second password, the hidden operating system loads with all the real hard stuff the user wants to hide. There could even be multiple hidden operating systems. It is a stunning idea that would become reality with TrueCrypt.

TrueCrypt included the ability to install a secret operating system. And like Le Roux's idea, the password decided what operating system to load. Unlike other encryption programs, there was nothing in a TrueCrypt container's header to indicate that it contained encrypted data. The system did not know in advance what was encrypted and what was not. It would attempt to decrypt the data and, if successful, conclude that it was dealing with an encrypted container. This meant the user could have multiple containers encrypted with different passwords on the same disk and even whole secret operating systems. The existence of the containers would be invisible to anyone unless they input the correct password for that container.

Le Roux's post shows that he was implementing this idea in the spring of 2003, almost a year before TrueCrypt. There were two reasons why the development stopped. First, as he admitted, he no longer had the time. Le Roux was fully occupied by his plan for his online prescription drug company. But there was a second, hidden reason: he had made things up with Hafner, and the two were working on a new project together.

Le Roux did not abandon his new encryption product but handed it over to David Tesarik. He probably thought that if he could arrange for others to develop the product, he would have plausible deniability with Hafner. It did not work out that way.

Tesarik participated extensively in the scramdisk group in 2002/3 under the name "Flare." He preferred open source software but was intrigued by DCPP and asked Le Roux several questions about the new product including the ability to run multiple operating systems. Flare was an intelligent programmer. His posts were to the point; despite his name, he avoided flame wars. Although he was not a native English speaker, he wrote excellent English.

By Oct 2003, Flare was running a modified and improved version of E4M: "Yes, I've been using a recompiled and bug-fixed version of E4M under Windows XP. 64-bit file pointer is used so maximum partition/container size is 18446744073 GB" (26 Oct 2003). Le Roux participated in the same thread and said he was also running a debugged version of E4M under Windows XP. When someone asked if he could post the files for those who were too poor to buy software, he replied: "sure I give you my wire details you send me $15K and it will be done" (30 Oct 2003).

Flare's program was almost ready by early December, although it did not have a name. When someone asked about problems with E4M, Flare came up with a list of issues before making a surprise announcement:

> "A sequel to E4M will be released soon. Regards, David." (4 Dec 2003)

A complacent Shaun Hollingworth treated Flare as a novice with no appreciation of the difficulties:

> "And many many hours of burning the candle at both ends may be required to deal with all of these [issues]... A competent programmer, should be able to deal with them given enough time however.

> But this is the reason why we are reticent to release the DriveCrypt source code...... UNLESS we can hide the solutions to these very problems...
>
> Why should we prevent our competitors (or would be competitors) going through the hell we did?
>
> Given that the DriveCrypt device driver is a direct development of the E4M driver, I know the answer to all these issues, and spent many many solitary hours dealing with them. But I am afraid I must keep the solutions to myself, as would anyone involved commercially...
>
> However some people appear to think it's 'easy'......" (4 Dec 2003)

Two months later, TrueCrypt was released. It worked as well as DriveCrypt and had revolutionary new features that put it ahead of DriveCrypt. The response from some in the Scramdisk group was instant:

> "Eat your heart out Shaun 'The Whiny Weiner' Hollingsworth [sic]. You can stick your DriveCrypt up your ass for good now. Now might be a good time to jump ship. SecurStar's future doesn't look good at all now. Hahaha..." (Anon, 2 Feb 2004)

Hollingworth and Hafner knew that only Le Roux could have solved the problems of getting E4M working under Windows XP so quickly. The "secret sauce" was the driver software Le Roux originally wrote for E4M and improved and rewrote at SecurStar. Hollingworth and Le Roux had "gone through hell" solving problems under the DriveCrypt development. Le Roux had obviously now supplied these drivers to TrueCrypt. Le Roux had betrayed Hafner again.

We will show that Le Roux was undoubtedly involved with the TrueCrypt Team. He posted to the scramdisk group under two pseudonyms, one of which was "Entropy". The two posters appeared shortly after the launch of TrueCrypt, with Entropy first posting the next day. All their posts were concerned with TrueCrypt. Entropy shows remarkable in-depth technical knowledge of both TrueCrypt and E4M. He claims to have gained this knowledge by reviewing the code for TrueCrypt. But more than one poster thought he was the developer of TrueCrypt.

The development of TrueCrypt 1.0 was supposedly stalled because of Hafner, and the product was officially withdrawn. However, it was still available. Another new poster "Thinker" (not Le Roux) linked to a site www.truecrypt.tk from which it could be downloaded. The .tk domain belonged to the island territory of Tokelau. Domains could be registered for free, which meant there was no payment that could be traced and no way of verifying the true domain owner.

When people lamented that TrueCrypt had been abandoned, Entropy reassured them that this was not the case: "Actually I am quite sure that the development *will* continue soon. ;-)" (15 May 2004). A few weeks later, TrueCrypt 2.0 was announced by Thinker.

It was attributed to the TrueCrypt Foundation rather than the TrueCrypt Team. There was and still is speculation whether the two groups were the same, but there is no reason to believe they were different. The name change was a legal manoeuvre to thwart Hafner and deflect any liability that might overwise fall on David Tesarik. As the TrueCrypt Team had halted TrueCrypt because of Le Roux's legal problems, it seems likely that Le Roux authorised the continuing development and deployment.

Entropy knew in advance that development was continuing, but denied that he had written TrueCrypt 2.0. His denial is believable. Le Roux had started the product and was a technical advisor and code reviewer but he was not the one coding TrueCrypt or making the final decisions. Nothing shows this better than the question of the licence.

Le Roux was no left-winger. Although he contributed to the open source movement, he never liked the "copyleft" GPL licence, which obliged any future development using the software to remain open source. As a libertarian, he issued E4M under a more permissive BDS licence. When TrueCrypt 1.0 was released, it was under the same E4M license. But surprisingly, TrueCrypt 2.0 was issued under the GPL licence! When Le Roux made his statement about the E4M licence a few weeks later, he expressed his displeasure:

> Certainly no permission has ever been granted to anyone to produce derived code and distribute it under a more restrictive license such

> as the GPL, any such product is not legal, and is simply a work of piracy. (16 Jun 2004)

So Le Roux is accusing the TrueCrypt Foundation of piracy! It added to Le Roux's own plausible deniability but was also a reproach. The next day, a bug fix, TrueCrypt 2.1, was issued. The GPL licence was withdrawn, and TrueCrypt 2.1 reverted to the previous E4M licence. There could be no clearer sign of Le Roux's influence on the TrueCrypt project.

SIXTEEN

RX LIMITED

Le Roux considered several ideas after his acrimonious break with Hafner in late 2002. We will see later that one of these ideas was a new decentralised digital currency, a "virtual coin", operating over a peer-to-peer network. Implementing this currency would involve years of development with an uncertain return. He was, as yet, far from solving some fundamental problems. So the virtual coin project was a long shot. He might never be able to get it working, and if he did, there was no guarantee that it would take off. If he could implement the virtual coin, get it taken up by enthusiasts and then find a wider audience, the payback could be extraordinary. Le Roux could even become richer than Bill Gates or Steve Jobs. But he had to keep his feet on the ground. His second kid was on the way (he would eventually have four with Lillian), and he needed to feed his growing family. So Le Roux put the virtual coin on the back burner. It would be four years before he had the time to work on it seriously.

As we have seen, he was also writing more encryption software, including one which, in other hands, would become TrueCrypt. Le Roux had to abandon the idea of a proprietary product because of the legal risk with Hafner, and an open source product offered no return at all.

So, Le Roux turned to two projects that offered better immediate profit potential: an online casino based in Costa Rica and a prescription drug company. He considered both but chose the pill idea, which he implemented through a company he named Rx Limited.

Ratliff came across three different stories as to how Le Roux got turned on to the pill idea and was unsure which to believe. The first is that Le Roux got the idea from his biological father, who he met in 2003, and who was arrested for selling drugs with false prescriptions in South Africa. But Le Roux once got into a fit of rage in front of Hafner at the mere mention of his biological father who he called "a shit". He was furious that his father had copied his idea and opened his own online pill operation. Le Roux once hinted that he had considered assassinating his own father. So we can rule out the father as the source for Rx Limited.

The second theory is that Le Roux was given the idea by the Costa Rican casino operators Hafner introduced. The online gambling space was already becoming crowded, and the online pill business presented a new opportunity. Although Le Roux did not move to Costa Rica, he did have an involvement with internet gambling. In 2010, he would set up a gambling start-up called The Betting Machine in Costa Rica. He also established a call centre there. So it is likely that this story contains at least a grain of truth.

The third explanation was that Le Roux got the idea from the Taggart brothers, Tomer and Boaz, who he met on an online forum. Tomer lived in the US and Boaz in Israel. Certainly, the two were involved in establishing a call centre in Israel in the early days. Moran Oz, who worked for Rx as early as 2005, told Ratliff that Tomer and Boaz had informed the staff that they owned the business along with a mysterious silent partner, a programmer who handled the technical side with a team of developers in Romania. Oz was surprised when Boaz suddenly left the company without a good explanation. Then, in 2007, he received an email from a person he had never heard of before—Paul Le Roux—announcing that Tomer had also left and that he, Le Roux, was in charge.

It is a puzzling story that suggests that the origins of Rx Limited are more complex than they appear. It shows Le Roux as just one part of the operation and perhaps not even the primary mover at first. However, it seems likely that the Taggart brothers were exaggerating their role to their employees. At some point, they were moved aside. Bought out or told to leave?

Ratliff was unsure which story to believe. However, another completely different account given by the prosecution sentencing document could only have come from Le Roux himself. The sentencing documents allege that Wilfried Hafner (the prosecution spelt the name Heffner) operated an illegal prescription drug company called Atlas Pharmacy alongside SecurStar. Atlas sold drugs in the US that had been sourced from a Brazilian wholesaler. Hafner asked Le Roux to do some programming work for Atlas while at SecurStar. Hafner obtained the drugs by bribing staff members of the wholesaler, and on one occasion this got him arrested in Brazil. He had to contact Le Roux, who urgently wired over $40,000 so Hafner could bribe local officials to end the investigation. After this experience, Hafner exited Atlas Pharmacy, and Le Roux established his own pill business. Le Roux even pleaded guilty to a money laundering count in respect of the $40,000. It was a very minor item on his charge sheet.

Hafner vehemently denied the whole extraordinary story to Shannon. She believed him because she had come to trust him and because the supposed year, 2004, contradicts the fact that Le Roux fell out with Hafner in 2002. However, many dates in the sentencing documents are out for this period. For example, Le Roux supposedly began working for SecurStar in 2003, whereas it was actually in 2001. A wrong date does not mean that the story is untrue.

Le Roux had certainly started his Rx Limited business by 2004. He talked to many people about it in 2003, claiming that it was intended as a legitimate operation to serve US consumers who faced drug prices much higher than in other parts of the world. The Internet pharmacy service would give the US consumer convenient, cheaper, and private access to prescription drugs. Rx Limited did not directly handle any drugs itself. Licensed US pharmacies fulfilled orders. The customer would complete a questionnaire to be reviewed by a doctor who would issue the prescription. The doctor could consult with the patient by telephone if necessary. Rx Limited paid them a fee for each prescription issued. No prescription, no fee.

To the customer, everything appeared legal and above board. The websites were professional and included a 24/7 toll-free number. Payment was by American Express, Visa, or Mastercard. A prescription would be issued by a doctor, and the drugs came from US pharmacies and were sent by FedEx for next-day delivery. Although the customer had to answer a few questions, no one would know if they were lying. It was very easy to get whatever pills they wanted.

Was it legal? Le Roux had obtained a written legal opinion. The lawyer had been cautious but advised Le Roux that if he wanted to proceed, he should avoid selling any drug that was on the Controlled Substance list. The illegal supply of such drugs was a federal offence, essentially drug dealing. Drugs not on the Controlled Substance list were regulated by State law, which was usually vague. And if a non-controlled drug was issued illegally, it would only be a misdemeanour offence. A few states had explicitly outlawed prescriptions based on patient questionnaires, and the lawyer advised Le Roux not to sell to customers in these states.

So, in theory, Le Roux had a good case that he was not breaking the law. The practice was rather different. Rx Limited issued pills to whoever wanted them. An algorithm allocated customer orders to doctors and pharmacists. Doctors did not have access to a patient's medical records and rarely phoned a patient. They mainly just approved the order, typically issuing hundreds of prescriptions daily. The pharmacist would not have any way of communicating with the doctor or the patient. They just packed the drugs, printed address labels off the system and gave the package, along with a large number of other orders, to the FedEx man who came to collect them.

Recruiting the pharmacies was relatively easy. They were typically small, failing businesses. Rx Limited was not generous with its payments, and the pharmacist typically only got a margin of $3.50 per order. But it added up as they could fulfil hundreds of orders a day. Doctors were more of a problem. As government pressure on the internet pill shops grew, it was difficult to find doctors foolish or desperate enough to write the prescriptions. Some of the doctors Rx hired had fake qualifications, or their licence had expired. One was a dentist.

Rx Limited first came to the DEA's notice in Oct 2007. Ratliff tells this part of the story best. Two relatively new Diversion Investigators, Kimberly Brill and Steven Holdren, uncovered Le Roux's operation. They worked from an office in Minneapolis, a world away from the glamorous gun-carrying DEA field agents who targeted drug barons. "Diversion" was the illegal sale of prescription medicines by crooked pharmacists and doctors. It all started when the pair were looking for online pharmacies selling a controlled substance, phentermine. After making an undercover online drug purchase which arrived by FedEx, they identified a pharmacy in Chicago supplying the substance. It was a routine case, but they decided to subpoena FedEx for details of the shipping account used by the pharmacy. When the spreadsheet came, they were amazed to see thousands of transactions involving customers and pharmacies throughout the US. They had uncovered a shipping account belonging to a company called Rx Limited.

The odd thing about this story is that Rx Limited never knowingly supplied controlled substances. So the investigators stumbled upon the Rx account by accident. More subpoenas to FedEx enabled them to see the full scope of the operation, identifying over a hundred pharmacies supplying the drugs. A technician happily took them through the whole process at a supposed routine inspection of one pharmacy. Rx Limited provided the computer and the software, a slick, custom-designed system called PCMS. Documentation was downloaded over the internet and PCMS handled the whole process right up to printing the shipping labels.

Working backwards through the chain, the investigators identified a website, acmemeds.com associated with Rx Limited. Once they had one site, they could find many more by googling blocks of text and phone numbers. But here they hit a snag: none of the sites were selling a controlled substance. It all smelled illegal to the agents, but was it? Rx Limited may have been breaking the spirit of the law, but was it breaking the letter?

One of the drugs Rx Limited supplied, Fioricet, was not a controlled substance itself but contained an ingredient, acetaminophen, that was. There was a possible legal case that this made Fioricet a controlled substance. It was little more than a technicality, but it allowed the two agents to justify an investigation that would last years with little apparent result.

Ironically, Le Roux also had concerns over Fioricet. He asked an employee in Israel to phone the DEA to confirm the status. They were told that Fioricet was not a controlled substance. But nothing was put in writing.

The DEA investigators next turned to the domain records for the websites. They identified two private name servers used for many of Rx Limited's websites; Cartadmin.com and SystemsCA.com. Behind them was a domain registrar, ABSystems. It was not a public service—Rx Limited had its own private domain registrar. ABSystems had registered thousands of domain names, all related to pharmacy and most with Rx in the name.

The investigators discovered that Rx Limited was a vast web of complexity: domain names, companies, and people. The company employed a team of programmers and operated call centres in Israel and the Philippines. The websites were promoted through services such as Google ads. The investigators were astonished at how anyone could keep track of it all. They had followed a few faint clues to the man who seemed to occupy the centre of the web, a programmer called Paul Le Roux. He had taken pains not to leave a trail back to himself but had made a few mistakes, such as hosting his E4M domain on ABSystems.

At the end of 2004 or early 2005, Le Roux relocated from the Netherlands to the Philippines. His wife was not happy in Holland, and the Philippines offered a warmer climate. For Le Roux, the chief advantages were cheap labour, freedom of operation, and an abundant supply of attractive women available to purchase in one way or another. Le Roux would stay together with his wife for a few years, but their marriage was doomed from the moment they moved to the Philippines. He continued to support her and their four children after the inevitable divorce.

Another attraction of the Philippines was that the government, the police and the military were corrupt at all levels. Le Roux was free with bribes. Some were necessary to stay in business, whereas others bought him additional protection and influence. He felt comparatively safe from US prosecution and had established an intelligence network in the Philippines government to give him early warning of any moves against him.

Alongside the websites, Le Roux operated a large outgoing telesales operation. Most customers needed repeat prescriptions, and Rx had a volume of information about them, including their telephone numbers. (Ironically, the customers' details were probably safer on Le Roux's encrypted servers than on just about any other company's systems at that time.) Le Roux set up another, larger call centre in Makati, Philippines, where he soon had over a thousand people working. He had a poor opinion of his Filipino staff, calling them "monkeys", and preferred to import his managers from Israel.

Rx Limited was now a giant money-making machine. Drugs were high-value items. There was no physical inventory, and the investment requirements were modest. It was millions and millions of pills and millions and millions of dollars for Le Roux. He would admit in court to have made $300 million from Rx Limited over several years.

A glimpse at Rx Limited's astronomical margins comes from a table embedded in a website, RxPayouts.com, aimed at affiliates. In 2006, one of the biggest sellers, Tramadol, retailed for almost four times the cost price with a margin of $70 per sale (for orders of 90 tabs). The other two best sellers, Fioricet and Soma, had even higher margins of $90 to $100 per sale. Rx Limited's costs would have to come out of these margins, but when you consider they were fulfilling millions of orders a year and paying pharmacists $3.50 per sale over cost price, the profit Le Roux was making becomes understandable.

Yet, the business was coming under pressure as the US government tried to squeeze online pharmacies out of existence. The main lines of attack were the banks, payment processors and shipping companies. Visa, Mastercard and FedEx demanded that Rx provide legal opinions that its business was legitimate. Le Roux had obtained letters of opinion from the attorney he consulted when he first established the company. But by 2006, that attorney refused to give the letters he needed. Le Roux turned to a crooked lawyer who knowingly gave him false opinions in return for a high fee, $10,000 per letter, which rose to $35,000 as Le Roux grew more desperate.

American Express and Discover changed their policy so that only companies with a valid pharmacy license could make online sales. So Le Roux got one of his biggest pharmacy partners to open an account in their name, which he used for Rx Limited. In 2011, FedEx closed the Rx Limited account because they had been told the company was selling controlled substances. Le Roux opened a new account and began using other shipping services.

Google was also turning up the heat, refusing advertising to websites that sold certain drugs. Le Roux found a clever way around this. He got his programmers to display a sanitised version of the websites to internet queries coming from the IP addresses of the Google offices. Everyone else saw the actual website with the offending drugs.

Le Roux also began diversifying his marketing methods using spam. He had innovative methods of obtaining leads. He employed two Canadian computer hackers to target the servers of medical centres and steal patient details. He was resorting to increasingly illegal actions to keep Rx Limited in business.

I wanted to find out the truth about the origins of Rx Limited and whether it had involved Hafner, who had furiously denied the whole story to Shannon. Had Le Roux made it all up to get revenge on Hafner? It was a twenty-year-old cold case, but the internet preserves information like a fly trapped in amber. Armed with the Wayback Machine and DomainTools, I set out to discover what I could find.

Identifying Atlas Pharmacy was easy. There was an online prescription drug website Atlas-Pharmacy.com at the right time. The Wayback Machine shows that it was in operation by Jun 2003. The domain name had been registered as far back as 1998, but the registration changed on 13 May 2003 reflecting new ownership.

The site was primitive, just a long list of drugs with an order button next to each one. There was no phone number. The website was up for a little over a year before the Wayback Machine records disappeared. It reappeared sporadically but kept changing and must have been sold on.

The new registrant in 2003 was recorded as Andy Thompson, and the contact address was a Seattle box number. I soon realised that registrant details were rarely useful because the operators of such sites would not put their own names and addresses down. The dates already disproved some aspects of the prosecution story. Le Roux could not have been employed by SecurStar while working on Atlas because he had left by Oct 2002, and Atlas was not in operation until May 2003.

Hafner had given Shannon a story of a complete break with Le Roux in 2002, but there were some puzzling aspects. Hafner supposedly directed Le Roux to casinos in Costa Rica while he was still working at SecurStar. But why would Hafner point his very talented chief technical officer towards other business opportunities when he needed him at SecurStar? It makes more sense if Le Roux had already left the company and Hafner had a finger in the Costa Rican casino pie. He could not trust Le Roux with SecurStar's intellectual property, but Le Roux could still be useful.

Then there is Hafner's story of Le Roux's rage when he had asked him about his biological father. Le Roux only found out that he was adopted in 2003, which is when he made contact with his biological father and mother. So this conversation couldn't have taken place before 2003. And yet, the two were supposed to have made a complete break. Hafner was not telling Shannon the whole truth. Why not?

An early sign of what was to become Rx Limited came from Le Roux posting to groups such as misc.entrepreneurs looking for people to front activities in the U.S.:

> "I'm looking for U.S. citizen /green card holders to help me opening bank accounts/ and companies for foreign citizens in the U.S. this is a quick way for you to make bucks, with very little work on your part, genuine people only" (28 Feb 2003)

And a few days later:

> We are European based private investors looking for a US citizen or green card holder to help us setup a new company based out of Florida, we will do all the paper work we need your help to comply with US law. But we know nothing in this world is free, so we will pay you up to $500 to help us. Please only genuine people. No time wasters. (2 Mar 2003)

So already in late Feb 2003 Le Roux was taking steps to establish his pill business. This was months before he could have begun coding the Atlas-Pharmacy website, as the domain was only registered in May. So the story that Le Roux came upon the pharmacy idea after developing the website for Atlas-Pharmacy at SecurStar is untrue. But note the phrases Le Roux uses in his request for business fronts—"European based investors" and "we". Le Roux is not doing this alone. Are his partners Hafner and his investors?

The next step was to trace exactly when Le Roux set up his early pharmacy sites. Ratliff included a long list of domains, almost all starting with Rx. But as I checked through, it became apparent that many of these domains had never been used, and all the others had been established much later than 2003/4. The list was useless for identifying early sites.

I then tried searching for pharmacy sites operating in 2003/4 with "Rx" in the name. I came up with a connected group of sites such as RxDrugs.com, RxDrugsonline.com, AmericanPharmacy.com and Rx-pain-pills.com. They all gave the same phone number, were linked to a Florida company, and had the same business model as Rx Limited. The customer would fill out a questionnaire, a doctor would issue a prescription, and a U.S. pharmacy would fulfil the order for next-day delivery. Customers could pay through a range of methods, including American Express, Mastercard and Visa. One of the domains, Rx-pain-pills.com, was even registered to Rx Limited's offices in Makati City in 2010.

It looked like I had found Le Roux's early sites, but it was a false lead. As I delved deeper, it became clear that these did not belong to Le Roux. As for Rx-pain-pills dot com, it had been abandoned by its initial registrants for several years before being reregistered by Rx Limited.

The exercise told me what was original about Rx Limited—nothing. Some sites active as early as 2001 were using the same business model. Le Roux's websites even had a generic resemblance to these earlier sites with their reassuring doctors-in-white-coats photos. So why was Rx Limited so successful compared to its very many competitors? Le Roux thought bigger than everyone else. He scaled his business and was more professional. Le Roux was brilliant at walking the thin grey line between the legal and illegal. Rx Limited was legitimate to outsiders and even many people working in the operation. It had its own call centres and programmers and operated in plain sight in places such as Israel and the Philippines. Yet, Le Roux was careful to keep his operations outside the long reach of the U.S.

So far, I had not found a single site active in the early days, so I turned to some more domains from Ratliff's and Shannon's books. Ratliff gave the two earliest domains as RxPayouts.com and BillRx.com, both registered in Dec 2003. RxPayouts.com was registered to a Florida address, but the name servers were directed to RxLimited.com in Jan 2004, with other known Le Roux servers, such as Cartadmin.com and Server72.com, appearing later. However, neither site was used immediately. RxPayouts only became active in 2006, and BillRx not until 2010. And neither was customer-facing. RxPayouts was aimed at affiliates who would operate their own websites and refer customers to Rx. Limited. Its promise of the "highest payouts in the industry" was reinforced by a picture of a wheelbarrow full of money. Affiliates earned 60% commissions on the difference between the retail and cost price.

The list of early Le Roux domains from Shannon's book was also imperfect but more helpful. Some domains did not seem to belong to Le Roux at all, others were much later. However, three early sites could be linked to Le Roux: acmemeds.com (active Aug 2004), BuyMedsCheap.com (active Feb 2005) and Your-Pills.com (active May 2004). They all gave the same toll-free phone number: 877-479-2455.

It was Your-Pills dot com that helped unravel the real story of Le Roux's early operation. The name server history proved it was a Rx Limited site:

Date changed	Server
9 Feb 2003	Name-services.com
4 Jun 2003	Metathinking.com
30 Jan 2004	Rxlimited.com
2 May 2004	cartadmin.com
28 Oct 2004	Server72.net

....

The first server belongs to the popular registrar eNom.com. The last three are all Le Roux's name servers. The domain was registered very early, on 8 Feb 2003, which is the first evidence of Le Roux's interest in the pill business.

But the real bonus came from the Wayback Machine, which recorded a temporary home page for Your-Pills. This was packed with hundreds of keywords, which was the way SEO worked in the early 2000s. Alongside pharmacy and drug search terms were items such as "Pamela Andresen", "Brittney Spears", and "The Matrix Reloaded". The page had clear links to SecurStar, including the odd sentence "Also on our page you find more about DriveCrypt" as well as search terms "DriveCrypt" and" Hard disk encryption". It looked as if someone had started with a list of search terms to drive leads to SecurStar and modified it for the pharmacy business. The most significant discovery was a list of 56 pharmacy domains, each proving to be an early Rx Limited website.

I now had 57 sites, including Your-Pills. Going through the list with the Wayback Machine yielded a picture of Rx Limited's activities in the early days. The results are shown in Appendix 2. All the sites went live within a few weeks, from 18 May 2004 to early June, except for two unused domains and one exception. The majority of these sites showed the full Rx Limited business model right from the beginning, with toll-free phone numbers, drugs supplied by US pharmacies, and next-day delivery.

One surprise was that 18 sites used another model, posting orders from foreign wholesalers to the US using international mail. One group of 6 sites used a different phone number and sourced the drugs from India, suggesting that these sites were operating as affiliates. The remaining 12 sites used the Rx Limited toll-free number and did not specify the overseas source.

It is all very reminiscent of the prosecution story that Hafner was sourcing his drugs from a wholesaler in Brazil. You could not import such drugs en masse to the US, so customer orders would have to be fulfilled either from Brazil or some other South American country.

The one exception among the 57 domains was pills24-7.com, which became active on 1 Apr 2004, several weeks before the others. The website was relatively crude; it offered 3 or 5-day delivery options with the drugs sourced from US pharmacies. And there was no phone line. The picture that emerges is that Rx Limited first went active with this preliminary site in April, with the full operation in place by 18 May 2004 after which all the other sites quickly became active. This is a long gestation period considering Le Roux had registered the first site as long ago as 8 Feb 2003 and was advertising for people to front a company a few weeks later.

Something must have come in between, and it was surely Atlas-Pharmacy. Can we definitely connect Atlas-Pharmacy to Le Roux or Hafner? The name server history is typically more informative than the registrant details. Your-pills and many of the other 57 sites show the same pattern; a change to Metathinking.com in Jun/Jul 2003, then Rxlimited.com in late Jan 2004, followed by Cartadmin.com around May 2004. Le Roux also used Metathinking.com and Rxlimited.com for the E4M website, which enabled the DEA investigators to follow a trail to Le Roux. If we look at the Atlas-Pharmacy name servers, we find a different history, except for one name in common. It also used Metathinking.com from Jul 2003 until Jan 2004, just like the Rx Limited sites.

As Metathinking was a private server, it proves Le Roux was linked to Atlas-Pharmacy. The registrar details for Metathinking dot com were unusually enlightening: the domain was registered to a UK company called Metathinking Ltd. The UK company register showed that Metathinking Ltd was established in 2002 by the same Pete Chown behind Skygate. (It was this link that first led me to Skygate). Metathinking's first set of accounts recorded an investment of £4,000 in fixed assets, presumably the server on which Atlas-Pharmacy and Le Roux's domains were hosted. (There is no suggestion that Chown was involved in the pharmacy business, and only Atlas-Pharmacy was operational while Metathinking was the name server.)

Le Roux had a business relationship with Chown, but so did Hafner if he were the client for Caveo. Was Hafner also linked with Atlas-Pharmacy? We can compare Atlas-Pharmacy's name server change history in 2003/4 with Hafner's SecurStar.com:

Date changed	Atlas-Pharmacy	SecurStar
14 May 2003	Handsonwebhosting.com	Hrnoc.net
4 Jun 2003	Hrnoc.net	
14 Jul 2003	Metathinking.com	
18 Jul 2003		Liquidweb.com
20 Jan 2004	Host-age.ro	

The name servers for both Atlas-Pharmacy and SecurStar were changed on 14 May 2003. SecurStar went to Hrnoc.net and Atlas-Pharmacy to Handsonwebhosting.com, a hosting service used by an internet shop software product. If the original intent was to use this software for the pharmacy operation, it was abandoned, and a few weeks later, Atlas-Pharmacy also went to Hrnoc.net. Then, in July, both sites were moved within four days. SecurStar went to Liquidweb.com, where it stayed for 13 years, and Atlas-Pharmacy to Metathinking.com. For six weeks, the name server of both sites was Hrnoc.net, which belongs to a web hosting company called HostRocket. It was a small outfit (only 1 in 100,000 domains are hosted on Hrnoc.net), so it is unlikely to be a coincidence.

I believe that this history shows that both SecurStar.com and Atlas-Pharmacy.com were managed by the same person in the summer of 2003. This was almost certainly Le Roux: the prosecution document said he had developed the Atlas-Pharmacy website. So Hafner really was involved in Le Roux's introduction to the pharmacy business although the prosecution story was wrong in some important respects. Le Roux left SecurStar long before Atlas-Pharmacy was active and registered pharmacy websites months before he could have done any programming on Atlas-Pharmacy.

A joint venture between Le Roux and Hafner would explain why Le Roux was the one who wired $40,000 to get Hafner out of jail in Brazil. We also see the same Atlas-Pharmacy business model of sourcing drugs from foreign wholesalers on at least twelve Rx Limited sites. There must have been other investors involved. Le Roux had no money, yet he launched his Rx Limited operation at scale in April/May 2004, with only Atlas-Pharmacy coming earlier. The story of the Taggart brothers running the call centre in Israel before Le Roux replaced them in 2007 shows that business partners were involved in the early days. Were Hafner's Costa Rican online casino operators also behind Rx Limited in some way?

This brings us to the mysterious group Le Roux called "the Brazilians". He would often talk to his subordinates about the Brazilians who were able to arrange assassinations using their criminal connections in Colombia. Le Roux implied that they were the people he reported to and were behind Rx Limited. After his capture Le Roux betrayed almost everyone, but, as far as we know, he never said anything about the Brazilians. Ratliff was not sure they existed—he thought Le Roux was bluffing to scare his people. However, the fact that Hafner was sourcing the drugs for Atlas-Pharmacy from Brazil gives Le Roux's stories credibility.

We can now set out a timeline:

By Oct 2002	Le Roux leaves SecurStar
8 Feb 2003	Your-pills.com registered
28 Feb 2003	Le Roux begins advertising for people to front the business
13 May 2003	Atlas-Pharmacy.com acquired

June 2003	Atlas-Pharmacy active - joint venture Le Roux/ Hafner
July 2003	Pharmacy sites, including Atlas-Pharmacy moved to Metathinking dot com
By Oct 2003	The first 57 domains that will belong to Rx Limited have been registered
Dec 2003	The first domains with "Rx" in the name are registered but are not operational.
Jan 2004	Rxlimited.com name server becomes active. Sites moved away from Metathinking.com
2 Feb 2004	TrueCrypt launched, final break with Hafner
1 Apr 2004	Pills24-7.com, the first Rx Limited site, becomes active
18 May 2004	The remaining sites become active over a few weeks. Rx Limited is fully operational.

The timeline shows that the Rx Limited label was adopted at the end of 2003, several months after the first set of pharmacy sites was registered. It seems that Hafner's withdrawal prompted Le Roux to establish that company to implement operations that had been long planned.

Is it a coincidence that Le Roux moved all his sites, including E4M, from the Metathinking server to Rxlimited.com days before the TrueCrypt launch? Atlas-Pharmacy had already moved a week earlier to be hosted on a different, Romanian server from Le Roux's domains. One possibility is that Le Roux wanted to avoid any overt connection between Pete Chown and himself. Chown was a libertarian like Le Roux and was involved in the first iteration of E4M. Remember that poster, "Thinker", who was part of the early TrueCrypt project and announced TrueCrypt 2.0. Was Thinker connected to Metathinking?

When I found the early Rx Limited websites, I was surprised that none had "Rx" in the domain name, and yet almost every later Rx Limited site featured "Rx". Ratliff gives a considerable sample, including, for example:

Rx-4u-usa.com
Rx-billing.com
Rx-drugstore-meds.com
Rx-usa.net
Rxcheaperdrugs.com

The complete list goes on and on for hundreds and hundreds of Rx names. I had assumed Le Roux used Rx because it was the first and last letters of his name: **R**ou**x**. So I started by looking for drug sites with "Rx" in the name that were operational in 2003/4, expecting to find Le Roux's early sites. I found several sites, but none connected with Le Roux. I had not realised that Rx was the abbreviation for a prescription because it is not commonly used in the UK. This little bit of ignorance led to a key insight that others may have missed.

At some point, Le Roux will have noticed that Rx meant "prescription" and that it was also the first and last letter of his name. The early sites do not have Rx in the name because they all come from the time when Hafner was involved. After Hafner withdrew from the pills business at the end of 2003, Le Roux latched on to Rx and began using it as the name of his company. His first pill websites used the domains registered in 2003. Yet Le Roux could not resist using Rx in new domain names and it became dominant.

It tells us something about Le Roux. His name is very important to him, and he likes to flaunt it. But not openly. Le Roux enjoys being cleverer than the people he deceives. He does not crave recognition but keeps in the shadows while taunting his audience by putting his real identity right in front of them. With his Rx sites he was mocking his US investigators. Is Satoshi Nakamoto also mocking everyone with his name?

There is something else, a minor detail, that will become important. Le Roux did not use his initials but his name's first and last letters. In fact, he used the last letter as a pseudonym a year before he thought of Rx Limited.

SEVENTEEN

GOLDFINGER

With the cash flows from Rx Limited, Le Roux acquired the toys he had set his heart on in the South of France. He purchased a private jet and a yacht. There were plenty of beautiful girls living in poverty in the Philippines who could be induced to put on bikinis and adorn his yacht. Le Roux could now live the life he had desired. But Le Roux was a hopeless, overweight workaholic without finesse or style. He rarely used his yacht and preferred to travel by scheduled airline. The jet was mainly employed for smuggling, with customs officials bribed to look the other way. There was no romance in Le Roux's nature, and his treatment of women was crude and appalling.

With Rx Limited's success, Le Roux encountered a new problem: what to do with the proceeds? His pill operation was generating tens of millions of dollars in free cash flow per year, and there was little opportunity to reinvest it in Rx Limited. The pill operation faced a finite operating lifetime before US authorities closed it down entirely.

Le Roux did not trust securities or bonds but liked to invest directly in physical assets. He acquired some trophy real estate in the Philippines for his own use, including twin penthouses in the prestigious Salcedo Park Twin Towers in Manila. From the top of one tower, Le Roux could look over to his apartment in the other tower. If the police or an assassin came calling at his address, he would see them from the other tower where he was actually living. A master criminal also needs a secluded and private location. So he had another property, a compound, by the coast.

He also bought properties far beyond Manilla, employing several individuals to find him houses and apartments in the Philippines and other nations. These properties were intended both for investment and his business activities. Le Roux preferred remote houses with easy access to the sea. These were ideal for smuggling goods and useful as safe houses if he was forced to flee from law enforcement.

Le Roux used very few of his many properties, but they were not empty. They housed his operatives and girls. In online conversations with his cousin, Matthew Smith, he called these women "his bitches". His attitude towards women in the Philippines was disturbing. He assembled what can only be called a harem. The Philippines had a bar-girl culture, and many women would have been interested in a rich man. But that was not enough for Le Roux. He treated his "bitches" like any other commodity. As a good businessman, he aimed to secure a good supply of pristine new product.

He took an employee from the call centre and gave him new duties. The man's new job was to go round the outlying villages and scout for suitable girls. He would negotiate with the parents, and if a deal were struck, he would take the girl back to Manilla to live in one of Le Roux's properties. Le Roux made the employee keep a spreadsheet so he could keep track of his harem. It would record essential information, such as the girl's name and medical details. When Ratliff first heard this story, he thought it was an exaggeration, but he tracked down the employee, who confirmed it was all true. The system was designed for maximum efficiency: Le Roux would have a constant stream of women on call without having to waste any time with small talk. He boasted to Matthew Smith about having sex with as many as three different girls a night.

It is a vivid demonstration of the way Le Roux treated other people. They were resources to be used and discarded when of no more use. With one single exception, no one came remotely close to being Le Roux's friend. He had no colleagues in his business, there was not a single person he trusted. Le Roux controlled every detail. His employees only ever saw their little slice of the action. Two men could be doing very similar tasks and never know of the other's existence. Le Roux was remarkably alone.

The one exception was a woman called Cindy Cayanan. After he split with his wife, she became his long-term girlfriend and, for all practical purposes, his new wife. She must have been ready to accept Le Roux as he was, including his many other women, for they stayed together to the end.

Le Roux liked property but loved gold. As a libertarian, he did not trust any government with his money. A bank deposit would be at constant risk of seizure, given the potentially illegal nature of Rx Limited's business. Le Roux was the son of a mining engineer brought up in a South African gold mining town. For a crime lord and money launderer, gold had the advantage of being untraceable. A legitimate gold bar with a serial number purchased from a Swiss refinery was useful because it could be traded legally. And if law enforcement discovered that serial number, the bar could always be melted down and recast.

Le Roux would source much of his gold through Hong Kong, where he had lived briefly after leaving Australia. The money would flow from Rx Limited through accounts held by his network of companies and into Hong Kong, where it would be used to purchase gold bars. There were no bank vaults for Le Roux—he stored the bars in stash houses before they were loaded onto a yacht for transfer to the Philippines. Le Roux also acquired diamonds. These commodities were the destination of the majority of the Rx Limited cash.

If you hold gold yourself, you need to provide security. Le Roux hired mercenaries. In the Philippines, he had come across a British ex-soldier called Dave Smith, who claimed to have been in the elite SAS regiment. He hailed from Northern Ireland and now, like many ex-soldiers, worked in "security". Smith had fetched up in the Philippines and was recruited by Le Roux to head up his mercenary operation. He was a terrible choice who would lead Le Roux into increasingly illegal activities. Smith was the conduit for former soldiers from America and other Western nations to enter Le Roux's employ as his private army. He was thoroughly corrupt and would cheat and betray Le Roux.

One of Smith's recruits was Lachlan McConnell, a Canadian in charge of security for the Hong Kong operation. Many of his duties were mundane. Gold was not the only thing that had to be safeguarded. Le Roux operated his companies through "dummies", proxies who were company directors and whose names were on the bank accounts and registration documents. This ensured anonymity but had its dangers—the proxies had to be kept in line. McConnell would babysit these individuals when they had to open an account or sign some papers. The presence of a mercenary would help focus the dummy's mind on obeying Le Roux's instructions.

Not all of Le Roux's gold was bought as gold bars from legitimate suppliers. He also went directly to the source, preferring illegal operations in developing countries such as irregular African gold mines in Ghana and the Congo. He used his cousin, Matthew Smith, from Le Roux's birthplace of Bulawayo in Zimbabwe, to help him acquire this gold.

Smith recruited two gold experts, the Hahn brothers, Andrew and Steve. They negotiated purchases and assayed the gold for purity. The arrangement went wrong when the brothers used $1.5m of Le Roux's money to buy 80 kg of gold from Zambia. When they returned to Zimbabwe, they found that the gold was fake. The Hahn brothers swore they had been tricked and the samples had been switched. Le Roux did not believe them. He concluded they were lying and had stolen his money.

Le Roux wanted to have the brothers killed. It was irrelevant whether they had stolen the money or been tricked. They had lost the gold and had to pay with their lives. Dave Smith, however, smelled money. He was sure the brothers were lying and wanted to retrieve the money. He came up with a plan.

Le Roux told Matthew Smith and the Hahn brothers to fly to Manila to explain the missing gold. They obeyed, which was very unwise. Dave Smith had a small quantity of cocaine secreted in Andrew Hahn's bag. Andrew was arrested at the airport and held in custody. He would spend the next two and half years in a Philippines prison before the charges against him were finally dropped.

Le Roux told Steve that Andrew would only be released when the money was recovered. He was then sent back to Zimbabwe to find the missing $1.5m. When he did not immediately return the money, Le Roux sent one of his mercenaries for additional motivation. This was Joseph Hunter, a decorated former US Army sniper who Dave Smith had recruited. Hunter was tall, muscular, and in perfect physical shape, the opposite of the sedentary and flabby Le Roux. He looked the part of an assassin, and everyone was scared of him, including the other mercenaries. Hunter remained a soldier at heart, with a need to obey orders. He was fanatically loyal to Le Roux. After visiting Steve Hahn to warn him about returning Le Roux's money, Hunter asked him to drive him back to the airport. On the way, he shot Hahn in the hand. Bizarrely, they continued to the airport together.

But Steve Hahn could not return money he did not have. He told Le Roux that Matthew Smith and another cousin had taken the money. Le

Roux had Hunter and another mercenary surveil Smith as an assassination target. But the other mercenary refused to carry out the job, and Le Roux had second thoughts about killing his own family. Eventually, he compromised by telling Hunter to fire-bomb Matthew Smith's house.

Having his house burnt down caused Matthew Smith to break with Le Roux permanently. He had been essential in negotiating deals in Africa. Many of these were for gold, but Le Roux also had logging operations in the Congo, Vanuatu, and Mozambique. The Congo was one of the main focuses of his unconventional business activities up until his falling out with Smith. Logging seems a very odd business for Le Roux, but he told his employees it was for money laundering on behalf of the "Brazilians". These logging operations were now abandoned.

Matthew Smith lived in fear of Le Roux's assassins, expecting them to appear at any time. But he survived his cousin's reign of terror to become one of Ratliff's major sources. It was from Smith that a vital clue connecting Le Roux to Satoshi emerged. Le Roux had used Smith to help him acquire valid passports, including a diplomatic passport from the Democratic Republic of the Congo. He would never have imagined that this passport would become public knowledge, but Smith passed a photo to Ratliff. It is shown below:

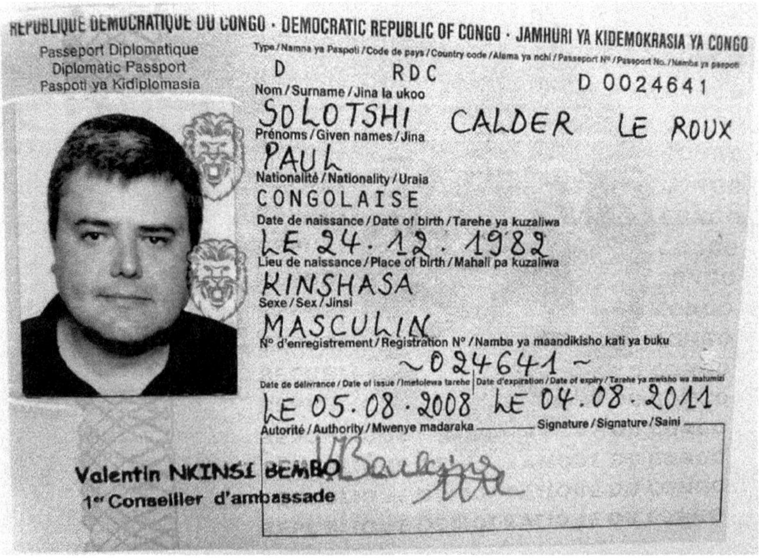
REPUBLIQUE DEMOCRATIQUE DU CONGO · DEMOCRATIC REPUBLIC OF CONGO · JAMHURI YA KIDEMOKRASIA YA CONGO

Passeport Diplomatique
Diplomatic Passport
Paspoti ya Kidiplomasia

Type / Namna ya Paspoti / Code de pays / Country code / Alama ya nchi / Passeport N° / Passport No. / Namba ya paspoti
D RDC D 0024641

Nom / Surname / Jina la ukoo
SOLOTSHI CALDER LE ROUX

Prénoms / Given names / Jina
PAUL

Nationalité / Nationality / Uraia
CONGOLAISE

Date de naissance / Date of birth / Tarehe ya kuzaliwa
LE 24.12.1982

Lieu de naissance / Place of birth / Mahali pa kuzaliwa
KINSHASA

Sexe / Sex / Jinsi
MASCULIN

N° d'enregistrement / Registration N° / Namba ya maandikisho kati ya buku
~024641~

Date de délivrance / Date of issue / Imetolewa tarehe
LE 05.08.2008

Date d'expiration / Date of expiry / Tarehe ya mwisho wa matumizi
LE 04.08.2011

Autorité / Authority / Mwenye madaraka

Signature / Signature / Saini

Valentin NKINSI BEMBO
1er Conseiller d'ambassade

Le Roux obtained this passport by bribing an official with $100,000. It is a diplomatic passport that could enable Le Roux to get through customs without being searched. It could also be used to claim diplomatic immunity. The passport gives all of Le Roux's real names (Paul Calder Le Roux) along with another name, Solotshi. The place of birth is shown falsely as Kinshasa in the Democratic Republic of Congo. The day and month of birth are correct, but the year 1982 makes him ten years too young.

When Ratliff published the passport photo in a magazine article about Le Roux, the striking similarity between the Solotshi and Satoshi names was picked up by some internet posters. And the dates are similar. The passport was issued on 5 Aug 2008, and the Satoshi Nakamoto name was first used on 20 Aug 2008.

Ratliff was sceptical that Le Roux was Satoshi. Matthew Smith and another carrier had travelled to the Congo with $100,000 strapped to their chests. He told Ratliff that the Solotshi name had been added by the official who wanted Le Roux's name to sound more Congolese. It makes sense that the official wanted a Congolese name, but that does not mean Le Roux was not involved in choosing the name. Smith may not have known the whole story or may have forgotten the details of something that happened years before.

Solotshi is an odd name for the official to choose. It is Congolese but very rare. The "Forebears" website rates it as the 23,516th most common name in the Democratic Republic of the Congo, with one occurrence for every quarter of a million people. Apart from the Congo, it appears a few times in South Africa. If you wanted a random name to make a passport sound more convincing, you would choose something familiar. Why pick an incredibly rare name? Because it has a hidden meaning.

The first name on the passport is Paul, so the full name is:

Paul Solotshi Calder Le Roux

Here, we have the first clue to decoding Satoshi. Look at the name above carefully. Can you see an English meaning in Solotshi?

EIGHTEEN

EMPIRE

In the summer of 2009, Satoshi lost interest in Bitcoin. It looked like a failure, with no momentum, a handful of miners, and almost no transactions. Even an enthusiast like Hal Finney ceased mining after a few months. We have seen that after Satoshi ironed out the early bugs in the first couple of months, he stopped programming altogether, only restarting in October. During that summer, he told Malmi how busy he was with other things.

It was in the summer of 2009 that Le Roux commenced his career as a master criminal. Getting involved in highly illicit activities made little business sense. He had carefully established Rx Limited by skirting the law without overtly breaking it. The company was a massive cash cow, so why go into other activities carrying a much greater risk?

Perhaps we should look at this differently. Le Roux was a megalomaniac who was always going to break out into high criminality. Bitcoin had restrained him, offering the possibility of controlling the world currency. In 2009, those hopes were dashed. He must have thought he had been wasting his time. So he turned to his other ideas and ambitions.

There had been warning signs; Le Roux had recruited mercenaries, surveilled family members for possible assassination, and had wanted to kill the Hahn brothers. He was motivated by the knowledge that his cousins, including Matthew Smith and the Hahn brothers, had stolen $1.5 million from him. This would be a recurring theme for Le Roux, who committed his worst crimes in the belief that the victim had cheated him. Le Roux saw himself as administering justice.

He may have thought he had nothing to lose and that he was already deep in trouble with the US from Rx Limited. If so, he was wrong. The company had been under investigation by the Minnesota branch of the DEA since 2007. Ratliff presents the Minnesota agents as the unsung heroes who built the case, but only to have it swept away at the last minute by the high-profile team who set up the sting operation. Shannon gives a very different picture: even as late as 2012, the Minnesota investigators could not persuade a prosecutor to go after Le Roux.

The Rx Limited case was largely built upon the dubious claim that Fioricet was a controlled substance. This was tested in court when prosecutors, using evidence from Le Roux, charged Rx Limited's senior managers, including Moran Oz. The prosecution withdrew the Fioricet charges when they failed to satisfy the judge that it was a controlled substance at the time Rx Limited was operating. The long DEA investigation of Rx Limited had been conducted under a false premise.

It got even worse for the prosecuting team and the DEA when the judge threw out the entire case due to a lack of evidence. Whether Le Roux would have been treated so favourably had he been on trial rather than his managers is another matter. But it is unlikely the US could ever have brought him to trial on Rx Limited's activities alone.

There was a close parallel to Le Roux's legal situation. A Canadian going under the name Calvin Wilson had an apartment just across the road from Le Roux's head office in Makati City, Manila. Like Le Roux, Wilson was operating a "grey" area business that earned most of its money from the US—in his case, online gambling. Wilson was even richer than Le Roux. His real name was Calvin Ayre. He would later emerge as the financial backer of Craig Wright and his claims to be Satoshi Nakamoto.

Information about Calvin Ayre's residence in Manilla came from the Panama Papers. Under the name Wilson, he gave the Roxas Triangle address as a director and shareholder of Elegant Step Group, established in the British Virgin Islands. Ayre's sister, Anita, was also a director and shareholder of this company. Roxas Triangle is several hundred yards from Le Roux's twin penthouses in Manila. Contemporary press reports confirm that Ayre was living in the Philippines as Calvin Wilson.

Ayre was the son of a pig farmer and had started his online casino business under the Bodog brand in 2000. He cultivated a playboy image, always photographed surrounded by scantily dressed young women. The girls came from poorer countries such as the Philippines. The images conveyed a not-so-subtle message to his target market of susceptible young men: play my casinos, and you too can have all the chicks and live a lifestyle like mine. The grim reality was different. Online gambling was addictive; it led to financial problems, bankruptcies, ruined lives and, in the worst cases, suicide.

Like Rx Limited, Bodog was operating in a market shielded from respectable competition because it was probably illegal. And like Rx Limited, Bodog expanded very rapidly and generated a mountain of cash. In 2006, Ayre was named a billionaire by Forbes magazine and was pictured on the cover sitting on his motorcycle. It was his high point. Ayre's legal difficulties were mounting, and in 2012, he was formally indicted in the US for operating an illegal gambling operation and became a fugitive from justice.

Ayre was more astute than Le Roux at dealing with his legal problems. He had the foresight to establish his main business base in Antigua. With a population of less than 100,000, a billionaire could secure significant influence on that island. It helped that the Antiguan government had a strong interest in protecting its online gambling industry against US interference. Antigua gave Ayre a much-needed shield during his protracted battle against US legal overreach.

From a position of strength, Ayre's lawyers negotiated a sweetheart plea bargain deal. In 2017, he pleaded guilty to one criminal misdemeanour charge, and the other, more serious charges, were dropped. He was sentenced to a fine of $0.5 million and a year of unsupervised probation in Antigua. A more painful penalty was his agreement not to seek the return of $66 million that the US had seized from his accounts.

With the acquisition of Wright's insolvent companies, Ayre pivoted to cryptocurrency. It was a natural evolution. Cryptocurrency shares many of the characteristics of online gambling. Like gambling, crypto trading is an addictive activity that promises great riches. Most people lose money, while those who own the casino can make a fortune.

Could Le Roux have made his peace with the US in a similar way? On the face of it, it would have been much more challenging for a US prosecutor to make a case against Rx Limited. There was always that troubling issue of whether the company's operations were even illegal.

A fascinating question is whether Ayre knew Le Roux. They lived physically close to each other in Manila. They were both rich and owned online businesses, placing them in legal peril with the US. They both ran major call centre operations in Makati City. We would have expected them to have at least been acquainted. However, it is very unlikely that Le Roux would have told Ayre about Bitcoin. And we know Ayre only met Wright in 2015 through their mutual connection, Stefan Matthews. We can conclude that Ayre was not involved in the early years.

Le Roux's real criminal career started with a ship, the Captain Ufuk. He had become interested in the arms trade, establishing a company called Red, White & Blue Arms in Manilla. There was certainly a thriving market for guns in the Philippines. It was rife with violent crime and faced a guerrilla insurgency in its outlying districts. Red, White and Blue opened a retail outlet in the city, complete with a firing range. Le Roux always thought big and wanted to establish a large international arms supply business. But his first trial shipment for Red, White & Blue went disastrously wrong.

Le Roux had sent Bruce Jones, an amiable British sea captain from Bristol, to purchase an old cargo ship, the Ufuk, in Turkey. With a Georgian crew, Jones sailed the Ufuk to Indonesia, where the arms in crates were loaded under police supervision. Hunter joined the ship to provide protection, and Jones and his crew sailed the boat to the Philippines. But instead of putting into port, Le Roux ordered Jones to anchor in a remote location. Jones sensed that something was wrong. Previously, he had been employed by Le Roux to transport gold from Hong Kong to the Philippines. He did not want to get involved in anything illegal. So when a boat, the Mou Man Tai, unloaded most of the arms he left with it and was replaced by a new captain. The next day the Ufuk was raided by Philippine customs, who discovered the remnants of the arms shipment.

The Ufuk became a national scandal in the Philippines although, ironically, the arms were intended for a warlord allied to the government. Bruce Jones was ready to testify, and Le Roux's companies were exposed to unwanted attention. It was a major headache for Le Roux who had previously managed to stay under the radar. He even appeared in an indictment as "Johan a.k.a. John Paul Leraux", an illustration of the degree to which people in the Philippines knew him under his Dutch "Johan" identity.

The ship was a fiasco that absorbed Le Roux's time to extinguish the fires. He had to pay hefty bribes to make the case go away.

It is here that we find a significant coincidence. Remember that the Patoshi miner ran continuously except for a curious ten-day gap. Those ten days happen to correspond with the Ufuk episode.

Ratliff reports that the ship was boarded by customs officials on 19 Aug 2009 and the guns were taken off the previous day. Shannon gives the additional information that the arms were loaded up in Indonesia on 10 Aug. Patoshi was inoperative between 14 Aug 2009 22:37 and 24 Aug 2009 22:04. Around the time as he restarted the miner, Satoshi responded to an email from Malmi, his first communication for weeks. Most likely Patoshi had crashed and Satoshi either did not notice or was too busy to fix the issue.

Le Roux was certainly busy. The Ufuk was his first venture into illegal arms trade and became his greatest crisis to date. He would have been fully occupied dealing with the aftermath of the seizure from the 19 Aug. But his problems with the shipment had started before that. Was he too distracted to care that his automatic Bitcoin miner had crashed?

There was one loose end to the Ufuk affair. Bruce Jones would not stop talking and even gave an interview on television. Dave Smith told Le Roux that he could buy Jones' silence for 7 million Philippine Pesos, which Le Roux paid to Smith's prostitute girlfriend. Le Roux would claim not to have known what Smith was intending.

In Sep 2010, Bruce Jones left his house for lunch with his Filipina wife and toddler. As they were driving back, a motorbike drew alongside and then moved ahead to cut them off. A gunman dismounted and fired through the driver's window. Bruce Jones was hit several times and died. His wife took a bullet in the back but survived. The child was unhurt.

Smith told Le Roux that Jones would no longer be a problem, and Le Roux read in the newspapers what had happened. Le Roux had crossed another line. The programmer had become a murderer. There was no going back now—but then he was always moving forward.

Le Roux's next move was one of his most audacious—establishing a military base in war-torn Somalia. There are two accounts of his motivation.

In one version, he intended to establish a tuna fishing industry. This is less absurd than it may seem. Le Roux was always ready to exploit a natural resource, and Somalia's lawlessness gave an opportunity for an organisation that could provide security to the fishermen and processing plants.

The second version was that the tuna operation was a cover for Le Roux's real intentions. Somalia was outside the long reach of the US or any international agency. It was the ideal place to establish a supply base to ship arms worldwide. If Le Roux could establish an armed presence in Somalia, it could also serve as his personal refuge, where he could be immune from Western attempts to arrest him.

Most likely, both versions are true. Le Roux would never pass up on an opportunity and would have seen multiple uses for the Somalia base. He recruited a mercenary who went under the pseudonym Felix Klaussen or, as he was known in Le Roux's organisation, Jack Andresen. (Note the coincidence that he was given the same surname as Gavin Andresen.) Unlike many other mercenaries, Jack would not undertake murders or physical intimidation for Le Roux. His first job was to find and vet potential coastal properties for purchase in dangerous areas such as Papua New Guinea. He worked for Le Roux because he loved the beach life in the Philippines. But when Le Roux appointed him to go to Somalia and run the operation under the cover of a security company, Southern Ace, he agreed. Like others, he found it impossible to resist the adrenalin rush that Le Roux's projects provided.

There was no functioning central government in Somalia. Le Roux established his operation in Galmudug state, an area under pressure from the expanding Al-Shabaab militant Islamic group. If the operation achieved scale, he could shore up Galmudug against Al-Shabaab and win influence over the government. The idea was to establish a base, a compound, in the outer areas of the inland city of Galkayo, which had a functioning airport. Later, the operation would expand to the coast with its tuna industry. The logistics of this coastal move proved formidable, and it was eventually abandoned. Le Roux revealed to Jack his Plan B which may always have been his Plan A: the compound would become a distribution centre for his arms trading and illicit drugs operations.

Jack was typical of Le Roux's employees in one respect. Many were given grey zone assignments that they thought were legal, only to be sucked into something criminal. It was now clear to Jack that Le Roux's plans for Southern Ace were illegal, and he knew the Americans would not be happy. But he faced a more immediate threat than the US legal system. Somalia was one of the most dangerous areas of the world. Somalian piracy was at the forefront of press coverage. But the whole country was lawless. Any Westerner in Somalia was assumed to be working for the US government. Jack had to keep the contractors and experts Le Roux sent safe and recruited local fighters to provide security. At one point, Jack's small army fought a pitched battle with Al-Shabaab, who were attempting to capture the compound. When Jack asked Le Roux to provide funds for medical assistance for his injured fighters, Le Roux refused. He told Jack to dump them in the desert. The men were easily replaceable, so there was no point in wasting money on them. Jack managed to get them free treatment.

Perhaps the most extreme story about Le Roux was his attempt to take over a sovereign state. The state in question was the Seychelles Islands. Le Roux did indeed contemplate the possibility. Hunter investigated the prospect of taking over the government with a team of mercenaries. He concluded that as few as thirty men would be required if they struck when all the senior officials and army officers attended a sporting event. Le Roux dismissed the plan as unrealistic. Even if a coup succeeded, allied nations would rapidly dispatch forces to reclaim the islands.

Eventually, Le Roux abandoned Somalia. Establishing a viable base had been much more complex and expensive than Le Roux had anticipated. An arms depot like the one he envisaged would become a very attractive target for Al-Shabaab. Le Roux's Somalian activities were also attracting unwelcome attention. A 2011 UN report described the activities of Southern Ace in an appendix. It said the operations started in 2009, with the Al-Shabaab battle in Nov 2010. When the compound was abandoned, it was overrun by locals. Crucially, the report named the owner of Southern Ace as Paul Calder Le Roux.

The Somalian operation sowed the seed for Le Roux's eventual downfall. Jack left Le Roux's employ when he risked getting deep into illegal activities. He then heard from his former mercenary colleagues that Le Roux had placed him on the hit list. Le Roux wrongly believed that Jack had stolen three hundred thousand dollars from him. Jack was not foolish enough to return to the Philippines. He settled in Dubai with a new girlfriend. But every day, he feared for his life. He knew that the fanatically loyal Hunter could find him even in Dubai. And so Jack phoned a CIA number and left a message that he had information about Le Roux and his criminal activities. He expected an agent to call back quickly to debrief him and provide protection. However, he heard nothing more. The call had disappeared into the CIA bureaucracy. But it had been logged.

As well as arms, Le Roux was getting into the illicit drugs business. Le Roux developed his drug operations using two individuals; an Irishman, Phillip Shackles and Scott Stammers, a British national. They attempted to produce methamphetamine but could not get it to crystallise. So Le Roux secured a supply through a contact called Kelly. It came from North Korea via Asian triad gangs. Le Roux also hoped to buy a North Korean submarine but decided that the price of $5 million was too high for the vessel on offer.

Le Roux found it easier to source cocaine. He even bought some from corrupt Philippine law enforcement officials who were recycling seized drugs back to criminals. The quality, however, was poor. In 2012, he was successful in buying South American cocaine that he intended to sell to Asian markets. He planned to import the cocaine using a sailing yacht called the JeReVe. The cocaine was loaded at Peru and hidden in the ship's hull. The captain of the JeReVe was a Slovakian mobster who went by the name Ivan Vaclavic. He would sail the boat with a single crew member. The two men were to cross the Pacific to the Philippines, taking two months at sea.

The voyage of the JeReVe is an abiding nautical mystery. The ship was found in Nov 2012 beached on a shallow reef offshore the island of Tonga. Strapped to the helm was a partially decomposed body which had been worked over by seagulls. The corpse was identified as the crew mate, Milan Rindzak, from Slovakia. He had died from severe trauma to the head. There was no sign of Captain Vaclavic. The 200 kilos of cocaine, worth approximately 90 million dollars in street value, was safely stored within the hull.

There had been a severe storm leading up to the beaching, and the obvious explanation was that the captain had been washed overboard, with Rindzak killed by impact with the boat while trying to control it. But there was more than that to the mystery.

Ratliff reports that the DEA had placed a tracker on board the ship—they had been alerted by monitoring Le Roux's phone calls—but it had ceased transmitting before the storm. By this time, Le Roux was in custody, and the DEA asked him to call the ship by satellite phone. The captain had given him a mysterious message: "My car is broken down. You have to send a car for me." As "car" was code for the ship, Vaclavic's message meant there had been trouble before the storm struck. Evidently, he was stranded somewhere. Le Roux next contacted Vaclavic's wife, who told him that her husband had been captured by "the fish people", which must have meant pirates.

Theories abound. Perhaps Vaclavic had been captured by pirates who had also murdered Rindzak. But if so, why had Vaclavic not turned up? And why was the cocaine left on board the ship? Or perhaps it was Vaclavic who had murdered his crew mate. But why would Vaclavic leave Rindzak on the ship and abandon the cocaine? All he had to do was push the body overboard and sail on. No one needed to know that he had killed Rindzak.

There is a simpler explanation. Vaclavic and Rindzak found the DEA's tracking device and thought it had been placed on board by Le Roux. They disabled the device and hatched a plan to steal the cocaine. When Le Roux called on the satellite phone, Vaclavic told him the boat had "broken down". Vaclavic also told his wife the story of being captured by pirates. The intention was to make Le Roux think the boat had been lost at sea. Vaclavic and Rindzak would then sail JeReVe to another destination, sell the cocaine and dispose of the ship. But nature, or an act of God, intervened. There was a bad storm. Vaclavic was swept overboard, and Rindzak was killed at the helm when his head struck the boat. Did it happen like this? There is no proof, but it fits the facts better than any other theory.

We will return to the name "Solotshi". Although it is Congolese, it has an English meaning revealed by moving the "t" to the end:

Solotshi = Solo-shit

So, the name on the passport is actually Paul "Solo-shit" Calder Le Roux. It is a piece of self-deprecating humour. Le Roux was a computer geek who happened to be a master criminal. As a teenager, he was antisocial, and as an adult, he spent his days in front of a computer screen, hardly ever venturing outside. He ran his criminal empire solo, consulting no one, telling no one his plans, and communicating his orders mostly by phone or email.

As for the "shit", that is how everyone saw him. Le Roux's relationship with others was illustrated in the trial of the Rx Limited managers. Jon Wall was Le Roux's shipping manager and had worked closely with him for years. When asked to list Le Roux's friends, he was stumped. He could not think of a single name. Did Le Roux have any friends? Wall replied, "Not really":

Q: "Okay, do you know why?"
Wall: "I guess people didn't like him very much."
Q: "Why?"
Wall: "He was unpleasant to be around often."

In all of Le Roux's extensive operations employing thousands of people, no one could be called a close colleague, let alone a friend. He had no confidants. He kept his cards close to his chest. Le Roux micromanaged everything. There was no single person, let alone a management team, with whom he could discuss his plans. He gave orders and never consulted or asked for advice, which is perhaps why he made some very bad decisions.

It is hard to think of a more appropriate nickname for Paul Le Roux than "Solo-shit". That he put it on his passport shows the dark sense of humour that occasionally flickers across his emails.

In the same month, Aug 2008, that Le Roux was fixing on Solotshi, "Solo-shit", the Bitcoin creator had fixed on Satoshi Nakamoto. Solotshi is a genuine Congolese name, and Satoshi is a good Japanese name. But if Solotshi was chosen for its hidden English meaning, how about Satoshi?

Significantly, we can do the same trick of moving the "t" to the end:

Satoshi = Sao-shit

On the face of it, this does not mean much. “Sao” is “saint” in Portuguese, so this would be “Saint-shit”. It might be ironic, but why would Le Roux use “saint” in Portuguese? We will put this puzzle aside and look at the second name.

Nakamoto is a perfectly good Japanese name. But can you also see something in English in that name?

NINETEEN

BOND VILLAIN

Le Roux was the closest we have to a real-life Bond villain. A good Bond villain is much more than a mere criminal. Whereas most criminals are stupid, a Bond villain is highly intelligent. They have their own organisation, their own mercenary mini-army, and most of all, they think big. Le Roux made no secret of his ultimate goal to control a country, to be its king. He had in mind his native continent of Africa.

It was not an unrealistic ambition. There are always African countries teetering on the brink of chaos. If Le Roux could shore up a failing regime, he could be the puppet master behind the scenes and eventually the outright ruler. The two things a dictator most needs are arms and money. Le Roux set out to build an empire in illicit arms and illicit drugs. Arms would give him power, and drugs would give him money.

This ambition was behind his Somalian adventure. Had he been able to establish a base financed by his arms and drugs trade, he could have developed his military capabilities. The failure of the Somalian compound gave him a bitter lesson in the problems he had to overcome. But Le Roux never worked on one avenue alone. In the same pivotal year of 2009 that he began in Somalia, he sent intermediaries to contact the Iranian government.

Iran was under severe international sanctions and Le Roux saw a profit opportunity. The initial approach was to buy weapons. Soon, however, Le Roux began to explore the possibility of developing weapons for the Islamic Republic. Originally, Iran wanted to buy high-quality components for their missile program. Such components were subject to rigorous export restrictions. Le Roux proposed developing technologies for Iran using only unrestricted and readily available components. Iran agreed to test this concept with two projects; a new explosive based on unmonitored materials and a missile guidance system.

Le Roux assembled a team of engineers from Eastern Europe in a remote Philippines location where they could conduct tests without scrutiny. At the same time as the Iran work, his engineers were building two submarines: a 10-metre one-man submarine and a larger 30-metre submarine. These were intended for smuggling chemicals, components, and arms.

By late 2010, Le Roux had developed an explosive based partly on a coffee sweetener. Work had also progressed on designs for a missile guidance system, which were sent to the client. Iran was impressed with the explosive but not the missile system. Le Roux was rewarded with $5m of gold bars. The transfer was made offshore and received by Dave Smith.

Le Roux doubled down on the missile program. Iran had given him another project: to analyse the performance characteristics of the US Phoenix missile system. It would seem that Le Roux's team succeeded in this. Indeed, Iran developed its own missile comparable to Phoenix a few years later.

The most ambitious program was to develop a cruise missile with a similar specification to the US Tomahawk using only readily available components that were not subject to export restrictions. The crucial element was the guidance system. Le Roux proposed hacking GPS in mobile phones to remove controls that prohibited its usefulness at higher altitudes and high speeds. Iran was intrigued. They wanted Le Roux's engineering team to be based near Tehran, but Le Roux was not having that. Iran might be using him, but he was also using them. A cruise missile would find many customers beyond the Islamic Republic.

Le Roux recruited his engineers from eastern European countries such as Romania, where he had established his first group of Rx Limited programmers. The engineers were housed in an office in Manilla, and began working on a missile system. Le Roux told them a cover story about developing a drone. Meanwhile, he imported components for his missiles from the US, including Honeywell jet engines for testing purposes. Le Roux was careful to avoid restricted exports so as not to alert the US to his plans. He was still taking an enormous risk.

When the US discovered what he was up to, they were bound to go after him. But his biggest threat was Israel, the intended target of Iran's missiles. The Israeli intelligence agency Mossad has a way of dealing with those who imperil the security of its people. Their reach is legendary and they have no scruples about assassinating enemies. Le Roux had a call centre in Israel and employed a large number of Israelis in his operations, including ex-members of the IDF. He would have been an easy target. Remarkably, neither the US nor Israel knew about his dealings with Iran or his cruise missile operation.

Had Le Roux succeeded in developing a cruise missile, it would have added to the chaos of the world. Le Roux would have had bargaining power with some of the world's most despicable regimes. And it would have been a stepping stone to something greater, for Le Roux was always moving on. To take over a small African country was not an impossible long-term target. But Le Roux ran out of time. The US captured him while he was still on his way up.

The Iranian gold that Le Roux received for developing the new explosive was blood money in more ways than one. The head of Le Roux's mercenaries, Dave Smith, received the gold by offshore transfer from an Iranian-controlled vessel. He decided to keep it. Smith lived a luxurious lifestyle well beyond what his boss was paying him. He drove a Lamborghini and a Mercedes, while Le Roux made do with a Range Rover. But his greatest crime was buying a boat bigger than Le Roux's own yacht. It did not take a genius to work out that Smith had his hand in the till. A former girlfriend of Smith's told Le Roux that he had stolen the Iranian gold and was planning to kidnap and kill Le Roux so he could get the rest of his money.

Le Roux set out to recover the gold and deal with Smith. He hired a South African former policeman and contract killer, Marius Malherbe, aka "Marcus", to help him. Le Roux started with Herbert Chu, a friend of Smith, who had been involved with unloading and storing the guns from the Ufuk. Le Roux and Marcus lured Chu onto a boat at Le Roux's compound by claiming he needed to stay low in an island safe house. When the boat was out at sea, Le Roux stunned Chu with a taser and threw him into the water. As Chu attempted to stay afloat, Le Roux interrogated him. Chu said that it was another friend, Chito, who was involved in helping Smith with the gold. Once Le Roux got the information he wanted, Marcus shot and killed Chu. They tied his body to the boat's anchor and sunk it.

Dave Smith was the next victim. Le Roux fed him a story about having to bury $2 million of cash at his coastal property. He knew that Smith would not be able to resist the lure of the money. So Le Roux, Smith and Marcus went together to bury the safe with the notes. While Smith was digging a hole, Marcus shot him in the head execution style. It did not go well, and Marcus had to shoot him again, with Le Roux joining in when Smith was already dead. They took Smith's body out to sea in a small boat. As they had nothing else available, they used the outboard motor to sink the corpse. Then, they had to row all the way back. Le Roux reported the motor stolen in case the body was ever found.

The next target was Chito. He was lured to Le Roux's coastal property, forced onto a boat and taken out to sea. He told Le Roux that Smith had sold the gold. As Le Roux was about to stun him, Chito jumped into the sea to escape. A ferry boat was fast approaching, and they were concerned that someone would hear Chito's shouts, so Marcus shot him with a gun equipped with a silencer. He tied the body to the anchor and sank it.

Le Roux paid Marcus $25,000 for each murder. He only recovered around a quarter of a million dollars of the gold money. Hunter was promoted to take Smith's place as head of the mercenary unit. Le Roux gave him a list of further targets for assassination.

Le Roux had discovered that one of his most trusted employees, Del Rosario, the manager of Red, White & Blue, had also been stealing from him. Le Roux had used Del Rosario on sensitive assignments, including initial contact with Iran. But his employee had siphoned off millions of dollars by inflating supply invoices for Red, White and Blue and the price of real estate purchases. Such hidden "commissions" were a regular part of business in the Philippines. But Le Roux was infuriated and decided to kill Del Rosario. He made the mistake of telling Del Rosario this on the phone. His former manager fled, and so Le Roux's wrath fell instead on two pawns: Noemi Edillor and Catherine Lee.

The first target was Edillor, former purchasing manager for Red, White & Blue, who had inflated invoices for Del Rosario's scam. Le Roux instructed Hunter that she should be interrogated for information about del Rosario and then killed. Hunter employed two mercenaries, Chris DeMeer and a man called Daddy Mac for this job. Le Roux met the two of them and authorised the hit, which was carried out in Jun 2011. Using a ruse, they picked up Edillor in a van. Her body was found later by her husband in a pool of blood on the sidewalk near her home.

It was a professional killing, but the hitmen had not extracted any information from Edillor. They both quit afterwards, leaving Hunter to find a new kill squad. Le Roux was impatient—he had a long list of targets for assassination. In desperation, Hunter settled on two Americans, Adam Samia and Carl Stillwell. Both were amateurs without any military training. Samoa talked tough and had long shown an interest in "wet work", meaning murders. Dave Smith recruited him, but he was sent back home after getting into trouble with the Philippines police over a fight with a bar girl. Stillwell was Samia's close friend, business partner and wargame buddy in their home town of Roxboro, North Carolina. He owned a gun shop and claimed to be a former US Army Ranger but had never been anywhere near the military.

The two flew to the Philippines and were given Le Roux's list of targets. Top of the list was Dazl Silverio, a woman who worked for Rx Limited, but Samia and Stillwell could not find her. She had several houses, and one was two hundred miles from Manilla. They asked for another target and were given a "target package" consisting of photos and addresses for Catherine Lee and two others. Lee was a real estate agent Le Roux believed had inflated property prices with Del Rosario. The would-be assassins contacted her, posing as Canadians looking to make a house purchase. In the evenings, they studiously researched murder techniques on the internet.

Le Roux had given them use of a Toyota Innova van that belonged to Rx Limited. They arranged for Catherine Lee to accompany them in viewing some houses. Lee got into the back seat with Samia while Stillwell drove. Their instructions were to shoot her almost immediately and dump the body out of the car. But the two tough guys could not pluck up the courage to do the deed. So they drove around all day, visiting houses and enjoying themselves with Lee's pleasant company. Hunter was furious. They had left behind a trail of witnesses who had seen them with Lee.

They continued to delay while Lee accompanied them on other house viewings. Hunter was fast losing patience. Finally, on 12 Feb 2012, they asked Lee if they could view more expensive properties outside Manilla. Catherine Lee once more hopped into the van's back seat alongside Samia. Night was falling as they returned to Manila. Samia pulled out a gun. As Lee looked at him in shock, he shot her twice in the face, a bullet under each eye.

Samia and Stillwell had no idea how much blood could come from a body. Everything was soaked. Nor did they have any plan for disposing of Lee. So they drove around for hours, well into the night, with the murdered woman's corpse in the back of their van. Finally, they dumped her on a rubbish tip, where the body was found the following morning.

It was a messy, incompetent hit, yet they got away with it—for a while. The police circulated sketches of the two men seen with Lee, but they looked nothing like Samia and Stillwell. Le Roux had some employees retrieve the blood-splattered vehicle. He had it reupholstered and supervised the cleaning himself.

Samia and Stillwell were paid $35,000 each for the killing. Samia boasted online that it was easier to put down a person than a dog. Later, Stillwell would buy a Harley Davidson motorbike that he called "Blood Money". Surprisingly, Le Roux continued to employ the two. He needed them. He had a long list of people he wanted dead and no one else to execute them. His next target was Fitch Penalosa, a low-level employee of Rx Limited. The two surveilled Penalosa but seem to have lost their early enthusiasm for the hit business. Instead of carrying out the murder, they took a plane back to the US "to file their taxes". Hunter assured Le Roux that they would return, but they never did.

This was a severe hitch to Le Roux's assassination plans. He was forced to delay while Hunter rebuilt his murder team. In the future, Hunter would only employ trained professionals, but it was hard to find the right men. Unbeknownst to Hunter, Le Roux would be in custody by the time he was ready.

Le Roux's final murder was carried out by a mobster called John Nash. Dave Smith had given him hit jobs, but Nash was not able to deliver. He owed Le Roux money and now asked if any of the hits were still available. Le Roux gave him the name of Bruce Jones' lawyer, Joe Frank Zuniga, who Le Roux believed had cheated him in the Ufuk affair. Zuniga, who was actually a friend of Nash, disappeared in Jul 2012 after attending a meeting in the Subic Bay area with two men from the Ocean Adventure theme park. A witness reported seeing a man being hustled into a car that morning. One of the attendees at the meeting was the theme park's head of security—John Nash. Le Roux credited the bounty for Zuniga against Nash's debt.

In total, Le Roux has admitted to seven murders. All but one were people he believed, wrongly or rightly, had cheated him of money. The exception was Bruce Jones, who could not keep his mouth shut. Several others had close escapes, and there is no doubt more would have been victims if Hunter had been able to assemble a hit team before Le Roux's arrest. As for Hunter, he organised the hits but never carried any out. Although he was a sharpshooter, he always left others to pull the trigger, even if that meant relying on such idiots as Samia and Stillwell. Le Roux was less squeamish. He was involved in three of the murders. For him, it was all very personal.

The extreme criminality of Le Roux's actions from 2009 onwards is puzzling, but perhaps we see what was always there, lurking in the shadows. There is an abiding mystery around "the Brazilians". In late 2011 or early 2012, Le Roux relocated from the Philippines to Brazil. The reasons why he made this move are obscure. It seems that things were getting too hot for him in the Philippines. In one story, he had problems with local Chinese drug gangs because he was stepping on their turf. In another, politicians were growing less accommodating in suspending various police investigations into Le Roux. Or could it have had something to do with the Brazilians? Whatever the reason, he relocated to Rio de Janeiro.

Long before this move, Le Roux talked about the Brazilians. He said they had connections in places like Colombia and could call on some unpleasant people to enforce their business agreements. Le Roux told his people that his logging and gold operations were money laundering on behalf of the Brazilians. When the Hahn's stole the gold money, Le Roux stressed that the Brazilians would bring in people from South America to solve the problem. As the "problem" would include Le Roux, he was very keen that they did not lose any money.

In 2009, Moran Oz was told that Le Roux was opening a new call centre with some Brazilian partners. It was a ruse to get Oz on a boat with Dave Smith and two supposed Brazilians. Once out at sea, they threw Oz into the water, and Smith fired bullets around him. Le Roux believed that Oz was cheating him and wanted to teach him a lesson. The Brazilians were fake in this case, but it shows how Le Roux's mind was working.

The South Americans emerged again with the murder of Dave Smith. When Le Roux explained to a friend of Smith's in 2010 why he had to eliminate him, he said: "I have partners in Colombia. Dave was stealing from me. I don't take care of this, they take care of me." Le Roux never achieved his ambition of a partnership with Colombians, so this must mean the Brazilians who would call on their Colombian partners.

When the Minnesota DEA began investigating Le Roux's phone records in 2008, they found he was making many calls to several countries, including Brazil. However, unlike the other locations, Le Roux had no operations in Brazil. And we have that story about Hafner sourcing the pills for Atlas-Pharmacy from Brazil.

The Brazilians could explain Le Roux's surprising evolution into complete criminality. Perhaps he was immersed in this world of drugs and murder for hire from the very start. If a criminal cartel had been behind the pharmacy operation, Le Roux would have been chosen for his technical ability and for being a respectable front. He had no criminal record, a good CV and even security clearance from the British government. Who better to lead an operation that existed in the grey zone? So perhaps Le Roux started as a pawn. Even a Bond villain has to start somewhere.

The name "Nakamoto" includes the English abbreviation "aka"—"Also Known As". Is this a coincidence? Le Roux used many aliases. He told everyone involved in his criminal and "grey zone" activities to always use an alias. The abbreviation "aka" appeared in police notices about Le Roux. It would be typical for his sense of humour to embed "aka" in a name that was an alias.

Le Roux loves to play games with us. But perhaps "aka" was more than a game. At age thirty, Le Roux obtained his full birth certificate and discovered that he had been adopted. It "shattered his whole world". What shocked him most was that his biological mother had recorded his first name as "unknown". As he told a relative: "She could have put down any name, but she put unknown." Does this account for the importance he attached to his name in later life? He used many variations of his name as aliases. His pharmaceutical business went under the banner Rx Limited, supposedly meaning a prescription but also a play on the first and last letters of "Roux". He used Rx in the names of literally hundreds of pharmacy websites owned by Rx Limited.

So we might see the "aka" in his Bitcoin alias as an ironic comment on the "unknown" of his birth certificate. The baby with no name is now a man with many names.

We have decoded two parts of the name, and we can now see that "Satoshi Nakamoto" is:

Sao-shit N aka moto

There are obvious problems. The "N" does not fit, and we must discard it. Le Roux had to ensure that the Bitcoin creator's identity could not be penetrated. So he had to work within the constraints of a valid Japanese name. Coding a hidden English meaning is difficult with such a constraint and is bound to be imperfect. The "N" must go, which gives us:

sao-shit aka moto

On the face of it, this does not make much sense. Sao could be a "saint", but what about "moto"? That does not seem to mean anything.

Le Roux was clever. Putting your real name in an alias makes it easy to decipher. People will tend to look for things like anagrams. We must think outside the box. The two unknowns, "Sao" and "Moto", are like the clues in a cryptic crossword.

So what name, phrase or expression does "Sao" conjure up?

TWENTY

THE STING

In 2008, the notorious Russian arms dealer Viktor Bout was captured by a sting conducted by the Special Operations Division of the DEA. Bout has been called the Walmart of the international arms trade. He supplied arms to anyone who could pay, including insurgents, drug dealers and third world dictators. He would even work for Western governments, helping arm the groups they supported.

The DEA had been given wide powers under the Patriot Act, which criminalised the use of drug money from anywhere in the world to finance terrorism anywhere in the world. The Act was particularly severe on Surface to Air Missiles—SAMs—which could bring down US helicopters and passenger jets. It could be seen as outrageous overreach—yet another attempt by the US to impose its laws on the world. But if the US did not do it, then who would? International criminals like Bout and Le Roux knew how to live in the gaps between legal systems.

Bout had been caught by a DEA sting operation. It was a typical DEA takedown: Find or plant an informer within the target's organisation. Dangle a deal they can't refuse in front of their nose and get them to travel to a third country to conclude the deal. Choose a host country that has no qualms about the US extracting a foreign national. The supposed counterparty is a front established by DEA agents, and the target is arrested and put on a plane to the US.

The bait to entice Bout was a deal with FARC involving the supply of an enormous quantity of weapons, including hundreds of SAMs. The *Fuerzas Armadas das Revolucionarias de Colombia* (FARC) started as the armed wing of the Colombian Communist Party. They evolved into an insurgency that controlled significant territory and was responsible for much of Colombia's cocaine production. The US was trying to stop

FARC's drug production. Bout was told that the SAMs would be used to bring down US helicopters. All he had to do was travel to Bangkok to complete the deal. The DEA recorded his conversations with the supposed FARC operatives, and Thai police arrested Bout.

At this point, things went awry. Bout, a former Russian soldier, had strong connections with the Kremlin, and his extradition from Thailand was not straightforward. Many questioned whether the US was exceeding its proper jurisdiction. Sting operations always carried a whiff of "entrapment", where a person only committed a crime because law enforcement agents enticed him into it. Was Bout a criminal or just a businessman dealing in an unsavoury line of goods? Eventually, the case was decided in the DEA's favour, and Bout was extradited from Thailand in 2010. As FARC was listed as a terrorist organisation by the US and drew their financing from the drug trade, his conviction was a slam dunk. Bout was sentenced to twenty-five years in prison. He was released early in 2022 by the Biden administration in exchange for basketball player Brittney Griner, who had been detained in Russia for smuggling a small quantity of drugs in her baggage.

Le Roux intended to move into the space left by Bout's arrest. He was determined not to repeat Bout's mistakes. He told Jack, who ran the Somalia operation that it was important for the top man never to get personally involved in deals. Ironically, he would be caught in a similar sting operation to that which trapped Bout. And Jack would be the traitor.

Shannon had extraordinary access to the DEA team and from her book we get an insider view of the sting operation. Ratliff's research on Le Roux is impressive: he travelled the world talking to people who had known Le Roux. However, his contacts in the DEA were with the Minnesota branch regarding the Rx Limited case and his lack of an inside line on the sting is evident. Ratliff portrays the Minnesota team as the heroes who first drew attention to Rx Limited and Le Roux and built the case patiently for years. Then, at the last minute, the Special Operations Division snatches the case away from them, carries out the sting and makes the arrest. With Le Roux in custody, the Minnesota agents were frozen out. Shannon gives a very different perspective.

The DEA Special Operations Division had been alerted to Le Roux by the United Nations report on his activities in Somalia under the guise of his companies Southern Ace and La Plata Trading. Two agents, Cindric and Stouch, took on the case and ran with it. The two worked for the leader of the team, Lou Milione, who had started as a professional actor, a skill that came in useful in undercover work. Milione had a stellar record at the DEA. He had been involved in the takedown of arms dealer Monzer al-Kassar and was responsible for the Viktor Bout case. Now in charge of the Africa team, he recruited Stouch and then Cindric. The two had worked together at Baltimore and formed a formidable combination, perhaps because they were very different personalities. Stouch, the athlete, was totally focused on whatever target he had set himself. Cindric wandered everywhere and wanted to know everything. He would then put the pieces together to build a case that would stand up in court. By coincidence, Cindric's father had been a mathematician and distinguished cryptographer.

The three were looking for a new challenge when they came across Le Roux. As they delved deeper, they knew they were on the trail of a very special type of criminal. When you get to know them, most criminals are deeply boring individuals. They might be psychotic and violent, but that is it. And they are not the brightest of people. South American drug lords have a certain class, but even they were pretty superficial. Le Roux was different. He was highly intelligent, a cryptographer no less. The team joined the dots together: Somalia, arms dealing, drugs running. He was planning something big. Le Roux was on his way up, whereas Bout had been going down.

Cindric and Stouch had already begun to track Le Roux's African activities before they knew about the Minnesota investigation. They had received vital information from the Australian police who had been sent anonymous emails from someone who called himself Persian Cat. The emails documented Le Roux's murderous activities around the Ufuk and his bribery of Philippine officials. Persian Cat was clearly someone who had been in Le Roux's organisation. He could even give bank account numbers. Most sensationally, he alleged that Le Roux was involved in arms deals with the Iranians.

As the investigation was proceeding, Milione received a request originating with the Minnesota team to investigate a company called Rx

Limited and its boss, Paul Le Roux. The DEA Special Operations Division did not go after pill-pushing companies. These cases were complex and time-consuming, and it was virtually impossible to secure a conviction. They were not even under the jurisdiction of the DEA unless they involved controlled substances. The Rx Limited case had only been referred to the SOD because of its extraordinary size. A single Hong Kong bank account had received $276 million, and the total operation was believed to be much greater. Milione would still have rejected the case, except it seemed to be the same Paul Le Roux.

The Persian Cat information was fascinating but anonymous, and they had no way of contacting the source. (Most likely Persian Cat was Le Roux's former manager Del Rosario.) The DEA team needed a way into Le Roux's operations. Given his obsession with secrecy and using unbreakable encryption in his communications, this seemed impossible. But a lucky break came when a computer search by a CIA official discovered a logged call about Le Roux made a year earlier. The name and number of the caller were passed to the DEA. Cindric dialled and found himself talking to a man with a foreign accent. They had made contact with Jack, aka Felix Klaussen. Jack was living in Dubai with his new girlfriend, but was still in fear of Hunter's assassination squad.

Cindric and Stouch persuaded Jack to meet with them in Larnaca, Cyprus for a long private talk. They met at Dubai airport to take the plane together to Cyprus. Jack was tall, dark-haired, athletic and shaking with fear. He was constantly on the lookout for Hunter. Jack only began to relax in the Hilton in Cyprus. They debriefed him for two days, and he gave them everything he knew about Le Roux's operation. He described Le Roux as a narcissist and sociopath. No one even knew what Le Roux was thinking. He controlled everything himself.

The two agents suggested Jack should return to Le Roux. It was an extraordinary risk for Jack to take, but he was determined to bring down Le Roux and Hunter and live his new life without fear. He had proved in Somalia that he was no coward.

A few weeks later, he called Le Roux and asked for his old job back. Amazingly, Le Roux agreed but cut Jack's salary as a punishment for leaving. It was a big mistake for Le Roux to take back someone he had once put a hit on. A weak spot in Le Roux's character was underestimating others. He made the same mistake with Dave Smith and Del Rosario. Not all his employees were "monkeys": some could scheme and plan and act for themselves. Le Roux reemployed Jack to go around the world making deals. Jack was just too useful for Le Roux. He had no one else with Jack's combination of intelligence and toughness. But Jack had something Le Roux never allowed for—moral scruples. He wanted to work for the good guys, perhaps the real reason he took the enormous risk of returning to Le Roux's operation.

The DEA had their inside man and only needed an angle. They had to dangle some bait in front of Le Roux that would cause him to disregard his own rules and become personally involved. Everyone has their weak spots, something they want so badly that they become complicit in fooling themselves. Fraudsters, policemen and spies understand this. For some men it is money, for others women. For Le Roux, it was the Colombians.

Le Roux was always fascinated with the Colombian drug lords. He had been trying to make contact but had never secured a partnership. Did his interest go back to his mysterious Brazilian partners who had contacts in Colombia? If so, Le Roux wanted a direct relationship with Colombians of his own. A raid on Le Roux's operation in Hong Kong discovered a warehouse full of ammonium nitrate fertiliser for bomb-making, tens of millions of dollars in gold, and a handwritten note with directions to a meeting in Buenaventura, Colombia, with Luis Caicedo Velandia, the secretive head of one of the largest cocaine cartels with links to FARC.

Now, Jack dangled a potential connection via an Israeli businessman to a Colombian cartel that wanted to refine Cocaine in Liberia. Why Liberia? Working through Jack, the DEA had managed to get Le Roux turned on to the idea of Liberia as a potential venue for his operations. It was a useful flag of convenience for shipping and had good access to the Middle East and Europe. Law enforcement was weak, and officials were open to corruption. Le Roux didn't know that the DEA had developed a good relationship with the Liberian head of national security, who wanted to stamp out the narcotics trade.

Jack told Le Roux that the Colombians were planning to ship permanganato, half made cocaine, to Liberia where it would be fully processed. He also gave Le Roux a list of chemicals that the Colombians were trying to source. Cindric and Stouch were careful to leave Le Roux to join the dots. The chemicals showed him that the cartel was planning to manufacture meth. Le Roux took the bait. He came up with the idea of supplying the Colombians with his own formula, "cooks", and a clean room. In return, he would get a supply of cocaine and meth. He would also be able to tap into the Colombian's supposed network of corrupt Liberian officials to build his own base of operations in the country.

The relocation to Rio de Janeiro was an uncomfortable move for Le Roux. It was harder for him to bribe officials in Brazil, and he would not have anything like the influence he had enjoyed in the Philippines. Unbeknown to him, his phone calls were being monitored by Brazilian police and passed on to the Americans. However, extradition from Brazil was tricky. And Le Roux had a secret plan to prevent it entirely. He had assembled a new harem of Brazilian women and was busy trying to get at least one of them pregnant. The Brazilian police discovered that he was timing the women's visits to correspond to the fertile point in their periods. The father of a Brazilian child could not be extradited, and Le Roux succeeded in having at least one child by a Brazilian woman.

It was vital for the DEA team to get Le Roux to travel to Liberia. Fortunately for them, he was eager to check out the country. Jack met Le Roux in Rio to give the DEA recorded evidence. Although Le Roux had no hitmen in the country, this was potentially dangerous. Jack was unconcerned because he was now Le Roux's golden boy. In addition to the Colombian deal, he brought in another prospective deal, this time with the Shan State Army, a rebel group in Myanmar. They wanted an order for arms, including SAMs, intended for use against US and UN aircraft. Le Roux never questioned why Jack was suddenly so productive. The Shan deal was another DEA-contrived fiction. The sentence for supplying SAMs was twenty-five years.

Jack was wired up for the Rio meeting, which was held in Le Roux's apartment. He saw Le Roux's new child and a plump woman, presumably the child's mother. The two men settled down for a lengthy discussion. Le Roux showed an amazing command of detail for the proposed Liberian operation. At one point, the recording device began to peek out of Jack's sleeve. As Jack pushed it back in, Le Roux noticed. But Jack passed it off as a diving device. Le Roux was so set on the romance of the Liberian deal that he accepted this without comment. He was busy thinking about ways of using the Colombians to get opioid drugs into the US. By the end of the meeting, the DEA had a treasure trove of incrementing evidence against Le Roux. Now, all they needed was the man.

Cindric and Stouch were assembled in Monrovia, Liberia, along with Jack and a former Colombian drug trafficker who had done a plea bargain with the DEA. The team had already secured an expulsion order for Le Roux so they would not have to go through a tiresome extradition procedure. Everything was ready. But Le Roux kept delaying. Would he really come? Finally, on 25 Sep 2012, he flew into Monrovia from Rio with his girlfriend Cindy Cayanan

The two were put up in a deluxe room in the Palm Spring Resort hotel. It was about as luxurious as you could get in Liberia. Most importantly, it was walled and private. The DEA agents had the room next door and had planted a bug in Le Roux's room in a vase of flowers. They were not recording his conversations but simply wanted to ensure he did not run away. Shannon gives an unforgettable account of Le Roux having very loud sex with Cayanan on his last night of freedom. There can be no surer proof of the author's extraordinary access to the agents.

After breakfast, Le Roux met with Jack and told him about a new arms deal with the Iranians, who would supply him with just about anything, provided he could find some African general to front the deal. The only thing he could not get from Iran were SAMs. They would not sell SAMs because they could be used to bring down an airliner. Le Roux, though, was working on potential suppliers because he badly wanted the Shan State as a client. They were a source of opium that could be turned into the finest heroin.

The two of them went to the meeting with Diego, the supposed Colombian drug lord. He acted the part well, and they discussed the meth and cocaine deal. Le Roux could not help talking about arms deals and his murder of Dave Smith. Diego and Le Roux sealed the deal with a handshake. The DEA had everything they needed.

Back in his hotel room, Le Roux was working on his laptop and Cayanan relaxing when there was a knock on the door, "Room service". Cayanan answered, and Liberian National Security agents stormed into the room, shouting that Le Roux was under arrest. He made a dive for his computer, but Cindric got there first. Le Roux collapsed on the floor in passive resistance. The DEA agents struggled with him while the Liberian kept threatening to shoot him. When they had finally succeeded in cuffing Le Roux, he tried another tactic. He offered to bribe the Liberians with anything they wanted if they let him go. But this would never happen with the US agents around and the eyes of senior politicians on the case.

Cayanan was detained but released later. Le Roux was destined for the plane to the US and was determined not to get on it. He did everything he could to resist without fighting or hitting anyone. At the police station, he kept offering bribes, but there were no takers. He even apologised to Milione, "I really don't want to get on the plane." It took twelve men to carry the protesting but inert Le Roux to the van that would take him to the airport. He shouted out the whole time that he was being kidnapped. He had a point. There was no judge, no legal process, just a pre-signed order from the deputy president.

Eventually, they got Le Roux on the plane. Milione had threatened that nasty things would happen to him if he kept resisting. But Le Roux stopped as soon as he was on the plane because there was no point any more. He was heading to the USA. Strapped quietly into his seat opposite the agents, his marvellous brain got working on the problem. He saw how Jack had betrayed him. Le Roux had a weak hand, but he would play what cards he had.

Before the plane touched down, he was negotiating. He knew he had to give the agents something greater than himself, which was a problem because he was the top man. So, he offered them Iran and North Korea.

Le Roux's cooperation with the DEA was extraordinary. Besides his former wife, girlfriend and children, Le Roux betrayed everyone. Why did he do it? If it were to get a lenient sentence, he would be disappointed. The judge was astonished at the catalogue of his crimes and ignored the prosecution's request for a reduced sentence. Le Roux was given twenty-five years in prison. He is not due for release until 2037 and, even then, faces potential extradition to the Philippines for the seven murders he authorised.

What was Le Roux thinking about on that plane? His trump card was Bitcoin. It was a card he must never allow the DEA to glimpse, the one secret he would never tell. The DEA agents must never guess they had the famed Satoshi Nakamoto in custody.

We must consider the price action to understand Le Roux's actions regarding Bitcoin. There was no price for 2009 and much of 2010; Bitcoin was valueless. By the end of 2010, it was worth cents. Rationally, Le Roux was wasting his time on Bitcoin. However, in 2011, the first signs were showing that Satoshi's vision of the potential of Bitcoin had not been misplaced. The price peaked at over $30 before falling back. Patoshi's Bitcoin holdings would have been worth around $50 million at that peak, a significant sum even for Le Roux. A few months later, the price went back down to $2. At the time of Le Roux's arrest, the price again climbed and hovered around $12.

As he flew towards the US, Le Roux would have known that his criminal activities were over and his organisation was toast. Bank accounts and assets would be confiscated. Perhaps he could retain ownership of some gold if it was stashed somewhere that could be kept secret from the DEA. But many people in the Philippines and worldwide would search for that gold. He could secure some properties but would be left with a fraction of his former wealth overall.

That left Bitcoin. It was still not worth much, but the potential was real. Le Roux's Bitcoins were beyond anyone's reach. If he could keep possession of his keys, he could one day become the world's richest man, even in jail. It was a long shot, but it was all he had left. It was vital to have connections with the outside world. He sacrificed his people to get that connection.

Who would have known that Le Roux was Satoshi Nakamoto in late 2012? It is unlikely that Hal Finney ever knew, for Le Roux had no reason to tell him. The one person we can be sure of was Dave Kleiman, who had mined Bitcoins for Satoshi and knew his true identity. And it was Kleiman who was best placed to control Satoshi's Bitcoins. It helped that he was respectable, a former soldier and policeman no less, with good connections to the security establishment and the FBI. But Kleiman was sick and in hospital, which is where his friend Craig Wright comes in. We will see the evidence later that Wright also had a connection with Le Roux.

Le Roux got a message to the TrueCrypt team and must have also contacted Kleiman. Communication was very difficult, and it would have been little more than that he was in captivity and needed Kleiman's help. Remember that email header: Wright and Kleiman were discussing "Bond villains" in Oct 2012. Wright claimed that the two had planned the establishment of Coin-Exch as early as the end of 2012.

To get better communication with the outside world, Le Roux told the DEA almost everything about his criminal operations. And he may have built up Hunter's role as a dangerous assassin on the loose. Le Roux helped the DEA with a sting operation to capture Hunter and his kill team, as well as the drug runners. It would be the most complex operation ever conducted by the DEA. The fact that Le Roux was now in a US prison had to be kept secret from his own people. This was possible because Le Roux really did operate as "solo-shit". He gave his orders via the Internet or the phone, and his people rarely saw the boss-man in person. The sting was coordinated for 25 Sep 2013, precisely one year after Le Roux flew into Liberia. All news about Le Roux's capture was blanked out for that year and beyond.

On that September day, the DEA would make ten arrests on three continents. Le Roux had ordered Hunter to arrange the assassination of a DEA agent and his informer in Monrovia, Liberia. Hunter was in Thailand, where he briefed and sent off the two mercenaries he had selected for the job. Also in Thailand were five members of Le Roux's gang involved in trading North Korean Meth. Finally, two more of Hunter's mercenaries had been sent on a mission to Estonia. These were all dangerous people, and the arrests had to be timed simultaneously.

The thrilling story of this complex takedown is told in Shannon's book. But in truth, it was a minor sideshow. The individuals arrested were pawns, not kings. Hunter, whose nickname was Rambo, is presented as a huge potential threat. Shannon says that the agents were concerned that he might continue killing, either like a zombie obeying kill orders Le Roux had given him in the past or by working for another criminal. In her words, "If he were inclined he could break out in a one man killing spree." Which is absurd. Hunter never directly carried out any murder for Le Roux. The one time he was ordered to injure someone, he shot him in the hand. Hunter was an ex-soldier who obeyed orders and passed them on to his subordinates. But he never wanted to be personally involved. Had he known Le Roux was captured, he would have drifted off into another security job.

There is no doubt that Hunter got what he deserved. He organised murders, and his capture and long sentence were justice. But what about the other mercenaries? The two men assigned to kill the DEA agent were Tim Vamvakias, a former US military policeman, and Dennis Gogel, a German who had served in the armed forces. Vamvakias was a long-time member of Le Roux's mercenary squad, predating even Hunter. Gogel was much younger, still in his twenties. A keen bodybuilder, he looked like a heavily tattooed Greek god but had more muscle than brains. The only crime he had committed was conspiring to kill the DEA agent and his informer. And that was a purely imaginary crime concocted by the DEA.

Gogel was a despicable individual who said he was looking forward to carrying out the murders, but how can we be sure he would really have done it? He was only recruited for Hunter's kill squad months after Le Roux had been captured. The DEA operatives even reviewed his CV, which Hunter passed to Le Roux for approval. Gogel was only a would-be murderer because the DEA had set him up.

Samia and Stillwell were certainly guilty. Even though they knew of Le Roux's detention and Hunter's arrest in late 2013, they stayed put in Roxboro, convinced they had nothing to fear. They were justified in one respect: the US had no jurisdiction over the murder of Lee in the Philippines. And the Philippines police had so many homicides to deal with that they did not go to the trouble of issuing an extradition warrant. But the American government was not going to allow two of its citizens to get away with murder. The two had discussed plans for Lee's execution with Hunter while they were still in the US. This made them liable for conspiracy to commit homicide. They were indicted and arrested in Jul 2015, having had over eighteen months warning. Samia was called in by the police for a supposed routine gun license signing and arrested. As for Stillwell, he was pulled over by the local cops. In his trailer home, police found 159 guns and a digital memory card with shots of Catherine Lee's face and body covered in blood.

Hunter, Samia and Stillwell were all convicted of conspiracy to commit murder and murder-for-hire in 2018. Le Roux was the star prosecution witness.

We have seen that Satoshi Nakamoto carries the hidden meaning "sao-shit aka moto". So what does Sao mean other than the Portuguese for Saint?

There is, in fact, no English word beginning with "Sao". If you have thought of a name or expression with Sao in it, you have probably come up with "Sao Paulo", the largest city in Brazil.

Le Roux relocated to Brazil in 2012, but his mysterious connections with the country certainly go back further than that, probably starting as early as 2003 with Atlas Pharmacy. The idea that Sao Paulo, "Saint Paul", had the same name as himself would have appealed to the narcissistic element of Le Roux's personality.

Sao Paulo is our clue. It tells us that we must substitute the second part for the first:

Paul-shit aka moto

We are getting somewhere! "Paul-shit" is a close analogue to "Solo-shit", Solotshi, used in the passport. We are left with one final puzzle. What is the meaning of "moto"?

If we are correct with Sao Paulo, then "moto" should follow the same rule. We need a name, phrase, or expression with "moto" as the first part. It helps to know the tech scene that Le Roux was so familiar with in the 1990s and early 2000s.

TWENTY-ONE

A PERFECT MATCH

We can now compare Le Roux to our Satoshi profile. The evidence in this chapter cannot prove the case by itself. A perfect fit of profile does not guarantee that a person is Satoshi, but it suggests strongly that they are. We will take each item in turn.

1. Satoshi was a programmer with years of experience.

At the time Bitcoin launched, Le Roux had 15 years of professional programming experience. He had worked for clients in Britain, Australia, Hong Kong, and the US. Most significantly, he launched his own open source encryption product and handled numerous bug fixes and requests for support. He then did it all over again for SecurStar's proprietary products. In terms of his ability, Le Roux was always regarded as an exceptional programmer.

Undoubtedly, Le Roux had the expertise to write the Bitcoin software. He had already done everything that Satoshi would have to do for the Bitcoin launch. It was all second nature for him.

1a. Satoshi learnt his coding informally or by working for small outfits. He may have worked as a one-man-band.

Le Roux had minimal formal training. He started programming at fourteen on a Commodore 64 and was largely self-taught. He preferred solo development, as he showed in his open source software and products such as DCPP.

He mainly worked professionally as an independent contractor. He started his career with Barratt Edwards in the UK, a company with ten employees, and went back to them after returning from Australia. He spent brief spells at two other companies, Crypto-Solutions and SecurStar, both tiny.

2. Satoshi programmed in C++ on a Windows computer.

Le Roux was always a Windows programmer, first and foremost, and his language of choice was C++. His website for Software Professionals in 2000/1 puts Windows programming in C++ at the top of his expertise, followed by cryptography.

It is not that Le Roux could not program in other languages. He was familiar with Unix and Linux operating systems and was excellent at assembly language. His posts show a strong preference for Windows for pragmatic reasons: there were many more PCs in the world running Windows than any other operating system.

2 a. Satoshi most likely learnt his C++ programming when he was young.

Le Roux must have learnt C++ in the UK when he was around twenty. His formal South African programming certificate was in C and COBOL. However, a CV he placed online at age twenty-two puts his primary expertise as programming in C and C++ and shows more C++ projects (four) at Barrett Edward than either C or assembly language.

2 b. Satoshi was a painstaking coder who wrote dense, compact code. He may have worked close to the metal or on electronics products.

As well as C++, Le Roux specialised in writing assembly code. This involved working close to the metal, below the operating system level. He was certainly painstaking, spending months on a 500-byte driver for his encryption products. Hafner commented on how good Le Roux was at this and how it differentiated him from other programmers. It is unsurprising that a person skilled at writing byte-level code should write compact code that others find "insane."

And Le Roux worked on at least one electronics product. He posted that he was looking for investors to manufacture a device for phone encryption.

3. Satoshi was not an academic.

Le Roux would have found coding the program much easier than writing the paper. He did not have a college degree, just a programming certificate. Coding was second nature to him, but writing a white paper was something he would not have done before.

We should not underestimate the power of the autodidact. A self-taught person can bring a high level of creativity to a field, but their lack of formal training will also be apparent. Le Roux had read and studied academic papers and books on cryptography. He also aspired to be an author and had been working on his writing style. Satoshi did a good job on the paper, but there are abundant signs that he was self-taught, like Le Roux.

4. Satoshi was an expert in the practical application of cryptography but not an academic cryptographer.

There can be no contention that Le Roux meets this condition. His first encryption program, Caveo, was written in 1997, ten years before Bitcoin and evolved into the open source program E4M. In 2000, he began working for Crypto-Solutions in London, developing encryption programs for use by the UK government and military, which had some of the highest standards for computer security in the world. He would have liaised with GCHQ in this work and had the result audited by that agency.

After leaving Crypto-Solutions, he joined SecurStar as their chief technology officer and built another application, Drive Crypt Plus Pack, from scratch. It was well received by the experts on the very critical Usenet group. One expert said that Le Roux and Shaun Hollingworth were the best programmers he knew. While at SecurStar, Le Roux was also working on a device to encrypt phone calls.

After leaving SecurStar, Le Roux had the idea for what became TrueCrypt. He began working on a product, but as he was busy with Rx Limited, he passed it on to other programmers. TrueCrypt became the number-one disk encryption product for a decade. Under the bonnet, TrueCrypt was primarily E4M. Le Roux was involved in TrueCrypt, giving technical assistance, reviewing the code, and posting under other names, including Entropy.

Le Roux remained interested in cryptography during his Rx Limited period. The company used advanced cryptographic techniques on its servers, and Le Roux developed his own cryptographic protocols. He specified that his employees' laptops should be preloaded with TrueCrypt.

5. Satoshi was a revolutionary thinker with the viewpoint of a high-tech entrepreneur.

Throughout his career, Le Roux was full of ideas. But he did not just have ideas. He had the ability of a high-tech entrepreneur to find solutions to problems and put his ideas into action.

He showed his original approach in E4M and TrueCrypt. Hafner summed up his work for SecurStar: "He is one of the smartest and most consequential technical person [sic] I know. Many people have cool ideas, but Paul also knows or finds a way to transform those ideas into reality."

Le Roux's creative mind came to full, evil fruition in his criminal enterprises. He approached his grey zone or outright criminal enterprises like a high-tech entrepreneur. He continuously learnt by putting his ideas into practice—move fast and break things. Rx Limited is the proof of this ability. Many people operated pill operations, but none had the scale or financial success of Rx Limited. It employed thousands of people and made hundreds of millions of dollars in profit. But Le Roux was never satisfied. He was propelled forward by his intellectual curiosity and his need to excel. They led him to dark places.

Whether building a submarine to smuggle drugs or developing a new explosive using only unmonitored ingredients, Le Roux relished new technical challenges. His attempt to hack mobile phone systems to build a cruise missile control system is typical James Bond villain.

6. Satoshi was not a cypherpunk and was unfamiliar with most previous attempts at creating digital currencies.

Le Roux was not a cypherpunk and never belonged to the cryptography mailing list. His interest in cryptography arose from a privacy perspective, specifically its use in hard disk encryption and communications. He would have approached digital currency from the angle of his existing expertise in cryptography.

7. Satoshi was familiar with the gold market and likely a gold investor.

Le Roux grew up in a gold-mining town, and his father was a mining engineer. With the success of Rx Limited, he had a large amount of cash to invest. Gold was his favourite investment to the point of obsession. In addition to buying gold bars in Hong Kong, he would acquire gold from illicit producers in Africa and elsewhere. His gold investing would have been very successful because the first decade of the 2000s was an era of rapidly increasing gold prices.

Le Roux also faced the difficulties of owning gold. As a criminal who ran the risk of asset confiscation, he preferred keeping his gold in his stash houses guarded by mercenaries. The advantages of "digital gold" would have been very obvious to Le Roux.

8. Satoshi was a native speaker of British English but used a mix of British and American spellings.

Le Roux grew up in Zimbabwe and South Africa, two places that spoke British English. He then worked for years in England before moving to Australia, Hong Kong and then back to England, all of which spoke British English. However, Le Roux was very international in his outlook. He moved to the Philippines, which would have spoken US English, and was heavily involved in marketing to the US. It is no surprise that he picked up US spellings.

More than this, Le Roux loved to play games with his identity. After starting his criminal activities, he lost his South African accent and spoke in a strange combination of British and American English. He could assume a British, American, South African or Dutch persona. Le Roux loved the ambiguity this created. Those who worked with him were often doubtful of his true nationality.

9. Satoshi was a libertarian.

Le Roux was certainly a libertarian. He wrote against intrusive government surveillance on the E4M website:

> "Privacy is becoming harder to find in the world. Today everyone, everywhere is monitored all the time, by everything from the close circuit recording system at the local store, to digital imaging systems at banks, the subway, and street corners. Governments issue social security numbers, national insurance numbers, Medicare numbers, ID numbers, passport numbers, tax numbers, and so on. Some governments even go as far as fingerprinting citizens, as part of the numbering regime." (2 Feb 2001)

He developed E4M "to combat these intrusions, preserve your rights, and guarantee your freedoms into the information age and beyond." This was followed by his involvement in TrueCrypt, a tool of libertarians of both the left and right-wing varieties.

Not that Le Roux was ever left-wing. He was an Ayn Rand type of libertarian, resenting any constraint on his behaviour by governments, society or the establishment. He aimed to make as much money as possible by bending or breaking the rules.

10. Satoshi disliked the "copyleft" GPL license and was not against closed-source code.

Le Roux always hated the GPL license. He issued E4M under the more permissive BDS licence, which was also used for TrueCrypt 1.0. In numerous posts to the scramdisk group, he defended the use of closed-source software alongside open source. For example:

> "I think these people don't understand that open source applications=dead end as far as innovation is concerned. Yes there is great open source out there, Linux, all the cool GNU stuff, GNOME, KDE, OpenSSL, Apache, but most of these are written by hobbyist's and cannot/will not make the mainstream unless someone can find a business model to fit them around. Yes OpenSSL/Apache have made the big time thanks to people like IBM. But Apache uses the BSD style license (like E4M) which is more business friendly, and which allow their incorporation into IBM's closed source web offerings, it's difficult to see a viable business model emerging from the GNU GPL stuff."

When TrueCrypt 2.0 was issued under the GPL license, Le Roux called it "a work of piracy." Whoever controlled the release corrected this mistake the very next day with the issue of TrueCrypt 2.1, which reverted to the previous licence.

11. Satoshi was an established expert at hiding his identity, which suggests involvement in criminal activities.

Le Roux was an expert at hiding his identity. He used aliases throughout his business and a web of companies with proxies as officers and directors. As early as 2003, Le Roux recruited proxies and established impenetrable internet addresses. However, he made mistakes early on and left a large digital footprint with Rx Limited. He was not careful enough in the beginning. Hosting the E4M site on the same name servers as his pharmacy sites, for example, was a rookie mistake which gave investigators a thread to follow.

By 2008, Le Roux was very good at the game. After all, he practised this every single day. Le Roux also loved assuming a false identity to fool people. There is no doubt that Le Roux could have constructed the almost impenetrable Satoshi Nakamoto alias.

12. Satoshi had megalomaniac ambitions and was deceptive in advancing his plans.

Le Roux was a megalomanic whose ambitions were unlimited. Unlike most megalomaniacs, he would work at putting these ambitions into effect. Le Roux was the unusual type who could conceive the concept of a new world currency, solve the problems, develop the software, and patiently work online with a group of outsiders lurking in their basements to build momentum.

Le Roux was certainly deceptive. He would deceive people professionally and for sheer fun. Le Roux would never tell people more than he found useful. A favourite trick was to tell part of the truth in such a way as to lead people to a completely false idea. Much of what Satoshi said and did also fits this pattern. For example, he used special software to mine Bitcoin while keeping that significant fact hidden.

13. Satoshi was constantly busy with some other activity. In particular, he was doing something else that required all of his time and energy in the summer of 2009.

Le Roux was busy running Rx Limited while Satoshi was developing Bitcoin. In the summer of 2009, Le Roux began building his criminal empire. Things went badly wrong with the Captain Ufuk episode, which required all of his attention to put out the fires. In the same fateful year, 2009, he established his compound in Somalia and made contact with Iran.

14. Satoshi had an interest in online casinos.

Hafner introduced Le Roux to online casino operators in Costa Rica who could need a programmer. Whether he did anything with them or not, Le Roux was thinking of online casinos. He likely began some trial software development in 2002/3 when he had spare time before becoming fully engaged in Rx Limited. Le Roux later set up an online casino in Costa Rica called the Betting Machine.

15. Satoshi was not a US citizen.

Dave Kleiman described the person he was working with mining Bitcoin as a "foreign guy". This certainly fitted Le Roux, a citizen of South Africa and Australia who also spent time in Britain, Holland and the Philippines. Le Roux would hide his origins, and many people who knew him were unsure of where he came from. It is unsurprising that Kleiman should think of him as a foreigner rather than giving him a specific label such as South African, Australian or British.

16. Satoshi was rich (but not a super-rich billionaire) and owned multiple properties.

Kleiman told Ira that his "foreign guy" partner was rich but not super-rich (in the context of a conversation about Mark Zuckerberg). Le Roux was perhaps richer than Kleiman knew. Most of his wealth was invisible, tied up in gold. His inner circle would have known Le Roux's wealth came from Rx Limited. But Le Roux tried to avoid overt connections to that company because of its illegal activities. What was most visible was his yacht, his jet, and his properties. These were good, but certainly not in the billionaire class. The properties were the most significant sign of Le Roux's wealth because he had a worldwide portfolio. It is understandable that Kleiman would think of Le Roux as a property owner. Kleiman actually told Ira more about the rich foreign guy than just his properties, but unfortunately, Ira did not recall the whole conversation.

The fit of the two profiles is excellent, extending to the general and specific points. Le Roux combined his ability as a highly creative problem solver and the helicopter viewpoint of the high-tech entrepreneur with in-depth technical skills, including Windows C++ programming and cryptography. It is exactly the same combination as Satoshi. No other Satoshi candidate comes anywhere close to matching this skill set. On the basis of the profile alone, we can have a high level of confidence that Le Roux is Satoshi.

The fit is much better than for any other known candidate. Consider, for example, Nick Szabo. He certainly satisfies some of the criteria; he is an expert cryptographer, a revolutionary thinker and a libertarian. But he was also a cypherpunk. And he fails other tests. He has never worked as a professional programmer and did not, as far as I know, program in C++ on Windows. He has an academic and legal background and would have found the paper much easier to write than the software. He is a US citizen, not a "foreign guy", and has no connection to Britain or areas under British influence. He is neither a megalomaniac nor deceptive and certainly not a criminal who is expert at hiding his identity. Szabo is a nice guy.

It is easy to be blinded by the preconception that the inventor of Bitcoin must have been someone previously involved with cryptocurrencies.

Satoshi/Le Roux had almost no knowledge of previous attempts at crypto when he came up with the initial idea for Bitcoin. Many people find it hard to conceive of people like Le Roux who, without formal training, can absorb the knowledge to do the things they do—whether it is developing a new explosive or a new concept of money. We live in the bureaucratic age of the corporation and the university where everyone needs a few relevant degrees to do anything.

What about the few clues that Satoshi left us? Some support Le Roux as Satoshi, while others may appear contrary. The time zone information is confusing. Satoshi's code commits and his Malmi emails indicate UK time, including British Summer Time. Some early emails appear to show a time zone of +8 hrs corresponding to south east Asia including the Philippines, but this is the time zone of the AnonymousSpeech servers in Asia.

The two versions of the white paper contain metadata recording a time zone of -6 hrs (Apr 2009) and -7 hrs (Oct 2008). One is consistent with US Mountain Time allowing for daylight saving, the other with Pacific Time. One theory is that Satoshi moved from the West coast to the Mountain Time area. But it seems more likely that Satoshi was manipulating the time zone to represent California but made a mistake in the second version of the paper.

There is little doubt that Satoshi was deceiving us with these time zones. He seems unable to decide whether to use the UK or Western USA as his supposed location. Perhaps he intended us to think he was a Californian pretending to be British!

As Le Roux was running an international business, there is no reason why he should use local Philippines time on his computers. Rx Limited sold exclusively to the US from the main call centres located in Israel and the Philippines, so it would make good sense for Le Roux to operate his business on US time.

How about the timing of Satoshi's posts? There were virtually no emails to Malmi between 3 pm and 11 pm Philippines time, with the peak coming between 2 am and 3 am. These times correspond to a void between 11:00 pm and 6:00 am in the US, with a peak in the morning. Other studies point to the same consistent picture. Proof that Satoshi lived in the US and was not Le Roux?

Le Roux lived a nocturnal existence. Witness after witness said that they hardly ever saw him in daylight. He had a habit of waking his employees by phoning them in the middle of the night. So Le Roux was awake and active during Satoshi's peak email time. He must have taken his main sleep in the day, which is consistent with the afternoon void.

This nocturnal existence might seem odd, but it made good business sense, which is all that mattered to Le Roux. The best time for him to sleep was after lunch and through the afternoon. The Rx Limited call centre employees had to keep US time so the Philippines business would have been active from the evening, all through the night, and into the morning. Le Roux could communicate with his employees or connections in the US or South America any time from the evening to the next morning. The evening would also have been an excellent time to talk to Israel and Africa. And either the mornings or evenings were suitable for the Philippines or East Asia. Visits to his harem girls would have been most convenient in the evening, early night or dawn. This left the early morning hours as the prime time for Bitcoin work.

It is very different from Saint Satoshi, who lives on the West Coast, gets up early, works hard in the mornings, and is always tucked up in bed by 11:00 pm. Bad boy Satoshi sleeps in the afternoons after an unhealthy lunch of hamburgers and fries, deals with his criminal enterprises in the evenings, has exploitative sex, and then codes through the dark hours of the night.

How about that IP address in Jan 2009 indicating Covad Communications in Van Nuys, California? There are many ways Le Roux could have arranged this. He could have parked his private jet at the large General Aviation airport in Van Nuys while he launched Bitcoin. It might be objected that the criminal Le Roux would never have ventured into the US. However, Le Roux was not a criminal then and was not wanted by US law enforcement. Rx Limited was under investigation by the DEA team in Minneapolis but remained very active in the US, where it had employees and operated through a network of pharmacies. The DEA could not shut Rx Limited down directly but was using back routes such as the payment processes and shipment companies. The Minneapolis team were nowhere near getting an indictment against Le Roux personally, and this remained the case even in

2012. As for Le Roux's extreme criminal enterprises, they were all in the future.

However, Le Roux wouldn't have needed to go anywhere near California to operate K5 from Van Nuys. He was not some guy working in his basement. He had a network of hundreds of computers in the US. It would have been trivial for him to operate the software remotely on a computer run by an Rx Limited employee or pharmacy. Alternatively, he could have used a server in a server farm or perhaps Covad's remote VPN service for business users.

We know that Satoshi was deceptive. He appears to have planted clues pointing to California. Which means he must have been a long way from California.

Then there is the issue of Satoshi's double spacing between sentences Le Roux was a habitual single spacer. We have seen that Satoshi's excellent grammar and spelling indicate he used a grammar and spelling checker for every communication. He only had to set the spacing to double in his software, and single spacing would be automatically changed to double spacing. Satoshi's double spacing tells us nothing.

Turning to the positive evidence, Le Roux was in Holland until 2004, which would explain the time zone of +1 hour in some early Bitcoin modules. This is no small point. It is very hard to explain why other potential candidates would have this time zone unless we allow Satoshi to be multiple people.

Then there is that obscure 1999 paper on time-stamping that seems to have led Satoshi to Haber and Stornetta and the early concept of the blockchain. It was presented at the 20th Symposium on Information Theory in the Benelux, held in Belgium on 27-28 May 1999. Le Roux had moved to the Netherlands, part of Benelux, by 2001. It is not impossible he attended the 1999 conference as the wife he married that year had Dutch citizenship, and they were relocating to London around then. More likely, he could have become aware of the paper later through his Dutch connections.

Satoshi's instructions to Malmi about keeping accounts are reminiscent of Le Roux. He told Malmi to email him a simple account with the amount of each item and the balance. Le Roux would ask his people to record similar information in a spreadsheet. The amounts involved with Malmi would have been utterly insignificant to Le Roux, but he loved to micro-manage. He was mean with expenses and kept track of every dollar. And Satoshi wanted the money to last because he was taking a risk every time he sent funds to Malmi.

Then there is the matter of style. I have read and studied every Satoshi and Le Roux communication I could find, and they are very similar stylistically. They both think the same way. They are business-like and to the point. Their comments are always intelligent (I omit the twenty-two-year-old Le Roux's Australian posts here) and use the least number of words necessary to get their point across. They are both good communicators but not remotely flowery. They do not lose their temper and are usually helpful. At times, Le Roux is more aggressive, which is unsurprising as Satoshi is an act. Satoshi reads to me like Le Roux on his very best behaviour.

We also learn from Matthew Smith via Ratliff that Le Roux had an unexpected ambition to be an author. He worked hard at his writing style and published at least one travel piece. This would explain why Satoshi, who saw himself as a coder and as not being good with words, exhibited a surprisingly good writing style.

There are some coincidences in phraseology between the two. When Malmi suggests paying companies small amounts of money to use Bitcoin, Satoshi is dismissive:

> "$100-200 is chump change if they're a serious company, it would only make us sound small." (21 Jul 2010)

Le Roux used the same expression, "chump change" when threatening to kill his cousin Matthew Smith for taking $52,000. Ratliff had access to an online exchange in which Le Roux said it was "chump change...BUT it is a matter of honor".

Most significantly, they both like to use the phrase 'for the masses", and at one point Satoshi seems to refer obliquely to Le Roux's E4M—Encryption For the Masses. It was a favourite phrase of Le Roux's, and he used it in other contexts. For example, the email about his proposed phone encryption device was headed “voice encryption box (STU-III for the masses)”.

Satoshi’s most striking use of the phrase came in a discussion following the Bitcoin release:

> “Then strong encryption became available to the masses, and trust was no longer required. Data could be secured in a way that was physically impossible for others to access, no matter for what reason, no matter how good the excuse, no matter what. It’s time we had the same thing for money.” (P2P Foundation, 11 Feb 2009)

Here, Satoshi talks about how “strong encryption became available to the masses” which reads like an allusion to E4M. Specifically, he says that data would be “physically impossible for others to access” which must mean disk encryption, like Le Roux’s products. Satoshi sees Bitcoin as the next logical step following on from such encryption “for the masses”. Had Satoshi moved from disk and data encryption to cryptocurrencies?

This is not Satoshi’s only use of the phase. He uses it in a private email to Malmi:

> “I like his [NewLibertyStandard’s] approach to estimating the value based on electricity. It’s educational to see what explanations people adopt. They may help discover a simplified way of understanding it that makes it more accessible to the masses. Many complex concepts in the world have a simplistic explanation that satisfies 80% of people, and a complete explanation that satisfies the other 20% who see the flaws in the simplistic explanation.” (16 Oct 2009)

It can be argued that Le Roux was engaged in a massive criminal enterprise while Satoshi was dealing with software updates, addressing users’ issues in the forum, and fixing bugs. Surely, they cannot be the same person? And why would Satoshi get involved in arms dealing and drugs when he had confidence that Bitcoin would become something huge?

Such arguments are based on the false premise that Satoshi was always convinced that Bitcoin would be a success. In reality, he almost gave up on

Bitcoin in the summer of 2009, precisely when Le Roux's attention turned to his grand criminal schemes. We can see this expansion as triggered by the release of his intellectual energies from Bitcoin.

Le Roux would always progress multiple projects simultaneously. Throw mud at the wall and see what sticks. It is the method of the modern entrepreneur. We must remember that Satoshi left Bitcoin behind in 2011 to work on other things, so Satoshi certainly had more than one iron in the fire. Even in April 2011, he seemed to consider Bitcoin a relative failure. By that April, the Bitcoin price had increased to around $1. Satoshi's confirmed holdings would have been worth around $1 million, chump change to Le Roux. Ironically, the price surged after Satoshi's exit to over $30, which valued the Patoshi Bitcoins at $35 million, before falling to the $2-$6 region. It climbed again in late 2012 and was at around $12 when Le Roux was captured.

But would Le Roux, a crime lord, spend his time dealing with routine updates and bug fixes? This is not at all surprising. He had started programming at fourteen, around 1986, and had been a professional since 1992. Even at Rx Limited, Le Roux seems to have started by running the programming side, with others managing the call centres, only taking full control in about 2007. This was when he would have started working on Bitcoin. A leopard might be able to change its spots, but not overnight. Programming had been Le Roux's life, his vocation for the previous twenty-three years. Of course he would keep coding.

The main development work on Bitcoin took place in 2007-8, a relatively settled period for Le Roux. His activities concentrated on the online pharmacy business, which was well-established. Ratliff gives an account of Le Roux shortly after he moved to the Philippines. It comes from a potential recruit for the security side of his business. They expected to find a typical crime boss, but Le Roux was very different: a large, pale, overweight man sitting alone in a small room in front of a screen surrounded by computer servers. No one knew what he was working on, and no one dared ask.

After Le Roux's experience with the Captain Ufuk, it is unsurprising that Satoshi returned to coding in Oct 2009. His second period of involvement lasted a little more than a year. During this time, Le Roux was still based in the Philippines, dealing with the aftermath of the ship, the operation in

Somalia, developing arms for Iran and his burgeoning illegal drugs trade. Satoshi often said he was busy, and this was very much the impression of those who worked with him. He had a habit of being silent for a while and then dealing with a volume of emails all at once. Le Roux's employees were very familiar with this same pattern of behaviour. They would not hear from him for weeks or months, and then he would suddenly contact them with an urgent flurry of activity.

It is a chilling thought that Le Roux was embarking upon his first murders while Satoshi was posting to the group and politely assisting people with the Bitcoin software. Could this really have been the same man? There are hints that it was.

In a Bitcoin forum posting, Satoshi considered what to do if someone stole gold from you. It was a thought experiment he used to justify a proposed implementation of escrow accounts:

> "Imagine someone stole something from you. You can't get it back, but if you could, if you had a kill switch that could be remote triggered, would you do it?" (11 Aug 2010)

The language is disturbing, although Satoshi's "kill switch" meant killing the thing stolen, not the thief. He continued, "Imagine if gold turned to lead when stolen. If the thief gives it back, it turns to gold again."

Le Roux was struggling with the same problem of someone stealing his gold. Dave Smith was using Le Roux's gold to fund his exorbitant lifestyle. Le Roux's solution was his own "kill switch". He lured Smith to a beach to bury some cash and took along his hit man, Marcus. As Dave Smith dug the hole, Marcus shot him in the head. But the first shot did not kill Smith, and the gun jammed. Dave Smith lay on the ground screaming in fear and agony while a pack of feral dogs came to investigate. Le Roux drove the dogs away while Marcus attempted to un-jam his gun. The assassin then calmly put more bullets into Smith's head, silencing the screaming man forever. Le Roux was anything but calm. He picked up an automatic weapon and sprayed the dead man with bullets, almost hitting Marcus with his lack of control. It was around this time that Satoshi stopped posting to the forum. He would soon disappear for good.

TWENTY-TWO

SATOSHI NAKAMOTO

We are left with the puzzle of "moto". If we follow the pattern of "Sao", which leads us to "Sao Paulo" and hence "Paul", we need a name or expression starting with "moto". We will then take the second half. A UK motorway service station company operated under the brand Moto in 2008. It is unlikely to have been at the forefront of Le Roux's mind and has no second part. Another possibility is the sport of "motocross," which involves low-powered motorbikes on dirt tracks. This was essentially a British sport at the time without much wider international recognition. There are some obvious words starting with "moto", such as motorcycle, motorcar, etc… But these involve "motor" rather than "mo-to" and do not sound the same.

We are left with only one name starting with "Moto" which would have been widely familiar internationally in 2008—Motorola. In the 1980s and 90s, Motorola stood for mobile communications. It was the pioneering technological leader and offered the first mobile cell phone, a brick-like device installed mainly in cars. Like many other tech companies, its huge technological advantage leaked away. It was still the market leader in mobile phones until 1998, when Nokia upstaged it. The brand exists today as a shadow of its former self.

Le Roux started working in the 1990s when Motorola was one of the world's greatest tech companies, involved both in mobile communications and computers. By the 2000s, the company was in decline but still a household name with a significant market share. "Motorola" gives us the expression we are looking for. We must follow the same rule of substituting the second part for the first. This gives:

Paul-shit aka rola

We now need to switch around the two syllables of "ro-la":

> Paul-shit aka La Ro

It is not perfect, but Le Roux had to work within the confines of an authentic Japanese name. It was vital not to connect Satoshi Nakamoto to himself. He would have succeeded had Ratliff not uncovered that Solotshi passport.

We can summarise the steps in transforming Satoshi Nakamoto into Paul Le Roux:

> Satoshi Nakamoto

Move the "t":

> Sao-shit Nakamoto

"aka" = "also known as", discard the "N":

> Sao-shit aka moto

Substitute last for first from "Sao Paulo" and "Motorola":

> Paul-shit aka rola

Switch "rola" syllables:

> Paul-shit aka La Ro

For:

> Paul Le Roux.

The steps are not random. Moving the "t" comes from the Solotshi passport issued fifteen days before Satoshi first appeared. "Sao Paulo" and

"Motorola" are the only common expressions for an English speaker that start with Sao and Moto. In both cases, we substitute the last part for the first.

It is all very clever. Le Roux knows that people will look for things like anagrams, so no part of his name appears in Satoshi Nakamoto. Like a cryptic crossword, we have to use sao and moto to suggest something else, which leads us to the name.

Could it be chance? I have tried to torture numerous random names to give something indicating Paul Le Roux and never succeeded. There is no easy way of putting a probability on this arising by chance. It must be many thousands to one. Satoshi Nakamoto is Paul Le Roux.

TWENTY-THREE

BITCOIN ADDRESSES

If something is true, we would expect to find plentiful evidence for it. We have seen some of the evidence that Satoshi is Le Roux. It is time to hunt for more.

A good place to start is Satoshi's writings. He wrote a lot. Surely, he must have given himself away at least once? There are many hints, such as the tantalising clue of "encryption... available to the masses". But this can be explained in other ways. If Satoshi does mean E4M, he may have been a user of Le Roux's program rather than Le Roux himself.

When I read Satoshi, I constantly felt that Le Roux was standing behind him. But other people may have other opinions, and we need something definite.

A Satoshi email of 12 Jan 2009, three days after Bitcoin was launched, sent a tingle down my spine. The context is the very first transaction with Hal Finney. Satoshi sent Hal some Bitcoins, and Hal sent them back to him. This required Satoshi to give Finney an address. It started like this:

1NSwywA5...

All addresses at the time commenced with "1", but Satoshi's attention is drawn to what comes after:

> "I have just thought of something. Eventually there'll be some interest in brute force scanning Bitcoin addresses to find one with the first few characters customised to your name, kind of like getting a phone number that spells out something. Just by chance I have my initials."

Reading this, I thought, "I bet he did it!"

Satoshi noticed that the address he has given Finney starts with the two capital letters "NS," which are the initials of Satoshi Nakamoto. As they are reversed, this may have been an accident and not deliberate. But it gave him the idea of customising an address to a name. Later that day he carried out some experimental transactions moving one Bitcoin to an address and then on to another (transaction time 12 Jan 2009 07:16). The second address is interesting:

15NUwyBYrZcnUgTagsm1A7M2yL2GntpuaZ

Not how the "5" looks like an "S" which would make it his initials in the correct order. Most likely he has just looked down a list of addresses and chosen one that resembles "SN". However, the next step would be to write a program to produce customised addresses.

You can't just choose any address you want because the address is generated by an algorithm seeded by essentially random numbers. Instead, you have to generate a large list of random addresses. You then write a program to review the addresses and select any that reflect your name. Le Roux specifically says, "the first few characters customised to your name". He is not thinking of the entire name but something like a few initials. Le Roux would surely not be able to resist the temptation to do this. He loved to put his ideas into action.

We can be sure that Satoshi did write such a program. The miner M254 is Satoshi. We know this because the Bitcoins mined in block 360 were combined with Satoshi's Bitcoins from block 9. The Bitcoin mined by M254 miner were transferred to five addresses, two of which give evidence of customisation. M254 mined about one in 50 blocks, but on one occasion it mined two blocks, 501 and 506, in quick succession. On 16 Jan 2009, these two blocks were transferred into another address:

1**33**f**ZZ**z**NN**bHL5VSuCWrUkLW2oL9ZPJELbY

The two blocks make a doublet and the address features three doublets starting with two threes! How unusual is this pattern? The chance of an address starting with three doublets after the "1" are actually very low—1 in 195,000. In this case the doublets are spaced out by a "f" and a "z", but the pattern is still very clear and unusual. Satoshi would have had to generate something of the order of 100,000 addresses to find one such pattern. The particular characters 3, Z and N are unlikely to have any significance. If you wanted to find three doublets with specific characters you would have to generate of the order of 38 billion addresses.

It proves that Le Roux was playing with patterns in addresses just days after he mentioned the idea to Hal Finney. But did he generate addresses customise to his real name? He had already shown narcissism in his abundant use of "Rx", standing for "Roux", for pharmacy sites. He had referred to his own name cryptically through "Satoshi Nakamoto". But neither case is obvious. Le Roux enjoys flaunting his name in front of people, knowing they will not see the pattern

If Satoshi had customised an address to his real name, it could provide the elusive evidence tying him to Le Roux. Satoshi had many addresses, most of which were produced automatically and randomly by Bitcoin mining. But could there be one or more "vanity" addresses he had generated by his "brute force scanning"?

On 14 Apr 2009, Satoshi wrote an email to Mike Hearn in which he suggested a similar transaction to the one he had done with Hal Finney. If Hearn sent him some Bitcoin, Satoshi would return them with an additional Bitcoin. For this transaction, Satoshi also sent Hearn his Bitcoin address—it was different from the one he had used a few months earlier!

1PhUXucRd8FzQved2KGK3g1eKfTHPGjgFu

Note how this address starts:

1**P**h**UX**

All addresses started with "1" at this time, so the first character is a capital P, followed by a lowercase h and then a capital U and X. Here it was! Satoshi had written about the "first few characters customised to your name". The first three capitals indicate the first and last two letters of a name:

Paul Le Ro**ux**

Only the capital letters are important, and we must ignore the lowercase "h" in between. In Satoshi's first address, the N and S were both in capitals, so it would be consistent to indicate the name using capitals. The "h" visually divides the first letter from the last two.

Le Roux cannot make the address obvious. He should never have tried to customise an address at all. But it was given in a private email, and Le Roux probably never thought it would be kept, let alone published. Besides, who would think of looking at a name's first and last letters? It is the trick he had already used with Rx Limited.

Could it be coincidence? The probability that the first three capitals are three specific letters is 1 in 13,824. (Calculated as 1 in 24^3.) This does not allow for other combinations of letters, such as PLR, PRX, PAX, or LRX. Assuming ten such possibilities, the probability of a chance result is less than 1 in 1,000.

What makes this particularly significant is:

1. Satoshi signalled the idea of customising a name in advance
2. This is one of the rare times he gives another person a Bitcoin address.

From the address 1**P**h**UX**ucRd8, we can work out the pattern Le Roux is using:

1. Consider only the capitals; ignore everything else (such as the "h")
2. Use the first ("P") and last ("UX") pattern.
3. Start the address after the "1" with a significant capital ("P")

Let's look at the second example of a customised address from the miner M254 which can be definitely linked to Satoshi. As well as the doublet address 133fZZzNN, this miner used another customised address. On 24 Jan 2009 the miner transferred the final 10 M254 Bitcoins to address:

1PxeCXMZBuXHt4CqWWEQ7Kwgdyob9P955L

Using the rule of only looking at capital letters we have the sequence 1**P**xe**CX** standing for **P**aul **C**alder Le Rou**x**. Once again it ends in X and this time we have Le Roux's two initials.

The customisation is subtle so as not to give the game away. It is all a matter of probability. I decided to test this empirically. First, a few numbers. Although these two Satoshi addresses each used three capitals, the simplest case is two capital letters. The first character after the "1" must be a capital initial. The possibilities are "P" (Paul), "C" (Calder), "L" (Le) or "R" (Roux). As there are 58 possible characters in a Bitcoin address, the probability of the first character after the initial "1" being one of these four is 1 in 14.5. The second capital letter must be the "X" that ends Roux—it does not matter where it occurs in the address. The probability of that is 1 in 24. (Not 1 in 26 as might be expected because "I" and "O" were not used in the Bitcoin addresses.) Multiplying these two probabilities gives the probability of a two-letter combination arising randomly as 1 in 348. So even a two-letter combination is quite unlikely.

It would be significant to find such a two-letter combination in a particular address. But if we look at hundreds or thousands of addresses, we are going to find examples arising by chance. I tested this by going through many hundreds of random coinbase addresses. Every now and then, a two-letter combination such as "1C__X" for Calder Le Roux would appear, but as expected, these were rare. And I never saw a single three-letter combination.

This exercise had an unexpected consequence. My brain was trained to look for these patterns. So when I read an email with multiple combinations in a small list of Bitcoin addresses, it jumped out at me:

To: Craig S Wight
From: Dave Kleiman
Subject: Re: Scripted Money
Received: Tue, 8 Jan 2013
All is good.
I will arrange this as soon as possible Craig.

We will have one of the others do up the financials and accounts for Professor Rees.
Dave

Hi Dave,

I have the notes and code from Prof Rees. Have no idea why he did not publish all this. Some of the work is remarkable and when you add the code for automata… Astounding.

I do not think Prof Rees knows what we offered him, not really, but we made the deal so it stands. Can you make sure that the others in the trust (I will talk to Uyen) know to use 1LXc28hWx1t8np5sCAb2EaNFqPwqJCuERD to make light of Dr Rees's contribution. Use this as a marker for his part.

I have already set up the following for payment.

I will have Uyen arrange to transfer ownership formally to him at this rate of the day on the 30 Jun 2013. This way we pay Dave Rees the first 19,470.12 BTC for work he had done for the prior. You will get the details of this from the following addresses:

146mH689Kn1yPqvWzkZHa4EfhEyhYcTWML
153R6qYmjySgwaQpQjKv7pb2nEN5cg8RJq
1CXnCzV78381AJQtxHYihF7kzoixtoncKE
1PbXw8aP5PymdQUM29UyimhgnFykut5p2W
1P5759ZaUX44MHEsiJgWckBMNAEJbGu7SY
168Rc6wJdL4chWhEUQwyywi4sHub6erf2s
19dQ2xfrK5GEUahG6Cv87XDRK7W6YFnGFx

Make sure that trust does its part to get this to him and formally list it all. I know that we a long way from getting this out, but he needs to get rewarded for what he did and I do not know if he really cares. He seems a little…well he is not really focused on being paid so please make him or Joan take it no matter what!

1LXc28hWx1t8np5sCAb2EaNFqPwqJCuERD is recorded for Strassan, make sure this links to David.

Craig

The emails came from Craig Wright's computer and were submitted as evidence in the discovery phase of the Florida trial. There are eight Bitcoin addresses mentioned in this email, and three of them fit the pattern of addresses customised to Le Roux's name:

1LX… for **L**e Rou**x**
1CX… for **C**alder Le Rou**x**
1PbX… for **P**aul Le Rou**x**

The chance of any one arising at random is 1 in 348. The probability of at least three among eight addresses can be calculated from a binomial distribution as 1 in 6,515.

But that's not all. There is another address among the eight that strictly fails our criteria but which is highly significant. 1**P**5759**Z**a**UX**4… starts with a P but has a Z as the second capital letter. However, it contains the same pattern P…UX as the Satoshi address 1PhUX… The probability of this sequence arising in the first four capital letters in a random address is 1 in 3947. We have 8 addresses, so the probability that one of the eight has this sequence is around 1 in 500. Note also how this address comes next to the other two customised addresses in the list.

We have two improbabilities: one of 1 in 6,500 and another independent improbability of 1 in 500 arising from the same list of eight addresses. The chances of this arising at random are three million to one. We can rule out coincidence. These Bitcoin addresses have been customised to Le Roux's name using the same method Satoshi used.

The email purports to be an instruction given to Kleiman about transferring Bitcoins to the third man in the Satoshi team, Professor Rees, using a Bitcoin address that starts with 1LX_. The email is a forgery produced by Wright as fake evidence for the ATO. Wright only mentioned Rees as the third man after the professor's death in Aug 2013. And Wright's supposed trust was not even a figment of his imagination in Jan 2013. How, then, to explain the coincidence of these Le Roux addresses?

Wright tends to start his forgeries and flights of fantasy with something real. We know that Kleiman was working for Satoshi. So it is likely that Wright had access to something from Kleiman, perhaps an actual email from Satoshi to Kleiman outlining certain Bitcoin transactions. Wright has taken aspects of this into his forgery.

Wright says in the email that Uyen will transfer ownership of the Bitcoin to an address belonging to one of Wright's companies, Strassan, which was supposed to stand for Rees. A formal deed of assignment of Bitcoin from another of Wright's companies, Hotwire PreEmptive Intelligence, to Strassan was submitted at the trial. It is dated 30 Jun 2013 and signed by Wright's intern, Uyen Nguyen. The three addresses customised to Le Roux's name come first in this assignment. The list of addresses matches the email except that the address 19dQ2x… is repeated three times and there are two new addresses 1JzzLX… and 1M7ccm. The assignment has obviously been compiled from a blockchain transaction:

13 Aug 2013 18:12

Inputs	
1JzzLXxuwn45S9HvBqAhkhWa3GhyG3zm64	0.35
168Rc6wJdL4chWhEUQwyywi4sHub6erf2s	2198
19dQ2xfrK5GEUahG6Cv87XDRK7W6YFnGFx	9999
1P5759ZaUX44MHEsiJgWckBMNAEJbGu7SY	1418
1PbXw8aP5PymdQUM29UyimhgnFykut5p2W	723
1M7ccmVnWpvKa41RGf7H8wS6thy5Tt3bad	4943
1CXnCzV78381AJQtxHYihF7kzoixtoncKE	4971
153R6qYmjySgwaQpQjKv7pb2nEN5cg8RJq	4915
19dQ2xfrK5GEUahG6Cv87XDRK7W6YFnGFx	1
19dQ2xfrK5GEUahG6Cv87XDRK7W6YFnGFx	417.569
146mH689Kn1yPqvWzkZHa4EfhEyhYcTWML	4927
Outputs	
1LXc28hWx1t8np5sCAb2EaNFqPwqJCuERD	34,512.819
13ts4NovccXoQxzrn9syxtM5kgR5XDFyJ2	0.1

Also relevant is a transaction that took place 15 minutes earlier:

13 Aug 2013 17:57

Inputs	
15LyEDxzU9r4P5xRkFque1vcVG8NwJq4Xh	0.36

Outputs

1JzzLXxuwn45S9HvBqAhkhWa3GhyG3zm64	0.35
1LXc28hWx1t8np5sCAb2EaNFqPwqJCuERD	0.01

This transaction is the first time that the 1LXc28… address is used. It appears alongside a second new address, 1JzzLX... that also features an "LX". This transaction must have been a trial for the primary transaction minutes later because the 0.35 in 1JzzLX... was transferred to 1LXc28… and the address was not used again. A trial would make sense, as 34,512 was moved to 1LXc28 in the primary transaction.

What are we to make of the "J" in 1JzzLX? Le Roux loved to assume a Dutch identity for which he used the name Johan Le Roux. Many employees in the Philippines knew him as Johan. So:

1JzzLX is **J**ohan **L**e Rou**x**.

The email deviates from the actual transaction in several details. Most significant is the amount of 19,470.12 Bitcoins, which does not correspond with the actual transaction. Nor can you get this number by summing some selection of addresses used in the transaction.

It is possible that Wright has edited a genuine email from Kleiman. The date of 8 Jan 2013 is shortly before Kleiman's first leave of absence from the hospital and his subsequent burst of activity. What is the origin of the Bitcoin in the 1LXc28 transaction? The Bitcoin in six addresses can be traced back to a most unusual transaction that took place on 27 Jan 2011. That day 400,000 Bitcoins were assembled into single address:

1AYtnRppWM7tWQaVLpm7TvcHKrjKxgCRvX

This was by far the largest accumulation of Bitcoin in one address up to that time. Later that day the 400,000 was divided into two groups of 250,000 and 150,000. The Bitcoin in the 1LXc28 transaction can be traced back to this second group which used the address starting 1LYJHS. These Bitcoin were soon moved to another address:

1NMDHMGjJBZjNfAEjvASPjUvT5kwFsHe9U

Then on the 1-2 Mar 2011 the 150,000 Bitcoin were divided into 34 slices each for a different number of Bitcoin between two and five thousand. The order of the slicing divides the Bitcoin into three groups:

- 3 slices created 1 Mar 2011 and not moved until 5/6 Feb 2014.
- 23 slices created 2 Mar 2011 and not moved until 21 Dec 2013.
- 7 slices created 2 Mar 2011 and moved at various times. This group of 32,423 Bitcoins includes the Bitcoin moved into 1LXc28 and 10,000+ Bitcoin moved into MtGox.

Many of the Bitcoins from this last group ended up in 1LXc28:

1M7ccm	4943
1CXnCz	4971
153R6q	4915
1PbXw8	723 (from 1JNxaj)
146mH6	3172 (from 1DmKhz)
1P5759	1418 (from 1Gmryy and other inputs)
Total	20,142

To return to the origin of these Bitcoins, where did the 400,000 in 1AYtnR come from? It was MtGox. Such a large amount was consolidated in a single address because of the sale of the exchange. In Jan 2011, Jed McCaleb was desperate to move on from MtGox. He had founded the exchange just six months previously in Jul 2010 "as a lark". It had grown amazingly fast and McCaleb was beginning to understand the risks and problems of running an exchange. So he approached Mark Karpeles, a French contract programmer living in Japan who was working on a MtGox project. McCaleb offered Karpeles generous terms to take the exchange off his hands, asking for just an earn out from future profits and a small minority share.

Karpeles was a terrible choice. He was completely out of his depth managing an exchange, never implemented even the most basic of financial controls, and lost most of MtGox's Bitcoins to hacks which went on for years without his noticing. The MtGox users only got back some of their Bitcoins because Karpeles forgot about a cold wallet containing 200,000 Bitcoins which survived untouched.

Karpeles wasn't solely to blame though. The first hack took place on 1 Mar 2011 during the handover period when a hacker drained the hot wallets of 79,956 Bitcoin into the notorious 1Feex address which was later claimed by Craig Wright.

McCaleb did not want to give all the Bitcoins to Karpeles straight away. So a few weeks before the hack he consolidated most of the cold wallets into 1AYtnR to give that huge total of 400,000. He then split these Bitcoins into two. The first amount for 250,000 he kept under his control. 165,000 was his own Bitcoin and the rest was paid back into the exchange later. The other amount, of 150,000, was set aside because it belonged to a large client. It is the source of the Bitcoins that eventually found their way into 1LXc28.

The 150,000 was first moved into the address 1LYJHS and then onto 1NMDHM, which must have been the transfer to the client. The client waited a month before processing the Bitcoin, starting just a few hours after the 1feex hack.

What was the origins of the 150,000? It could have been purchased on MtGox—the exchange accepted Liberty Reserve. But as the supply of Bitcoin was very limited, it is more likely that the Bitcoin were moved in and out of the exchange to confuse the trail. Looking at all the sources of the 1LXc28 Bitcoins shows evidence of mining activity. These sources are:

- 150,000 Bitcoin from MtGox.
- 1,755 Bitcoins added in 4 Mar 2011 from a total of several thousand Bitcoins mined between the end of Sep 2010 and Feb 2011.
- 2,200 Bitcoins from address, 168Rc6 which consolidated 44 mined blocks between 24 May 2011 and 26 Nov 2011.
- 10,417 Bitcoins from address 19dQ2x. The source of these Bitcoins is complex but certainly includes some additional Bitcoins from MtGox.

We can see here the evidence of mining between end of Sep 2010 up until 26 Nov 2011. A further four blocks, mined and moved to an address, 1D7vvy, connected to 1LXc28, takes the mining up 20 Mar 2012.

The 1,755 Bitcoins mined at the end of 2010 and beginning of 2011 were part of a much larger total, of which 4,624 ended up in another address starting with LX:

1**LX**7**SUPB**WDQ7MshgdVhwK3iDNwhLszMH1A

(Does SUPB = superb?)

Further evidence of mining comes from 7,000 Bitcoins moved into 1NMDHM, the address which held the 150,000 Bitcoins, and out again in five matching transactions. Digging down into the source of the Bitcoin reveals a web of complexity which is the consolidation of a large mining operation, only a small part of which found its way in and out of 1NMDHM. However, we can't be sure whether the Bitcoin was mined by the owner of the 150,000 or purchased from a miner.

The obvious interpretation is that the 150,000 represents Bitcoin mined up to Sep 2010 by a mining operation which continued, with ever diminishing results, until early 2012. It was far easier to mine Bitcoin in late 2009 and early 2010 when the difficulty level was low, and substantial totals could have been achieved in that period.

How many Bitcoins did the owner of 1LXc28 control? We can identify c.180,000. The question is whether this is the total or the tip of the iceberg.

Let us return to the mystery of how a group of addresses customised to Paul Le Roux's name came together in a transaction and the Wright email. Let's consider when these addresses were first used:

1CXnCz	2 Mar 2011
1P5759ZaUX	10 Jun 2011
1PbXw8	4 Jun 2013
1JzzLX	13 Aug 2013
1LXc28	13 Aug 2013

How to account for this odd pattern of addresses created over more than two years and mixed in with non-customised addresses? We know that in early 2009, Satoshi generated a large number of random addresses and wrote a program to extract addresses customised to his name. He kept it subtle and non-obvious, looking only at capitals and using the last and first pattern. He used at least two of these addresses under his Satoshi identity, but would have quickly seen he was taking an unnecessary security risk. However, he must have kept the customised addresses. They became mixed in with some non-customised addresses and shared with whoever was managing his non-Patoshi Bitcoin.

The person carrying out the slicing operation must have moved to this list of addresses for the final slices, and the same list was used for subsequent operations on these Bitcoins. Another possibility is that the 150,000 was being divided between different people, in which case the person owning 1LXc28 only had control of c.32,000 in the last slices. More likely it all belonged to the same owner but was managed in different silos.

Even if the 1LXc28 addresses were customised to Le Roux's name, can we be sure that Wright did not come across the transaction by chance? Wright has claimed ownership of dozens of addresses containing a total of 650,000 Bitcoins. Wright has never given cryptographic proof of ownership of any of these addresses and has been proven not to be the owner of several. Wright must have obtained his information from a rich list of addresses and from the blockchain. Most people who have looked into Wright's Faketoshi act have come to believe that he had no real connection to Satoshi and derived all his information from such publicly available sources. Did he come across the 1LXc28 transaction in the same way?

The proof that he had non-public information about 1LXc28 comes from that total in the email: "This way we pay Dave Rees the first 19,470.12 BTC for work he had done…". If Wright had taken the transaction from the blockchain he would have given the correct total of 34,512. He even quoted the correct amount for 1LXc28 in an Oct 2013 email to the ATO. So why did he give a different total in the Kleiman email? Appendix B shows that the figure Wright quoted does make sense. It is the sum of the last four slices of the 150,000 together with additionally mined Bitcoin from the end of 2010 and beginning of 2011. By rounding some figures up and others down we can get to the precise figure of 19,470.12 But this total was only valid between 2 Mar and 4 Mar 2011.

It seems that the 19,470.12 was allocated to a Satoshi silo after the slicing operation on 2 Mar 2011. The 1LXc28 transaction was based on this silo but some changes were made and Bitcoins mined or purchased later were added in. The address 1M7ccm that was omitted from Wright's email but included in the transaction, is one of the changes that were made.

The obvious source of Wright's information is through Kleiman. There is nothing surprising about Kleiman mining Bitcoin. What is unusual is Ira's story that he was mining for the rich foreign guy who can only be Satoshi, for no one else was interested in acquiring Bitcoins at that time. This points to Kleiman mining on behalf of Satoshi no later than Nov 2009.

Was he the only one? Another miner with a strange story is Michael Mancil Brown from Tennessee who went under the name knightmb. He appeared in the forum from nowhere on 12 Jul 2010 but was clearly already an expert miner having started in early 2010. He contributed hundreds of posts over several weeks before disappearing again in August, although he reappeared a few times years later. His main contribution was testing the new faster clients that were being developed and he had several interactions with Satoshi who recommended his version of the blockchain for resuming after the overflow bug.

His main claim to fame was on a thread where posters were revealing how much Bitcoin they owned. He posted a partially blanked out screen shot showing 371,067.36 Bitcoins. Later knightmb explained that he mined his Bitcoin through a server farm:

> "In case anyone was curious, the servers were made up of about 330 64bit 8-core Xeon processor systems that all ranged from Linux to Windows along with another 20 special systems that ranged from 8 to 64 core systems running various flavors and windows and Linux. After the end of this month, it will just fall back to a half dozen 8-core servers to keep the daemons running for testing and keeping the BitCoin network going of course." (28 Jul 2010)

So he had 350 servers running over 3,000 cores, a massive setup for the time. But is he telling the truth? His story kept changing. He claimed to have bought his computer power from Amazon in the cloud, but the numbers he quoted would imply a mining cost of up to a million dollars when Bitcoin was worth almost nothing. He then claimed that Amazon was too expensive and he had rented the servers from different server farms on the cheap. Later he reverted to his Amazon story.

Even stranger, knightmb claimed to be mining on behalf of some mysterious investors linked to a bank who wanted the Bitcoin to back a card they were planning. The card would allow Bitcoin to be used in places like Walmart. But no bank would have invested in such an idea in early 2010 when Bitcoin was unknown outside a tiny group of geeks. When he briefly returned to the forum the next year he gave more details:

> "So they invested about $12k to either generated or buy Bitcoins for the first part of 2010. My part was to simply compile some versions of Bitcoin that could run on the Amazon cloud service. They rented a ton of CPU time and basically generated BTC non-stop for a while." (16 May 2011)

The budget of $12k is ridiculously low for his claimed mining setup. And as well as mining Bitcoin he claimed to have purchased Bitcoin from other forum members. However, the project had been put in hibernation and the investors allowed him to buy the Bitcoins for just $5,000 in May 2011, even though they would have been worth millions of dollars by that date. And what happened to those Bitcoins? They evaporated into thin air. Michael Brown said he had given them away including "a large portion … to WikiLeaks".

By 2012, Brown was desperate for money. He came up with a hair-brained scheme to blackmail the presidential candidate Mitt Romney over his tax returns. Using the name of the Austin Powers character Dr Evil, he claimed to have hacked into PWC's office and obtained copies of Romney's past tax returns. He supposedly sent copies of the encrypted returns on flash drives to the Republicans and Democrats and invited them to post a million dollars in Bitcoin to one of two addresses: one address to release the private key, and one address to destroy it. It was quickly determined by PWC that no hack had taken place. The Secret Service examined the flash drives and found the username "knightmb" along with Brown's wife's name "Katheryn" and a picture of a neighbour's two cats. He was raided by the secret service on 14 Sep 2012 and jailed for four years for blackmail in 2014.

Michael Brown is clearly a liar. Take that screenshot showing a balance of 371,067.36 Bitcoins. This was forged because no single address had anything like that number of Bitcoins at that time. The story about buying the Bitcoin for $5k is absurd as is the story of how he lost those same Bitcoins—WikiLeaks never received more than a few thousand Bitcoins in total donations. However, knightmb was certainly mining a significant quantity in 2010. An address 1LUPDXYf9XD9Ee1AqCuM3gZCA3ZMKgTcgw which can be linked to him and probably belonged to him received a total of 110,000 Bitcoins. At least 36,000 found their way into that 400,000 MtGox address 1AYtnR.

The most interesting aspect of his story is that he was mining for someone else. He never told anyone who these investors were, nor the identity of the bank. There was no reason for knightmb to have made this story up. It ties in with Ira Kleiman's account of Dave mining for the "rich foreign guy" just a few months earlier than knightmb's own mining in 2010. The only person interested in early 2010 in acquiring a large volume of Bitcoin was Satoshi who needed to replace his Patoshi output. And knightmb claimed to know a lot about Satoshi:

> "Back in 2009 when Satoshi still did personal e-mails to members, it was pretty easy with a tracking pixel to pinpoint where he was at the time even though he used a foreign e-mail server. His Mac was using a plain vanilla e-mail client that would load the pixels from the same place for every message he read from me, so if the search is where was he at the time years ago, I can shed some light on that." (14 Mar 2013)

> "I have many communications with him from years ago that only he would know about and has never been made public. If someone came

> forward claiming to be him, I could easily verify since I know what PC he was using, what part of the world he was living in, etc. before he started to actually try to be anonymous on the net. I can't say if he is alive or dead right now, but he could easily verify being alive at least with me because he would still know how to contact me." (28 Oct 2013)

Can we trust anything knightmb says? Did he really put a pixel in his emails? It seems unlikely that such a simple trick would get past Satoshi's defences, but who knows. Michael Brown, unlike Kleiman, does not appear to have known Satoshi's identity. But he is a good candidate to be another Satoshi miner.

It may be helpful to summarise the important points in this chapter:

- Satoshi told Hal Finney about his idea for customising the first few letters of an address to indicate a name. This involved generating a large number of addresses and using a program to pick out addresses of interest.
- Satoshi did this. The address he quoted to Hal Finney starting 1NS may be coincidence, but he also used an address starting 15N indicating Satoshi Nakamoto. Miner M254 who can be identified as Satoshi used the address 133fZZzNN involving three doubles for a doublet transaction. Such a statistically unlikely address must have been customised from a list of c.100,000 random addresses.
- In April 2009, Satoshi quoted an address starting 1PhUX to Mike Hearne which has been customised to **P**aul Le Ro**ux**.
- This establishes the "first and last" pattern which only takes into account capital letters.
- As early as Jan 2009, the miner M524=Satoshi used an address 1PxeCX for **P**aul **C**alder Le Rou**x**.
- We find five similar addresses customised to Le Roux's name in a list of addresses quoted by Wright as reserved for an allocation made to the "third man" who was Satoshi. The actual transaction took place on 13 Aug 2013 and was made to the customised address 1LXc28 which stands for **L**e Rou**x** and is a close equivalent of Rx for **R**ou**x**.

- Most of the Bitcoins for this transaction are derived from 150,000 Bitcoins from MtGox set aside for a single large client in Jan 2011 and split into slices on 1 Mar to 2 Mar 2011. There is evidence for an extensive mining operation that continued into 2012.
- Wright had a genuine source not derived from the blockchain for the prospective 1LXc28 transaction because his email quotes a total which has been calculated from addresses allocated to a Satoshi silo between 2 Mar and 4 Mar 2011.

It is the third man who interests us. Wright has mentioned several names in conjunction with this third man. One of them is Paul Le Roux.

TWENTY-FOUR

THE THIRD MAN

From the start, Craig Wright talked about Satoshi as being three people. A mysterious third man invented Bitcoin along with himself and Kleiman. There was absolutely no reason for Wright to bring in a third man, and yet it has been a recurring element of his story. The identity of this individual has varied over the years. Initially, Wright said the third man was Professor Rees.

Wright started naming Rees as someone involved in Bitcoin a few days after his death on 13 Aug 2013. On 9 Oct, he wrote an email to the Australian Tax Office, giving a list of Bitcoin addresses that he claimed were under his control. The list only gave the address and balance, information easily obtainable from public sources.

He wrote to the ATO:

> "The addresses are in my control now as a matter of fate and other circumstances. David Reese and David Kleiman have both been essential parts of this project."

Wright goes on to describe Dave Kleiman as his best friend and "Reese" as a friend of his grandfather. "Both of these gentlemen who I had the good fortune to call friends passed away this year." If Rees were such a good friend, it would be strange for Wright to misspell his name.

Professor David Rees was a mathematician who had worked on a major cryptography project for the British government. Could he have been part of Satoshi? There is a problem: that cryptography project was the Enigma decoding at Bletchley Park in the Second World War! Rees was ninety-five when he died, and there is no evidence that connects him with Bitcoin.

The ATO wrote to Rees' four daughters, two of whom were also professors, to confirm Wright's statements. The daughters said their father had not been involved with computers or cryptography since the 1940s. Wright had claimed that Rees had given him his unpublished research, but there was no such research. Rees had had dementia for years before his death and could not have been involved with Bitcoin. His daughters had been handling all their father's financial affairs, correspondence and emails. They had never heard of Wright.

After this put-down, Wright ceased mentioning Rees. But the third man was a recurring theme in his accounts. Gavin Andresen recalled meeting Craig Wright in 2016 for the first time:

> "I think we had a conversation about the person of Satoshi actually being three people — being Dave Kleiman, Craig Wright and some other mysterious person who I never asked about." (26 Feb 2020)

Ira Kleiman's legal team were keen to identify the third man who could supply vital evidence about Dave Kleiman's involvement with Bitcoin. When the lawyers travelled to London to take Craig Wright's deposition, Ira's counsel, Devin Freedman, put the question directly:

> "QUESTION: What is the identity of number three?"
> "ANSWER: I can't answer that on national security grounds."

Freedman had never come across a national security objection before. There were other questions that Wright also refused to answer on the same grounds of national security. But this one was the most important. As Freedman put it: "That third person could be the star witness of the trial who could say Dave Kleiman and Craig Wright told me they partnered up to be Satoshi Nakamoto."

A hasty phone call was arranged with the judge, who ruled that only the US government could assert a national security objection. The defence counsel must find out the circumstances from Wright and approach the Government for confirmation. One of the defence lawyers, Zaharah Markoe, travelled to London to meet Wright to determine the national security issue. She needed to know the names of the US government officials to approach. But Wright was not forthcoming. The whole thing was becoming a logistic nightmare. Her frustration was apparent at the discovery hearing:

> "And we have spoken with the client about that and we said, look, you've got to give us something. You've got to give us names and contact information, or you've got to give us a contract that says you're not allowed to talk about this."

The discovery hearing was held in Florida before Judge Bruce Reinhart on 11 Apr 2019. When they reached the national security objection, Wright's attorney Amanda McGovern began by setting the background: "And it basically goes to this question, Your Honor, that the individual, the identity of the individual that had some, I guess involvement early on, involves issues of personal safety." The defence was also concerned with the intense interest in the case by "the internet". Every document was combed through, and every development was breathlessly reported. She then described the safety concern:

> "There is a legitimate concern about identification of individuals that have been incarcerated as a result of things that have happened and some of those related parties are not incarcerated. So there is a safety concern."

The judge was not convinced. Wright was testifying under oath and must answer the questions unless he had legal "standing". McGovern continues:

> "This is an individual who was involved before Dave Kleiman was involved. So this is really it goes back to Dr Wright's initial involvement. And you know, in order to be completely candid about every single person that was involved, it would require disclosure of this individual. So the standing simply is not wanting to disclose that information for personal safety."

Markoe added some more detail:

"And the concern, as I understand it, that the client has is there is involvement among himself and others in activities that resulted in the incarceration of an international crime lord, if you will, who has associates that are not incarcerated. And there are safety concerns about the disclosure of his own involvement and the involvement of others in those efforts to bring this individual into custody."

As an argument, it is bizarre. In Judge Reinhart's words, Wright is saying, "I don't want to" answer the questions because of some "super secret international drug lord". The judge said he was willing to consider a protective order so the information could be given in camera and kept out of the public record to protect Wright's safety: "And the folks on the Internet can try all they want, but they are not getting it."

But the folks on the internet did get it, and the name was Paul Le Roux.

The defence produced a document in which Wright answered three of the plaintiff's questions. The public release of the document was heavily redacted.

1. The first question concerned the identity of a third person on a video call made to Dave Kleiman when Wright was in New York in 2011. Wright had said this individual was irrelevant to Bitcoin but was now ready to name the person. The name is redacted.

2. The second question was about the supposed software Dave and Craig had worked on together. Wright claimed that this had been distributed to a number of sites including some associated with the United States government. He had been unwilling to disclose any details of this software for national security reasons. But now he said his software was used to apprehend two master criminals whose names were redacted.

The defence lawyers, however, failed to redact the second part of a note that went over the page. This enabled the first criminal to be identified as Paul Le Roux.

3. The third question was the identity of the third person in the email to Lou Kleiman. The document disclosed that Wright had testified

that this individual had worked as an informer for the United States Government and that Wright did not know if he was still alive or dead. The third person's involvement in Bitcoin had ceased in 2007 before Dave Kleiman became involved in 2008. But now Wright was ready to name the mysterious third man: "This individual went by the codename of [redacted] and was an anonymous data source for [one line redacted]." Wright only knew this individual's "codename" and had no means of contacting him. Like much of what Wright says, it is nonsense that defies common sense.

Wright's reply was not enough, and Freedman got the court to agree to a second deposition of Wright on 28 Jun 2019. Some of this deposition is in the public domain, which helps us fill in some redacted elements.

The answer to the first question, the third person on a video call when Wright visited New York in 2011, is revealed to be Gareth Williams. The Gareth Williams affair was front-page news in the UK, and Wright lived in London. Williams was a brilliant young man whose life has been overshadowed by the bizarre circumstances of his death. He was an exceptional mathematician who gained a first-class university degree at the tender age of 17. After achieving his PhD, Williams was recruited by British intelligence to work at GCHQ in Cheltenham, England. He lived modestly and quietly, his favourite occupation being long walks in the pleasant countryside around Cheltenham. So it was a shock when his naked and partially decomposed body was found in a zipped up and padlocked bag in a bath in the London flat where he had been staying for work—he was just 31. The police discovered that Williams had an interest in bondage and cross-dressing and concluded that his death was an act of self-bondage that went wrong. However, there was speculation that Russian agents had actually murdered Williams. It was known that Russian assassins had been active in Britain, and a speciality was making murders look like suicide.

Wright claimed that Williams had been working on a theory that the Russian President Putin was funding the Clintons via Russian oligarchs. Williams wanted to use Wright's software to break into servers in the US to uncover crucial evidence. Wright had helped train Williams, and they were now tracing the movement of money. Williams had agreed to remove all evidence of Wright as Satoshi in return for using his software. Williams was supposedly involved in the development of Bitcoin and was the only person, apart from Kleiman, who knew that Wright was Satoshi.

Wright's stories always change, and Williams is now the "third man." By the time of the deposition, the mysterious individual known only by code name had completely disappeared from Wright's account.

It is all incredible, a mishmash of the various political obsessions and conspiracy theories circulating at the time. We can be sure that Williams did not have a conference call with Wright in early 2011 because he died in Aug 2010. Someone who put the redacted document together seems to have noticed this embarrassing contradiction, as there is a note that Wright now thought the meeting happened earlier than in 2011. But in the deposition, the meeting was back to 2011.

The second criminal mastermind captured with Wright's claimed involvement turned out to be the notorious Russian arms dealer, Viktor Bout. As we have seen, he was apprehended by the DEA in a sting operation remarkably similar to that which ensnared Le Roux. When asked what Wright had contributed to the capture and prosecution of Bout, he replied: "I created software to break encryption and to put in back doors in systems to allow capture of data." In reality, Wright couldn't program, and Bout was betrayed by an insider.

When Wright was asked whether the US government had reached out to him for his help in these high-profile cases, he answered "no." How, then, did he get involved? "I had contacts with people like Mr. Williams, who worked for GCHQ." So Wright was not officially working for any government in his fantastic achievement of bringing down both Viktor Bout and Le Roux. He was working off the record and could offer no names to support his claims.

Unsurprisingly, Wright's defence attorney wanted to shut this conversation down, so she objected to the line of questioning, and the judge upheld the objection.

Wright changed his story with every repetition. He initially said that disclosing the third man would have national security implications involving an "international crime lord". In the written document submitted a few weeks later, one crime lord had turned into two: Le Roux and Bout. The national security implications had changed into Wright's personal security. And now Wright was saying that Le Roux and Bout were only involved because he had supplied software used in their capture. The man known only by codename had disappeared into thin air. And the third man on the conference call was now Gareth Williams.

When asked what this video call had to do with Satoshi, Wright replied that only Dave Kleiman and Williams knew he was Satoshi and that Williams had agreed to help him cover his tracks by removing information on the internet. The deposition continued:

> "Q. Was Mr. Williams involved in Bitcoin in any way beyond helping you -- beyond agreeing to delete the records of you belonging to Satoshi?
> A. Yes.
> Q. How was Mr. Williams involved?
> A. Mr. Williams was a very good mathematician, and I used his skill of knowledge in analyzing graph theory in associated with the creation of Bitcoin and some of the mining algorithms that I was planning to implement."

So Williams was supposedly part of Satoshi to the extent of giving some technical assistance to Wright. However, Gareth Williams could not possibly have been on the video conference in early 2011 because he had died the previous August. Nor could the video conference have occurred as early as the summer of 2010, when Williams was still alive: this would conflict with both Craig and Lynn's testimony. We will see that Wright's blog entries at the time enable us to tie down his New York visit to between 24 and 30 Jan 2011.

There are problems with Wright's story that he supplied software to capture Bout and Le Roux. Most obviously, Wright could not code. His story is also inconsistent with what he said previously when he was unable to name the third man because of the crime lord's activities, which involved "national security" concerns. Yet in his new version,

Bout and Le Roux are not connected in any way to the third man, so why bring them in?

Wright knew he had said too much and substituted Gareth Williams in place of the real third man. But Gareth Williams could not have been on the conference call because he was dead. And Viktor Bout could not have been on the conference call because he had been captured in 2008. Clearly, Wright was not involved with Bout's capture: at the time, he was a computer auditor with BDO accountants in Australia.

The original question was about the identity of the third man, the person who had supposedly invented Bitcoin along with Wright and Kleiman. Wright said it involved an international crime lord and refused to answer on national security grounds. Of the three names Wright gave in his written deposition document, only Le Roux could have been on the conference call. Wright tries to confuse the issue, but he had told too much of the truth. The third man is Paul Le Roux.

Wright's legal team submitted the document about the third man under seal to the court on 18 Apr 2019. Five days later, on 23 Apr 2019, Wright published a blog post called "The Immovable", in which he compared himself to the "church of the immovable ladder".

This is the Church of the Holy Sepulchre in Jerusalem, the supposed location of Jesus' resurrection and one of Christianity's holiest sites. On the exterior, there is a small ladder standing on a ledge against an upper window. A workman forgot to take it down in 1728, so why is it still there? Several denominations have argued over the control of the church, and they have never been able to agree on who has the authority to remove the ladder. So it stays.

Is there a hidden meaning in Wright's comparison? The ladder is not supposed to be there. It is an accident that has become an immovable feature. Wright is hinting that he plays the same role in Bitcoin.

In his blog post, Wright revealed the real reason that he invented Bitcoin. It was not because of the financial crisis: "The reality is Bitcoin is not anti-bank, it is not anti-government, and in fact, it is not even anti-central bank." The aim was to end "criminal manipulation" of the financial markets. The real targets were "Web Money, Liberty Reserve and a group of criminals associated with things such as the Russian Business Network (RBN)". The Russian Business Network suffered from ISPs withdrawing their services in 2007, but others continued in operation:

> "Others such as RX Ltd trading a bit longer. They survived because of the growth of Liberty Reserve and associated money-laundering organisations."

Wright repeated something almost identical in an interview on 27 Apr 2019. In both cases, Wright says that he invented Bitcoin to bring down Liberty Reserve and the criminal organisations that depended upon it. He names only one: Rx Limited. So Wright is claiming he set up Bitcoin to bring down Le Roux!

Liberty Reserve was a digital currency service based in Costa Rica and closed down by the US in 2013. The service allowed users to remain essentially anonymous by not performing checks on the user's identity. It issued "Liberty dollars" and "Liberty Euros" pegged to each respective currency. Wright portrays Liberty Reserve as a criminal scam which allowed people like Le Roux to launder their money. Wright appears to be firmly against Liberty Reserve. Yet he also claimed to have been a customer who lost significant money when it was closed down.

To make sense of all this, we need to return to the events of April 2013.

After Le Roux was captured, he was held in a prison in Brooklyn. Every weekday morning, the DEA agents would take him either to a Manhattan courthouse or the Brooklyn Bridge Marriott hotel, where they would debrief him. Le Roux would return to prison in the evening. He communicated with his organisation and was allowed to use his laptop, but his keystrokes were recorded by DEA technicians.

Le Roux was full of ideas and schemes, and the DEA agents began to fall under his spell. According to Shannon, Cindric and Stouch seriously considered allowing Le Roux the freedom to make contact with Iran or North Korea and perhaps even visit Iran. It was never going to happen. The DEA could not take any chances with Le Roux, and Milione vetoed the idea.

That brings us to the entry in the prison's system that recorded Le Roux as released on 9 Apr 2013. If this was not an admin mistake, then Le Roux must have been released into DEA custody—there is no way they would have allowed him back into the wild. It must have been a longer time away from prison than the regular daily routine. The DEA were up to something that required Le Roux's presence.

We know that Wright was in New Jersey on 13 Apr and could have arrived as early as 11 Apr. When he returned home, his behaviour changed dramatically, and he became very interested in Bitcoin. Wright started building his business empire almost immediately and had suddenly acquired a lot of money. We have suggested that Wright met Satoshi or his representative on that trip and that Kleiman may have attended if his health permitted.

We can pinpoint Wright on 13 Apr to a "dive bar" in Oak Ridge, NJ 07438, which may have been The Daily Planet. This semi-rural area would make sense as a location for the DEA to take Le Roux. It was close to New York, where the DEA agents were based, and it would be easier to control and guard Le Roux in a hotel or other venue in that area rather than the city.

Le Roux could have taken advantage of his time out of prison and arranged to contact Wright without the DEA's prior knowledge. For example, they could have arranged to meet "accidentally" at a hotel or bar. Or someone else could have been present at the meeting who could then act as an intermediary. But there is another intriguing possibility.

Consider things from Le Roux's perspective. His urgent priority was to keep control of his Bitcoin keys. The obvious person to turn to was Kleiman, who had previously managed his Bitcoin transactions. It helped that Kleiman was a trustworthy individual. Unfortunately for Le Roux, he was also seriously ill, so he had to involve Wright. It was vital for Le Roux to open a good line of communication between himself and the two men he had selected to manage his Bitcoin. How could he do this? Le Roux was a genius who thought outside of the box. Rather than trying to get messages out to Kleiman and Wright, why not bring them in?

Let us assume they had both worked for him in the past. He could represent them to the DEA as two honest computer experts who were familiar with his systems. They could even be sent in physically to his operation to gain control of his computers for the DEA. It would have helped that Kleiman was a US citizen, ex-army, ex-police, and in good standing with the FBI. If Kleiman and Wright were working for the DEA, then Le Roux would have ample opportunity to communicate with them.

Evidence for this scenario comes from Wright, who has repeatedly claimed to have been an "agent of influence" for the US. He would not disclose the identity of the third man because it involved issues of "national security". Wright's stories change all the time, and he has claimed to have been an agent for the CIA and, in an alternative version, an agent for ICE (US immigration). But his main claim is that he helped bring down Le Roux's empire and Rx Limited, and Bout as well, by undermining their computer systems. He could only have done that by working with the DEA, although he never named them.

Wright starts with something real, which he elaborates in ridiculous ways. Is it possible that he really did work briefly for the DEA on the Le Roux case? Some of the DEA team that took down Le Roux were also involved with Bout's capture. It would be natural for Wright to exaggerate his role and extend it to Bout to distract attention away from Le Roux. But if Wright worked for the DEA, it would have been Le Roux's idea.

A few days after visiting New Jersey, Wright established Coin-Exch, a Bitcoin exchange joint venture with Kleiman. But Kleiman tragically died almost immediately, and Wright had to implement the plan alone. He suddenly had access to a great deal of money. Where did it come from?

Wright has maintained that the initial funding came from internet casino groups via Kleiman. He has mentioned a vague "Playboy group", but this is clearly not the Playboy organisation. The funds came via the same Liberty Reserve he associated with criminal organisations, including Rx Limited. Wright has written openly in his blog claiming that he and Kleiman produced software for grey-zone casino operations run by criminals. He has backed up these stories with forged emails between himself and Kleiman. As neither Kleiman nor Wright could program, we cannot take his account at face value. But significantly, he created a picture in which these casinos supposedly paid him through Liberty Reserve.

We can deduce that Wright got the funds for his business expansion in 2013 from an online casino operation via Liberty Reserve. We know Le Roux was associated with online casino operators in Costa Rica and established his own casino. So Le Roux could have arranged the transfer of funds intended for Coin-Exch.

Here, things went badly wrong. On 24 May 2013, the US took down Liberty Reserve. Depositors were wiped out without compensation. Wright claimed to have lost substantial amounts from the closure. There would have been a brief window of opportunity to transfer funds before the US took this action, but Wright soon ran out of money.

If there was an arrangement between Wright and Satoshi, it did not last. Wright must have seriously upset the Bitcoin creator. He may have clung to the forlorn hope that Satoshi would relent and send him the keys. This would explain Wright's more absurd stories, such as the bonded courier. But Satoshi is not the forgiving type.

We have suggested that Wright's statements point to Le Roux being the real "third man". We have seen how in Jan 2011, Wright, Kleiman and the third man had a video conference in New York. What happened next was truly bizarre. Wright, the Australian ex-computer auditor, travelled from New York to Venezuela and then to the Colombia border area. He made contact with the FARC guerrilla movement and was shot.

TWENTY-FIVE

CRAIG WRIGHT IS SHOT

When Wright travelled to New York in Jan 2011, it was not his ultimate destination. He continued on to Venezuela and Colombia, where he was shot by the FARC terror movement. We can piece together the basic story from Wright's accounts of this episode. Essential elements of the story can be cross checked. It cannot be dismissed as fantasy.

The second deposition in Miami continued with this South American trip:

"Q. Dr Wright, you participated in a videoconference with Dave Kleiman while you were in New York City sometime in 2011, correct?
A. Yes.
Q. An individual by the name of Gareth Williams was at that meeting; is that correct?
A. He wasn't at that meeting.
Q. Where was Gareth Williams?
A. He was in the UK."

Wright clarified that Gareth Williams was "formally of MI6" and "of GCHQ" and had participated in the call from the UK. Dave Kleiman had participated from Florida. The deposition continued:

"Q. What was the purpose of your trip?
A. I was on my way to Venezuela.
Q. What were you going to do in Venezuela?
A. I was doing forensic work.
Q. For who?

> A. I was doing forensic work with a group associated with ICE. We were tracking movement of money associated with FARC and FARCV.
> Q. What is ICE?
> A. ICE is customs enforcement here in the U.S."

Wright claims to have been working with US Customs and Immigration Enforcement, ICE. The US government had not approached him for this work, but he said he was working informally through people such as Gareth Williams.

Wright gave his deposition in Jun 2019. A few months earlier, he wrote about this trip in a blog article dated 9 Feb 2019. This was around the time he told his lawyers in London that the video conference with the third man in New York at the beginning of 2011 involved an "international crime lord":

> "I was offline for much of January 2011. During the time, I had travelled to Venezuela where I was working with a 'Jawbreaker' team. The work was focused on stopping the tracking of humans for the sex trade. I was in 'prevention.' I did not bring people to justice, I worked with teams to stop things, permanently."

Wright says he was working with the "Jawbreaker" team of SAD agents, the elite Special Activities Division of the CIA. Wright did not "bring people to justice" but worked with those who "stop things, permanently". So Wright is claiming to have been part of a murder squad that conducted extrajudicial killings.

There is an inconsistency between the two accounts in that the Special Activities Division of the CIA had turned into ICE by the time of the deposition. In one account, he is tracking the movement of money for ICE; in the other, he is stopping human trafficking for the sex trade with SAD. Wright's blog post continues:

> "My 'Blind Date' in Venezuela had me progressing west to the border of Colombia. It was my last operation of the type. I was

shot twice, and evidence of it is likely to still exist on the Internet for all my efforts to have destroyed it. I met with Colombian El Departamento Administrativo de Seguridad (DAS) agents, as my job was accessing systems and information, and on the occasion, it was related to an operation associated with garnishing evidence against FARC-V. Before, I was what some people would call an 'agent of influence.'"

So Wright claims to have been shot twice while investigating FARC-V while working with Colombian security forces. The odd expression "Blind Date" implies that Wright did not know what he was letting himself in for. A security consultant would be expected to work in a safe location, perhaps police headquarters or a plush hotel. But Wright's account makes it clear he was in the field:

"I was a pastor for a time. But, the images of what I have done, what I have seen, and the cruelties I have witnessed in the world led me to abandon the position."

Note the strange wording "images of what I have done". He continues:

"I have witnessed children as young as 10 with AK-74s and women who have been forced to watch the death of their children knowing that other members of their family are being held and, if they try to escape, will be killed."

So Wright must have visited FARC-controlled territory. He claims he could no longer dream: "In some ways, it is a reaction to some of the things that I've seen." Wright says, "I'm not ashamed of my past, but I never wanted to talk about it." Some bits, though, are "darkened dirty parts", which he now wants to pour some light on. It is all very odd. From his own account, he is a James Bond like figure fighting the forces of evil, a hero of our times. But he does not seem proud of his actions. It reads almost as if he were trying to make some kind of confession.

Much of the post is concerned with people trafficking for the sex trade:

> "People smuggling, sex slavery, and many forms of illicit exchange exist in the modern world."

He claims to have invented Bitcoin to stop these evils:

> "I designed and created Bitcoin to stop the need for people like me — people who worked with SAD operatives and even those acting in the tracing of funds."

This is not the only time that Wright talked about the circumstances that caused him to stop being a pastor in early 2011. In his Florida deposition, he claimed that his loss of faith was due to the activities of Malmi and Theymos. Specifically, he accused Theymos of using Bitcoin to set up a service to exchange child pornography for drugs. Neither Malmi nor Theymos were involved in any such scheme. Both had prominent roles in administering the Bitcoin forum and controlling bitcoin.org, so Wright may have thought, wrongly, that they were in cahoots with Satoshi. He may be projecting Satoshi's actions onto them.

One obvious question is whether it is all a fantasy. It certainly reads like fantasy. Why should a computer professional go undercover in FARC territory? Even if Wright had worked on such a case, it would have been in a backroom capacity. However, Wright has not made it all up. We have independent evidence that he was shot.

At this time, he and his wife Lynn were having a hard time. For a start, the couple were in a difficult financial position. Craig had been made redundant from his last job at BDO and, by 2011, had run out of money:

> "In 2011, I had no idea what to do. I had sworn I would never go back to the work I was doing overseas, and I had applied for a formal role as an officer in the military police which luckily I did not follow up on. I left an excellent job at a chartered accounting firm, BDO, taking a golden-handshake redundancy that funded me for a time. The redundancy was offered in December 2008, and it is how I was able to spend 2009 working and burning down my savings."

Craig and Lynn were now living on their farm, but it was not a happy time for their relationship. They started divorce proceedings in Oct/Nov 2010, although they continued to live together for a while due to a lack of funds. Divorce would not have helped Wright's finances. He had gone through "two years of earning very little but spending a lot on my research". Later, in 2011, he was to describe in his blog how he had come down to living in a rented apartment.

This is the background to Lynn's court deposition in the trial. She was asked specifically about the time that Craig was shot:

> "I think it was - it might have been 2010, because I think we were still - I think we were still in the house in - living together here. Because I remember getting the phone call and then when he got back, so but we - that was coming close to the time we were separating."

Lynn was not clear on the exact location of the shooting, but it was somewhere in South America or Central America. She was asked if she knew what he was doing there:

> "No, not really. I mean, he - he went to do some work but I - I don't know what it was as, again, we were - we were pretty much having trouble communicating about anything, then."

Lynn's account confirms Wright's story that he was shot in South America. She comes over as a truthful, level-headed witness, and had no motive for lying. Lynn is unsure of the exact date but thinks it might have been 2010. She is certain it was while they were still living together because she can remember taking the call.

Craig dates the divorce proceedings from Oct 2010, whereas Lynn says it was Nov 2010. But they certainly still lived together into 2011. Wright has repeatedly said that the trip and video call were in Jan 2011. So, the two accounts are consistent, allowing for a bit of haziness on the date of something that happened years before.

Additional confirmation comes from Wright's blog. In 2011, his main blog was called "Cracked, inSecure and Generally Broken" and had the snappy sub-title "The ravings of a SANS/GIAC GSE (Compliance & Malware)". He started the blog in 2006 and was a prolific blogger. Although Wright later deleted the whole blog, it can be recovered from the internet archives stored on the Wayback Machine. Wright had a habit of editing old posts, adding new backdated posts and deleting old posts. So it is essential to consider the date the archive's web crawler captured a post.

The posts from Jan 2011 confirm that Wright did fly to New York. He posted on 24 Jan 2011 about "Internet in the air". He is flying from SFO (San Francisco) to JFK (New York) on a business trip: "I am not flying economy as this is a work trip and I have laptops and other things sprawled all over the place in my mobile office structure. Having power in business and first was always a turn on for me and a justification as I can generally pay for the cost of the flight in billable hours as well as arriving relaxed."

Several days later, he took a second flight out of New York and found his business class seat was broken. He posted no less than three times about his broken seat while in the air:

> Sunday, 30 Jan 2011: "Please accept our apology".
> Sunday, 30 Jan 2011: "DO NOT FLY UNITED AIRLINES!".
> Sunday, 30 Jan 2011: "Why US airlines are losing money and loyalty".

Then, when he landed, he posted again about the economic consequences of his broken seat:

> Sunday, 30 Jan 2011: "Why the economy is slowing, one of the many reasons."

This last post starts, "I was on a United Airlines flight from JFK to NYC today". Wright flew into New York on 24 Jan 2011 and flew out again on 30 Jan 2011. This enables us to confidently date the video conference between 24 Jan and 30 Jan 2011. We should note that this includes 27 Jan 2011 when the 150,000 Bitcoins were removed from MtGox. Were these Bitcoins discussed on the conference call?

Where did Wright travel to on 30 Jan? His statement that he flew from JFK to NYC makes no sense, as they are both codes for New York airports.

Either Wright has made a mistake, or the post was edited later to hide the ultimate destination. However, the blog is consistent with Wright's deposition that the destination was Venezuela.

Wright was travelling Business class from Australia to South America via New York. That would have been an expensive trip when he was running out of funds. Who was paying for that journey?

Over the next two weeks, Wright would be a prolific blogger. He made 23 blog posts up to 14 Feb, primarily on economic matters. And then silence. The next blog post was not until 9 Jul, and there was no hint of why he had been silent for so long. There was a supposed post on 27 Mar 2011, "Rant", about his company, Integyrs Pty Ltd, going into receivership because the Australian Tax Office refused his claim for research refunds: "Bitcoin has value. It is not a hobby." However, the Wayback Machine shows that this post was added in 2014 and backdated.

Wright did not blog after 14 Feb 2011 for five months, by far his most extended silent period. Previously, he had been blogging more than once a day, so this may indicate the time that he moved further west in Venezuela and into Colombia and was shot.

On 14/15 Feb, he exchanged emails with Dave Kleiman about registering W&K Info in Florida. Analysis of the timing shows that Wright's computer was set to Australian time. This does not necessarily mean that Wright was in Australia, as keeping a computer set to the home time zone while travelling is convenient.

Most blog posts between 30 Jan and 14 Feb are on Wright's economic views and give no clues about his activities. He would later claim to have deleted the internet evidence of the shooting, and he did delete a large number of posts made in 2011 and early 2012. He gave a series of webinars in late 2011/early 2012 in association with Charles Sturt University with the title "Cyber (Crime, espionage, terror)". Wright later deleted everything from his blog relating to this lecture series, about 10-15 posts. They can be recovered but are nothing more than invitations and dead links to join webinars and podcasts. However, we will see later that the crucial slides from this presentation are available.

One intriguing post had a URL ending in "/assassination attempt". The URL is generated by the post title when saved, but this title is actually "character assassination attempt". Someone had reviewed Wright's recent book and found extensive plagiarism. Wright's defence was that it was all due to an innocent mistake on his part. According to his blog post, others were saying that the accusations against him amounted to a "character assassination attempt". The post reads contrived, and the URL suggests that it started life as an account of his shooting before being quickly changed to character assassination.

The most significant deletions were three posts made in the critical period between 30 Jan and 14 Feb. These are:

Friday, 4 Feb 2011: "Cybercrime."
Sunday, 6 Feb 2011: "FARC, Gold, cyber and terror."
Monday, 7 Feb 2011: "Why gold?"

The "Cybercrime" post is innocuous and was probably deleted because of its title. "Why gold" advocates a return to the gold standard. Wright has become very interested in gold at this time. A post on 4 Feb was also about gold, with the intriguing title: "Looking for people interested in starting a new revolution in payments." Wright has devised a solution to fiat currencies—but not Bitcoin! He proposes "a payment measure in the form of PayPal that offers a currency exchange mechanism and a gold-based currency". He is looking for others "interested in starting an online gold trading system along the lines of PayPal". What a strange post for Satoshi to make!

The critical post is "FARC, Gold, cyber and terror". It confirms that Wright is either in Venezuela/Colombia or has been there in the recent past:

> "In Colombia and Venezuela, FARC (and FARC-V) have been taking over gold mines illegally. These are a better source of income than the traditional means of cocaine trading. First, cocaine has devalued in recent years and next, it is far more difficult to smuggle."

FARC was best known as a significant exporter of cocaine. However, Wright's description of FARC taking over much of the gold mining industry at this time is accurate. Wright says that FARC continued to be involved in the people trade. "The illegal gold mines are manned by slave labour and serviced by forced prostitution." Child soldiers are recruited for FARC forces, and other children are used in the sex trade.

Other accounts confirm Wright's description of FARC and gold mining. A report on the illegal mining industry shows a similar situation in 2015/6. Some 80% of gold mined in Colombia and 80%- 90% in Venezuela was produced illegally. Criminal gangs and paramilitary organisations dominated the mining. FARC was a major player and would take a substantial slice of every piece of the gold mining action in the territories it controlled.

Where there was illegal gold mining, there was also human trafficking. Much of the labour force had been trafficked and were basically slave labour. They were prevented from leaving by the criminal gangs and FARC soldiers. The mining employed child labour, particularly in narrow tunnels and cleaning gold with poisonous mercury. Women and underaged girls were trafficked on a mass scale to provide sexual services for FARC soldiers and the predominantly male workforce. Mining conditions were appalling, and the work was dangerous. The threat of death, whether through accident or assassination, was ubiquitous.

Awareness of the problem developed when the DAS security service produced a report on the issue on 28 Sep 2011. A newspaper, El Espectador, picked up on the report and published an article that drew wider international attention. Wright made his blog post several months before these reports. It supports the conclusion that he was in Venezuela and Colombia and had first-hand knowledge.

In his later accounts of his "blind date", Wright never mentions gold. Yet it was central to FARC's activities and something that Wright was interested in at the time.

In his 2011 blog post, Wright says that criminal groups are exploiting the situation by exchanging software and distribution capabilities to FARC in return for illegally mined gold:

"The link to crimeware is twofold.

1 Gold is used to purchase the services and software of the criminal groups.

> 2 People taken into the sex trade by these groups are abused and filmed for sale and digital distribution."

The criminal groups are also involved in laundering the gold:

> "The knowledge and expertise of the criminal hacker groups has been for sale for a long time. The ability to move gold and to launder it through these groups has resulted in a rise in the ties between cyber-crime and cyber terror."

He continues about the advantages to the criminals of child pornography:

> "As these links grow stronger over time, the profits from gold and online sexual exploitation of abducted women and children will form a stronger basis for terror funding than the drug trade.
>
> The nature of the activities also creates an ongoing revenue stream. Once an individual has signed up for a child porn service offered by the cyber-criminal groups, they cannot leave."

As the mere possession of child porn is illegal, anyone who pays for the service becomes a cash cow. The actual software is produced by programmers recruited locally:

> "So, how do you turn gold into US$, add a cybercrime group. Because there are few good computer jobs available in Colombia and Venezuela, hackers can earn more from working on such software than with legitimate businesses."

The strange thing about this is that tech is not required to launder gold, and there is no evidence that FARC was interested in cybercrime. They were, after all, a revolutionary political movement and may have had severe objections about filming children engaged in sexual activities for the benefit of a decadent Western audience. Gold is gold, an elemental metal, and it is easy to disguise its origins. You just need to move it through intermediary corporations and refiners. Le Roux, of course, was an expert at this. He loved to source gold from illegal mines where he could buy it cheaply.

Where did Wright get his information for the scenario he is describing? Is it something he learned from contacts in Venezuela, or some kind of prospective scheme, or just his own ideas as to what might happen? The crucial question is the identity of the criminal groups. But Wright does not name any names. As FARC would be supplying both the gold and the women and children to be abused, what would the criminal group contribute? It must be the software and distribution.

The talks Wright gave later in 2011 presented his trip to South America under the guise of conducting research for a non-profit called the Global Institute for Cyber Security Research (GICSR) based at Cape Canaveral, Florida. Wright had been appointed to a position as Asian Pacific Director of GICSR in 2011, a position which he resigned in Feb 2012. His role was to establish relationships with other organisations in the Australia region with the idea of founding a local centre of excellence for cyber-security. He was an unpaid volunteer representing the organisation in Australia, not a researcher funded to go to South America. And he could not have conducted research for GICSR in Feb 2011 because it was not established until Jun 2011. In Wright's CV he claimed to have been appointed in Apr 2011, but both dates are months after his time in Venezuela.

Wright also mentions his trip to South America in an application he made for a court internship:

> "I have engaged in extensive research into the abduction and trafficking of persons across South America. In particular this research has looked at the changing trafficking environment where individuals are abducted for economic sex crimes such as the filming and sale of child pornography within western nations. These projects were done under funding from DHS and ICE and involved research within Venezuela, Panama and Colombia."

Here Wright says he was conducting research under funding from the US DHS and ICE. There is no evidence that Wright did any work for either of these organisations. He applied for unrelated research grants from the

Department of Homeland Security but they were all rejected. His CV talks up his role in GICSR to an absurd extent including "executive level relationships with the National Security Agency (NSA), Department of Homeland Security (DHS) and North American Space Agency...". (Note the incorrect "North American Space Agency" for NASA.) This is fantasy as Wright was never part of the management team of the US based GICSR, but their representative in Australia. Wright went on to use his brief GICSR relationship for an identity theft in which he pretended to establish a GICSR trust in Belize including the sale of a software product for $32 million to GICSR with funding provided by NASA. GICSR had never purchased anything like that and did not have any business relationship with NASA.

The presentation Wright gave at the end of 2011 under the guise of GICSR incorporated two slides confirming that Wright was in Venezuela in Feb 2011:

> "In Feb this year, we interviewed and spoke with people in organised cyber-groups in Venezuela.
>
> Without the ability to be extradited, many of these people are surprisingly open about what they do.
>
> In Venezuela groups are moving from people smuggling to the production and sale of rape and child exploitation videos.
>
> What is surprising is that many US citizens who purchase such illicit goods are dumbfounded when they are extorted!"

It is absurd to suppose that an unemployed Australian computer auditor just took a flight to Venezuela, asked around and found some cyber-criminals who told him all the details of their evil schemes. If Wright is not making it all up, and the evidence suggest he is not, then he must have had contacts in Venezuela. The GICSR slides are silent about certain issues: that Wright was shot, that he was in FARC territory, and that the criminal scheme involved gold.

Further confirmation that Wright was involved with FARC in 2011 comes from a post "The Economy is screwed?" he made later that year. In this post, he mentioned some "failed economies" he had witnessed:

> "I worked in Mumbai for a time. There I saw the world's largest slum. I saw people leaving to work and support families they see once a year at best. I saw the garbage heaps in Manilla. I saw the Congo and Farc controlled places in Venezuela.
>
> I saw Somalia and even Arch Angel [Archangel, Russia] in what was touted as an industrial powerhouse of a failed socialist country." (2 Sep 2011)

Here is confirmation that Wright had visited FARC controlled territory in Venezuela. Wright had no reason to lie: it is a minor aside in a post about something completely different. Some other places he lists alongside FARC-controlled Venezuela are interesting because they are associated with Paul Le Roux. Manilla was Le Roux's and RX Limited's home base, although it is not surprising that an Australian should visit the capital of the Philippines. More unusual is the Congo, where Le Roux had gold mining and logging interests. However, there might be other reasons why Wright would travel to the Congo.

The real stand out is Somalia. It was perhaps the most dangerous place in the world. Anyone visiting Somalia would require a hefty level of protection, meaning armed soldiers. No legitimate Western companies were operating there. A Westerner would not visit Somalia unless he was working for a government or aid agency. An exception was Le Roux's Southern Ace which had its own private army based in a compound in Somalia starting in late 2009.

What skills did Craig Wright have that might be useful for Le Roux? Certainly not as a mercenary, although Wright did consider joining the military police. Nor was he the "Jawbreaker" assassin type. Wright was good at one thing—setting up computer systems, hardware and software. He presented himself as a genius computer scientist, but his CV shows that he was really a "computer guy". Le Roux intended the Somalia compound to be the hub for his arms and drugs business. Jack, who was running the Somalian operation, was tasked with protecting the technical personnel Le Roux sent to Somalia. If Wright did work for Le Roux in Somalia, which is unproven, it would have been to install a computer system. The compound was supposedly a tuna fishing enterprise, so this work would not have been illegal.

The evidence supports Wright's story that while visiting New York in Jan 2011, he had a video conference with Kleiman and the "third man". He then travelled to Venezuela and moved on to FARC-controlled territory on the Venezuela/Colombian border area. He made contact with FARC and was shot.

After being made redundant at the end of 2008, Craig Wright was running out of money. Le Roux loved to prey upon people who were at a loose end and financially desperate. He had a nasty habit of sending people on what they thought were legitimate or grey zone missions only to find themselves up to their neck in criminality. Wright described his time in Venezuela/Colombia as a "blind date" suggesting that he had no idea of what he was letting himself in for.

It should be emphasised that there is no proof that Wright was working for Le Roux on this visit to South America. However, we cannot believe Wright's own explanation that he was an undercover agent working for the CIA/ICE and the Colombian DAS. His story keeps changing and is unverifiable. US government agencies are never going to use an unemployed Australian computer auditor on such a sensitive mission.

The emotional trauma that Wright claims he suffered as a result of his FARC mission is more believable. Wright has been strangely persistent in his Satoshi act, and I believe he is motivated by a deep hatred. He wants to obliterate Satoshi and write him out of his own invention. And more than that, he wants to destroy Bitcoin. That is the implication of his persecution of the Bitcoin core developers and of his attempt to gain copyright over the Bitcoin file system. If he had succeeded, he would have been able to shut down Bitcoin completely and substitute his own Bitcoin variant, BSV. Then he really would be Satoshi.

Was the criminal scheme that Wright described something Le Roux was considering? The fundamental difficulty was the distribution of illegal material risk-free to the ultimate consumer. This would involve encrypted communications, encrypted storage that was undetectable by law enforcement, and, most challenging of all, untraceable payment. Satoshi/Le Roux was an expert at all three requirements. In TrueCrypt and Bitcoin, he had already developed the most advanced solutions for two of the three. If he could go a step further and bring it all together, he could create the ultimate ultra-hardcore pornography business. The obvious market would be paedophiles. But there are other possibilities involving even more extreme material.

Le Roux loved to corrupt people. Imagine if he had succeeded in developing an illegal pornography service where the clients could get whatever they wanted, no matter how extreme, in a way that was completely impenetrable to the police. It would not just give Le Roux money—it would give him immense power. His client list would be eminently blackmailable.

Could even Le Roux be this bad? Or is it just a Wright fantasy? Certainly, Le Roux treated his own harem girls as a commodity. And there is one clue that Le Roux was thinking of people trafficking. Shannon reports that Cindric once asked Le Roux what he would do when he left prison. He is not going to reply truthfully to the DEA agent. But his answer is revealing. He planned to enter a new business area: "Girls… Yeah you know the Arabs. They want the girls."

It may be helpful to summarise Wright and Kleiman's involvement in Bitcoin:

- It started with Kleiman working for Satoshi mining Bitcoin no later than Nov 2009. This collaboration continued until early 2012 and would have resulted in a substantial amount of Bitcoin mined in 2009/2010.
- Kleiman was also responsible for organising Satoshi's non-Patoshi Bitcoin, a considerable task given the number of addresses involved.
- Even before Wright had involvement with Bitcoin, he may have been associated with Le Roux. Wright has given various contradictory explanations for the "third man" on a video conference call with himself and Kleiman in New York in Jan 2011. The only name he gave that is feasible is Le Roux.
- Wright shows knowledge of Bitcoin in 2011, but was unlikely to have been involved until 2013.
- When Le Roux/Satoshi was incarcerated in Sep 2012, his priority was to secure his Bitcoin holdings. To this end, he was extraordinary

cooperative with the DEA, which gave him access to the outside world.

- The natural person to help him keep control of his Bitcoin wealth was Kleiman. However, Kleiman was sick and in hospital and so Wright was also involved. Kleiman discharged himself in Mar 2013, perhaps in preparation for a meeting with Le Roux or his representative.
- Wright travelled to America for this meeting and was in New Jersey on 13 Apr 2013. Le Roux is recorded as released a few days earlier and was presumably on a DEA mission. He may have planned to bring Kleiman and Wright into the DEA operation to shut down Rx Limited.
- Immediately after his journey to the USA, Wright registered a new company in Australia, Coin-Exch, which was intended to be a Bitcoin exchange joint venture with Kleiman.
- Most likely Coin-Exch was planned as a front for Satoshi's Bitcoin holdings. This would involve presenting Wright and Kleiman to the world as two members of a mysterious Satoshi team with Le Roux staying in the shadows as the "third man". (There would be nothing illegal about this as Satoshi had acquired his Bitcoins legitimately.)
- Everything changed when Dave Kleiman died just a few days later. Wright now took the plan forward on his own, He suddenly had access to a lot of money, perhaps financing from Le Roux channelled through Costa Rican casino operations and Liberty Reserve.
- However, Liberty Reserve was taken down by the US. And Wright soon lost credibility with Satoshi due to his incompetence and his grandiose plans which went far beyond Coin-Exch. So Wright had to fall back on financing his business with tax claims.
- Wright continued with the story that he was one part of Satoshi, along with Kleiman and another man, and had control of immense Bitcoin wealth. This developed over the years into his claim to be Satoshi and the sole inventor of Bitcoin.

TWENTY-SIX

X INVENTS BITCOIN

X meant something to Le Roux. It is the last letter of his name, something he could hide behind. We find it in Rx Limited and his customised Bitcoin addresses.

A mysterious poster named "x" came up with the idea of Bitcoin several years before Satoshi. (The poster used a small x either because capital X was already taken or because a small x was more relevant, perhaps because it was the last letter of his name. The use of a small letter for a name is awkward, so I have used capital X for the poster in what follows.) X posted their idea to the p2p Usenet group and another unexpected Usenet group—uk.finance:

> "Virtual peer to peer banking:
>
> I have this idea of a future with virtual peer to peer banking. A kind of decentralized and secured system. Gone would be the times that governments and banks can track and interfere with our money transfers. Or even interfere with the total amount of money on earth. My envisioned system would have a fixed total amount of money. But each money unit (say virtual coin) is divisible indefinitely. So a kind of deflation would replace inflation. The total value of the money in the world would be a fixed number. It poses no problem for liquidity, because the currency can be divided anytime. However maybe people will not spend their money much, because it's value will increase often. Other problems raise in the areas of security, malicious use, and how to come towards such system from current systems? These are just ideas, I like to hear comments or about net resources on this subject." (9 Dec 2002)

X would have been disappointed with the response. He was met with derision: "You are a crazy man (woman)..." was the curt response of a German poster, although they added a smiley face. OneGuy said, "I want some of what you're smoking!" The response from "wwf" was more hostile: "Good idea ben Laden."

A poster called Matt thought that X's scheme would cause massive inflation because it was not backed by anything:

> "What you don't understand is how money gets its value. It gets its value by having a stack of some metal, ore, etc. i.e. if you have a $1 bill, it represents one dollar worth of gold, silver, of whatever."

Another poster, "Reflector," pointed out that currencies are not actually backed by gold anymore. "Miner" offered a different criticism, misunderstanding the nature of a peer-to-peer system: "It would require way too much cooperation and communication between different countries and governments that want nothing to do with another, not now, or ever."

X's response to these objections was polite and thought-provoking:

> "Maybe the community can bypass the old powers (countries and governments). It wouldn't be a revolution, but rather evolution. Slowly a new p2p system might take over. The current monetary systems were mainly backed with gold (not anymore now, to my knowledge). Maybe the underlying values of a virtual peer to peer system could be other scarce resources, relatively easy to exchange via internet. Examples are: computer processing power, bandwidth and data storage. These resources would make a limited peer to peer money exchange system possible. Limited to the total real life value of all these resources. However from that point other resources could back up the virtual currency..." (10 Dec 2002)

No one was positive. Only "Reflector" was not hostile and mentioned a scheme in Hong Kong using Octopus cards. X replied:

"It is a step in the right direction indeed. Now replace the system operator by a secure peer to peer system. And replace the underlying currency with something else, or slowly uncouple the underlying currency. Then it would be the system of my ideas…" (10 Dec 2002)

In these posts, X outlines several of the main features of Bitcoin:

It is peer-to-peer, eliminating the need for a central third party.
It would gradually replace government-sanctioned currencies, and there would be no future need for banks.
There is a fixed total amount of virtual coins.
Each coin is infinitely divisible, providing the necessary liquidity.
Deflation would replace inflation and the value of the virtual coins would appreciate.

X also thinks of the profit potential: "maybe people will not spend their money much, because it's value will increase often." In the second post, he is groping towards the idea of the proof of work. He suggests using internet resources to back the currency instead of something like gold. These resources include "computer processing power". It is not yet the elegant concept employed by Bitcoin, but it is a first step from which X could have developed the Bitcoin proof of work following exposure to Adam Back's Hashcash.

X must have come up with his idea independently of earlier attempts to develop a crypto-currency. He is looking for "net resources" and pointers to help build the idea. This rules out all the favourite candidates, such as Adam Back, Nick Szabo, Hal Finney and Wei Dai. No cypherpunk would ask for "net resources" from Usenet groups such as p2p and uk.finance. The early innovators were already engaged at a much more advanced level. And none of them would have any reason to post to the uk.finance group except perhaps Adam Back, who was British. And X can't be Back because he had already developed the elegant hash cash proof of work. X is an innovative thinker ignorant of earlier work that went in the same direction.

The posts were first brought to light in 2014 by a Reddit poster "slapded". There was a lot of excitement with over 200 comments, the great majority agreeing that X was Satoshi. One poster summed it up succinctly —"Yep. Totally found him. Satoshi's real name is X"!

Was this the chink in Satoshi's armour, a post made before he erected his anonymity barriers? The hunt for X was on. It was determined that X was using an internet provider, xs4all.nl, operating in the Netherlands. X was also active in other Usenet groups. In one such group, X said he was Dutch. No one had expected Satoshi to be Dutch! Everyone who had examined Satoshi's communications concluded that he was a native English speaker. However, some independent evidence supported a Netherlands connection: early Bitcoin modules recorded the time zone as UTC + 1 hour.

A Dutch Satoshi living in Holland in the early 2000s ruled out all the favourite candidates. People concluded that X could not be Satoshi after all. Only later did a plausible candidate emerge who had been living in the Netherlands at the right time—Paul Le Roux.

It is worth looking at some of X's other posts, for they are illuminating. One question is whether they are all by the same person. X is not a unique username, and there could be different people using X in newsgroups over the years. However, we can identify a set of posts made between 9 Dec and 23 Dec 2002 by "x" with a similar style, which came from an ISP that can be identified from multiple posts as xs4all.nl. They are obviously the same person.

X came up with another innovative idea posted to the p2p group just ten days after his virtual coin post. In this new post, he described a system of internet communications that could not be eavesdropped by a third party such as law enforcement:

> "Anonymousity [sic] through encrypted p2p pool
>
> Maybe the following network situation enables a reasonable means of anonymousity on the regular internet: Imagine a p2p network in which each time you (or your browser or another application) send an IP request to the "normal" internet a local IP daemon on your host will randomly select a peer in the available p2p pool. The request is sent encrypted (RSA) to the random peer and there the peer decrypts the request and executes the request for you on the normal (insecure,

> eavesdrop-unprotected) internet domain. When the peer gets a response of the single request it encrypts the response and sends it to the original requestor. Now you have a kind of semi-anonymous proxy. However, it is naive to trust the proxy peer (just like any proxy) so your local IP daemon sends each request to a different random peer. So even if a peer wants to do malicious things with your transmitted data, it only has control over a small amount of your data: a single webpage transmission, or a single email (encrypted if you like), a single newsgroup posting, etc etc. To increase the anonymousity the method could be extended to allow multiple hops. Then you send your request through n peers. Through RSA each peer on the route only knows the IP address of the previous and next peer on the route. Only the last peer can read the actual IP request, while only the first peer knows the requestor's IP address. Of course malicious peers are able to propagate information about you (your IP address, the request or the response). However, a number of peers must now cooperate to do that. If n=20 and the peers you choose are sufficiently random (e.g. geographically) the chance that 20 peers cooperate to [disclose] your data would be rather small. How about that? Or is the system doomed to fail? Or is the system unnecessarily complex, i.e. are there better ways to ensure anonymousity?" (19 Dec 2002)

X is describing a system similar to the Tor browser. The idea uses multiple nodes to transmit an encrypted message from node to node. Only the last node knows the ultimate destination, and only the first knows the sender's IP. Tor stands for "The Onion Router" and is a famous/infamous tool for ensuring anonymous communication. The onion refers to multiple levels of encryption, with each node unwrapping one layer of the onion but not knowing what came before or after.

Tor is the means of accessing the dark web to acquire drugs, weapons or child pornography, with transactions often settled in Bitcoin. It is also a lifeline to free information and communications for millions living under oppressive regimes. Within ten days, X has outlined the two primary tools beloved by internet criminals and libertarians!

But X did not invent Tor. The principles for the browser were developed in academic work in the mid-1990s, and the prototype of Tor was launched Sep 2002, a few months before X's post. The trial was confined to just a few users, and not many people would have heard about the project in Dec 2002. None of the responders to X's post mentioned Tor. X has come up with the idea independently.

The problem of finding enough people to volunteer as nodes was raised in the discussion. Another objection was that the system would be very slow. X's responses make it clear that he envisaged a general system for point-to-point communications:

> "YES, however I would like more a system that not only is limited to remailing but rather a system that gives you more general anonymous point to point IP connections (via peer to peer pool). An interesting detail is that if each peer never "interprets" (on machine or human level) the request nor response and only relays it, then legally it would be harder to punish him if he relayed an illegal internet communication. Because he couldn't know about it." (20 Dec 2002)

This is the legal argument protecting those who operate Tor nodes. They cannot know what is being transmitted through their servers because everything is encrypted. X anticipated the same argument in his scheme.

X uses poor English, odd phrases, and misspellings. He sounds nothing like Satoshi or Le Roux. Note the strange word "anonymousity", which is not a real word at all. When someone pointed this out, X replied that he was Dutch:

> "I'm not a native English speaker (but Dutch). I made the word from the stem "anonymous" according to the geek way: [...] The word sounds nice for Dutch people, almost intimate :)" (20 Dec 2002)

X indeed shows every sign of not being a native English speaker. But is it all an act? He does seem to take it too far.

One link with Le Roux is that X is an extreme libertarian obsessed with privacy. All his posts are concerned with escaping from under the foot of authority and the oversight of Big Brother. He is engrossed in ensuring completely anonymous communications and putting transactions out of the reach of government:

> "Yes, performance will be a pain in the ass. If one wants to download porno one better sticks to soon-to-be-extensively-monitored-an d-moderated-regular-internet-connections. About "anonymousity": what if they (ISPs, Big brother, or even worse) record all data you download and upload. It is not as expensive as you think for a big user group. Because many download the same files. An eavesdropping big brother just hashes the stuff and couples the hashes to your IP (and personal ID?)." (21 Dec 2002)

These groups would then have "15 years of all your (and all your peers) communications, which they can use for marketing, blackmailing, etc. In the meanwhile you are crying about not bothering about privacy earlier…". Look past the broken, childish English and you can see that X is highly intelligent. To save storage space, he has the idea of hashing files with user identification to preserve evidence of who was accessing what files—potentially illegal/pornographic—without having to save the entire file multiple times. It is all very similar to how the blockchain uses hashes to incorporate an image of the previous block.

Most people who posted to these groups were libertarians of some sort, but both X and Le Roux take this to extremes:

> "Isn't it a good practise to don't trust people? See Machiavelli (link expires 500 years ago)." (21 Dec 2002)

X's posts are centred on peer-to-peer (p2p), a hot topic at the time. It was under attack by copyright holders and government. Napster had led the way with its hugely popular free audio file-sharing service before it was forced to close down in Jul 2001. Napster's weakness was that it had been a centralised system with a head that could be cut off. X knew that it was better to use a completely non-centralised system. Such was the thinking behind Bitcoin.

The day after his virtual coin post, X posted about the future of p2p on the p2p group, going through various scenarios. It was, in his own words, "a step by step possible future of battle between copyright owners (big brother, etc) and freedom fighters (p2p)". For each privacy idea, there was a matching response by Big Brother. It is illuminating to consider x's ideas for robust p2p systems:

> "p2p users switch to encrypted systems, third parties (eg governments or copyright owners) simply cannot detect who is sharing what."
>
> "encrypted connections through satellites of foreign countries are used."
>
> "p2p will get a new meaning: wireless p2p: each p2p user connects wireless and encrypted with other p2p users. ISP's and centralization in general are bypassed."
> (10 Dec 2002)

All these solutions involve encrypted communications. X even has the idea of individuals connecting directly to each other wirelessly without an ISP. By using encryption, their communications could not be eavesdropped. You can envisage a new internet based on such a system that is entirely outside government control. It would completely undermine copyright, censorship and any other restriction on communications and information exchange. And if you could combine this with X's virtual coin, a large slice of economic activity could disappear beyond the reach of regulation and taxation. It is a virtual paradise or dark web nightmare, depending on your point of view. But as X points out, governments could simply outlaw such wireless communications. Even foreign satellites can be shot out of the sky.

At this time, Le Roux had spent years writing disk encryption software, which is the one topic that X does not mention. When someone suggested "there are many ways to hide files", X gave an unusually terse reply: "I agree".

X is full of ideas:

> "An idea: How about p2p radio. There are many radio streaming providers on internet. But if we distribute radio via p2p networks, we could be independent of these providers." (10 Dec 2002)

In another thread on the same group, a poster, Jeff, complained that 75% of the songs he downloaded from Grokster came out wrong and suspected that the copyright holders' association RCIAA was uploading "crap" as a tactic to disrupt file sharing. X came up with the idea of users attaching feedback to files, such as "real" or "fake", and adds a comment about hashes:

> "By the way... Is FastTrack using hashes for files? This should increase the possibilities to link this kind of metadata even more. I know EDonkey uses (used?) hashes." (10 Dec 2002}

The issue is much more complicated than just adding reviews, as X perhaps realises as he writes. How can you verify that the reviews are genuine? What is to stop the uploader of a fake or malicious file from attaching a pile of good reviews? It is part of a bigger problem of p2p networks: how can a user trust the content they are downloading? One solution was to use hashes from the SHA256 algorithm or something similar. The user's computer calculates the file's hash and compares it to the value from a trusted source. If they match, then the file has not been tampered with. A development of this idea is to use a Merkel tree, a hierarchy of hashes that can efficiently verify a database of files, such as an audio file split into many subfiles.

X's brief comment shows that he is familiar with the use of hashes by some p2p systems, and is considering how they could be used to authenticate reviews. This is a deep problem. You still need a trusted source for the hash to authenticate the file. Does that sound familiar? There is a close parallel between verifying p2p files and verifying crypto transactions. Hashes are one part of the solution. Bitcoin uses hashes and Merkel trees to ensure the integrity of the blockchain. It is the same structure used by some of the earlier p2p file-sharing systems. But it would take Satoshi years to remove the requirement for the trusted third party.

We started with Jeff's complaint that his "Beautiful Day" download came out as hip-hop, and ended up with the architecture of the Bitcoin blockchain. Often, real-life problems that seem very different are mathematically closely related.

X's posts lead us to an unexpected insight into the origins of Bitcoin: it emerged from p2p rather than earlier cryptocurrency ideas. Assuming that X is Satoshi, he must have continued researching his "virtual coin" and come across some of those earlier papers. Back's Hashcash gave him the missing piece, the proof of work towards which he was already struggling. However, the genesis of Bitcoin lay in the world of p2p ideas and applications that were circulating feverishly in the early 2000s.

Let us look at two of X's posts that link to Le Roux's areas of interest. One poster suggested that cash would soon be made illegal, but they could use scrip (he called it "script") instead. Scrip are notes issued by private banks, so this is not a great idea. X suggested gold instead:

> "Why all troubles. Let's use gold again. Buy PDAs with built-in weight balance for taxing. Melt gold in standard spherical sizes to do it even simpler. (Metric system please!)."

This is not easy to understand! It seems "taxing" is a typo for "testing". Like Le Roux, X had an interest in gold, although there is nothing remarkable about his suggestion of using gold rather than scrip. What is unusual is the emphasis on gold assay, testing its purity. This would not occur to most gold-bugs who acquire gold as coins or pre-fabricated bars. X suggests a PDA with an inbuilt weight balance. A Personal Digital Assistant was a device such as the Palm Pilot that many of us carried around in the early 2000s before the iPhone. If gold were in "standard spherical sizes", it would be easy to calculate volume. If the PDA had an inbuilt scale, it would know the weight and calculate the density to check if it matched gold. The comment about using the "metric system" refers to replacing the traditional measure of troy ounces, which introduces an unnecessary complication.

X has given a very technical reply. Le Roux came from a gold town and was the son of a gold-mining engineer. In a few years, he would be occupied with the problem of testing his own gold.

The second post is in an "Anonymous cell phone" thread about acquiring a burner phone that could not be traced. Several people made helpful suggestions about where to buy such a phone, and one poster cautioned about the dangers: "Just remember that by calling phone numbers you provide clues to your identity. So depending on how you want to use the phone you may want several phones for calling different people." X added his comment:

> "And you are subject to eavesdropping by Echelon or whatever name they give those Big brother systems. Voice identification systems will be far more abundant (-cheap) in the near future. So save anonymous calling via a telephone exchange: forget it. The answer to this is public/private key encryption not issued by a third party but generated by yourself or by well known open source software. But hehe see this on phones soon?" (22 Dec 2002)

"Echelon" is the "Five Eyes" surveillance program led by the United States. Echelon was something of an obsession to Le Roux to the extent that he even called his security company "Echelon Associates". Here is Le Roux writing about Echelon on the E4M website:

> "Project ECHELON shows the extent to which major world governments have gone to invade everyone's privacy. The UKUSA agreement between the U.S, U.K, Canada, Australia & New Zealand facilitated project ECHELON, which intercepts global phone calls, faxes, and email messages transmitted via satellites, if certain "key words" are detected the communication is recorded for later analysis by the intelligence agencies of the respective governments."

X says that Echelon is developing software to identify specific voices, which would enable them to tie individuals to calls even if those calls are made by untraceable phones. He suggests using encrypted communications instead of voice communications through normal phone systems.

Note the final sentence: "But hehe on phones soon?" Presumably, "hehe" is supposed to mean LOL. X suggests that a phone encrypting all its communications could escape eavesdropping provided the user-controlled the encryption and not the phone network provider. Such a phone is unlikely to become available because governments would hate this idea. And even if such a phone were marketed, the user could never be confident that the encryption did not have backdoors. So it was safest to do it yourself or use "well-known open source software".

The user would need a device to encrypt conversations before relaying them over the phone network. As it happened, Le Roux had been working on just such a device. He posted about his idea to sci.crypt a year earlier:

> "Hi is there any interest out there in a voice encryption box which will basically would allow a standard phone/fax to plug into it and go secure with another similar unit. The units would offer:
>
> * AES 128-bit for voice encryption
> * G723.1 voice compression
> * 1024-bit DH using interlock protocol for key agreement
>
> The units will be about the size of an external modem, and AC powered.
>
> We would like to create a voice encryption unit for the masses and would price the unit at about $150.
>
> Is there any demand out there?
>
> We are also looking for investors, we currently have the electrical design for the above device, but have not yet decided to go ahead yet, because first: we need to know what the demand is likely to be like, and secondly: we need investors who want to be part of our exciting new hardware security company." (14 Oct 2001)

Le Roux must have spent considerable time on this device in 2001, presumably with Hafner at SecurStar, although nothing seems to have come of it. One problem is that both parties in the call need one of these units. The market was likely to be limited, and many potential customers would be criminals.

Several years later, Hafner manufactured such a phone. Shannon reports an intriguing conversation between him and Le Roux about financing this project. Hafner claimed to have been emailed by Le Roux out of the blue and not to have known about Rx Limited and the programmer's newfound wealth. This is unbelievable as Hafner was involved in Atlas-Pharmacy. More likely, Hafner contacted Le Roux as they had worked previously on a similar device. Le Roux wanted a business plan before investing. Hafner's normal investors were not the type to read business plans, and he claimed to have walked away from the deal. It seems more likely that Le Roux rejected him.

Hafner said about Le Roux, "he came with some, how do you say, interesting, innovative ideas." The same was true of X. He only posted for a few weeks, but suggested several striking ideas:

A virtual coin to replace the world's monetary systems which anticipated many of the features of Bitcoin.
A system for anonymous and untraceable p2p communications which prefigures Tor.
The idea of using direct p2p communications over wireless networks.
The concept of p2p radio stations.
The idea of hashing files together with user id to preserve proof.
Using gold to replace cash with ideas for testing the purity of gold.
Encrypting phone conversations to avoid surveillance.

Some of these ideas, such as the Tor idea, were already being done. Others were impractical. One of them would give rise to cryptocurrency.

X's last post was made the day before Le Roux's thirtieth birthday. Le Roux was at a crossroads: it was that critical time in life when people take stock of their progress and experience the disappointment of how far they have fallen behind their earlier ambitions and dreams.

Le Roux had spent years developing state-of-the-art open source encryption software, and it must have seemed to him that he had little to show for it. He was living with his wife and kids in a small flat in Rotterdam. He had broken with Hafner and was back looking for contract work.

Analysis of Le Roux's posts on alt.security.scramdisk for late 2002 and early 2003 show that he was dividing his time between the Netherlands and South Africa. In the Netherlands, Le Roux used a different mail domain, "wxs", than X's "xs4all". So if Le Roux was X, he was trying to disguise his identity, at least to the extent of going to a coffee shop to send his X posts.

X claimed to be Dutch. Le Roux was not Dutch but would often adopt a Dutch identity. The Le Roux family had Dutch ancestry: "I also have some Dutch ancestry, my name in fact is the Dutch spelling of a French surname." (Le Roux, 11 Nov 1995). He grew up in Krugersdorp, where most white people spoke the Dutch variant Afrikaans as their first language. He lived in the Netherlands. Later, in the Philippines, he went under the name Johan Le Roux, and many people thought he was from Holland.

Le Roux loved to put on an act and deceive people even when there was no reason. So X's Dutch nationality and poor English could be a deliberate attempt to hide his real identity. Expressions such as "anonymousity" are suspiciously over the top. Would a poor English speaker really communicate like this? The problem with pretending is the tendency to lapse into your everyday style. X actually can communicate perfectly well in English, as a couple of examples show:

> "My proposal is about cases in which you want to be anonymous. This is technically (and socially) very different a concept from sharing sheer computing power (or data). However, maybe some interdisciplinary knowledge can be shared."

> "Yes. That is a better earning concept than copyright. However we still have to be able to share without commercials too. It's just more a matter of freedom, not just a matter of getting around copyright. I think p2p has the future not only for sharing copyrighted media, but also for many other future decentralized moderator less systems for exchanging freedom of speech, money transfers, secure private data storage, authentication etc etc."

It is strange that someone who appears to struggle with English can communicate these complex topics so well. These particular extracts could certainly have come from Le Roux or Satoshi.

X's spelling is particularly poor, perhaps deliberately so. But then Le Roux's spelling and English were often poor when trolling Australian groups in his early twenties. And Le Roux's English would have improved substantially between 2002 and 2008 because, at this time, he had an ambition to be a writer. We can see both X and Satoshi as Le Roux putting on an act: for X, he uses poor English as an imagined Dutch speaker; for Satoshi, he puts on his best polished English by employing a grammar and spelling checker.

How can we be confident that X is Le Roux? Le Roux used two aliases in Usenet groups that can be identified. One of them happens to be X.

TWENTY-SEVEN

X AND ENTROPY

Le Roux mostly posted under his real name before Bitcoin. The only exceptions are connected to TrueCrypt when he had to hide his identity because of the dispute with Hafner. The evidence lies in the archive of the alt.security.scramdisk Usenet group. Le Roux sent more posts to this group than to any other. He apparently stopped posting to this group in Oct 2003, except for his final farewell post in Jun 2004. But he actually continued participating under two aliases.

TrueCrypt 1.0 was launched on 2 Feb 2004 and supposedly abandoned two days later because of the Hafner copyright dispute. A new poster to the scramdisk group called Entropy appeared on 3 Feb commenting on the TrueCrypt launch thread. Another poster, X, started posting in Apr 2004. We will show that both Entropy and X are Paul Le Roux.

TrueCrypt 2.0 was released on 9 Jun 2004. It was attributed to the TrueCrypt Foundation rather than the TrueCrypt Team responsible for TrueCrypt 1.0. This change was obviously to give cover against Hafner's actions, and there is no reason to doubt that the same people were involved. Several new posters, including Entropy and X, had appeared in the scramdisk group with the launch of TrueCrypt. Some gave detailed technical replies to questions about TrueCrypt and obviously had some involvement in the TrueCrypt project, although they denied this. One poster, "WinTerMiNator", speculated that all the new arrivals were one person:

> "Hello, Crow = X = Entropy = ... what else?
>
> Are you the author of TrueCrypt? In that case, it is schizophrenic to want to stay anonymous and want to get all the gratitude for it!" (8 Jun 2004)

He thought that the new posters were all David Tesarik:

> Maybe are you David T. = flare253, author of TrueCrypt 1.0, living in Czech republic, fond of J. S. Bach, webmaster of a web site with only a picture of an angel, and a very big traffic (of course, there is a hidden entry to this web site)…" (8 Jun 2004)

In his next post, he took it further and added the observation that all the mysterious TrueCrypt posters used the same news service:

> "Crow = X = Entropy = H2O = Anonymous = Flare253 = The TrueCrypt Team = David Terasik [sic], who uses Teranews for posting and Xnews/5.04.25 as Newsreader." (8 Jun 2004)

Crow thought the idea that he was involved in TrueCrypt was hilarious. Others pointed out that Teranews was a very popular way of posting anonymously. While this is true, it is still an unlikely coincidence that all the new TrueCrypt posters use the same service. It indicates they are linked but does not necessarily mean they are all the same person. The Czech programmer David Tesarik was the only acknowledged member of the TrueCrypt team. But others must have been involved and they kept their identities secret. Flare is David Tesarik, who openly used this name in discussions several months before launching TrueCrypt. Some, like Crow, were probably not involved.

WinTerMiNator was right about one thing: X and Entropy are the same person, but not David Tesarik. Entropy and X have an identical style and use identical arguments, and one will continue an argument that the other started. For example, in two separate threads, they argue whether law enforcement could prosecute people for having a hidden TrueCrypt file on their computer. They both maintain that in "democratic countries", no one could be prosecuted for simply having a file of apparently random numbers on their computer, even though any computer forensic expert would know it was an encrypted directory. They both suggest having a program on the computer to generate random numbers for plausible deniability. They even use the same hypothetical case. Here is Entropy responding to "nemo_outis":

> "In democratic countries speculations are not sufficient. I can speculate that you are a serial killer. Anyone can make up anything. However, the essential thing is to be able to prove it. You do not need to be afraid of my speculations, because they are just speculations and nothing more." (13 Mar 2004)

And here is X using exactly the same example, that nemo_outis is a murderer, two months later:

> "I am an expert and my expert opinion is that nemo_outis killed my best friend. But I cannot prove that. It is just my opinion. Do you think that we could get nemo_outis in prison? Without any evidence, just by persuading the judge (come on, it is *very* likely that he killed him!)" (2 May 2004)

Entropy does give us one small clue to his identity:

> "In the country where I live (Europe, but not the UK), our constitution grants us the right to refuse to testify if you believe it could harm you." (17 Mar 2004)

This narrows things down a little: Entropy speaks English as a native and yet lives in a continental European country—note that he only says he lives there, not that it is his home country. Le Roux was living in the Netherlands at the time of this post.

How can we be confident that X and Entropy are Le Roux? All three use a very similar business-like style, which is similar to Satoshi. None give an inch in argument or ever apologise for anything. Not that this was unusual in the masculine environment of computer Usenet groups where it was almost expected that participants would trade insults. But their curt replies show an unusual degree of control. Others throw their toys out of the pram or concoct long arguments about why they are right and their opponent an idiot. But not X, Entropy or Le Roux. All three are short, rational, and to the point. But they certainly don't give out a warm fuzzy feeling.

Style can hardly decide the issue. In substance, the views of both Entropy and X are remarkably similar to those of Paul Le Roux. One example is the GPL licence. Both Le Roux and Satoshi disliked this licence, and so did X:

> "TC and SD [scramdisk] are open source, which is enough. GPL is not anything we should look for or care about." (18 Apr 2004)

And Entropy also:

> "E4M and TC are properly open source too. IMHO, GPL is more restrictive than E4M license. What I really like about E4M and TrueCrypt is that they use salt, which makes them much more secure than Scramdisk (and I suppose DriveCrypt too)." (13 Feb 2004)

This post brings up the revealing subject of "salt". This was a longstanding issue of contention between SecurStar's two programmers: Le Roux and Shaun Hollingworth. Salt is an additional protection against hackers. It is a random number combined with a password before it is hashed. The advantage of salt is that it makes a dictionary attack using a precomputed series of hashes much harder.

Satoshi was familiar with the concept. He mentioned salt while floating an idea to make Bitcoin more anonymous on the Bitcoin Forum:

> "The inpoint signs a hash of its associated next outpoint and a salt, so it can privately be shown that the signature signs a particular next outpoint if you know the salt, but publicly the network doesn't know what the next outpoint is." (11 Aug 2010)

Le Roux was enthusiastic about salt, but Shaun Hollingworth considered it unnecessary. When Hollingworth was asked if DriveCrypt Plus Pack included a salt, he replied: "It is likely to, as Paul is rather fond of them... " (4 Apr 2002). While Le Roux's DCPP included salt, Hollingworth's DriveCrypt did not. Even when the two were working at the same company, there was competitive rivalry between them. With the launch of

TrueCrypt there was an open feud between Le Roux on one side and Hafner and Hollingworth on the other.

In the post above, Entropy does not mention Hollingworth by name but takes a little dig at him. Hollingworth's two products, Scramdisk and DriveCrypt, do not include salt and are, therefore, less secure than Le Roux's products, E4M and TrueCrypt.

Sam Simpson was a programmer who had become involved with Scramdisk. He became involved in a discussion with Entropy who was also strongly in favour of salt:

> "Salt has been invented to protect crypto systems from dictionary attacks. You probably know that dictionary attack is the most feasible and the most probable one. Nobody is going to brute-force SD containers." (13 Feb 2004)

Simpson replied that it would be impractical to attack Scramdisk in this way because of its slow response time but made an admission:

> "With hindsight, not salting passphrases for Scramdisk was an oversight...."

To which Entropy replies:

> "...or incompetence and a lack of knowledge"

Sam Simpson's response to Entropy's provocation was relatively mild:

> "I look forward to seeing your (lack of...) cryptography prowess one day ;)" (13 Feb 2004)

Entropy is accusing Shaun Hollingworth of incompetence, which seems incredibly arrogant from an unknown new poster to the scramdisk group, named after Hollingworth's product. Unless, of course, that poster is Le Roux.

Another revealing exchange involving Entropy and X came about after a poster reported a bug in TrueCrypt under the heading "Random pool weakness in TrueCrypt." He had not been able to contact the TrueCrypt team and so posted the report to the scramdisk group. Entropy responded with an authoritative reply:

> "You probably did not mean predicting the output, but knowing the values that have been generated. You forgot one important thing: Knowing the output of the random number generator does not help an adversary in any way. The output is used to generate the master key when creating a new volume. This master key is stored in RAM *every* time the volume is mounted anyway, so an adversary would gain nothing if he grabbed the output of the random number generator while you are formatting the volume." (13 May 2004)

I have repeated this in full to show the degree of Entropy's expert knowledge of TrueCrypt. He is also very protective:

> "And one last comment, IMHO you should avoid sensational subject lines like "Random pool weakness in TrueCrypt" when, as you said, you are not sure whether you are right or not." (13 May 2004)

This is harsh! The poster reviewed the TrueCrypt code and found something genuinely wrong even though it did not have security implications. Other posters defended him, and X joined the argument, posting 19 minutes after Entropy and taking an identical line:

> "In my opinion, it was a *very* bad message and exactly the kind of message we should all dislike. OTFE [On The Fly Encryption] is a very sensitive area and when you post such an alarming message (that can potentially spoil a good product's name), you should at least know what you are talking about. He is just a perfect example of a guy who writes faster than thinks." (14 May 2004)

Entropy claims to have reviewed the code of TrueCrypt, which is why he knows so much about it. When asked, he knew all the differences between TrueCrypt and its predecessor, E4M:

> "The differences between the source code of E4M and Truecrypt match the change log (version history) that is in the manual. Apart from these well-documented changes, there are some minor changes (variables were renamed, etc.)
>
> Those who assumed that Truecrypt has the same basic structure, techniques, etc., were right. It is improved and bug-fixed E4M (plus several new functions). The only incompatibility with E4M is the volume format (E4M volumes have unencrypted headers, which makes them identifiable)."

The random pool weakness bug went back to E4M. When Paul Le Roux first posted about E4M under the name "Abacus", he announced that he was collaborating with Peter Gutmann to support his "MDC/SHA implementation and his 'IV scrambler' for sector by sector unique IV generation" (13 Oct 1998). Gutmann was a distinguished academic computer scientist from New Zealand. His random number methodology had been incorrectly implemented in E4M and hence TrueCrypt. Gutmann participated in the scramdisk group and posted about the correct implementation. X replied:

> "BTW, E4M does it the same way as Truecrypt. Truecrypt only improves things a little by applying SHA1 each time a byte is added to the pool.
>
> PS - It is sad that you used E4M too (if I recall correctly) yet you have not found time to review its source code (not even to make sure your own PRNG specs have been correctly implemented.)" (15 May 2004)

X is saying the bug is Gutmann's fault! TrueCrypt has inherited the bug from E4M, and if Gutmann had reviewed E4M properly, it would have been found long ago. The mask has slipped. X is emotionally involved in this argument. How could he possibly know that Gutmann had never reviewed the E4M source code and the implementation of his specs in 1998? Only Le Roux would know this. It was Le Roux's perpetual gripe that no one reviewed E4M except those who wished to copy it.

X, like Entropy, understands the issue. When asked whether TrueCrypt is secure, he gives a confident reply:

> "Yes, it is. This is just that the PRNG specs have not been implemented in its entirety. But it does not affect the security of TC or TC containers." (19 May 2004)

It is obvious that Entropy/X was involved in TrueCrypt. Entropy's response to a comment that no one will fix bugs as TrueCrypt 1.0 had been abandoned confirms this:

> "I wonder why you are so sure that nobody will fix them. You suppose that all programmers are dead?" (14 May 2004)

He is even more definite when someone raises the issue of the copyright conflict with SecurStar:

> "If it is done anonymously, there will be no problems with SS. You really are pessimistic. Actually I am quite sure that the development *will* continue soon. ;-)" (15 May 2004)

Entropy knows that TrueCrypt development is resuming soon: only Le Roux could authorise new development. And Entropy was proved right. Within a month, TrueCrypt 2.0 was launched. The coincidence did not go unnoticed and a poster "Phillip J. Fry" speculated that Entropy was the author of TrueCrypt 2.0:

> "There have been several side comments by an individual in here who said he was quite sure that somebody was about to fix some bugs in TC and release it. It doesn't take too much effort to connect the dots." (8 Jun 2004)

Entropy denies this:

> "I made such a comment. However, Truecrypt 2.0 is not my work. I did not even know that TC 1.0 corrupted data. Good job whoever did it." (11 Jun 2004)

He is probably truthful in saying that he did not program TrueCrypt 2.0, but his reply is disingenuous. Entropy is part of the TrueCrypt project.

The crucial issue is whether we can be sure that X is Le Roux. The decisive evidence comes in a thread "Scramdisk and Windows XP". It starts with Phillip J. Fry saying that E4M was forced to remove scramdisk compatibility:

> "The exact format of the scramdisk volume belongs to Shaun and he won't allow anybody else (such as e4m, Truecrypt, etc.) to create a program that is compatible with it. That's why e4m had to remove scramdisk compatibility back in v2.0." (24 May 2004)

X jumps in to tell us the real story, which involves salt:

> "This is not correct. Paul Le Roux removed Scramdisk support when he found out that Scramdisk was not as good as he had thought (no salt etc.) plus E4M ran on Windows 98 too after he swapped source code with S. Hollingworth (Scramdisk Win98 code was used for E4M and E4M WinNT code was used for Scramdisk) so he no longer felt the need to support SD containers." (25 May 2004)

How could X know everything about Le Roux's reasons for removing scam disk support five years ago? X must be Le Roux. "Phillip J. Fry" responds:

> "In that case I stand corrected. However, at the time people were saying it was because Shaun had 'requested' it. Scramdisk support was in e4m very very briefly." (25 May 2004)

X realises that he has gone too far and tries to explain how he knows so much:

> "Yes, according to some sources there was a request from him. What I wrote was basically what I had read on the official E4M site a couple of years ago." (25 May 2004)

No one is going to remember what they read on a website "a couple of years ago". And then jump in angrily to correct a misunderstanding about Le Roux's motivations. Not unless they are Le Roux himself.

Meanwhile, Shaun Hollingworth has been stung by X saying that Scramdisk was "not as good as he [Le Roux] had thought":

> "That is not true either. Paul Le Roux decided HIMSELF to remove SD support, when I make SD work with NT.... I didn't ask him to do it. The nuances of Scramdisk encryption, were not at all considered when he decided to remove the support.,
> Shaun.;"
> (26 May 2004)

X retaliates by correcting Shaun:

> "Were not at all considered? Well then let me quote from the E4M official site:
> 'As E4M has more sophisticated Pkcs-5 key setting, and faster cipher implementations than Scramdisk, support for Scramdisk will be phased out when E4M supports Windows 95/98.'" (27 May 2004)

There is no doubt that X is Le Roux in this argument.

Shortly after the launch of TrueCrypt 2.0, Le Roux made his final statement to the group. After that, Entropy and X more or less disappeared, although X made a final post on 30 Aug 2004. This was around the time Le Roux relocated to the Philippines.

To summarise, X posted his idea of a virtual coin with several distinct similarities to Bitcoin in Dec 2002. He was no cypherpunk: he posted the idea on the UK finance group and was ignorant of previous attempts to develop a cryptocurrency. At the same time, X posted other innovative ideas, demonstrating a wide breadth of thought. Like Le Roux, he had a technical interest in gold and voice encryption over a phone. Like Le Roux, X was an extreme libertarian who had the same obsession with privacy and encryption. X posted from the Netherlands, where Le Roux was living. He claimed to be Dutch, as did Le Roux.

Le Roux attached particular importance to the X that terminated his name. This is shown by Rx Limited and the Bitcoin address customisations, which invariably end with X. Most notably, Le Roux posted as X in connection with TrueCrypt. It is one of only two aliases he used before relocating to the Philippines in mid-2004 and commencing his criminal career.

Le Roux is X.

TWENTY-EIGHT

CONCLUSION

Satoshi is Paul Le Roux. It may be helpful to summarise the evidence. The Satoshi profile matches Le Roux perfectly. Satoshi was, first and foremost, a programmer and an expert in C++. Hal Finney said he must have learned this language at a young age. Le Roux specialised in C++ programming and first learned the language at around age twenty. By the time Bitcoin launched, he had fifteen years of professional programming experience. Satoshi was also described as a "paranoid" programmer due to his habit of writing dense, compact code, which few programmers could keep track of. Some have viewed him as working close to the metal. This also fits Le Roux, who spent years working on encryption software which required assembly code. On one occasion, he took 3 months to write code so compact that it fitted into 400 bytes. He also worked on an electronic device for encrypting phone signals.

Satoshi's other area of technical expertise was cryptography. Although he said he was no cryptographer, Satoshi shows great understanding and skill in the use of encryption technologies. Le Roux had no mathematical or computer science training, and probably no deep theoretical knowledge of cryptography. But he was an expert at the practical application of cryptography, writing a whole series of cutting-edge products for hard disk encryption.

Satoshi was no cypherpunk and was largely ignorant of earlier attempts at cryptocurrency. Although heavily involved in encryption, Le Roux did not belong to the cypherpunk mailing groups.

Satoshi wrote open source code, helped people run the software, and spent significant time over two years answering problems and dealing with bug fixes. Le Roux issued an open source product, E4M, doing the same things: answering queries, giving help and sorting out bugs. Le Roux, like Satoshi, could be remarkably helpful where software was concerned. He was also the force behind the revolutionary encryption software TrueCrypt; he had the original idea, gave technical support to the development, and ongoing financial support during his Rx Limited years. Patterns of behaviour tend to repeat. What he had done with E4M/ TrueCrypt, he could repeat with Bitcoin.

Satoshi was a highly innovative individual. Everyone who worked with Le Roux called him innovative and gave plentiful evidence both as a programmer and as a criminal mastermind of his creative out-of-the-box thinking. Satoshi did not just come up with a paper but a working program. Le Roux was remarkable for putting his ideas into action.

Satoshi had an excellent overview of the economic issues around Bitcoin. By 2007, Le Roux was much more than just a programmer. He was a business entrepreneur who had made hundreds of millions of dollars. His business may have been highly illegal, but he showed a good grasp of economic principles.

There are many clues that Satoshi thought like a gold bug and was a gold investor. Le Roux grew up in a gold-mining town as the son of a mining engineer. He had extensive gold holdings in his Rx Limited years, often sourcing his gold directly from illegal mines.

Satoshi was a libertarian and so was Le Roux.

Satoshi disliked the GPL "copy-left" licence in favour of more permissive licences, and so did Le Roux, who used the BDS licence for the same reason.

Satoshi included a redundant module in the Bitcoin program for a casino. Le Roux was interested in online casinos as early as 2002 and eventually launched an online casino in his Rx Limited years.

Satoshi was constantly busy, particularly in the summer of 2009. He had a habit of not communicating for weeks and then responding to all of his emails at once. Le Roux had to run his Rx Limited business, which employed thousands of people and was busy with many projects. In the summer of 2009, he was expanding into outright criminal activities. The Captain Ufuk affair meant he was fully occupied fighting fires in the late summer of 2009. Le Roux's employees were used to a pattern where he left them alone for weeks at a time, and then suddenly communicated constantly, just like Satoshi.

Satoshi was paranoid about his anonymity from the very beginning, and he was an expert at hiding his identity. It is astonishing that he made his defences impregnable to almost all attempts to unmask him. And he did it when Bitcoin seemed completely insignificant. Le Roux had this skill of hiding his identity. He made some mistakes in 2003/4 when he first started with Rx Limited. By 2008, Le Roux was an expert at remaining out of sight and making his operations untraceable.

Stylistically, Le Roux is very similar to Satoshi. They both write intelligent terse replies, to the point without wasting words. Satoshi's perfect grammar, spelling, and double spacing could have been achieved using a grammar and spell checker for every communication. Satoshi writes in British English with some American spellings. Le Roux grew up in an area of British influence, worked in London, and used a mixture of British and American English.

Then there are the specific links. On one occasion, Satoshi obliquely referred to Encryption for the Masses (Le Roux's E4M) and presented Bitcoin as the natural next step after that product and disk encryption.

Satoshi left the forum mysteriously two days after Farmer_boy posted about Satoshi's code looking just like TrueCrypt, which was primarily based on Le Roux's coding,

The Patoshi mining machine went mysteriously offline for ten days in Aug 2009, showing that Satoshi was either too busy to notice or was unable to fix the problem. The period corresponds to Le Roux's Captain Ufuk episode.

Le Roux is by far the best candidate ever put forward for Satoshi. Although none of the above points amount to proof, they build a high probability case when taken together. To make this case conclusive, we must turn to four independent strands of evidence that specifically link Le Roux to Satoshi.

First, is the passport using the name Solotshi, issued just fifteen days before Satoshi first appeared. The name is Congolese, but it is very rare. It has been chosen because it has a hidden English meaning, "Solo-shit". The full name on the passport is Paul Solo-shit Calder Le Roux, a piece of humour. This gives us the vital first clue that leads, via Sao Paulo and Motorola, to the meaning of Satoshi Nakamoto as "Paul-shit aka La Ro". This unambiguously ties Satoshi to Paul Le Roux and proves he is not some shadowy team.

The second strand of evidence starts with that post to Hal Finney for the very first Bitcoin transaction. He sends Finney his address starting with "1NS" and has the idea of personalising addresses by generating a large number of random addresses and selecting those whose first few characters indicate a name. We know he did this because he uses an unusual address involving three doublets that would require approximately 100,000 randomly generated addresses to find. The next time he gives someone his address, it starts with 1PhUX. The capital letters match the first and last two letters of **P**aul Le Ro**ux**.

This establishes a pattern; we must look at the capital letters at the beginning of an address, ignoring lowercase and numbers. Le Roux uses a first and last pattern rather than initials, as he did for his "Rx" brand, which takes the first and last letters of Roux. Satoshi uses a second customised address for Bitcoins mined by the non-Patoshi miner M254. It starts with the sequence 1PxeCX, standing for **P**aul **C**alder Le Rou**x**. Once again, it ends in X, and this time, we have Le Roux's two initials.

This leads to the third strand of evidence. A forged email by Craig Wright has an unusual number of addresses that can be linked as a personalisation of Le Roux's name. Any one of these addresses could have arisen through random coincidence, but the probability of so many coincidences in a small list of names is thousands to one. The email sets out a transaction to reward the "third man" for his contribution to Satoshi. The address to which the Bitcoins are transferred is 1LXc28h, which is customised to **L**e Rou**x** and a close parallel to Rx. In the email, the "third man" is Professor Rees, who was certainly not involved as he was in a nursing home suffering from dementia.

We have followed these addresses back to MtGox and 150,000 Bitcoins set aside for a large client. This amount was divided into thirty-four slices in early Mar 2011. The Bitcoins that have found their way into 1LXc28h all come from the final seven slices. Bitcoins from later mining have also been added together with an address containing over 10,000 Bitcoins from miscellaneous sources. Most likely, the 1LXc28h owner controlled the 150,000 Bitcoins along with significant holdings elsewhere. Unlike the Patoshi Bitcoins, these have been moved multiple times.

The email provides a definite link between Wright and Satoshi, and that link must surely involve Dave Kleiman. We can eliminate the possibility that Wright randomly came across the 1LXc28h transaction from a rich list of Bitcoin addresses. The email includes a total that does not relate to the final transaction in Aug 2013 but to the situation on 2 Mar 2011. Using figures valid at that time, we can get back to the precise total from a calculation that makes sense on that day, but not much later as various things changed. So Wright had access to some genuine information about Satoshi's Bitcoin holdings.

The link is undoubtedly Dave Kleiman. In Wright's forgeries, Kleiman always does the mining and moves Bitcoins. Jamie Wilson, who worked closely with Wright in early 2013, testified that Wright had told him Kleiman was into Bitcoin and mining before him. We know that Kleiman actively participated in the cryptography mailing list while Satoshi was posting. Most significantly, we have the evidence of an early email from Ira Kleiman, who recalled a Thanksgiving dinner in 2009 in which Dave told him he was making digital money with a "rich foreign guy" who owned properties. The description matches Le Roux rather than Wright. We also have an independent witness, BitcoinFX, who observed Kleiman operating a node online in early 2010. Then there is a to-do note found unencrypted on one of Kleiman's drives, which shows he was checking whether an address belonged to Satoshi.

We traced Craig Wright's involvement back to April 2013 when he travelled to New Jersey. Most likely, he met Le Roux or an intermediary on this journey. Although Le Roux was in captivity, he is recorded as "released" at this time, perhaps because he was involved in a DEA operation. After this visit, Wright suddenly had access to capital and established Coin-Exch, a prospective Bitcoin exchange that was intended to be a 50/50 operation with Dave Kleiman. However, Kleiman died very shortly afterwards, and Wright was left to carry on alone. Satoshi likely devised the original plan as a front for his Bitcoin activities, but Wright soon deviated with his own ideas and was abandoned by Satoshi.

A link between Wright and Le Roux comes from Wright's accounts of the events of Jan/Feb 2011. Wright flew to New York, where he had a conference call with Kleiman and the "third man" before flying on to Venezuela, where he made contact with FARC and was shot. In his deposition in the Florida court case, Wright initially said that he could not identify the third man because of national security concerns. He then changed his story and said the concern was with his personal security due to an "international crime lord" who had been incarcerated, and who was later identified as Paul Le Roux. The posts he made at the time were concerned with unidentified criminal groups who planned to produce software and services for the sexual exploitation of enslaved persons in return for FARC illegally mined gold. In another blog post, Wright confirmed he had been in FARC-controlled territory and also said he had been in Somalia.

The final strand of evidence concerns "X", who posted to the ukfinance and p2p groups about an idea for cryptocurrency in Dec 2002, six years before Bitcoin. The idea has remarkable similarities to Bitcoin, including a fixed total supply that is almost infinitely divisible. There is no proof of work yet, although X was already moving in that direction. In other posts, X came up with a number of innovative ideas, including a Tor-like browsing system. X showed technical knowledge of gold, and put forward ideas for encrypting phone conversations similar to a product that Le Roux had been working on. X posted from the Netherlands, where Le Roux lived, and said he was Dutch. Le Roux often claimed to be Dutch and went under the name Johan Le Roux in the Philippines.

Most significantly, we can identify just two online aliases used by Le Roux: Entropy and X. He posted under these aliases to the scramdisk group after the TrueCrypt launch. X was Le Roux, and he had the idea for Bitcoin as early as 2002. Le Roux was faced with a choice of projects to work on at the beginning of 2003. The one that won out was the online pill idea. It was not until 2007 that he could give time to the cryptocurrency project.

Why has Le Roux not received wider attention as the most likely Satoshi? His CV is a perfect fit and the passport evidence has been known for years. Put simply, Le Roux is a vast embarrassment to the Bitcoin industry and community. It is much better to describe the Le Roux scenario as a conspiracy theory, and it has certainly tended to attract conspiracy theorists. Other objections are that it is foolish to believe that a criminal like Le Roux could be Satoshi. Would a criminal mastermind have spent so much time giving software support and making bug fixes while running his empire? The force of these arguments disappears when we examine the actual evidence of Le Roux, the programmer, and see the striking parallels to Satoshi.

Bitcoiners prefer to advance an acceptable list of candidates, most prominently Szabo, Back and Finney. Although they are not Satoshi, they serve as acceptable placeholders, surrogates to fill a void. Often, the strategy is to say that Satoshi must be some mysterious collective and then hint at Szabo, Back or Finney being part of it. It's best not to be too specific.

I expect the Bitcoin community will react to the Le Roux case in three possible ways. Many will simply ignore it. The evidence will be brushed aside, and the usual suspects will be pushed forward. Satoshi-the-myth is just too valuable. The Bitcoin industry will not want the myth contaminated by Le Roux.

The second reaction would be to go further down the conspiracy rabbit hole. Le Roux's history gives ample material for such conspiracy theories. Some have already speculated that he was working as an agent for the US government. I don't believe he was. A more significant question is whether the US government already know he is Satoshi. Given that they have Le Roux in custody, we might expect them to know, but we should not underestimate bureaucratic inertia.

The third approach is to cast Le Roux as an anti-hero like Ross Ulbricht. Although Ulbricht was a criminal who commissioned murders, he has been transformed by the libertarian movement into a champion of liberty. A significant factor has been Ulbricht's harsh sentence of life imprisonment. Although the libertarians have only a few per cent of the vote, even that few per cent can count in a tight election such as in 2024. To win the libertarian vote, Trump promised to free Ross Ulbricht. Could Le Roux be lionised in the same way? His murders are the chief embarrassment. Unlike Ulbricht, Le Roux's hit jobs succeeded. It is difficult to make a hero of someone who had a woman shot in the back of a car, one bullet under each eye.

Would acknowledging Le Roux as the creator invalidate Bitcoin? In one sense, it does not. Bitcoin was an invention "in the air" waiting to happen. Many people were thinking along the lines of a digital currency.

Le Roux had the ability to solve the problems, evolve a practical system and put it into action. It is hard to avoid comparisons with another South African innovator, Elon Musk. The two are risk-takers wholly committed to achieving an apparently impossible objective. Society needs people like these. It is a tragedy that the anger lurking within Le Roux turned his genius in a criminal direction.

Bitcoin will likely just sail on and shrug off its disreputable founder. But the tearing down of Saint Satoshi will give rise to theological problems. The Bitcoin movement has the characteristics of a religion. Fiat is original sin. Everything wrong with the modern world is due to fiat currencies. Without fiat, there would be no war, no housing problem, no poverty, no socialists and no government. Bitcoiners are waiting for their own apocalypse when fiat will collapse in hyperinflation, bringing great suffering to the no-coiners. Hyperbitcoinization will follow. The world will be purified as Bitcoin becomes the universal currency.

Bitcoin is the one true faith against the heathens of the fiat banking system. However, heretics have arisen from among the Bitcoiners' own ranks. These heretics practice the dark arts of "crypto", any cryptocurrency other than Bitcoin. Their leader is the cursed Vitalik, who left the true faith to found Ethereum. Those who dabble in crypto are regarded as scammers, which, to be fair, is more or less true.

The real Bitcoiners hodl their Bitcoins. The word is a misspelling of "hold" and comes from a drunken rant by an early Bitcoiner who posted that he was always mistiming his trades and in future he was just going to "hodl". The faithful stack Sats and avoid the corruption of fiat and crypto. The ultimate test of faith is to hodl through a ferocious pullback. Only by being tested by fire will you get the reward of the bull market.

Bitcoiners tend to be crypto-anarchists: anti-conformist, libertarian and right-wing. They do not tell others what to do and do not accept that others should tell them what to do. They believe in free speech rather than hate speech laws and see tax as state-authorised theft. Bitcoiners are rebels at a time when the left has become the conformist establishment. There is Bitcoin culture and Bitcoin art, much of which would horrify the left-wing art establishment. Some of it (such as by the Bitcoin artist Madex) is very good.

To the Bitcoiners, Satoshi is the Messiah. Le Roux, however, did not create Bitcoin to make the world a better place. He invented it because he wanted to control the world, or at least some small part of it. We have suggested that his target may have been c.10% of the Bitcoin supply. He achieved 5.7% from Patoshi but was also mining through others. We can allocate an additional 150,000 and probably a lot more through this mining activity as well as purchases. Although the Patoshi Bitcoins have never been moved, these other Bitcoins were undoubtedly moved. We cannot say how much Le Roux still controls.

Le Roux designed Bitcoin to increase in value. He did not just program computers, he programmed human beings. He baked in an exponentially decreasing supply rather than an exponentially increasing supply, as expected of a fair system. Bitcoin was not designed to be fair, but grossly unfair, for only an unfair system could achieve the gains that Satoshi wanted. So he programmed in his greed loop, making it easy for him to acquire large volumes of Bitcoin in the early years while putting a speculative rocket under the Bitcoin price.

Money should be just an accounting system. Its purpose is twofold. First, to allow the specialised work of the individual to be exchanged for the goods and services produced by the broader economy. And second, to enable an individual to store the value of their work to be consumed at a later time. Suppose an existing monetary system A, such as dollars or gold, was to be replaced by a new system B. To preserve accounting integrity, units of B should be created to allow holdings in A to be transferred over at a fair equivalent value. So, the money supply in B would greatly increase as B was adopted. At the same time, the equivalent unit of A should be destroyed to avoid inflation in A. If this happened, there would not be any net creation of money in A and B combined. People's holdings in A would end up as equivalent holdings in B.

This is not how Bitcoin works. Almost all of the value has already been assigned to holders who have not worked for it. If A were to transfer over to B, this would cause a theft of the work represented by A into the hands of these early adopters. They would acquire vast wealth at the expense of everyone else. In Bitcoin theology, everyone would become richer, but this is obviously impossible. Instead, the wealth represented by A must be destroyed. How? By inflation caused by the transfer to B. This is the point that Bitcoiners miss. If hyperbitcoinization took place, it would cause the destruction of everyone else's savings. It would have to, for there can be no net creation of value from simply moving from one currency to another. The early adopters would gain immense unearned value, so someone else would have to lose it.

This is the original sin of Bitcoin. It is essentially an act of theft created by a criminal to make himself insanely rich at the expense of those who worked and saved. The mechanism is the greed loop. The problem in late 2009 and early 2010 was priming the greed loop with an initial large price increase. If Bitcoin continued to be worth nothing, Satoshi's supporters would lose motivation, and it would not attract new people. It seems he subsidised miners to increase the hash rate and the price to get things moving.

Satoshi designed Bitcoin so that most of the gains would go to the early miners, the early adaptors, and traders who bought Bitcoin from them. This would create vast fortunes, incentivising others to come in and providing further momentum for the price in an endless loop. Satoshi was rationally greedy. He could only maximise his own wealth by making others rich. He had to leave enough Bitcoin on the table, and his target was never to mine more than 50%. In 2009, he mined too much. In 2010 things changed rapidly. With the development of GPU mining even Satoshi was getting squeezed out by the second half of that year. His 2011 mining output would have been insignificant compared to his holdings. Satoshi had ruled the mining roost for little more than eighteen months, which seems too short to achieve 10% of total Bitcoin holdings—perhaps 7% is more likely.

Satoshi/Le Roux created the world's greatest speculative machine. He set it going on 9 Jan 2009. We have not yet seen where it might end.

APPENDIX A

Timing of the Malmi emails.

The following table shows the number of Satoshi emails in the Martti Malmi collection for each hour for three different time zones.

Hour	UTC (UK)	UTC – 8 hrs (California)	UTC + 8 hrs (Japan/Philippines)
00	8	0	8
01	6	0	8
02	3	0	16
03	8	0	16
04	6	0	9
05	12	0	9
06	8	1	8
07	1	6	7
08	0	8	8
09	0	8	6
10	0	16	3
11	0	16	8
12	0	9	6
13	0	9	12
14	1	8	8
15	6	7	1
16	8	8	0
17	8	6	0
18	16	3	0
19	16	8	0
20	9	6	0
21	9	12	0
22	8	8	1
23	7	1	6

APPENDIX B

The Wright-Kleiman email total

The Wright-Kleiman email deals with a transaction to address 1LXc28 reserved for the "third man" identified at that time as Professor Rees. The email is a forgery but contains several addresses customised to Le Roux's name. Most of the details on the email could have been taken from the blockchain record of a transaction that took place 13 Aug 2013 18:12. However, the email shows a total of 19,470.12 Bitcoins to be reserved for Rees which is strikingly different from the transaction total of 34,512.819. In this appendix we will show where Wright's total comes from.

The majority of the Bitcoin that ended up in 1LXc28 came from 150,000 Bitcoin set aside for a large client of MtGox. This was processed into 34 slices on 1 Mar to 2 Mar 2011. The Bitcoin that eventually found their way into 1LXc28 came from the last 7 slices. To get the Wright total we start with the final 4 slices:

1CXnCz	4,971 transferred to 1LXc28
15SF8a	4,658 moved 9 Jun 2011
153R6q	4,915 transferred to 1LXc28
1DmKhz	3,172 transferred to 146mH6 and then 1LXc28
Total	17,716

Three of the four slices ended up in 1LXc28. The final slice, 1DmKhz, was not moved directly into 1LXc28 but was combined with 1,755.66

Bitcoin from a mining operation and transferred into 146mH6 apart from the fraction of 0.66 which went to a separate address.

Suppose we add this additional mined Bitcoin to the total for the last four slices. This gives 19,471.66 which is close to 19,470.12. We can do better! Looking at the addresses that were combined, one has the fraction 0.12. By rounding other fractions up or down we get the precise total:

Last 4 slices	17,716
Additional mining added to 146mH6 on 4 Mar 2011:	
16sg8v	750
1KPSUx	22.12
1nodcQ	2 (exact 2.90)
1GEKNV	383 (exact 382.95)
176NJz	597 (exact 597.69)
Total	19,470.12

The lack of consistency in the rounding is very typical of the real world. People write down a figure without the fraction, or round it up, or include the fraction, and then combine all these in one total.

The total made sense in a brief time window:

- After the slicing had been completed at 2 Mar 2011 22:06.
- Before the 146mH6 transaction on 4 Mar 2011 15:09. This changed the rounding so that the total calculated after this transaction would have been 19,471.

There were more significant changes later:

- In June 2011, 15SF8a was combined with Bitcoin from another address and sent to MtGox. As it was no longer available for the 1LXc28 transaction, it seems to have been replaced by another slice, 1M7ccm, which was not included in the Wright email but present in the actual transaction.
- The final transaction in Aug 2013 had multiple changes including

the addition of later mined Bitcoin and the miscellaneous address 19dQ2x, which is why the final total of 34,516 was much larger than 19,470.

Conclusion

The Wright-Kleiman email total of 19,470.12 was not taken from the blockchain but from a schedule prepared between 2 Mar and 4 Mar 2011 by the person involved in the slicing operation. The schedule recorded Bitcoin reserved for a Satoshi silo. Subsequent events led to several changes between this schedule and the 2013 transaction.

APPENDIX C

Rx Limited early websites

The table in this appendix shows the 57 earliest active pharmacy sites associated with Le Roux and Rx Limited. They were essentially all registered before Oct 2003, although most did not become active until May/June the following year. The list of domains has been identified through SEO pages set up before some sites became active. With the exception of Atlas-Pharmacy and the last site listed, all the domains were included in Wayback Machine captures on 1 Oct 2003 for the domains Cybergp.com, EUChemist.com and No-prescription_drugs.com.

The earliest registered site would seem to be cybertabs.com which was reactivated on 9 Feb 2003 having previously been used as a US based IT recruiting site. The name server history suggests it was intended as the original pharmacy site before being replaced by Atlas-Pharmacy. (The name server was set to Handsonwebhosting.com on 12 May 2003. Atlas-Pharmacy was activated and set to the same name server two days later, with Cybertabs.com moved away the following day.)

With a few exceptions the sites belonged to three generic types named here A, B and C. Within a type the sites were essentially identical apart from the name and images.

Type A sourced the drugs from US pharmacies, promised next day delivery, and used a toll-free 24-hour number, 877-479-2455. There were 35 type A websites including Your-pills.

Type B offered seven-day delivery with the drugs being sourced from a foreign country. Type B had the same toll-free number, 877-479-2455, as Type A and did not specify what territory the drugs came from. There were 12 Type B websites.

Type C offered seven-day delivery with the drugs being sourced from India and used a different number, 800-615-4168. There were 6 Type C websites.

The main exceptions are:

Atlas-pharmacy.com which was alleged by the prosecution in Le Roux's trial to have been owned by Wilfred Hafner. As explained in the text, it is more likely to have been a joint venture between Le Roux and Hafner.

Pills24-7.com which was the prototype Rx Limited site. Initially it did not have a phone number, but was later moved to type A.

Domain	Active by	Type
Atlas-pharmacy.com	26 Jun 2003	Exception
Pills24-7.com	1 Apr 2004	Exception (A)
Your-pills.com	18 May 2004	A
Anxiety-attacks-drugs.com	20 May 2004	B
Anxiety-disorder-drugs.com	-	Not used in 2004
Best-drug-store.com	2 Jun 2004	A
Best-online-drug-store.com	27 May 2004	A
Best-online-drugs.com	9 Jun 2004	A
Best-online-pharmacy.us	23 May 2004	A
Best-perscription-drug.com	23 May 2004	A
Buy-best-drugs.com	24 May 2004	A
Buy-cheap-drug.com	18 May 2004	B
Buy-cheap-perscription-drugs-online.com	25 May 2004	A
Buy-cheaper-drugs.com	5 Jun 2004	A
Buy-klonopin-online.com	22 May 2004	A
Buy-online-drugs.com	4 Jun 2004	A

Buy-online-pills.com	19 May 2004	B
Buy-online-valium.com	20 May 2004	B
Buy-pain-relief-drugs.com	19 May 2004	C
BuyCheapDrug.com	19 May 2004	B
BuyOnlineValium.com	4 Jun 2004	A
Canada-pills.com	18 May 2004	C
Cheap-drugs-for-you.com	22 May 2004	A
Cheap-drugs-pharmacy.com	26 May 2004	A
Cheap-meds-online.com	23 May 2004	A
Cheap-online-pharmacy.com	22 Jul 2004	A
Cheaper-drugs-online.com	19 May 2004	B
Cheaper-pills-online.com	25 May 2004	A
Cheapest-meds-online.com	18 May 2004	B
Cybergp.com	20 May 2004	B
Cybertabs.com	13 May 2004	B
Drugs-without-prescription.com	18 May 2004	C
EUChemist.com	18 May 2004	B
First-online-pharmacy.com	23 May 2004	A
Medicines-shop.com	23 May 2004	A
Meds-for-you.com	25 May 2004	A
Medtabs.com	-	Not used
Net-drugs-store.com	4 Jun 2004	A
No-prescription-drugs.com	30 May 2004	B
Offshoremeds.com	22 May 2004	C
Online-cheap-drugs.com	5 Jun 2004	A
Online-cheap-pills.com	5 Jun 2004	A
Online-diazepram.com	4 Jun 2004	A
Online-drugs-for-you.com	24 May 2004	A
Online-valium.com	26 May 2004	A
Pharmacy-medication.com	12 May 2004	C
Pharmacy-online-drug.com	24 May 2004	A
Pharmacy-online-medicine.com	26 May 2004	A
Store-drugs.com	26 May 2004	A
The-best-online-pharmacy.com	25 May 2004	A

The-best-pharmacy.com	2 Jun 2004	A
The-cheap-pharmacy.com	4 Jun 2004	A
The-cheapest-pharmacy.com	2 Jun 2004	A
The-top-pharmacy.com	22 Aug 2004	A
Top-drug-store.com	26 May 2004	C
UKDrugStore.com	20 May 2004	B
Women-health-drugs.com	10 Jun 2004	A

Notes:

"Active by" is the first date the Wayback machine records the active site, which is not necessarily the day the site was created.

REFERENCES AND NOTES

For more information and updates please see:

SatoshiEnigma.com
X/Twitter: @SatoshiEntropy

This is a book about the early internet age. The primary sources were internet forums, USENET groups, mail lists, Wayback Machine records, Twitter/X posts, Reddit, the blockchain, and online court documents. Referencing such informal and disparate sources is awkward, and including a comprehensive list of long URLs in a print book is of dubious value. I believe the best way to present this material is through an online site with links or copies of the original material as appropriate. Such a site can be updated quickly to allow for developments and news.

There were, however, a few traditional resources used which I list here.

Bibliography

Two books on Le Roux were vital:

Evan Ratliff, *The Mastermind: The Hunt for the World's Most Prolific Criminal* (Bantum Press, 2019).
Elaine Shannon, *Hunting LeRoux* (Michael Mann Books, 2019)

Other useful books:

Jonathan Bier, The Blocksize War: The Battle for Control Over Bitcoin's Protocol and Rules (Amazon, 2021)

crrdlx (Ed.), *Kicking the Hornet's Nest: The Complete Writings, Emails, and Forum Posts of Satoshi Nakamoto, the Founder of Bitcoin and Cryptocurrency* (Mill Hill Books, 2nd Ed. 2019)

Mark Hunter, *Ultimate Catastrophe, How MtGox Lost Half a Billion Dollars and Nearly Killed Bitcoin* (Content.Ed, 2024)

ACKNOWLEDGMENTS

I would like to thank my family, and in particular my wife Angela. I first began researching Satoshi in 2019 and dived in deep during the pandemic lockdown. The actual writing of the book took almost the whole of 2023 and 2024. Throughout this long gestation, I have enjoyed the patience and support of my wife and family.

One of my daughters, Rose Laurie and my son, James Laurie, both IT professionals, gave their time to proofread and comment on the work. Their contributions are greatly appreciated.

Euan Monaghan, who typeset the book and got it ready for publication, was as helpful as ever.

A special thank you is due to Wolfgang Wester, an expert on the forensic study of early Bitcoin mining. His contributions and comments on X (formerly Twitter) greatly improved my understanding of the early miners. His amazing work deserves more recognition than it has received.

Finally, I would like to thank all the internet archivists who have preserved vital information from the recent past. Without resources such as the Internet Archive Wayback Machine, Google Groups archives, CourtListerner.com and the archives at the Satoshi Nakamoto Institute, this book would not have been possible.

www.ingramcontent.com/pod-product-compliance
Lightning Source LLC
LaVergne TN
LVHW022259060326
832902LV00020B/3174